SCHOOL OF
ORIENTAL AND AFRICAN STUDIES
UNIVERSITY OF LONDON

London Oriental Series
Volume 25

LONDON ORIENTAL SERIES · VOLUME 25

THE FINANCIAL SYSTEM OF EGYPT

A.H. 564–741/A.D. 1169–1341

BY

HASSANEIN RABIE

Lecturer in History, Faculty of Arts
University of Cairo

LONDON
OXFORD UNIVERSITY PRESS
NEW YORK TORONTO
1972

Oxford University Press, Ely House, London W. 1
GLASGOW NEW YORK TORONTO MELBOURNE WELLINGTON
CAPE TOWN IBADAN NAIROBI DAR ES SALAAM LUSAKA ADDIS ABABA
DELHI BOMBAY CALCUTTA MADRAS KARACHI LAHORE DACCA
KUALA LUMPUR SINGAPORE HONG KONG TOKYO

ISBN 0 19 713564 1

PRINTED IN GREAT BRITAIN
AT THE UNIVERSITY PRESS, OXFORD
BY VIVIAN RIDLER
PRINTER TO THE UNIVERSITY

FOREWORD

EGYPT is in many ways a special case in medieval Islam. In an age of shifting frontiers and transitory regimes, Egypt stands out as a country—a political entity—sharply defined by both geography and history, with a degree of administrative cohesion and continuity unparalleled elsewhere in the Islamic world. For this reason, as well as because of a favourable climate, Egypt has also preserved a wealth of documentation, which makes possible the study of Egyptian institutions with a detailed accuracy rare in pre-archival historical research.

The topic which Dr. Rabie has chosen for his monograph is of self-evident interest and importance. His themes are taxation, financial administration, and money, with special attention to the *iqṭāʿ*; his period runs from the rise of Saladin to the death of al-Malik al-Nāṣir Muḥammad ibn Qala'un, spanning the last years of the Fatimid Caliphate, the whole of the Ayyubid era, and the establishment and consolidation of the Mamluk Sultanate. The study thus deals with some of the central institutions of the Muslim state, and analyses their development through a period of major change.

Dr. Rabie has attempted a difficult task, and accomplished it with distinction. Combining the skill and care of the palaeographer and philologist with the discipline and perception of the economic historian, he has produced a monograph of outstanding merit. It is a pleasure and a privilege to introduce and commend it to the reader.

BERNARD LEWIS

London
30 October 1970

CONTENTS

ACKNOWLEDGEMENTS

FIRST and foremost, I should like to express my deepest gratitude to my supervisor at the School of Oriental and African Studies, Professor Bernard Lewis, without whose learned guidance, constant encouragement, and indefatigable help I should not have been able to overcome the difficulties that faced me in the course of my work. I shall never forget what I owe him in every respect.

I am also grateful to Professor P. M. Holt, Professor J. M. Hussey, Professor C. E. Bosworth, and Mr. M. A. Cook for their invaluable comments on my work; to Professor S. A. Ashour of Cairo University, who gave me every possible encouragement; to the late Dr. S. M. Stern, who put at my disposal a valuable fragment of a Geniza document; to the late Professor M. M. Ziada for his kind interest in my work; and to the late Professor E. E. El-Arini for lending me the 29th volume of Nuwayrī's *Nihāyat al-arab*.

I would also like to thank Mr. J. D. Pearson and the staff of the Library of the S.O.A.S.; Dr. Helene Loebenstein, the director of the Papyri Department of the Österreichische Nationalbibliothek, Vienna; and the librarians and staff of these institutions: the British Museum Library; the University Library, Cambridge; the Bodleian Library, Oxford; the Bibliothèque Nationale, Paris; the Manuscripts Department of the Österreichische Nationalbibliothek, Vienna, and the Bibliotheek Der Rijksuniversiteit, Leiden; the Ayasofya, Beyazit, Köprülü, Nuruosmaniye, Süleymaniye, and Topkapı Sarayı Libraries in Istanbul.

Thanks are also due to Dr. Anna Irene Falk for her translation of German and Italian works; to Mr. A. F. Shore of the Department of Egyptian Antiquities, British Museum, for the translation of some Coptic texts, and to Mr. P. Hunt for his translation of G. Vernadsky's booklet from the Russian.

I should also like to express my thanks to Cairo University for awarding me four years' study leave, which enabled me to devote myself unreservedly to the preparation of the present book, and to the Central Research Fund Committee (University of London) for the grant which covered my maintenance expenses during my stay in Vienna.

I am extremely grateful to the School of Oriental and African Studies, University of London, for accepting this work for the London Oriental Series and for bearing the costs of its publication.

Finally I thank my wife who, with infinite patience and endurance, stood by me during these years of research.

H. M. RABIE

LIST OF ABBREVIATIONS

AI	*Ars Islamica*
BEO	*Bulletin d'études orientales*
BFA	*Bulletin of the Faculty of Arts, University of Alexandria*
BFLS	*Bulletin de la Faculté des Lettres de Strasbourg*
BIE	*Bulletin de l'Institut Égyptien (d'Égypte)*
BIFAO	*Bulletin de l'Institut Français d'Archéologie orientale*
BSOAS	*Bulletin of the School of Oriental* [*and African*] *Studies*
BSRGE	*Bulletin de la Société Royale de Géographie d'Égypte*
CIA	*Corpus Inscriptionum Arabicarum*
CHE	*Cahiers d'histoire égyptienne*
EC	*L'Égypte contemporaine*
EHR	*The Economic History Review*
EI[1]	*Encyclopaedia of Islam, 1st edition*
EI[2]	*Encyclopaedia of Islam, 2nd edition*
HJAS	*Harvard Journal of Asiatic Studies*
IC	*Islamic Culture*
JA	*Journal asiatique*
JAOS	*Journal of the American Oriental Society*
JEH	*Journal of Economic History*
JESHO	*Journal of the Economic and Social History of the Orient*
JNES	*Journal of Near Eastern Studies*
JQR	*Jewish Quarterly Review*
JRAS	*Journal of the Royal Asiatic Society*
JSCL	*Journal of the Society of Comparative Legislation*
MIDEO	*Mélanges de l'Institut Dominicain d'Études orientales du Caire*
MIE	*Mémoires de l'Institut d'Égypte*
MMIA	*Majallat al-Majmaʿ al-ʿIlmī al-ʿArabī*
MMII	*Majallat al-Majmaʿ al-ʿIlmī al-ʿIrāqī*
MTM	*al-Majalla al-Tārīkhiyya al-Miṣriyya*
PO	*Patrologia Orientalis*
RCEA	*Répertoire chronologique d'épigraphie arabe*
REI	*Revue des études islamiques*
REJ	*Revue des études juives*
RFSE Univ. Istanbul	*Revue de la Faculté des Sciences économiques*

RHC	*Recueil des historiens des croisades*
RHES	*Revue d'histoire économique et sociale*
ROL	*Revue de l'Orient latin*
SI	*Studia Islamica*

SYSTEM OF TRANSLITERATION OF ARABIC CHARACTERS

Consonants

ء	' (except when initial)	ر	r	ف	f
ب	b	ز	z	ق	q
ت	t	س	s	ك	k
ث	th	ش	sh	ل	l
ج	j	ص	ṣ	م	m
ح	ḥ	ض	ḍ	ن	n
خ	kh	ط	ṭ	ه	h
د	d	ظ	ẓ	و	w
ذ	dh	ع	'	ي	y
		غ	gh		

Long Vowels		*Short Vowels*		*Diphthongs*	
ا and ى	ā	ـَ	a	ـَ و	aw
و	ū	ـُ	u	ـَ ي	ay
ي	ī	ـِ	i	ـِيّ	iyy (final form ī)
				ـُوّ	uww (final form ū)

ة	a
ال	(article) al

I

A CRITICAL SURVEY OF THE SOURCES

THE student of the financial system of Egypt (564–741/1169–1341) has to rely on sources which can be divided into the following eight main groups: A. The Cairo Geniza documents; B. the Vienna papers; C. documents preserved in the Personal Status Court in Cairo (the *Maḥkama* collection); D. Egyptian documents found in a number of European centres; E. works of contemporary Egyptian historians and writers containing financial material; F. records of travel; G. coins; H. inscriptions.

A. *The Cairo Geniza documents*

The Geniza is well known to scholars.[1] It provides useful evidence about such aspects of the Egyptian financial system in the period under study as the *iqṭāʿ* system, taxation, and the monetary system.

Documents referring to the *iqṭāʿ* are not numerous in the Geniza. However, they are important as they furnish information not to be found in the literary sources on such matters as relinquishment of the *iqṭāʿ* by a *muqṭaʿ*, or the functions of certain officials administering the *iqṭāʿ*.[2] Some fragments relate to the famous caravan road between Qūṣ and ʿAydhāb, and to entry permits for merchants.[3] A number describe the *jawālī* tax, specifying its amount and methods of collection, and demonstrating what a heavy burden this tax imposed on non-Muslims.[4] Mention of the *mawārīth ḥashriyya* occurs frequently in the Geniza, as every death had to be reported

[1] Cf. Goitein, article *Geniza* in *EI*²; id., 'L'état actuel de la recherche sur les documents de la Geniza du Caire', *REJ*, troisième série, i (cxviii) (1959–60), pp. 9–27; id., *Studies in Islamic history*, pp. 279–94; id., *Med. Soc.*, i, pp. 1–28; there is a tentative bibliography of Geniza documents in existence, which consists of two parts: a list of all published Geniza records with details of their publication, and a list of books and articles in which such publications are contained: S. Shaked, *A tentative bibliography of Geniza documents*, Paris–The Hague, 1964.

[2] See below, pp. 57, 65.

[3] See below, p. 101 n. 1, p. 106 n. 2.

[4] See below, pp. 109–110.

immediately to the officials of the *dīwān*. They throw light on the greed with which the authorities often seized the estate of a deceased person even if he left an heir.[1] Finally, evidence found in the Geniza is invaluable for the study of the monetary system. It provides information on the depreciation of certain silver *dirhams* issued during the period under review as well as the acute monetary crises of the period.[2]

Another important aspect of the Geniza in this respect is that it is not limited in provenance to Cairo or Fusṭāṭ, where it was kept until 1889–90, but includes numerous documents from the Egyptian countryside and small towns. Most of them are informal, and their authors include rich and poor alike. Consequently, the overall picture they provide is comprehensive, fairly accurate, and free from the exaggerations that are so common in the literary sources. Furthermore, it contains documents addressed to the chancery. According to Dr. Stern, they found their way into the Geniza through Jewish clerks employed in the chancery who used to discard papers into the lumber-room of the Synagogue.[3] It might also be assumed that some of these documents were purchased by Jews, when Saladin came to power and sold the Fāṭimid library and archives.

Research on the Geniza records is complicated by the fact that most of them derive from the Fāṭimid period, some from the Ayyūbid period, but only a very small quantity from the Mamluk era. The majority of the fragments are undated, and there is the ever-present danger of relying on an undated fragment from the Fāṭimid period for evidence for a later period. Caution is therefore advisable with undated documents. Besides, it is necessary to differentiate between the kinds of script used not only under the Fāṭimid, Ayyūbid, and Mamluk rule, but also under previous dynasties. It must also be borne in mind that the financial system of Egypt was by no means static, but subject to fluctuations of many kinds.

The fact that the Geniza is not an archive but, in the words of Professor Goitein, 'a kind of waste-paper basket, into which discarded writings were thrown often after they had been torn apart,

[1] See below, pp. 130 and n. 8, 131.

[2] See below, pp. 167–8, 176, 179–181, 188 n. 1.

[3] Stern, 'An original document from the Fāṭimid chancery concerning Italian merchants', *Studi . . . Levi Della Vida*, ii (1956), pp. 531–2.

and in which all its contents were mixed up topsy turvy',[1] constitutes another difficulty, as one leaf of a document may be found in Cambridge, another in Oxford, and the third be lost altogether.

The third obstacle lies in the very nature of the Geniza papers. Paper was expensive and people used the free spaces and margins of documents for notes of various kinds. Besides, the Geniza papers are often hard to decipher, as the documents have suffered extensively from the ravages of time, the writing having faded because of the poor quality of the ink, and the paper being frequently wormeaten.[2] As to the language, the majority of the documents in the Cairo Geniza, though in Arabic, are written in Hebrew characters, or as Mann says, in 'Jewish Arabic, which was the native language of the Egyptian Jews'.[3] This presents additional difficulties since types of Hebrew script vary according to the country, time, social class, and profession of the writer.[4]

The last, but not the least, difficulty is that the Geniza, though not necessarily all its documents, derives from a single minority community. The advantage of the Jewish origin of the Geniza is that Jews lived not only in Cairo or in the main ports and towns such as Alexandria, Damietta, and Qūṣ, but also in the Egyptian countryside, and played a great financial role in trade and monetary matters. The disadvantage of its Jewish minority origin lies in the limits it imposes on the validity of the evidence supplied. The Geniza lacks information on most aspects of financial history, such as financial administration in the *dīwān*s or such taxation as did not apply to members of the Jewish community, despite the fact that a number of the documents in question were written by Muslims and Christians who stood in some relationship to Jews.

B. *The Vienna papers*

In a paper submitted to the Conference on the Economic History of the Middle East in July 1967, Professor Bernard Lewis has pointed out that, though papyrus was gradually supplanted by paper in the tenth century, little is known about the range and

[1] Goitein, 'Letters and documents on the India trade', *IC*, xxxvii (1963), p. 189; id., *Med. Soc.*, i, pp. 7–8.

[2] Goitein, 'The Cairo Geniza as source for Mediterranean social history', *JAOS*, lxxx (1960), p. 92; id., *Med. Soc.*, i, p. 7.

[3] Mann, *The Jews in Egypt and in Palestine*, i, p. 242.

[4] Cf. Goitein, *Med. Soc.*, i, pp. 14–16.

iqṭāʿ over a long period did not give the *muqṭaʿ* any rights of ownership over the cultivated land in the *iqṭāʿ*; another furnishes proof of the existence of the *dīwān al-amīr* mentioned in literary sources; two others contain references to the functions of the *shādd* or *mushidd* in the *iqṭāʿ*.[1] Still others are extremely helpful in the study of forms of taxation such as the *kharāj* tax, the assignment of fisheries to *ḍāmins*, or the *jawālī* tax.[2] A number of fragments were found valuable in dealing with financial administration. Among them is one which proves that there was a *dīwān al-khāṣṣ* under the Fāṭimids, and that the *jahbadh* was known in Egypt even before their advent.[3] There are many fragments in the collection which relate to such facts as the purity of the *nuqra dirhams*, the general prevalence of *dirhams* (possibly *waraq dirhams*) before al-Kāmil's reform of 622/1225, and the Egyptian preference for silver *dirhams* over gold *dīnārs* under al-Nāṣir Muḥammad, in spite of the influx of gold from the Bilād al-Takrūr.[4] These are but a few of the problems to which the indications found in the Vienna papers have proved relevant.

c. *The* Maḥkama *collection*

This group comprises the documents preserved in the Personal Status Court in Cairo (*Maḥkamat al-aḥwāl al-shakhṣiyya li al-wilāya ʿalā al-nafs*) and includes one document from the Fāṭimid,[5] two from the Ayyūbid,[6] and a considerable number from the Mamluk and Ottoman periods. Some of these documents are sizeable rolls, consisting of sheets of paper sewn together into strips which are often several yards long when unrolled. They are so long because the *wāqif*, in assigning a series of houses, shops, public baths, etc., in the form of *waqf*, often had to define the boundaries of each, and the provisions laid down by the deed of *waqf*, in detail.[7] In other cases, the buyer of property did not buy it from one seller

[1] See below, pp. 57, 64–5, 67.
[2] See below, pp. 74 nn. 2–3, 77, 88 n. 4, 108–9, 112.
[3] See below, pp. 143 n. 2, 159.
[4] See below, pp. 174–5 n. 4, 180 n. 2, 192.
[5] *Ḥujjat waqf* of al-Ṣāliḥ Ṭalāʾiʿ ibn Ruzzīk, *Maḥkama*, Box 1, no. 1.
[6] *Ḥujjat waqf* daughter of Jamāl al-Dīn Muḥammad, *Maḥkama*, Box 1, no. 4; *Ḥujjat tamlīk wa waqf* of Sadīd al-Dīn Abī Muḥammad ʿAbd Allāh, *Maḥkama*, Box 1, no. 5.
[7] Cf. *Ḥujjat waqf* of Sultan Lājīn, *Maḥkama*, Box 3, no. 17 and *ḥujjat waqf* of Sultan Baybars al-Jāshnikīr, *Maḥkama*, Box 4, no. 22.

only, but had to buy several parts from different owners, and often at different times. Thus one deed of purchase was added to another as soon as or before the property was assigned as *waqf*, so that the deed of *waqf* consisted of a number of successive deeds sewn together.[1] That is why in a single document signatures of different qadis and witnesses are found. The quality of ink and paper varies according to the time and the wealth of the *wāqif* in question.

Two defects detract from the usefulness of these documents for scholarly research. First, they are limited in range, since they consist, in the main, of *waqfiyyāt*, i.e. deeds of *waqf* for benevolent purposes.[2] It is therefore not easy to find agreements between merchants, lists of prices, or tax-collectors' notebooks, or even official *manshūrs*. Secondly, many of the documents are incomplete, and have been damaged through exposure to humidity, dust, and rats, by being kept on open wooden shelves for many generations.[3]

The *Maḥkama* documents are relevant in this context as they are informative on a number of aspects of the financial system of Egypt in the period under study. They are of the official type, that is of a kind not represented in the Geniza or in the Vienna papers. Those dealing with financial matters are of help in that they show how the *waqf* system supplied contemporary Egyptians, especially those who had daughters, with a means of avoiding the seizure of their property after their death by the *dīwān al-mawārīth al-ḥashriyya*.[4] Some are contracts of sale and purchase of houses, stables, shops, etc., and thereby useful for the study of financial and monetary matters.[5] In others there is evidence to show that, during the Mamluk period, the *dirham nuqra* was used as money of

[1] Cf. *Ḥujjat tamlīk wa waqf* of the qadi Ḥamza ibn Abī Bakr, *Maḥkama*, Box 2, no. 13.

[2] For the *waqfiyya* cf. Björkman, article 'Diplomatic' in *EI*². There are 28 deeds of *waqf* from the Mamluk period preserved in the collection of documents of the Ministry of *Waqf* in Cairo. Four of these documents derive from the Baḥrī Mamluk period. Two of them, nos. 1010 and 1011, dated 685/1286 and 686/1287 respectively, concern the *awqāf* of Sultan Qalāwūn, one on behalf of the amir Mughulṭāy al-Jamālī (see below, p. 142 n. 6) and the other, no. 881, dated 760/1359 on behalf of Sultan Ḥasan ibn al-Nāṣir Muḥammad. The remaining 24 documents derive from the Circassian period. For deeds of *waqf* cf. also Roemer, 'Documents et archives de l'Égypte islamique', *MIDEO*, v (1958), pp. 243–4; Ḥusayn, *al-Wathā'iq*, pp. 98–9.

[3] Cf. *Ḥujjat waqf* of Abī al-Ma'ālī Yāqūt, *Maḥkama*, Box 2, no. 8.

[4] See below, pp. 128–9, 131–2.

[5] Cf. *Ḥujjat bay'* of Barqūq ibn 'Abd Allāh, *Maḥkama*, Box 2, no. 10; see below, p. 190.

account in the deeds of *waqf*.[1] Some throw light on the significance of the functions of some officials of the financial *dīwāns*, such as the *wakīl bayt al-māl*, the *nāẓir*, the *mushidd*, and the *ʿāmil*.[2] Last but not least, the *Maḥkama* documents are important because the majority are concerned with ordinary people not mentioned in the chronicles—such as Badr ibn ʿAbd Allāh al-Ḥusaynī, one of the servants of the Prophet's tomb.[3]

D. *Egyptian documents found in a number of European centres*

This group consists of documents relating to Egypt found in many European centres, especially Venice, Genoa, Pisa, and Barcelona. These documents are mostly treaties, contracts, and letters which contain evidence about commercial relations between Egypt and these cities, and are written in Italian and Latin as well as Arabic. These documents have been preserved in public and private archives, but there is no comprehensive catalogue available to date of the documents referring to Egyptian relations with the Italian republics in the twelfth and thirteenth centuries. In spite of the work of Amari and others, the majority of the Egyptian documents in Italian archives still await publication.[4] Among the documents published hitherto are:

(*a*) Fourteen documents relating to commercial relations between Egypt and Pisa, published by Amari. Seven of them are in Latin, four in Italian, two in Arabic, and the last in Arabic and Latin.[5] These documents cover the period from 1173 to 1215. Most of them are letters from the Ayyūbid sultans or their deputies in Egypt to the rulers of Pisa, ordering certain kinds of goods, such as iron, timber, and pitch, or conferring privileges on and giving assurances to the merchants concerned. Unfortunately, apart from the sultan's promise that the taxes already levied would not be increased, tax rates are seldom mentioned, taxes imposed on imported or exported merchandise being rarely specified in this type of document.[6]

[1] See below, p. 188. [2] See below, pp. 148–9, 153, 155 n. 1, 158.

[3] *Maḥkama*, Box 4, no. 21.

[4] Cf. Gabrieli, *Manuale di bibliografia Musulmana*, pp. 255–8.

[5] Amari, *Diplomi Arabi*, pp. 60, 70–1, 81–2, 257–68, 282–90.

[6] Cf. Saladin's letter dated Rajab 570/January 1177 and al-ʿĀdil's letter of 3 May 1208; ibid., pp. 264, 283; see below, pp. 83 n. 5, 93 n. 1, 95 n. 1. The '*Délibérations des assemblées vénitiennes concernant la Romanie*' edited by Thiriet touches on certain financial aspects of the trade between Egypt and Venice, such

(*b*) Eleven documents published by Mas Latrie, and concerned with commercial relations between Egypt and Venice from 1205 to 1302, that is from the reign of al-ʿĀdil I to that of al-Nāṣir ibn Qalāwūn. This collection is very useful in the study of Egyptian trade in the period concerned. It contains, for example, two documents referring to the trade privileges conferred by al-ʿĀdil I and al-ʿĀdil II on Venetian merchants, which are illustrative of the principles underlying trade between Egypt and Venice.[1] In this collection, there are five documents from the reign of al-Nāṣir dated 2, 5, 7, and 18 August 1302, referring to trade with Venice, which indicate the facilities offered by al-Nāṣir to the Venetians in order to increase trade between Egypt and Venice.[2]

(*c*) A single published document concerning the trade between Egypt and Genoa in this period; it consists of a peace treaty between Sultan Qalāwūn and his son Khalīl on the one side, and Albert Spinola, the ambassador of Genoa, on the other. It is dated 2 Jumādā I 689/13 May 1290, and has been preserved, in its original Arabic, by the contemporary historian Ibn ʿAbd al-Ẓāhir.[3] It was published in 1827 by Silvestre de Sacy in France, and in 1873 by Amari in Italy.[4] This document is useful in that it gives information on the dangers of navigation in the Mediterranean in the last decades of the thirteenth century. However, it is not informative on Egyptian trade relations with Genoa.

as the reduction of the number of maritime convoys to Syria, Cilician Armenia, Cyprus, and Egypt to one per year; rules on navigation to and commercial operations in Alexandria; the Venetian prohibition to sell slaves to Egypt; and instructions to Venetian ambassadors to Egypt to demand satisfaction for past damages and to prepare new commercial agreements. However, it contains no mention of tax; cf. op. cit., pp. 38 no. XLVIII, 41 no. LV, 50 no. LXXXXVII, 62 no. CLI, 63 no. CLVIII, 66 no. CLXIX, p. 90 no. 44, p. 92 nos. 51, 53, p. 93 no. 56.

[1] Mas-Latrie, *Traités de paix et de commerce*, Appendice, pp. 70–6. These eleven documents include four previously published by Tafel and Thomas, *Urkunden zur Älteren Handels- und Staatsgeschichte der Republik Venedig*, ii, pp. 185–7, 336–41, 416–18, 483–9. This group of four documents consists of one from the reign of al-ʿĀdil I (composed at some not exactly ascertainable date between 1205 and 1218); one from the reign of al-ʿĀdil II, dated 1238; one from the reign of al-Ṣāliḥ Ayyūb, dated 1244; and one from the reign of al-Muʿizz Aybak dated 1254. Tafel and Thomas have also edited another group of documents, seven in number, five of which derive from the reign of al-ʿĀdil I, and the remaining two from the reign of Aybak; cf. ibid., ii, pp. 187–93, 490–2.

[2] Mas Latrie, pp. 82–8. [3] Ibn ʿAbd al-Ẓāhir, *Tashrīf*, pp. 165–9.

[4] S. de Sacy, 'Pièces diplomatiques tirées des Archives de la République de Gênes', *Notices et extraits*, xi (1827), pp. 41–6; Amari, 'Nuovi Ricordi arabici su la Storia di Genova', in *Atti della Società Ligure di Storia Patria*, v (1873), pp. 11–19.

Besides the documents found in Italy, there is a group of five documents concerning relations between Egypt and Aragon, published by Alarcón y Santón and Ramón García.[1] Four of them have been partially republished by Professor A. S. Atiya, together with a group of other documents, in a booklet entitled *Egypt and Aragon*. The fifth document, which defines the principles of trade exchange between Egypt and Aragon, is a treaty between Sultan Khalīl ibn Qalāwūn and Jaime II of Aragon dated 19 Ṣafar 692/28 January 1292, and has been preserved by Qalqashandī in the *Ṣubḥ al-aʿshā*.[2]

The documents contained in Atiya's booklet consist of six Aragonese and eight Arabic letters, exchanged between Jaime II and Alfonso IV of Aragon and Sultan al-Nāṣir Muḥammad between 699/1300 and 730/1330 in eight embassies. Though ostensibly written for the diplomatic purpose of fostering friendship between Egypt and Aragon, and ensuring a better treatment of the Copts and Eastern Christians in Egypt, these letters can be of some use to the student of Egyptian finance, since:

(1) they enumerate different kinds of gifts presented by the Mamluk Sultan to Jaime II, and thereby supply information on the kind of Egyptian merchandise which attracted the attention of the European countries;

(2) they specify the trade privileges granted to Aragonese merchants in the Mamluk sultanate, which are probably identical with those conferred on the merchants of other countries;

(3) they demonstrate the efforts of Sultan al-Nāṣir to increase Egyptian trade with other countries.

E. *Works of contemporary Egyptian historians and writers containing financial material*

This group consists of works of contemporary Egyptian writers who discussed aspects of the financial system of Egypt on the basis of personal experience gained while holding various offices in the different *dīwān*s. Hitherto known works of this kind are:

1. The *Kitāb al-minhāj fī ʿilm kharāj Miṣr* by Makhzūmī.
2. The *Rasāʾil* and the *Mutajaddidāt* by al-Qāḍī al-Fāḍil.
3. The *Kitāb qawānīn al-dawāwīn* by Ibn Mammātī.

[1] Alarcón y Santón and R. García, *Los documentos árabes diplomáticos del Archivo de la Corona de Aragón*, pp. 335–62.

[2] Qalqashandī, *Ṣubḥ*, xiv, pp. 63–70.

4. The *Kitāb kashf al-asrār al-ʿilmiyya* by Ibn Baʿra.
5. The *Kitāb tārīkh al-Fayyūm* and the *Kitāb lumaʿ al-qawānīn* by Nābulsī.
6. The eighth volume of the *Kitāb nihāyat al-arab* by Nuwayrī, together with four books from a later period, the *Kitāb ṣubḥ al-aʿshā* by Qalqashandī and the *Kitāb al-khiṭaṭ*, the *Kitāb shudhūr al-ʿuqūd* and the *Kitāb ighāthat al-umma* by Maqrīzī.

1. Kitāb al-minhāj fī ʿilm kharāj Miṣr *by Makhzūmī*

Professor Cahen has thrown some light on this manuscript, which is found under Add. 23483 in the British Museum Library, by tracing its author and title by means of comparison with other sources.[1]

Makhzūmī served in the Fāṭimid and Ayyūbid *dīwāns*. He reached the post of chief of the *dīwān al-majlis*, the main Fāṭimid *dīwān*, and it is probable that, being experienced in customs duties and the *jawālī* tax, he was given another important financial post at the beginning of the Ayyūbid period. He compiled the *Kitāb al-minhāj* in 565/1169–70, that is immediately after the conquest of Egypt by Shīrkūh and Saladin. In 581/1185–6 or later, he revised his book and added more information. This revised edition is worth mentioning because it contains useful data on the financial system of Egypt at the end of the Fāṭimid era and the beginning of the Ayyūbid period.[2]

The incomplete copy of the *Kitāb al-minhāj* of Makhzūmī in the British Museum covers the following five financial topics:

(*a*) The various categories of land in Egypt, times of cultivation and different sorts of plants and crops.
(*b*) The *taḥwīl* of the *kharājī* years 565 and 566.[3]
(*c*) The *dār al-ḍarb* (mint) in Cairo and Alexandria.
(*d*) The *muʿāmalāt*, which Makhzūmī divided into three groups: the *hilālī* tax, the *kharājī* tax, and other kinds of taxes.
(*e*) The *Dīwān al-jaysh* (army office).

[1] Cahen, 'Un traité financier inédit d'époque Fatimide-Ayyubide', *JESHO*, v (1962), pp. 139–59; id., 'Contribution à l'étude des impôts dans l'Égypte médiévale', *JESHO*, v (1962), pp. 244–78; id., 'Douanes et commerce dans les ports méditerranéens de l'Égypte médiévale d'après le *Minhādj* d'Al-Makhzūmī', *JESHO*, vii (1964), pp. 217–314. Ḥabīb al-Zayyāt ('al-Jawālī', *al-Mashriq*, xli. ii (1947), p. 12) stressed the importance of this manuscript in 1947. However, he seems to have been unable to identify its author and title.

[2] Cahen, 'Un traité financier', pp. 140–1; see Maqrīzī, *Khiṭaṭ*, ii, p. 460; for the *dīwān al-majlis* see below, p. 144 and n. 3.

[3] See below, p. 134.

The financial material provided is useful in several ways. Makhzūmī tries to find for each tax an origin in the *Sharī'a*. He states its amount and method of collection, and provides advice to the officials in charge of its collection on the preparation of their monthly and yearly lists.[1] The data on taxes on trade in Alexandria, Damietta, and Tinnīs as supplied by Makhzūmī are useful in this context, in that they have a bearing on the study of taxation.[2] The obvious importance of the *Kitāb al-minhāj* prompted Maqrīzī to quote it frequently in his *Khiṭaṭ*.[3] The usefulness of the manuscript is reduced by the loss of certain pages.

2. *The* Rasā'il *and the* Mutajaddidāt *by al-Qāḍī al-Fāḍil*

While he was the chief of the Fāṭimid *dīwān al-inshā'* (chancellery of state), al-Qāḍī al-Fāḍil helped Saladin to overthrow the Fāṭimid dynasty. Saladin trusted him and appointed him vizier, and he became his right-hand man in carrying through necessary reforms in the army and the system of taxation.[4] Apart from his *Rasā'il* (letters), al-Fāḍil wrote an administrative and historical work in the form of a diary, referred to in later works as *al-Mutajaddidāt* and *al-Muyāwamāt*.[5] Both are of importance for the financial history of Medieval Egypt.

Some collections of his letters are preserved in the British Museum Library, in Cambridge University Library, in Leiden, and in the *Kitāb nihāyat al-arab* of Nuwayrī.[6]

The four manuscripts in the British Museum contain some of the *rasā'il* or merely extracts from them. Two of the manuscripts are not relevant to the present study, as they were intended as

[1] Makhzūmī, fols. 142–54, 165–80; the writer follows Prof. Cahen in using the original Coptic numbers of the MS.; cf. Cahen, 'Un traité financier', p. 140 n. 1.

[2] See below, pp. 89 ff.; for Tinnīs cf. Ibn Bassām, *Kitāb anīs al-jalīs fī akhbār Tinnīs*, ed. al-Shayyāl in *MMII*, xiv (1967), pp. 151–89.

[3] Maqrīzī, *Khiṭaṭ*, i, pp. 100, 103, 247, 275–7; ii, p. 460; cf. Guest, 'A list of writers, books and other authorities mentioned by El Maqrīzi in his Khiṭaṭ', *JRAS* (1902), p. 118.

[4] Nuwayrī, xxvii, fol. 3; Ibn Qāḍī Shuhba, *Ṭabaqāt*, fol. 129^{r-v}; Ibn Khallikān, *Wafayāt*, i, pp. 357–9; Maqrīzī, *Khiṭaṭ*, ii, p. 366; Brockelmann, article 'al-Ḳāḍī al-Fāḍil', in *EI*[1].

[5] Cf. M. H. M. Ahmad, *Studies on the works of Abū Shāma* (Ph.D. thesis, London, 1951), pp. 163–6; id., 'Some notes on Arabic historiography', in Lewis and Holt, *Historians*, pp. 85–6; see also his introduction to the *Kitāb al-rawḍatayn*, i. i, pp. 21–2.

[6] There is another collection in Konya in the Yusuf Ağa Library; see Ahmad, 'Some notes', p. 86 n. 16.

models for the student of literature and eloquence and do not contain any financial material.[1] The third, Add. 25757, which is untitled and undated, consists of letters, mans̲h̲ūrs, and sijillāt from al-Fāḍil's pen. Some of them contain useful information about the iqṭāʿ, the zakāt, and the mawārīt̲h̲ ḥas̲h̲riyya,[2] while others throw light on trade in ʿAyd̲h̲āb and Alexandria.[3] The defects of this manuscript are incomplete text and bad script. The fourth manuscript, Add. 7465 Rich, lacks, like the first, both title and date. It contains only letters, most of which are addressed to Saladin and ʿImād al-Dīn al-Iṣfahānī. In some, which are addressed to Saladin, al-Fāḍil mentions such financial matters as the impact of war on the assignment of iqṭāʿs and cases of confiscation.[4]

The manuscript preserved in the Cambridge University Library is entitled Ins̲h̲āʾāt al-Qāḍī al-Fāḍil, and contains letters written by al-Fāḍil to his friends or in his capacity as Saladin's secretary. Neither these letters nor the Leiden MS. nor the rasāʾil utilized by Nuwayrī provide any financial material.[5]

The title of al-Fāḍil's historical work, the Kitāb mutajaddidāt al-ḥawādit̲h̲, is quoted forty times by Maqrīzī in the K̲h̲iṭaṭ.[6] Maqrīzī refers to it as Mutajaddidāt,[7] Mutajaddidāt ḥawādit̲h̲,[8] Taʿlīq al-mutajaddidāt,[9] Ḥawādit̲h̲,[10] and al-Muyāwamāt.[11]

Helbig, in his pamphlet on al-Qāḍī al-Fāḍil, suggests that these Mutajaddidāt derive from the files of the dīwān al-ins̲h̲āʾ in Egypt, especially from the journals of this dīwān which contained, inter alia, copies of important letters and descriptions of the more significant events of state.[12] Haq seems to be of the same opinion, as he describes the Mutajaddidāt as 'an official journal'.[13] However, an examination of the material from the Mutajaddidāt as preserved by Maqrīzī suggests a different conception. It was probably, as

---

[1] ʿUyūn al-rasāʾil al-Fāḍiliyya, MS. Add. 25756; and al-Fāṣil min kalām al-Qāḍī al-Fāḍil, MS. Add. 7307 Rich.
[2] Rasāʾil, fols. 9ᵛ–10ᵛ, 73ʳ⁻ᵛ, 118ʳ⁻ᵛ.
[3] Ibid., fols. 114ᵛ–17ʳ. [4] Rasāʾil, fols. 10ʳ, 112ᵛ–13ʳ.
[5] The Leiden MS. is entitled Fāḍiliyyāt al-Fāḍil (Cod. Or. 994, fols. 135–79); Nuwayrī, viii, pp. 1–51.
[6] Maqrīzī, K̲h̲iṭaṭ, i, pp. 249–50.
[7] Ibid., i, pp. 60, 86–7, 105, 108, 184, 281, 407, 413, 488; ii, pp. 5, 24, 107, 143, 198.
[8] Ibid., i, p. 107; ii, p. 143. [9] Ibid., i, p. 493; ii, p. 124.
[10] Ibid., ii, p. 164. [11] Ibid., i, p. 100.
[12] Helbig, al-Qāḍī al-Fāḍil, Der Wezīr Saladin's, pp. 41–2.
[13] Haq, 'al-Qadi-ul-Fadil and his diary', Proceedings and Transactions of the Tenth All-India Oriental Conference (1940), p. 724.

Ibn Khallikān states, a daily chronicle, very exactly dated and covering important events of the time.[1] A direct relationship with the *dīwān al-inshā'* cannot be assumed for two reasons. First, the *Mutajaddidāt* covers a period from 566 up to 594 (1170 to 98). It is known that, apart from a very brief interlude, al-Fāḍil occupied no position of power after Saladin's death in 589/1193. Thus the book cannot be said to express the official viewpoint. Secondly, the quotations from the *Mutajaddidāt* in the *Khiṭaṭ* are not of a uniform character, but have each a purpose of their own. Thus, for instance, the criticism of the deplorable condition of Egypt during the financial crisis of the year 592/1195–6 is hardly compatible with the character of an official journal.[2]

The quotations from the *Mutajaddidāt* in the *Khiṭaṭ* are helpful in the study of the following financial topics:

(*a*) The military *iqṭā'* system during the reign of Saladin.[3]
(*b*) The financial resources of Egypt from 585 to 588/1189–93.[4]
(*c*) The revenue collected by the *matjar* of Alexandria in 587/1191–2.[5]
(*d*) The *taḥwīl* of the *kharājī* year in 567/1171–2.[6]

3. *The* Kitāb qawānīn al-dawāwīn *by Ibn Mammātī*

Ibn Mammātī's father was converted to Islam during the reign of the last Fāṭimid Caliph al-'Āḍid, and became an important figure in the *dīwāns*. His son and successor in office, al-As'ad, rose to become the chief of the *dīwān al-jaysh* and the *nāẓir al-dawāwīn* under Saladin and his son al-'Azīz 'Uthmān.[7]

Maqrīzī states that Ibn Mammātī compiled the *Qawānīn al-dawāwīn* for al-'Azīz 'Uthmān in four volumes. The book which is extant today is merely a synopsis of the original.[8] According to his

[1] Ibn Khallikān, *Wafayāt*, i, p. 107; see also Dhahabī, *Tārīkh* (MS. Or. 52), fols. 109^{v}–10^{r}; 'Aynī, *'Iqd*, 'B', xiii, fol. 124^{v}.

[2] Maqrīzī, *Khiṭaṭ*, i, p. 105.

[3] Maqrīzī, *Khiṭaṭ*, i, p. 86.

[4] Ibid., i, pp. 87, 100, 107–10, 198, 249–50.

[5] Ibid., i, p. 109; for the *matjar*, see below, pp. 92–4.

[6] Ibid., i, pp. 281–3.

[7] Nuwayrī, xxvii, fol. 13; Kutubī, *'Uyūn* (Fatih), fols. 13^{v}–14^{v}; 'Aynī, *'Iqd*, B, xiii, fol. 160^{v}; Ibn Khallikān, *Wafayāt*, i, pp. 84–6; Yāqūt, *Irshād*, ii, pp. 244–56; Maqrīzī, *Khiṭaṭ*, ii, p. 160; for the *naẓar al-dawāwīn*, see below, pp. 149–50.

[8] Maqrīzī, *Khiṭaṭ*, ii, p. 160. According to the table of contents given by Ibn Mammātī himself in his introduction (*Qawānīn*, ed. Atiya, pp. 54–60) the book was compiled in fifteen chapters; the published book, however, is a summary of only ten. Unless the edition of al-Najjār is specially referred to, use was made of Prof. Atiya's edition.

own statement, Ibn Mammātī's motive in writing the book was twofold: to give proof of loyalty to the state whose officials would profit by his experience and knowledge; and to facilitate the task of the *kuttāb* by providing a handy textbook of financial administration.[1]

The *Qawānīn al-dawāwīn* provides five main items of financial information:

(*a*) An alphabetic list of the provinces and villages of Egypt.
(*b*) A description of the cultivated land, canals, plants, and crops of Egypt, including the dates of surveying and cultivating the land, the harvesting of crops, and the collection of taxes, as well as the amount of these taxes.
(*c*) Details of the work of eighteen *dīwānī* officials.
(*d*) Important data on different kinds of financial resources, which used to be drawn on in the author's lifetime.
(*e*) Information on the *iqṭāʿ* system.

Despite its usefulness, the *Qawānīn al-dawāwīn* is, in certain respects, an inadequate source. It says nothing of the area and the *ʿibra* of different provinces and villages, for fear of infringing what Ibn Mammātī calls '*asrār al-dawla*' (state secrets).[2] It provides information about the *dīwānī* officials, but not about the number and nature of particular *dīwāns*. The evidence on taxes is often limited, for example, the *zakāt* is described as defined in the *Sharīʿa*, not as what it had become in Ibn Mammātī's lifetime.[3] The evidence the book contains on the relationship between the *muqṭaʿ* and state, and on the taxes collected in the *iqṭāʿ*, is therefore inconclusive.

4. *The* Kitāb kashf al-asrār al-ʿilmiyya *by Ibn Baʿra*

All that is known about the author is that he is identical with Manṣūr ibn Baʿra al-Dhahabī al-Kāmilī. The name al-Dhahabī suggests that he was professionally concerned with the smelting and refining of gold. The *nisba* al-Kāmilī points to the relation between him and the Ayyūbid Sultan al-Kāmil. It also indicates that he wrote his book during the reign of this sultan, that is between 615/1218 and 635/1238.[4]

[1] Ibn Mammātī, pp. 52–3; Ahmad, 'Some notes', pp. 95–6.
[2] Ibn Mammātī, pp. 55, 84; for the *ʿibra*, see below, pp. 47–8.
[3] Ibn Mammātī, pp. 308–17.
[4] Ehrenkreutz, 'Extracts from the technical manual on the Ayyūbid mint in Cairo', *BSOAS*, xv (1953), pp. 423–4.

Professor Ehrenkreutz has divided the material of this work into two categories. The first is the historical material, consisting of all the items of information with a bearing upon the economic history of Egypt in that period, the second the bulk of Ibn Baʿra's work, which deals with technical matters, such as the quality of gold and silver ore, descriptions of chemical processes, the testing of gold, various instruments, tools, weights, and measures.[1]

In this respect, the book is important, since the author himself was employed in the Egyptian mint. Besides, data on the Āmirī *dīnār*, the Kāmilī *dīnār*, the *nuqra dirham*, the *waraq dirham*, etc., are very useful in dealing with the monetary system of Egypt in the period under consideration.[2]

5. *The* Kitāb tārīkh al-Fayyūm *and the* Kitāb lumaʿ al-qawānīn *by Nābulsī*

These two books are more relevant to the subject under study than Nābulsī's other works.[3] ʿUthmān ibn Ibrāhīm al-Nābulsī came from a Nabulsian family and was born in Egypt on 19 Dhū al-Ḥijja 588/26 December 1192.[4] During the reign of Sultan al-Kāmil, Nābulsī held administrative offices in Upper and Lower Egypt.[5] As can be inferred from an account in the *Tajrīd*, he became an important figure among the *dīwānī* officials in Cairo in 627/1229–30.[6] Victim of a calumny, he retired in 634/1236–7.[7] According to the *Tārīkh al-Fayyūm*, he was sent by Sultan al-Ṣāliḥ Ayyūb in 641/1243–4 to the Fayyūm province, where he spent two years investigating the financial system of that province, and wrote his book *Tārīkh al-Fayyūm*.[8]

This book is divided into ten chapters, the first eight being a

[1] Ehrenkreutz, 'Extracts', pp. 424–5.

[2] See below, pp. 165, 174 n. 4, 175 n. 1, 177.

[3] Nābulsī wrote three epistles, of which only one is known to survive, '*Tajrīd sayf al-himma*'; we know the titles of the other two: '*Ḥusn al-sarīra fī ittikhādh al-ḥiṣn bi al-Jazīra*' and '*Ḥusn al-sulūk fī faḍl malik Miṣr 'lā sā'ir al-mulūk*'. An untitled, incomplete MS. of the first epistle is found in the British Museum Library, Add. 23293; cf. Nābulsī, *Lumaʿ*, p. 31; id., *Fayyūm*, p. 14; Maqrīzī, *Khiṭaṭ*, i, p. 86; Cahen, 'Histoires coptes d'un cadi médiéval. Extraits du *Kitāb tadjrīd saïf al-himma*', *BIFAO*, lix (1960), pp. 133–50.

[4] Prof. Cahen's introduction to *Lumaʿ*, *BEO*, xvi (1959–60), p. 120.

[5] Nābulsī, *Lumaʿ*, p. 4.

[6] Id., *Tajrīd*, fols. 208^{v}–11^{r}.

[7] Id., *Lumaʿ*, pp. 39–42, tr. Cahen, 'Quelques aspects de l'administration égyptienne médiévale', *BFLS*, année 26 (1948), pp. 105–8.

[8] Nābulsī, *Fayyūm*, p. 3.

description of the province of Fayyūm, its climate, inhabitants, villages, mosques, monasteries, and churches. The ninth chapter deals with the total financial resources of the Fayyūm. The last chapter contains useful financial material about each village and city in Fayyūm. The author specifies the fiscal character of the village in question, whether *waqf*, *iqṭāʿ* of the sultan, or ordinary *iqṭāʿ*. For each *iqṭāʿ*, Nābulsī specifies the *ʿibra* and the different taxes collected from the *fallāḥīn*.[1]

The *Tārīkh al-Fayyūm* is pertinent to the subject under study for the three following reasons: (*a*) It is probable that the taxes which were collected in Fayyūm in the author's lifetime were much the same as in other Egyptian provinces; (*b*) it is unique in giving certain details of *iqṭāʿ* taxes and subordinate *iqṭāʿ* clerks; (*c*) part of the material was collected by word of mouth from clerks of the *iqṭāʿ*s and *waqf*s, so that it represents first-hand information, invaluable in this context.[2]

When he had retired, Nābulsī wrote the *Kitāb lumaʿ al-qawānīn* for Sultan al-Ṣāliḥ Ayyūb, to warn him of the negligence and dishonesty of officials with which his long experience in the work of the *dīwān*s had made him conversant.[3] This book provides useful information on the administration of the *matjar* at the end of the Ayyūbid period, the revenue from the mint, the functions of the *dīwān al-jaysh*, the *dīwān al-aḥbās*, and the *dīwān al-māl*, and *dīwānī* officials such as the *mushidd al-dawāwīn* and the *mustawfī*.[4] However, caution is advisable in utilizing these data, as Nābulsī composed this work in order to ingratiate himself with the sultan and boast of his experience in the *dīwān*s. He may also be guilty of many exaggerations in his accounts.

6. *The* Kitāb nihāyat al-arab, *by Nuwayrī*

Nuwayrī, born in 677/1279 in Akhmīm in Upper Egypt, was sent in 701/1302 to Damascus to supervise the sultani property in Syria. Two years later he was transferred to the *dīwān al-khāṣṣ*. In 710/1311, he became *nāẓir al-jaysh* (inspector of the army) in Tripoli, and was eventually appointed *nāẓir al-dīwān* in the Egyptian provinces al-Daqahliyya and al-Murtāḥiyya.[5] The

[1] Ibid., pp. 26–179. [2] Ibid., p. 23. [3] Nābulsī, *Lumaʿ*, pp. 3–6.

[4] See below, pp. 39, 93–4, 116–7, 147, 151–2, 156.

[5] Nuwayrī, xxviii, fol. 123, xxx, fols. 2, 18, 20, 45, 59, 77; Ṣafadī, *Aʿyān* (MS. A.S. 2962), fols. 93^v–4^r; Idfuwī, *Ṭāliʿ*, pp. 46–7; Ibn Ḥajar, *Durar*, i, p. 197; Ibn Taghrī Birdī, *Manhal*, i, pp. 361–2.

Nihāyat al-arab, which Nuwayrī dedicated to Sultan al-Nāṣir ibn Qalāwūn, consists of thirty volumes. Part of it is connected with his administrative activities, especially the eighth volume, which is of importance for any research on the financial system of Egypt in that period.[1]

The three main financial aspects covered in this volume are:

(*a*) The function of the *dīwān al-jaysh*, the only *dīwān* to deal with the registration, evaluation, and conferment of the *iqṭā*ʿs.[2]

(*b*) The nature and method of collection of taxes such as the *hilālī*, the *jawālī*, the *kharājī*, and the *marāʿī* taxes.[3]

(*c*) The duties of *dīwānī* officials.[4]

7. *The* Kitāb ṣubḥ al-aʿshā *by Qalqashandī*

Qalqashandī completed his studies in Alexandria in 778/1376–7, and joined, thirteen years later, the *dīwān al-inshā*ʾ in Cairo in 791/1388–9.[5] His office may have facilitated access to the material for his book, which comprises copies of *iqṭā*ʿ brevets, treaties between Egypt and other countries, and official letters containing orders and instructions.

Qalqashandī's data must be treated with great caution, as it was his primary intention to compose a handbook for the *kuttāb* of the *dīwān al-inshā*ʾ or, in the words of Professor B. Lewis, an 'encyclopaedic bureaucratic vade-mecum'.[6] Qalqashandī went so far as to supply models for all kinds of correspondence, even letters of congratulation, condolence, and blame.[7] One must therefore treat most of the documents in the *Ṣubḥ al-aʿshā* as chancery models and, consequently, less reliable than archival records.

The financial evidence contained in the *Ṣubḥ al-aʿshā* is useful since:

(*a*) It contains copies of some documents, treaties, *manshūr*s, etc., the originals of which have been lost. Some *taqlīd*s of appoint-

[1] Nuwayrī's work was very important for later historians, cf. Ashtor, 'Some unpublished sources for the Baḥrī period', *Studies in Islamic history and civilization* (*Scripta Hierosolymitana*), ix (1961), pp. 20–2.

[2] Nuwayrī, viii, pp. 200–17.

[3] Ibid., viii, pp. 228–64.

[4] Ibid., viii, pp. 298–305.

[5] Qalqashandī, *Ṣubḥ*, xiv, p. 111; Sakhāwī, *Ḍaw*ʾ, ii, p. 8; Ibn Taghrī Birdī, *Manhal*, i, pp. 330–1.

[6] Lewis, 'The use by Muslim historians of non-Muslim sources', in Lewis and Holt, *Historians*, p. 182.

[7] Qalqashandī, *Ṣubḥ*, ix, pp. 5–228.

ment describe the functions of such high financial offices as the *wizāra*, the *naẓar al-khāṣṣ*, and the *naẓar al-jaysh*.[1]

(*b*) It illustrates the nature of the *iqṭā'*. Qalqashandī has preserved three Fāṭimid *manshūrs*, three Ayyūbid *tawqī's*, and several incomplete *manshūrs* from the Mamluk period which shed light on some aspects of the *iqṭā'* system in Egypt during the period under consideration.[2]

(*c*) It supplies details of the resources of Egypt. Though the division into two categories, *shar'ī* (in accordance with the *Sharī'a*) and *ghayr shar'ī* (outside the *Sharī'a*) is not applicable to the period under study, the details given for different taxes and their methods of collection are useful in studying taxation.[3]

(*d*) It provides information about different kinds of coins.[4]

8. *The* Kitāb al-khiṭaṭ, *the* Kitāb shudhūr al-'uqūd *and the* Kitāb ighāthat al-umma *by Maqrīzī.*

Maqrīzī's *Kitāb al-khiṭaṭ* and, to a lesser extent, the *Kitāb shudhūr al-'uqūd* and the *Kitāb ighāthat al-umma* are more relevant to the subject under study than his other works. As he himself states, the material of the *Kitāb al-khiṭaṭ* is derived from three main sources; previous books, contemporary writings, and his personal experience.[5] The material derived from the first source is useful in three respects: it provides information on taxation, the *iqṭā'* system, and Mongol influence on the financial system.

Maqrīzī divides the financial resources of Egypt, *māl Miṣr*, into two kinds: *al-māl al-kharājī* and *al-māl al-hilālī*.[6] He gives details of the method of collecting the *kharājī* tax in Egypt from pre-Islamic times onwards, mentioning the amount of the *kharāj* in each particular period of Egyptian history. However, he tends to exaggerate in his figures. The data he gives on the different varieties of the *hilālī* and other taxes are useful in studying taxation.[7]

The material is particularly rich where the *iqṭā'* system is concerned. Maqrīzī seems to have utilized, besides earlier and contemporary works, also documentary sources, especially as regards the Nāṣirī *rawk*.[8]

[1] Ibid., xi, pp. 270–93, 316–19, 321–4; xiv, pp. 63–70; for the *wizāra*, the *naẓar al-khāṣṣ*, and the *naẓar al-jaysh*, see below, pp. 41, 138 ff.

[2] Ibid., xiii, pp. 131–99; see below, pp. 33–4.

[3] Ibid., iii, pp. 452–71.

[4] Ibid., iii, pp. 440–4.

[5] Maqrīzī, *Khiṭaṭ*, i, p. 4.

[6] Ibid., i, pp. 103–11.

[7] Ibid., i, pp. 81–7, 98–100.

[8] Ibid., i, pp. 83, 85–91, 95–8; for the Nāṣirī *rawk* see below, pp. 53–6.

The information derived from the Mongol Code, the Great *Yāsa* of Čingīz Khān, is useful in that it is indicative of the influence of Mongol institutions on Mamluk administration.[1]

In spite of the abundance of evidence of a financial kind in the *Khiṭaṭ*, the use of this book as a source carries with it some disadvantages. There are defects in the systematization and classification of the financial material.[2] Maqrīzī rarely criticizes the facts and figures on the financial resources of Egypt which he derives from other authors.[3] Despite the stress laid on the status of the Copts in financial administration, his information about the financial administration of Egypt is poor in such details as the different kinds of financial *dīwān* and the functions of their officials.[4]

The *Kitāb shudhūr al-ʿuqūd* is divided into three parts. The first deals with *al-nuqūd al-qadīma*, the ancient coins known in Arabia before Islam;[5] the second with *al-nuqūd al-Islāmiyya*, the Islamic coins which were in circulation from the time of the Prophet until the reign of the ʿAbbāsid Caliph al-Mutawakkil;[6] the third with the whole variety of coinage circulating in Egypt from the Islamic period until Maqrīzī's lifetime.[7] It is this third part which is of the utmost importance for the study of the monetary system of Egypt in the period under review, as it contains valuable data on the monetary crisis which occurred at the beginning of Saladin's reign; on Saladin's monetary reform of 583/1187; on al-Kāmil's monetary reform of 622/1225; and on the issue of Ẓāhirī *dirhams* by al-Ẓāhir Baybars in 658/1260.[8] Some of these data do not seem altogether reliable. Thus, for example, the information given about the alloy of the Kāmilī *dirhams* is contradicted by numismatic evidence.[9]

Financial material of value can also be derived from the *Kitāb ighāthat al-umma*, which is mainly concerned with a succession of epidemics in Egyptian history from the pre-Islamic period until 808/1405. Maqrīzī, who is not blind to the fact that some of these epidemics had far-reaching effects on the economic life of the country, refers to certain economic phenomena which accom-

[1] Maqrīzī, *Khiṭaṭ*, ii, pp. 220–2.
[2] Ibid., i, pp. 82 and 85.
[3] Cf. ibid., i, p. 99.
[4] Ibid., i, p. 69.
[5] Maqrīzī, *Shudhūr*, pp. 22–30, tr. S. de Sacy, *Traité des monnoies musulmanes*, pp. 5–12.
[6] Ibid., pp. 30–51, tr. S. de Sacy, pp. 12–34.
[7] Ibid., pp. 52–73, tr. S. de Sacy, pp. 34–59.
[8] See below, pp. 162, 173, 178, 186.
[9] See below, p. 180.

panied them, such as changes in the price of commodities and in the exchange rates of coins. He enlarges on the monetary crises which frequently occurred during such epidemics.[1] Pointing to the dangers connected with the increasing circulation of copper *fulūs*, Maqrīzī gives a short survey of the history of copper coinage, how it was recognized as valid currency under al-Kāmil, gradually increasing in importance until it predominated in Maqrīzī's own time.[2] These data are of great value for the study of the monetary system of Medieval Egypt.

F. *Records of travel*

Benjamin of Tudela, Burchard (or Gerard) vice-dominus of Strasburg, Ibn Jubayr, 'Abd al-Laṭīf al-Baghdādī, Ibn Sa'īd al-Andalusī, al-'Abdarī, Ibn Baṭṭūṭa, and al-Balawī, were the most famous travellers to visit Egypt in the period under study. They all left records of their travels which are important, in that they refer to a number of phenomena, which may have seemed to contemporary Egyptian historians too banal to be recorded in their chronicles.

1. Benjamin of Tudela visited Egypt while Saladin was al-'Āḍid's vizier. He mentions briefly some facts relevant to the finances of that time, such as the types of goods brought by merchants from Fezzan (south of Tripoli), and describes the market-places and inns of Cairo.[3]

2. Burchard (or Gerard), vice-dominus of Strasbourg ,was sent by Frederick I Barbarossa on a mission to Saladin in 1175. Arnold of Lübeck preserved Gerard's report of his mission to Egypt and Syria in his history.[4] His report contains some fiscal data, such as the statement that, in his time, alum was still mined in Egypt on behalf of the sovereign.[5]

3. Ibn Jubayr, who visited Egypt in 578/1183, mentions that he had to pay *zakāt* in Alexandria, and gives his impressions of the

[1] Cf. Maqrīzī, *Ighātha*, pp. 14–17, 36–8, tr. Wiet, 'Le traité des famines de Maqrīzī', *JESHO*, v (1962), pp. 15–17, 37–40.

[2] Ibid., pp. 47, 66–72, tr. Wiet, pp. 49–50, 65–71.

[3] *The itinerary of Benjamin*, English translation by M. N. Adler, pp. 68–9, 71; Arabic translation by E. H. Haddad, pp. 170–1, 173 and n. 1; Adler, *Jewish travellers*, pp. 61–2.

[4] Arnold of Lübeck, *Arnoldi Chronica Slavorum*, Lib. vii. 8, pp. 264–77; Lewis, 'The sources for the history of the Syrian Assassins', *Speculum*, xxvii (1952), p. 482.

[5] See below, p. 83.

Egyptian tax-collectors.[1] The information he gives about the exchange rate between the contemporary Egyptian *dīnār* and the Mu'minī *dīnār* of the Almohads is important in that it shows that Saladin maintained the old exchange rate of the Fāṭimids in spite of the debasement of his *dīnār*.[2]

4. ʿAbd al-Laṭīf al-Baghdādī gives a first-hand description of the epidemic which broke out in Egypt in 596/1200, and records its effects on the financial situation of Egypt at that time.[3]

5. ʿAlī ibn Mūsā, known as Ibn Saʿīd al-Andalusī, visited Egypt with his father in 639/1241–2, during the reign of al-Ṣāliḥ Najm al-Dīn Ayyūb. The father died shortly after their arrival in Egypt, leaving to his son the task of completing the *Kitāb al-mughrib*.[4] Ibn Saʿīd was surprised by the liveliness of the commerce in Fusṭāṭ, to which he devotes some space.[5] The remarks he makes on the black *dirham*s he found in circulation in Egypt at the end of the Ayyūbid period, their rate of exchange and their low value, throw light on the situation of the Egyptian silver coinage on the eve of Mamluk rule.[6]

6. Al-ʿAbdarī came to Egypt from the Maghrib around 688/1289, during the reign of Sultan Qalāwūn. Describing a journey to the Ḥijāz, al-ʿAbdarī records his impressions of Egypt, which are unfavourable throughout.[7] His remarks about the reprehensible behaviour of tax-officials in Alexandria can be credited, since they coincide with those of Ibn Jubayr.[8] These remarks, as well as the statement that the *kharāj* used to be imposed as soon as the Nile reached the height of 16 *dhirāʿ*,[9] contribute to our understanding of the method of tax collection in Egypt at that time.

7. Ibn Baṭṭūṭa, who visited Egypt in 726/1326 on his way to Mecca, touches in his *Tuḥfa* on the economic state of some towns in Egypt during the reign of al-Nāṣir Muḥammad.[10] The informa-

[1] Ibn Jubayr, pp. 39–40; see below, pp. 97–8.

[2] See below, p. 172.

[3] Baghdādī, *Ifāda* (ed. 1964), pp. 204 ff.; the English translation of this edition being unreliable, a facsimile of the Arabic original and the translation of S. de Sacy are used throughout.

[4] Z. M. Ḥasan, *Raḥḥāla*, pp. 121–2; id., the introduction to the *Kitāb al-Mughrib*, pp. 11–15.

[5] Ibn Saʿīd, *Mughrib*, i, p. 7.

[6] See below, p. 184.

[7] ʿAbdarī, fols. 49^r–82^v, ed. al-Fāsī, pp. 90–156; for al-ʿAbdarī cf. Zaghlūl, 'Mulāḥaẓāt ʿan Miṣr', *BFA*, viii (1954), pp. 108–9; M. Ben Cheneb and W. Hoenerbach, article 'al-ʿAbdarī' in *EI*².

[8] See below, p. 99.

[9] See below, p. 73.

[10] Ibn Baṭṭūṭa, i, pp. 27–113.

tion he provides on Qaṭyā and the port of ʻAydhāb is, to a certain extent, illustrative of contemporary methods of taxation.[1]

8. Al-Balawī visited Egypt in 737/1337 while on pilgrimage. A part of his book is devoted to the description of his Egyptian route.[2] He gives specific information about the amount he paid in tax and the methods of tax collection in Alexandria. The data concerning tax collection in Qaṭyā are less precise.[3]

G. *Coins*

In the words of Professor Grierson, the evidence provided by coins 'may fill in gaps in our evidence, or it may confirm and exemplify things that we know of from other sources, or it may correct the statements of literary sources'.[4]

Coins are a historical source of paramount importance for the student of economic history in that (*a*) they reflect the economic conditions of the time; for instance, the *dīnār* crisis of the first year of Saladin's reign reflects the economic uncertainty which prevailed at the beginning of the Ayyūbid period and had its effect on the army and taxation;[5] (*b*) they serve the needs of taxation and trade, a fact which enhances the value of the information on the variations in the standard of fineness of specimen coins of each sultan. Changes in the purity and amount of gold in the *dīnār* and of silver in the *dirham* were most frequently due to the economic situation. In this respect, the numismatic catalogues are sadly incomplete, merely giving the legend, image, size, and weight, but not the metallic composition of coins, which cannot be deduced from the information given.[6]

[1] See below, p. 101.

[2] Balawī, fols. 27r–75v; for al-Balawī cf. Ḥasan, *Raḥḥāla*, pp. 134–5; *Zaghlūl, Mulāḥaẓāt*, pp. 109–10.

[3] See below, pp. 99–102.

[4] Grierson, *Numismatics and history*, The Historical Association, General Series, G. 19, p. 8.

[5] See below, pp. 162, 165, 169 ff.

[6] See *Jean Sauvaget's introduction to the history of the Muslim East: a bibliographical guide, based on the second edition as recast by Claude Cahen*, pp. 55–7; Ehrenkreutz, 'Monetary aspects of medieval Near Eastern economic history', in Cook, ed., *Studies*, p. 46; S. Lane-Poole, *Catalogue of oriental coins in the British Museum*, iv, pp. 63–159, ix, pp. 326–49; id., *Catalogue of the collection of Arabic coins preserved in the Khedivial Library at Cairo*, pp. 203–55; Lavoix, *Catalogue des monnaies musulmanes de la Bibliothèque Nationale*, iii, pp. 173–347; see also Dr. Fahmī's description of the Ayyūbid coins preserved in the Museum of Islamic Art (Cairo), published as an appendix to his edition of Ibn Baʻra's *Kashf*, pp. 98–133.

Numismatic evidence often goes a long way to support information found in documentary sources, such as, for example, the data on the depreciation of the Fāṭimid *dirhams* found in the Geniza.[1] Data found in literary sources are sometimes confirmed by numismatic evidence, as in the case of the references to the intrinsic quality of the Kāmilī *dīnār* and the Ẓāhirī *dirham*, and sometimes refuted by it as in the case of the alloy of the Kāmilī *dirham*.[2] Chapter V of the present work illustrates the importance of evidence of this kind derived from a series of recent investigations of the alloy of Egyptian coins carried out by Professor Balog and Professor Ehrenkreutz.[3]

H. *Inscriptions*

Arabic texts written or carved on buildings, mosques, schools, tombstones, metal, wooden, or porcelain objects, do not yield as much detail as the literary sources, though they are authentic, first-hand documents contemporaneous with the events under study.[4] Professor B. Lewis points out two groups of inscriptions of particular interest to the economic historian: 'The first consists of the texts or summaries of *waqf* deeds, inscribed on pious foundations, to protect the service of God from the depredations of the state; the second deals with taxes, tolls, and levies of various kinds—usually in the form of the pious abolition of illegal taxes by a pious new ruler.' He also mentions inscriptions on metrological objects (weights, coin-weights, measure-stamps, vessel-stamps, tokens), and trade marks or certificates on manufactured articles, especially textiles and metalwork.[5]

Of the Egyptian inscriptions from the period under review, only a few provide financial information.[6] However, several have been

[1] See below, pp. 168–9. [2] See below, pp. 177, 180, 186.

[3] Cf. below, pp. 164–5, 168–9, 172, 175, 177, 180, 183–4, 186.

[4] Cf. Cahen–Sauvaget, *Introduction*, pp. 52–5; Bās͟hā, *Funūn*, iii, pp. 1351–64.

[5] Lewis, 'Sources for the economic history of the Middle East', in Cook, ed., *Studies*, p. 86.

[6] Unfortunately, most of the inscriptions with a bearing on the abolition of taxes and tolls derive from a later period; cf. *CIA*, Égypte, i, pp. 560–1, No. 373, p. 745, No. 539; Wiet, 'Les inscriptions arabes d'Égypte', *Comptes rendus de l'Académie des Inscriptions et Belles-Lettres*, 1913, p. 504; id., 'Un décret du sultan mamlouk Malik Ashraf Sha'ban à la Mecque', *Mélanges L. Massignon*, iii (1957), pp. 384–7; Darrāg, *L'Égypte sous le règne de Barsbay*, pp. 152 n. 1, 154–5; see also Sauvaget, 'Décrets mamelouks de Syrie', *BEO*, ii (1932), pp. 1–52, iii (1933), pp. 1–29, xii (1947–8), pp. 5–60; Bās͟hā, *Funūn*, i, pp. 87, 416, ii, pp. 513, 515, iii, pp. 1357, 1361.

found useful when dealing with the financial administration of Egypt: those containing fiscal evidence, and those referring to officials of financial *dīwāns* such as the *s͟hādd*, the *mutawallī* and the *ʿāmil.*[1] In one particular case, mention of *al-mus͟hārafa* in an inscription permitted the deduction that this office was Fāṭimid in origin.[2] In another case, evidence derived from inscriptions showed that Qarāqūs͟h, who supervised the execution of the Ṣalāḥī *rawk*, was also chosen by Saladin to supervise the construction of the citadel of Cairo.[3]

[1] See below, pp. 153, 155 n. 3, 158 n. 2.

[2] See below, p. 157.

[3] See below, p. 51 n. 5

II

THE *IQṬĀʿ* SYSTEM

A. *Introduction*

STATING that 'from the days of Saladin Yūsuf ibn Ayyūb until today, all Egyptian cultivated land has been assigned in the form of *iqṭāʿ*s to the sultan, his *ajnād* and his amirs', Maqrīzī implies that it was Saladin who introduced the military *iqṭāʿ* system to Egypt.[1] It is well known that Saladin and other Ayyūbids, as well as a number of amirs, had become acquainted with this practice while they served the Zankid dynasty. Moreover, Saladin found in Egypt, on the eve of the collapse of the Fāṭimid regime, an indigenous system of *iqṭāʿ* which he could neither wholly utilize nor ignore.

The main features of the Fāṭimid *iqṭāʿ* in Egypt are still ambiguous and need serious research. However, it appears that—before the reign of al-Mustanṣir—the Fāṭimid Caliphs sometimes conferred *iqṭāʿ*s upon high-ranking civil officials such as the viziers and the heads of the *dīwāns* (offices) in lieu of salaries. The sources mention, for instance, that the Egyptian and Syrian *iqṭāʿ* of the vizier Yaʿqūb ibn Killis provided him, during the reign of al-ʿAzīz, with 8,000 *dīnār*s yearly.[2] Musabbiḥī states that when, in 415/1024, the amir Shams al-Mulk, the chief of the *dīwān al-Kutāmiyyīn*, was replaced by ʿIzz al-Dawla al-Khādim, he asked the Caliph al-Ẓāhir to cancel his *iqṭāʿ* at the same time. The Caliph replied that an *iqṭāʿ* was a favour (*niʿma*) and as such could not be cancelled.[3]

It is worth mentioning that the *muqṭaʿ*s in this case were not committed to any military service, but were subject to the payment

[1] Maqrīzī, *Khiṭaṭ*, i, p. 97.

[2] Ibn Ẓāfir, *Akhbār*, fol. 54^{r-v}; Nuwayrī, xxvi, fol. 49; Ibn al-Ṣayrafī, *Ishāra*, p. 23; Dawādārī (*Durra muḍiyya*, p. 225) states that the *iqṭāʿ* of Ibn Killis yielded 100,000 *dīnār*s of revenue yearly.

[3] Musabbiḥī, MS., xl, fols. 148^{v}–9^{r}; it seems that the Fāṭimid office which administered the affairs of the corps whose soldiers belonged to a Maghribī Berber tribe, Kutāma, was the *dīwān al-Kutāmiyyīn*. For the Fāṭimid army cf. Qalqashandī, *Ṣubḥ*, iii, pp. 480–2; Canard, article 'Fāṭimids' in *EI*²; for other Fāṭimid *dīwān*s see below, pp. 144 ff.

of the *ʿushr* (tithe) of the *iqṭāʿ* revenue to the treasury.[1] This type of assignment of *iqṭāʿ*s to civil officials was known at the beginning of the 4th/10th century or even before, and has no particular fiscal character.[2] However—at this stage of their rule—the Fāṭimids do not seem to have imitated the Buwayhid military *iqṭāʿ* system.[3]

It also appears that, as a result of the confusion prevalent in Egypt during the reign of the Caliph al-Mustanṣir, soldiers were gradually substituted for civilians as tax-farmers. Professor Cahen states that this entitled them to receive localities of taxable value designated by the term *iqṭāʿ*. This taxable value could be reassessed from time to time, that is changed, increased, or diminished. Although the *muqṭaʿ*s were permitted to utilize the income of the *kharājī* land to their benefit, they had to pay a certain sum to the treasury, from which the soldiers received a supplement to their pay which distinguished them from Buwayhid soldiers.[4] It appears that the military service of the soldier who was also an *iqṭāʿ*-holder was performed, not in return for the benefits derived from his *iqṭāʿ*, but for the pay he received from the treasury. In fact, the prevalent system of paying soldiers in the Fāṭimid army was based on regular monthly pay.[5]

In the year 501/1107–8, both military and civilian *muqṭaʿ*s complained that the financial resources of the *iqṭāʿ*s were on the decrease, particularly as every *iqṭāʿ* suffered from *fawāḍil* (arrears)

[1] The term *ʿushr* (tithe) (plural *aʿshār* not *ʿushūr*) refers here to the rate of ten per cent collected from the produce of the cultivated land irrigated by running water or the rate of five per cent (*niṣf al-ʿushr*) on the products of the land which was irrigated by artificial means such as water-wheels. It is different from the sort of *ʿushr* (plural *ʿushūr*) which was euphemistically used to refer to certain illegal taxes, see Forand, 'Notes on ʿušr and maks', *Arabica*, xiii (1966), pp. 137–41.

[2] See for example Maqrīzī, *Khiṭaṭ*, i, p. 97; Dūrī, *Tārīkh al-ʿIrāq*, p. 29.

[3] The Buwayhid regime established an absolute military supremacy in the government. Army officers were granted *iqṭāʿ*s in lieu of salaries without even the obligation to pay tithes to the treasury. The Buwayhid *muqṭaʿ* would exchange the *iqṭāʿ*, at his own or the government's wish, if its revenue was no longer adequate, or for any other expedient cause; for details cf. Miskawayh, *Tajārib*, ii, pp. 95–100; Dūrī, 'Studies on the economic life of Mesopotamia in the tenth century' (Ph.D., London, 1942), pp. 33–8; id., *Tārīkh al-ʿIrāq*, pp. 30–2, 262–6; Cahen, 'L'Évolution de l'iqṭāʿ du IXe au XIIIe siècle', *Annales* (*E.S.C.*), viii (1953), pp. 32–8; id., article 'Buwayhids' in *EI*²; id., *Pre-Ottoman Turkey*, p. 39; Kabir, *The Buwayhid dynasty*, pp. 12, 139–41, 146–8; Bosworth, 'Military organization under the Būyids of Persia and Iraq', *Oriens*, xviii–xix (1967), pp. 159 ff.

[4] Cahen, 'Évolution', pp. 37–8; id., Review of Løkkegaard's *Islamic taxation*, *Arabica*, i (1954), p. 348.

[5] Musabbiḥī, fol. 243v; Ibn al-Ṣayrafī, *Ishāra*, p. 54; Nāṣir-i Khusraw, p. 53.

which were collected with difficulty. Al-Afḍal ibn Badr al-Jamālī tried to solve the problem by a cadastral survey of Egyptian cultivated land and a consequent reassignment of the *iqṭā*ʿs (the Afḍalī *rawk*).[1]

When al-Baṭā'iḥī became vizier to the Fāṭimid Caliph al-Āmir in 515/1122, he found that anybody could ask for an *iqṭā*ʿ grant, on condition that the share of the treasury was increased. Thus any existing *muqṭa*ʿ would be outbid. Al-Baṭā'iḥī issued a decree prohibiting the transfer of *iqṭā*ʿs so long as dues were paid without delay.[2]

It appears that al-Baṭā'iḥī's decree transformed the Fāṭimid *iqṭā*ʿ system. The *muqṭa*ʿs could no longer be transferred from their *iqṭā*ʿs if they regularly remitted a certain but possibly not uniform proportion of the revenue of their *iqṭā*ʿs to *bayt al-māl*. Those who were able to do so increased in power and wealth which enabled them to participate, together with their subordinates, in important military and political actions. What power the *muqṭa*ʿs came to possess is illustrated by the account found in available sources to the effect that Ibn Ruzzīk, who had come from Upper Egypt after the murder of al-Ẓāfir with a number of Bedouin and *ajnād*, was joined by the Egyptian *muqṭa*ʿs who came out in support of the new Caliph al-Fā'iz against his vizier ʿAbbās.[3] Later Ibn Ruzzīk himself was granted the village of Balaqs as an *iqṭā*ʿ.[4]

It also seems that the Fāṭimid *iqṭā*ʿ system developed gradually after the reassignment of some Egyptian *iqṭā*ʿs to amirs from Nūr al-Dīn's army before the collapse of the Fāṭimid regime. Quoting Ibn Abī Ṭayy, Abū Shāma states that, during Shīrkūh's first expedition to Egypt in 558/1163, the Fāṭimid vizier Shāwar urged some of the Zankid amirs to place themselves under his command. One of them was Khushtarīn al-Kurdī upon whom Shāwar conferred the village of Shaṭṭanawf as an *iqṭā*ʿ.[5] The sources also mention that when Shīrkūh became the vizier of al-ʿĀḍid in 564/1169, he conferred Egyptian *iqṭā*ʿs upon the amirs who came with him

[1] Nuwayrī, xxvi, fols. 81–2; Maqrīzī, *Khiṭaṭ*, i, p. 83; Shayyāl, 'Ṭarīqat masḥ al-arāḍī', in *Dirāsāt fī al-tārīkh al-Islāmī*, pp. 98–9; Rabīʿ, *Nuẓum*, p. 13; see below, p. 51.

[2] Maqrīzī, *Khiṭaṭ*, i, p. 84; for al-Baṭā'iḥī cf. ibid., i, pp. 462–3.

[3] Ibn Ẓāfir, *Akhbār*, fol. 89^{r-v}; Nuwayrī, xxvi, fol. 95; Maqrīzī, *Ittiʿāẓ*, fol. 146^{r}.

[4] *Ḥujjat waqf* Ibn Ruzzīk, *Maḥkama*, Box 1, no. 1.

[5] Abū Shāma, *Rawḍatayn*, i. ii, p. 424; see also Ibn al-Furāt, iii, fol. 200^{v}; Maqrīzī, *Ittiʿāẓ*, fol. 156^{r-v}.

from Syria. Saladin behaved in the same way when he succeeded his uncle Shīrkūh in the vizierate.[1]

Both these accounts indicate that the Fāṭimid *iqṭāʿ* system, which had been non-military, underwent a modification under the Zankid amirs who connected *iqṭāʿ* grants with military service. Thus, Saladin seems to have utilized the Fāṭimid *iqṭāʿ* in introducing the military *iqṭāʿ*, but did not adopt the Fāṭimid model as a whole. As Professor Cahen states, the Ayyūbid *iqṭāʿ* was freer economically than the Fāṭimid *iqṭāʿ*, in the sense that it was no longer subject to the tithes.[2]

Obviously, Saladin, some members of his family, and the new Zankid *muqṭāʿ*s in Egypt were accustomed to the Zankid military *iqṭāʿ* system in which the *iqṭāʿ* was conferred upon the *muqṭaʿ* mainly in return for military service.[3] Nūr al-Dīn used to cancel the *iqṭāʿ* of any amir who neglected his military duties. In 562/1167, when the majority of Nūr al-Dīn's amirs were hesitant to fight against the Fāṭimids and the Crusaders at al-Bābayn in Upper Egypt, the amir Sharaf al-Dīn Barghash threatened that, if they refused to fight, Sultan Nūr al-Dīn would cancel their *iqṭāʿ*s and demand the return of whatever revenue they had already derived from them. Thereupon they fought bravely until they won.[4]

It is worth mentioning that the Zankid *iqṭāʿ* was hereditary. When an amir died, Nūr al-Dīn used to confirm his son in his late father's *iqṭāʿ*. In cases of extreme youth of the new incumbent, the sultan would appoint someone to manage his affairs until he grew up. That was one of the reasons why the amirs showed great fortitude in war.[5] However, the military *iqṭāʿ* introduced by Saladin in

[1] Ibn Abī al-Hayjā', fols. 165^{r}–6^{v}; Maqrīzī, *Ittiʿāẓ*, fol. 164^{r}; Abū Shāma, *Rawḍatayn*, i. ii, pp. 402, 450; Ibn al-Furāt, iv. i, p. 67; Ibn Kathīr, xii, pp. 256–7; ʿIṣāmī, *Simṭ*, iv, pp. 6–7.

[2] Cahen, article 'Ayyūbids' in *EI*^{2}.

[3] For the *iqṭāʿ*s of Najm al-Dīn Ayyūb, Shīrkūh, and Saladin during the reigns of Zankī and Nūr al-Dīn cf. Ibn Abī al-Hayjā', fols. 161^{r-v}, 163^{v}; Ibn Abī al-Damm, fol. 152^{r}; Ibn Wāṣil, *Ṣāliḥī*, fol. 194^{r}; Ḥanbalī, *Shifā'*, fols. 4^{v}–5^{r}; Dhahabī, *Tārīkh*, (MS. Or. 5578), fol. 9^{v}; Ibn Qāḍī Shuhba, *Durr*, fol. 83^{r}; ʿAynī, *ʿIqd*, 'A', xii, fols. 136^{v}, 147^{v}; Ibn al-Athīr, *Atabaks*, pp. 214–15; id., *Kāmil*, xi, p. 225; Abū Shāma, *Rawḍatayn*, i. ii, pp. 330–1, 383, 428; Dawādārī, *Durra muḍiyya*, pp. 569–70; Ibn Kathīr, xii, pp. 232–3.

[4] Ibn Abī al-Hayjā', fol. 162^{v}; Ḥanbalī, Shifā', fol. 5^{r-v}; Nuwayrī, xxvi, fol. 100; Ibn Qāḍī Shuhba, *Durr*, fol. 81^{r}; Ibn al-Furāt, iii, fol. 213^{r-v}; ʿAynī, *ʿIqd*, 'A', xii, fol. 135^{v}; Ibn al-Athīr, *Atabaks*, pp. 237–8; id., *Kāmil*, xi, p. 214; Abū Shāma, *Rawḍatayn*, i. ii, pp. 364–5; Ibn Wāṣil, *Mufarrij*, i, pp. 150–1; Elisséeff, *Nūr Ad-Din*, ii, p. 608.

[5] Ibn Qāḍī Shuhba, *Durr*, fol. 10^{r-v}; Ibn al-Athīr, *Atabaks*, p. 308; Abū

Egypt did not conform entirely to the Zankid model to which he and his amirs were accustomed, for, though the resultant Ayyūbid *iqṭāʿ* was granted, exactly as the Zankid *iqṭāʿ*, in return for military service, it was not hereditary and did not confer on the *muqṭaʿ* any seigneurial autonomy over his territory.[1]

When the Mamluks came to power, they inherited the Egyptian *iqṭāʿ* system as it had developed under the Ayyūbids. After large numbers of Mongol refugees and exiles (*wāfidiyya* or *wāfidūn*) entered Egypt, the *iqṭāʿ* among other Mamluk institutions was affected by Mongol influence.[2] Unlike the Mamluks, who were bought as children and trained for special purposes, the Mongols were not slaves, but remained free individuals on whom the sultans conferred *iqṭāʿ*s in return for military services. The Mongols enjoyed great prestige owing to their extraordinary military prowess. It seems that they brought into Egypt their own tribal institutions, especially the Mongol Code (the Great *Yāsa*) of Čingīz Khān.[3]

Shāma, *Rawḍatayn*, i. i, p. 20; Ibn Wāṣil, *Mufarrij*, i, p. 280; Maqrīzī, *Khiṭaṭ*, ii, p. 216; Lambton, *Contributions to the study of Seljūq institutions* (Ph.D. London, 1939), pp. 263–4; id., 'Reflections on the *iqṭāʿ*' in *Arabic and Islamic studies in honor of Hamilton A. J. Gibb*, p. 372; Rabīʿ, *Nuẓum*, p. 9; for the Zankid *iqṭāʿ* under Nūr al-Dīn cf. Elisséeff, *Nūr Ad-Dīn*, iii, pp. 726–9.

[1] Cahen, article 'Ayyūbids' in *EI*[2]; see below, pp. 56 ff.

[2] Ayalon, 'The wafidiya in the Mamluk kingdom', *IC*, xxv (1951), p. 89; for the groups of *wāfidiyya* who immigrated into Egypt in the Mamluk period cf. Ibn Wāṣil, *Mufarrij*, fol. 406^{r-v}; Ibn Shaddād, *Rawḍa*, fol. 244^{r-v}; Ibn ʿAbd al-Ẓāhir, *Rawḍ*, pp. 961–2, 1003–5; id., *Alṭāf*, pp. 48–9; Shāfiʿ ibn ʿAlī, *Ḥusn*, fol. 42^{r-v}; Baybars al-Manṣūrī, *Zubda*, fols. 61^{r-v}, 129^{v}, 191^{r}–2^{r}; Dawādārī, *Durra zakiyya*, fols. 158^{v}–9^{r}; Nuwayrī, xxviii, fols. 16–17, 25–6; xxix, fols. 85–6; xxx, fol. 23; ʿUmarī, *Masālik* (MS. P.), fol. 116^{v}; Ibn Ḥabīb, *Durra* (MS. Marsh 223), i, fol. 196^{r}; id., *Tadhkira*, fol. 36^{r}; Ibn al-Furāt, vi, fols. 6^{r}–7^{r}, 33^{v}, 43^{r}; Ibn Abī al-Faḍā'il, pp. 424–7; Ibn Kathīr, xiii, pp. 234, 330, 343; Maqrīzī, *Khiṭaṭ*, ii, pp. 22–3; id., *Sulūk*, i, pp. 473–4, 500–1, 515, 712, 812–13, 950; ii, pp. 5–6, 515–16; tr. Quatremère, *Histoire des Sultans Mamlouks de l'Égypte*, i. i, pp. 179–81, 221–2, 240; ii. i, p. 59, ii, pp. 29–30, 228–9, 243; Ibn Ḥajar, *Durar*, iii, p. 263; Ibn Taghrī Birdī, *Nujūm*, viii, p. 60.

[3] Many of the Mongol immigrants spoke their own language in Egypt. For instance, the amir Ūrtāmish al-Ashrafī (died 736/1335–6) spoke and wrote the Mongol language. He was also familiar with the history of the Mongols, their literature, and the *Yāsa*; this emerges from two biographies of Ūrtāmish in Ibn Taghrī Birdī's *Manhal* under Ūrtāmish, vol. i, fol. 153^{r-v}, and under Ūtāmish, vol. ii, fols. 24^{v}–5^{r}; see also Ṣafadī, *Aʿyān* (MS. A.S. 2970), fols. 20^{v}–1^{r}; ʿUmarī, *Masālik*, (MS. A.S. 3434), fols. 129^{v}–132^{r}; ʿAynī, *ʿIqd*, 'A', xvii, fol. 103^{v}; Ibn Ḥajar, *Durar*, i, pp. 423–4; for the contents of the Great *Yāsa* cf. ʿUmarī, *Masālik* (MS. P. 2325), fols. 31^{r}, 34^{r}–6^{r} (MS. A.S. 3416), fols. 28^{v}–30^{r}; Ibn Kathīr, xiii, pp. 117–19; Maqrīzī, *Khiṭaṭ*, ii, pp. 220–1; Vernadsky, *O sostave velikoi Yasui Chingis Khana*, pp. 7–12; id., 'The scope and contents of Chingis Khan's Yasa', *HJAS*, iii (1938), pp. 337–60; Petis de la Croix, *The history of*

As Ibn Taghrī Birdī and Suyūṭī state, Sultan Baybars was an admirer of Čingīz Khān, whom he was eager to imitate. Thus, he encouraged the immigration of the Mongols with their special experience in Mongol administration, and introduced not only the Great *Yāsa* into the Mamluk state, but also many Mongol institutions, offices, and social customs.[1] Maqrīzī states that the law of the Mongol *Yāsa* used to be described, during the Mamluk era, by the term *sī-yāsa* which distinguished it from the *Sharīʿa*, so that finally the legal code of Egypt consisted of two parts, the *Sharīʿa* and the *sī-yāsa*.[2]

It appears that the Mongol influence on the Egyptian *iqṭāʿ* system was determined by the spirit of the Īlkhānid *iqṭāʿ* in Iraq. Dr. Khaṣbāk states that there were two types of *iqṭāʿ* in Iraq under the Īlkhānids: (*a*) *iqṭāʿ*s conferred upon members of the sultan's family, the holders of which had the right of ownership which permitted them to offer the land for sale or set aside part of it as *waqf* for religious and charitable purposes; (*b*) *iqṭāʿ*s whose holders had no right of ownership and which were not hereditary. Dr. Khaṣbāk suggests that the *muqṭaʿ* who administered his *iqṭāʿ* under the Īlkhānid rule had to send a part of the revenue derived from his *iqṭāʿ* to the government, or pay annually to the state, for a number of years, a contracted sum (*ḍamān*), undertaking to recover it himself from the revenue of his *iqṭāʿ*. He is also of the opinion that the Īlkhānids increased the assignment of cities, as well as of cultivated land, to the *muqṭaʿ*s in return for military service.[3]

A comparison of the main characteristics of the *iqṭāʿ* in the period under consideration with the main characteristics of European

Genghizcan the Great, Book I, vi, pp. 78–87; Riasanovsky, *Fundamental principles of Mongol law*, pp. 25–40, 83–6.

[1] Ibn Taghrī Birdī, *Nujūm*, vi, pp. 268–9, vii, pp. 182–3; Suyūṭī, *Ḥusn*, ii, p. 95; socially, the Mamluk amirs imitated the Mongols by eating horseflesh and wearing Tatar coats (*al-aqbiya al-tatāriyya*), cf. ʿAynī, *Badr*, fol. 30r, Dawādārī, *Durr fakhir*, pp. 182, 323; Ibn Kathīr, xiv, p. 157; Maqrīzī, *Sulūk*, ii, p. 288; Mayer, *Mamluk costume*, pp. 21–2.

[2] Maqrīzī, *Khiṭaṭ*, ii, p. 220; Poliak, 'The influence of Čhingīz-Khān's Yasa upon the general organization of the Mamlūk State', *BSOAS*, x (1940–2), pp. 862–4. Ibn ʿAbd al-Ẓāhir (*Alṭāf*, p. 54) states that Sultan al-Ashraf Khalīl ruled according to both the *Sharīʿa* and the *sī-yāsa*; for the term *sī-yāsa* cf. Ibn Taghrī Birdī, *Nujūm*, vi, pp. 268–9, vii, pp. 182–3; Khafājī, *Shifāʾ*, pp. 121–2.

[3] Khaṣbāk, 'Aḥwāl al-ʿIrāq al-Iqtiṣādiyya fī ʿahd al-Īlkhāniyyīn', *Majallat Kulliyat al-Ādāb*, University of Baghdad, iv (1961), pp. 130–2; id., *al-ʿIrāq*, pp. 103–6; for the Mongol influence on the Egyptian *iqṭāʿ* system during the Mamluk era see below, pp. 49, 61.

medieval feudalism shows that the *iqṭāʿ* system of the Ayyūbids and the Mamluks was not derived from any of the various types of feudalism found in Western Europe. One is inclined to accept the view of Professor Lambton that the circumstances which accompanied the rise and development of the *iqṭāʿ* system differed from those prevailing in Western Europe where feudalism was organized, and the results were consequently dissimilar.[1]

B. *The* iqṭāʿ *as a method of paying soldiers*

In return for the benefits derived from the *iqṭāʿ*, the *muqṭaʿ* had a number of obligations to fulfil. These consisted of military duties, such as providing troops in times of war, a number of non-military functions, such as supervision of cultivation, irrigation, and some personal service to the sultan. Considering the warlike character of the period, the *muqṭaʿ*'s military obligations were clearly the most important. The *muqṭaʿ* was responsible for the expenses of his soldiers and had to hold himself in readiness to join the regular army and head his troop in every expedition. The following anecdote is illustrative of the custom prevalent in the Ayyūbid period. ʿImād al-Dīn al-Iṣfahānī relates that, when Saladin's army reached al-Sadīr on the expedition to Ramla in 573/1177, an announcement was made in the camp that all troops should take sufficient supplies for a further ten days. The *sūq al-ʿaskar* (army bazaar) was established especially for this purpose. The excessively high prices charged tempted al-Iṣfahānī to avail himself of the opportunity to offer his own supplies for sale. He was, as he said, 'a man of the pen and not a man of the flag' (i.e. a writer, not a warrior).[2]

[1] Lambton, *Landlord and Peasant in Persia*, p. 53; for feudalism in Europe cf. Marc Bloch, *Feudal Society*, tr. from the French by L. A. Manyon (London, 1961); C. Stephenson, *Mediaeval feudalism* (Ithaca–New York, 1963). The complex and controversial question of feudalism in the Byzantine Empire is still under discussion; cf. G. Ostrogorsky, *Pour l'histoire de la féodalité byzantine* (Bruxelles, 1954); id., *Quelques problèmes d'histoire de la paysannerie byzantine* (Bruxelles, 1956); id., *History of the Byzantine state*, pp. 254–5, 276, 329–31, 371–2, 375 and n. 1, 424–5, 481 ff., 496, 527; *Cam. Med. Hist.*, iv. i, pp. 142, 240–1, 243–4, 290, 341–2, ii, pp. 33, 41–2, 77, 98–9; Hussey, *The Byzantine world*, 3rd ed., pp. 48, 56, 63, 65, 71–2, 89, 91–2 and n. 1; for Oriental *iqṭāʿ* as compared with European feudalism cf. Cahen, 'Réflexions sur l'usage du mot de "Féodalité" ', *JESHO*, iii (1960), pp. 15–19. The writer will refrain from the use of European terms such as feudalism, fief, lord, etc.

[2] Iṣfahānī, *Barq*, iii, fols. 8v–9r; id., *Sanā al-barq* (as abridged by Bundārī), fols. 188v–9r; Abū Shāma, *Rawḍatayn*, i. ii, p. 697; Gibb, 'The Armies of Saladin', in *Studies on the civilization of Islam*, p. 84; Rabīʿ, *Nuẓum*, p. 65.

This statement of al-Iṣfahānī is significant. It provides evidence that each soldier in the army was responsible for his personal needs for the duration of war. It seems that he would buy his supplies from the army bazaar with the pay which he had received from the sultan, if he belonged to the regular army; or from the *muqṭaʿ* if he belonged to the *muqṭaʿ*'s troop. This assumption is corroborated by two untitled and undated *tawqīʿ*s (brevets of *iqṭāʿ*s), of the Ayyūbid period, which have been preserved in *Ṣubḥ al-aʿs͟hā*. In the first *tawqīʿ*, the Ayyūbid sultan advised the *muqṭaʿ* to prepare himself—as far as he could—for military service, to keep only brave men and horses under his command and to exclude cowards. The second *tawqīʿ* contains the same admonition to the *muqṭaʿ*, with the addition of advice to attend to the outward appearance of his cavalry men, especially in respect of clothes and equipment.[1] The sources do not mention any kind of remuneration to the amirs who had been granted *iqṭāʿ*s in the Ayyūbid period. It would appear, therefore, that the sultan preferred to grant *iqṭāʿ*s instead of outright pay. Thus the *iqṭāʿ* became the main source of revenue to the *muqṭaʿ*. The latter paid the soldiers under his command, and provided them with the means to procure equipment and supplies from the revenue of his *iqṭāʿ*. Sometimes he even conferred part of his *iqṭāʿ* upon some of his *ajnād*, in lieu of payment.[2]

During the Mamluk period until the end of the reign of al-Nāṣir Muḥammad, the amirs received, in addition to the *iqṭāʿ*, one special payment, the *nafaqa*. It is worth noting that the *nafaqa* was not distributed regularly, but occasionally, mainly on the eve of a campaign.[3] Furthermore, the amount of the *nafaqa* by no means sufficed to cover the expenses of the amir and his mamluks during a war which might last for a long time. Professor Ayalon

[1] Qalqas͟handī, *Ṣubḥ*, xiii, pp. 148–52; during the Ayyūbid period, the brevet of the *iqṭāʿ* was known as *tawqīʿ* in contrast to the usage of the Fāṭimids who termed it *mans͟hūr*. During the Mamluk era, the brevet of the *iqṭāʿ* was called the *mans͟hūr*, cf. Ibn al-Ṣayrafī, *Qānūn*, pp. 109, 114, 133; Qalqas͟handī, *Ṣubḥ*, xiii, pp. 132, 144, 157; Björkman, article 'Diplomatic' in *EI*²; Dr. Stern states ('Two Ayyūbid decrees from Sinai', in *Documents from Islamic chanceries*, p. 14 n. 5) that the history of the word *mans͟hūr* is still rather obscure.

[2] See below, pp. 36–8.

[3] Baybars al-Manṣūrī, *Tuḥfa*, fol. 24ʳ; Nuwayrī, xxx, fol. 51; Ibn al-Furāt, vi, fol. 152ᵛ, vii, p. 41; Ṣafadī, *Nuzha*, fols. 68ʳ, 69ᵛ, 70ᵛ; Ibn Duqmāq, *Jawhar*, fols. 123ᵛ–4ʳ; Zetterstéen, pp. 58, 159; Maqrīzī, *Sulūk*, i, pp. 682, 724, ii, p. 499, tr. Quatremère, ii. i, pp. 26, 73; Ibn Tag͟hrī Birdī, *Nujūm*, ix, pp. 78–9; Ayalon, 'The system of payment in Mamluk military society', *JESHO*, i (1958), pp. 48–50, 57; id., article 'Ḥarb' in *EI*².

states that, in the Baḥrī Mamluk period, the *nafaqa* given to the various ranks of the army was as follows: an Amir of a Thousand only received between 1,000 and 3,000 *dīnārs*; an Amir of Forty (or *amir ṭablkhānā*) between 400 and 1,000 *dīnārs*. As to the *nafaqa* received by an Amir of Ten, there is no information. Other ranks, such as the *Muqaddam al-ḥalqa*, received 1,000 *dirhams*, and royal mamluks 500 *dirhams* each[1].

However, it would seem that, in spite of the *nafaqa*, the *iqṭā'* remained, in the Mamluk period also, the amir's main source of revenue. There is some evidence from the Baḥrī Mamluk period to support this assumption. It is stated by Ibn 'Abd al-Ẓāhir, Ibn al-Furāt, and Maqrīzī that in the year 662/1264, Sultan Baybars ordered the amirs and the *ajnād* to get ready for an expedition with their mamluks. The *sūq al-silāḥ* (equipment bazaar) in Cairo was crowded with the horses of the soldiers who were buying equipment. As a result, the price of iron and the wages of the smiths increased sharply. It may be deduced from this evidence that the amirs were responsible for financing the equipment of their soldiers from the revenue derived from their *iqṭā'*s.[2] Further proof that the *iqṭā'*s were conferred upon the amirs chiefly in exchange for military services, is supplied by three incomplete *manshūrs* from the reign of al-Nāṣir ibn Qalāwūn, also preserved in *Ṣubḥ al-a'shā*. Thus, for instance, a *manshūr* addressed to the amir Shams al-Dīn indicates that he was granted an *iqṭā'* mainly with his future military services in view. He had been one of the commanders during the war, and his services were obviously valuable.[3]

Equally prominent among the reasons which led to the conferment of the *iqṭā'*s on the chieftains of the Bedouin tribes in Egypt was military service. Besides supplying the army with auxiliary cavalry in case of emergency, these Bedouin *muqṭa'*s had to guard roads, to keep highwaymen in check, to transport crops, to supply post-horses at the post-centres, and to send horses as annual gifts to the sultan.[4] Before 577/1181, Saladin had conferred some *iqṭā'*s upon the Tha'laba tribe.[5] He may also have done so with regard to

[1] Ayalon, 'The system of payment', p. 49.

[2] Ibn 'Abd al-Ẓāhir, *Rawḍ*, p. 1023; Ibn al-Furāt, vi, fol. 45^{r-v}; Maqrīzī, *Sulūk*, i, p. 512, tr. Quatremère, i. i, p. 238.

[3] Qalqashandī, *Ṣubḥ*, xiii, pp. 173–4, 178–81.

[4] Ibn Wāṣil, *Mufarrij*, fol. 311^{r}; Shāfi' ibn 'Alī, *Ḥusn*, fol. 32^{r}; Nuwayrī, viii, p. 201; Poliak, *Feudalism*, pp. 9–10.

[5] Maqrīzī, *Bayān*, p. 23; Rabī', *Nuẓum*, p. 29.

some other tribes in various parts of Egypt. In 577/1181, while confiscating property belonging to the Bedouin tribes in the Sharqiyya province, he cancelled the *iqṭāʿ*s of the Judhām and Thaʿlaba tribes.[1] However, Saladin's successors assigned new *iqṭāʿ*s to Judhām, Thaʿlaba, and other Bedouin tribes. Thus, for example, Sultan al-ʿAzīz ʿUthmān conferred upon al-Sharīf Ibn Thaʿlaba al-Jaʿfarī an *iqṭāʿ*, the revenue from which amounted to 60,000 *dīnār*s yearly in 592/1195–6.[2]

As to the Mamluk sultans, their practice of conferring *iqṭāʿ*s on the Bedouin tribes in Egypt despite their hostile attitude indicates that they desired to secure their co-operation as auxiliary forces in many expeditions.[3] Consequently, the Bedouin tribes of Upper Egypt took part in the two expeditions which Sultan Qalāwūn had sent to Nubia in the years 686/1288 and 688/1289. In the first expedition, the tribes of Awlād Bakr, Awlād ʿUmar, Awlād Sharīf, Awlād Shaybān, Awlād al-Kanz, and Banū Hilāl participated.[4] From the *Kitāb al-tuḥfa al-saniyya* by Ibn al-Jīʿān—whose material is based on the *rawk* of 715/1315—one may deduce that the Bedouin tribes held a proportionately large share of the Egyptian *iqṭāʿ*s.[5]

Because the *iqṭāʿ* was the amir's main source of revenue, it appears that the number of *ajnād* commanded by individual *muqṭaʿ*s was limited by the *ʿibra* of the *iqṭāʿ*. Some corroborative evidence for this assumption is to be found in the *Kitāb al-kāmil*. When al-ʿĀdil, Saladin's brother, was acclaimed as sultan in the year 596/1200, he investigated the position of the *muqṭaʿ*s, especially the number of soldiers under their command. Ibn al-Athīr even states that this action weakened the loyalty of his *muqṭaʿ*s.[6] Besides,

[1] See below, p. 123.

[2] Maqrīzī, *Sulūk*, i, p. 132, tr. Blochet, 'C', pp. 88–9.

[3] One of several Bedouin revolts occurred in 651/1253, when they rose against Aybak claiming to possess a better right to power than the Mamluks, who were slaves by origin. Other risings of this kind occurred in 660/1262, 689/1290, and 701/1301–2; cf. Baybars al-Manṣūrī, *Tuḥfa*, fols. 6r–v, 76r; Kutubī, *ʿUyūn* (MS. Fatih), fol. 165v; Ibn al-Furāt, vi, fol. 3v; Maqrīzī, *Bayān*, pp. 9–10; Qalqashandī, *Ṣubḥ*, iv, p. 68; Maqrīzī, *Sulūk*, i, pp. 386–8, 471, 754, 920–2, tr. Quatremère, i. i, pp. 40–1, 177; ii. i, p. 110; ii. ii, pp. 186–90; Poliak, 'Les révoltes populaires en Égypte à l'époque des Mamelouks et leurs causes économiques', *REI*, viii (1934), pp. 257–65.

[4] Nuwayrī, xxix, fol. 11; Ibn al-Furāt, viii, pp. 52–3, 82–3; Maqrīzī, *Sulūk*, i, pp. 736–7, 749, tr. Quatremère, ii. i, pp. 90, 105; see Ḥasan, *The Arabs and the Sudan*, pp. 112–16.

[5] Ibn al-Jīʿān, *Tuḥfa*, pp. 15–45; for the *rawk* of 715/1315 see below, pp. 53–6.

[6] Ibn al-Athīr, *Kāmil*, xii, p. 103; for the *ʿibra*, see below, pp. 47–8.

both al-Makīn ibn al-ʿAmīd and Maqrīzī state that, in the year 627/1229, Sultan al-Kāmil, appointing the amir S̲h̲ams al-Dīn al-ʿĀdilī as his deputy for the Eastern provinces, conferred upon him the *iqṭāʿ* of al-Muwazzar in consideration for the provision of 100 cavalry. It is explicitly stated that it was granted to him in addition to his Egyptian *iqṭāʿ*. The sources state that his *iqṭāʿ* was augmented to enable him to support 350 cavalry, which means that he had to muster 250 cavalry in return for his Egyptian *iqṭāʿ* only.[1] Furthermore when, in 647/1249, the two sons of al-Malik al-Nāṣir Dāwūd handed over Karak to Sultan al-Ṣāliḥ Ayyūb, the sultan conferred upon al-Malik al-Ẓāhir an Egyptian *iqṭāʿ* of 200 cavalry, and upon his brother al-Malik al-Amjad, another *iqṭāʿ* of 150 cavalry. It appears that the *iqṭāʿ* of al-Ẓāhir provided him with sufficient revenue to cover the expenses of 200 cavalry, while the *iqṭāʿ* of his brother provided means to support 150 cavalry only.[2]

It seems that a limitation of the number of the *ajnād* to each *iqṭāʿ* continued during the Mamluk period. Professor Ayalon states that the number of mamluks an amir could take into his service was fixed, and new ones could only be introduced when some of the original number died or were cashiered.[3] There is some evidence in support of this statement. In the year 660/1262, the amir S̲h̲ams al-Dīn Aq-qūs̲h̲ al-Burlī entered the service of Sultan Baybars, who conferred on him an *iqṭāʿ* which made him amir of 70 cavalry.[4] Further evidence, supplied by Baybars al-Manṣūrī and Nuwayrī, shows that, in the year 702/1303, Sultan al-Nāṣir ibn Qalāwūn ordered all the amirs to increase the number of their mamluks by a quarter, in order to fight the Mongols. This can only be taken to mean that each of them had previously had a strictly limited number of mamluks.[5]

Concerning the share of the *ajnād* in the amir's *iqṭāʿ* during the Ayyūbid period, it is probable that each amir sometimes conferred small *iqṭāʿ*s upon some of his *ajnād*. According to the *Kitāb tārīkh al-Fayyūm* by Nābulsī, the village of Babīj Anqās̲h̲ was assigned

---

[1] Ibn al-ʿAmīd, *Akhbār*, p. 139; Maqrīzī, *Sulūk*, i, pp. 238–9, tr. Blochet, 'D', p. 256; Rabīʿ, *Nuẓum*, p. 36.

[2] Ibn Wāṣil, *Mufarrij*, fol. 358ʳ⁻ᵛ; Ibn Tag̲h̲rī Birdī, *Nujūm*, vi, p. 362.

[3] Ayalon, 'Studies on the structure of the Mamluk army', *BSOAS*, xv (1953), p. 459; the mamluks of the amirs were called *mamālik al-umarāʾ* or *ajnād al-umarāʾ*, cf. loc. cit.

[4] Maqrīzī, *Sulūk*, i, pp. 475–6, tr. Quatremère, i. i, p. 182.

[5] Baybars al-Manṣūrī, *Zubda*, fol. 234ʳ⁻ᵛ; Nuwayrī, xxx, fol. 6.

in the form of *iqṭāʿ*s to the amir ʿImād al-Dīn ibn Ṭayy and the *aṣḥāb* (*ajnād*) of the amirs Shihāb al-Dīn Khiḍr, Ḥusām al-Dīn ibn Abī ʿAlī, Rukn al-Dīn Khāṣṣ al-Turk, ʿAlam al-Dīn al-Sharīfī, Fārs al-Dīn Aqṭāy, Sayf al-Dīn al-Ḥamīdī, and Jamāl al-Dīn Aq-qūsh.[1] In another passage, it is noted that the village of Minyat al-Baṭs was conferred in the form of *iqṭāʿ*s upon the amir Rukn al-Dīn Khāṣṣ al-Turk, the amir Iftikhār al-Dīn Yāqūt al-Yamanī, and that a share in it was given to the *aṣḥāb* (*ajnād*) of three other amirs and a group of *ajnād al-ḥalqa al-manṣūra*.[2] Bamūya and Qambashā were conferred as *iqṭāʿ*s upon the *ajnād* of two amirs.[3] Furthermore, the hand-written *waṣiyya* of al-Ṣāliḥ Ayyūb to his son Tūrānshāh mentions that most of the *ajnād* had become pedlars and commoners. The sultan adds that each of these people had come to the amir wearing a *qabāʾ* (coat) and riding a horse, but the latter conferred upon him 'the *iqṭāʿ* of one of his brave soldiers'.[4] From this evidence, it appears that the Ayyūbid amir conferred specific portions of the cultivated land which constituted his *iqṭāʿ* upon some of his *ajnād*.

In respect of the share of the *ajnād* in the amir's *iqṭāʿ* during the Mamluk period, Maqrīzī states that it was specified in the amir's *manshūr* that a third of the *iqṭāʿ* was the share of the amir, and two-thirds the portion of his *ajnād*. The amir or his clerks were not permitted to augment the amir's portion at the expense of the *ajnād* without the latter's consent.[5] It is difficult to understand from Maqrīzī's statement whether this arrangement assigned to the *ajnād* a specific portion of the cultivated land of the amir's *iqṭāʿ*, or whether it gave them two-thirds of the revenue of the *iqṭāʿ*. It appears that—as in the Ayyūbid period—the amir set aside a part of his *iqṭāʿ* for his *ajnād* to enjoy the yield from its revenue. It is Nuwayrī's contention that each amir had to inform the *dīwān al-jaysh* (the army office) of the number, the names, and the size of the *iqṭāʿ*, which had been conferred upon each of his *ajnād*.[6]

As regards the share a mamluk had in his amir's *iqṭāʿ*, Professor Poliak's attempt to deduce, from an insufficiently authenticated

[1] Nābulsī, *Fayyūm*, p. 76.

[2] Ibid., p. 164.

[3] Ibid., p. 141.

[4] Nuwayrī, xxvii, fol. 92; Nuwayrī copied the text of this *waṣiyya* from the original, cf. ibid., xxvii, fols. 89–93; the material and colour of the *qabāʾ* (coat) depended on the rank of the person in question, cf. Mayer, *Mamluk costume*, pp. 13, 18, 22, 29, 59–61.

[5] Maqrīzī, *Khiṭaṭ*, ii, p. 216.

[6] Nuwayrī, viii, pp. 206–7.

table, that the annual allowance of an amir to each mamluk was between 183 and 605, or 200 and 1,333 *dīnār jayshī*, is not really successful.[1] Professor Ayalon says that 'nothing is known, for the sources keep completely, or almost completely, silent on this subject'.[2] Although Maqrīzī states in his *Khiṭaṭ* that every mamluk of the amir Baktāsh al-Fakhrī (who died in 706/1306) had an *iqṭā'* of 20,000 *dirhams* annually, and each of his *ajnād* had an *iqṭā'* of 10,000 *dirhams* annually, in addition to barley and meat, he refers to the lack of a stable criterion for the internal distribution of the benefits of the *iqṭā'*, saying that the share of the mamluk in his amir's *iqṭā'* depends on the latter's whim.[3]

There are indications to the effect that the mamluks were more attached to their *iqṭā'*s than to their amir. Ibn 'Abd al-Ẓāhir and other historians state that, when Sultan Baybars arrested the three amirs, al-Rashīdī, al-Burlī, and al-Dimyāṭī in the year 661/1262, he left their mamluks undisturbed in their *iqṭā'*s.[4] Also, when Sultan al-Nāṣir cancelled the *iqṭā'* of the amir Baktāsh al-Fakhrī, he left his mamluks in their own *iqṭā'*s.[5] One can only suppose that the mamluks were reluctant to leave land which, as they knew, was profitable, for an uncertain future. It is, however, difficult to find informed sources to prove this assumption.

As, in the period under consideration, the primary role of the *iqṭā'* system in Egypt was military, the *dīwān al-jaysh* was the only *dīwān* to deal with the registration, evaluation, and conferment of *iqṭā'*s.

As to the immediately preceding Fāṭimid period, Maqrīzī, quoting Ibn al-Ṭuwayr, states that the *dīwān al-jaysh wa al-rawātib* (army and pay office) was divided into two departments, one dealing with the army and the other with the *rawātib* (pay).[6] It appears that when the Fāṭimids increased the number of *iqṭā'*s, they formed a special department within the *dīwān al-jaysh* to take care of the affairs of the *iqṭā'*s. According to Qalqashandī, the *dīwān al-jaysh* consisted of three departments, each department bearing the name

[1] Poliak, 'Some notes on the feudal system of the Mamluks', *JRAS* (1937), pp. 102–3; for the *jayshī dīnār* see below, pp. 48–9.

[2] Ayalon, 'The system of payment', p. 62.

[3] Maqrīzī, *Khiṭaṭ*, ii, pp. 33, 216.

[4] Ibn 'Abd al-Ẓāhir, *Rawḍ*, p. 994; Nuwayrī, xxviii, fols. 24–5; 'Umarī, *Masālik* (MS. P.), fol. 112^r; Ibn al-Furāt, vi, fols. 27^v–9^v.

[5] Nuwayrī, xxx, fol. 38.

[6] Maqrīzī, *Khiṭaṭ* i, p. 401; it appears that the Fāṭimids abbreviated the title of this *dīwān* to '*dīwān al-jaysh*' only, cf. Ibn al-Ṣayrafī, *Ishāra*, pp. 35, 47.

'*dīwān*': the *dīwān al-jaysh*. a kind of war office as well as a military administration, the *dīwān al-rawātib*, the central pay office, and the *dīwān al-iqṭāʿ*.[1]

Makhzūmī states that it was the function of the *dīwān al-iqṭāʿāt* to deal with the *ʿibra* of the *iqṭāʿ*s, the *muqṭaʿ*'s affairs and the arrears in the provinces. He furthermore states that there was, in the *dīwān al-majlis*, a department supervising the work of the *dīwān al-iqṭāʿāt*.[2] This record is significant, because it supports the contention of Qalqashandī and Maqrīzī that the *ṣāḥib dīwān al-majlis* (the chief of the council office) and not the *nāẓir al-jaysh* (the chief of the army office) was considered competent in matters relating to the *iqṭāʿ*s.[3]

However, it seems that *dīwān al-rawātib* had been abolished by the time the Ayyūbids became rulers of Egypt, and the Fāṭimid *iqṭāʿ* had developed into a military system. This seems to have occurred after the vizierate of Saladin, at a date not mentioned in the sources. Consequently the *dīwān al-jaysh* or *al-juyūsh* became responsible for the affairs of the army and the *iqṭāʿ*s, under one official, the *nāẓir al-jaysh*.[4]

From an important text in the *Kitāb lumaʿ al-qawānīn* by Nābulsī, it would appear that the conferment of the *iqṭāʿ* constituted the essential function of the *dīwān al-juyūsh* during the Ayyūbid period. For its implementation, the *dīwān* could depend on receiving from the *dīwān al-māl* information about the financial condition of Egyptian provinces, especially of those farms which were irrigated by Nile water, stating to what extent the area under cultivation had increased or decreased. This information was obviously important in the evaluation of the *iqṭāʿ*s in question.[5]

It seems that as time went on the *dīwān al-jaysh* gained complete independence. It possessed its own information services concerning

[1] Qalqashandī, *Ṣubḥ*, iii, pp. 492–3, 525; Lewis, article 'Daftar' in *EI*²; Gottschalk, article 'Dīwān' in *EI*²; for the *dīwān al-iqṭāʿ* cf. Mājid (Magued), 'L'organisation financière en Égypte sous les Fatimides', *EC*, liii (1962), p. 49; id., *Nuẓum*, p. 116.

[2] Makhzūmī, fol. 190ᵛ; for the *dīwān al-majlis*, see below, pp. 144–5.

[3] Qalqashandī, *Ṣubḥ*, iii, pp. 493–4; Maqrīzī, *Khiṭaṭ*, i, p. 397.

[4] The *dīwān al-rawātib* was still in existence during the vizierate of Saladin, cf. *Rasāʾil al-Qāḍī al-Fāḍil* (MS. Brit. Mus., Add. 25757), fols. 43ᵛ–6ᵛ.

[5] Nābulsī, *Lumaʿ*, p. 23, tr. Cahen, 'Quelques aspects', p. 100; according to Buwayhid tradition, the *dīwān al-jaysh* controlled the military *iqṭāʿ*. The Buwayhid *dīwān al-jaysh* was concerned not only with military administration, but also with the *ʿibra* of each *iqṭāʿ* as well as the reassignment of vacant *iqṭāʿ*s. Cf. Cahen, 'Évolution', pp. 36–7; Lambton, 'Reflections on the *iqṭāʿ*', p. 368.

the *iqṭā*ʿs which consisted, in the Mamluk era, of five main registers: the *jayshī jarīda*, the *iqṭāʿī jarīda*, the special *jarīda*, one containing the number of every *muqṭa*ʿ's *ajnād*, and one, the last, vaguely termed the *ḥawṭa jayshiyya*.[1]

Thanks to the contemporary historian Nuwayrī, who held secretarial posts in some Egyptian *dīwān*s during the reign of al-Nāṣir ibn Qalāwūn, the contents of these five registers are known in detail:

The first of them contained the names of the *muqṭa*ʿs in alphabetical order. Each name was preceded by the date of the assignment of the *iqṭā*ʿ, and followed by a description of the manner in which it was conferred on the *muqṭa*ʿ. The list further contained the names of every commander of *ajnād al-ḥalqa*,[2] and specified the amounts levied on the Bedouin Arabs in return for the *iqṭā*ʿs. The most important item of information provided by this *jarīda* concerned the registration of the transfer of the *iqṭā*ʿ from one *muqṭa*ʿ to another, and a somewhat cryptic definition of the ʿ*ibra* of each *iqṭā*ʿ. This precaution may have prevented the officials from divulging the secrets of the ʿ*ibra* of any *iqṭā*ʿ without a special decree from the sultan.

The second register, the *iqṭāʿī jarīda*, gave the names of Egyptian provinces detailing their districts, villages, and main characteristics. It also specified the amount of the *hilālī* and the *jawālī* taxes, the ʿ*ibra* of the *iqṭā*ʿ, and the last financial revenue collected from it.

The third, special register, *jarīda khāṣṣa*, which was actually a branch of the *jayshī jarīda*, contained the names of the *muqṭa*ʿs whose *iqṭā*ʿs entitled them to the collection of taxes (*arbāb al-nuqūd wa al-makīlāt*). The importance of this *jarīda* was that it restated the rights of every *muqṭā*ʿ within his *iqṭā*ʿ according to his brevet, in order to avoid abuses and wrongs.

The fourth list contained the numbers of each amir's *ajnād*, their own names, and their *iqṭā*ʿs. The information which compiled this important list always came from the amirs' *dīwān*s in the *iqṭā*ʿs.

The last register was called *ḥawṭa jayshiyya*. According to a rather obscure text in *Nihāyat al-arab*, it was under this heading that the officials of the *dīwān al-jaysh* registered the *maḥlūlāt* and

[1] The common term for the army list was *jarīda*, cf. Lewis, article 'Daftar' in *EI*².

[2] *Ajnād al-ḥalqa* or *jund al-ḥalqa* (the troops of the *ḥalqa*) were a corps of free (i.e. non-mamluk) cavalry, cf. Gaudefroy-Demombynes, *La Syrie*, pp. xxiii–iv; Ayalon, Studies', i, p. 204; ii, pp. 448 ff.

the *tafāwut*. The term *maḥlūl* (plural *maḥlūlāt*) was used to designate a vacant *iqṭāʿ*. As to the term *tafāwut*, it denoted the revenue reserved to the *dīwān*s in the interval between the death, departure, or transfer of a *muqṭaʿ* and the assignment to his successor. The share of the *dīwān* was entered into the *ḥawṭa* and then sent to the responsible *dīwān* for ratification.[1]

The work of the *dīwān al-jaysh* was administered by a staff headed by the *nāẓir al-jaysh*. Among his functions, the *nāẓir al-jaysh* administered the assignment of the *iqṭāʿ*s, conducted correspondence regarding them, and it was under his supervision that the brevets of the *iqṭāʿ*s were drafted and recorded. Next in importance was the *ṣāḥib dīwān al-jaysh* (inspector of the army office), who appears to have been the deputy of the *nāẓir*. Other subordinate clerks, *shuhūd. kuttāb*, recorded details of the *iqṭāʿ*s under the supervision of the above two officials.[2]

C. *The* iqṭāʿ *as a method of collecting taxes*

The *iqṭāʿ* in Egypt—during the period under consideration—was one of the means of collecting taxes. A considerable part of the taxes was collected by the *muqṭaʿ* from the *iqṭāʿ*, to cover the cost of troops and to meet expenses connected with the irrigation and cultivation of the *iqṭāʿ* lands.

It seems that, until 715/1315, the taxes collected in most of the *iqṭāʿ*s were of two kinds, those collected under the supervision of financial *dīwān*s on behalf of the sultan, such as the *zakāt*, the *jawālī* tax, and the *mawārīth ḥashriyya*, and those collected by the *muqṭaʿ*s for themselves and their *ajnād*, such as the *marāʿī* tax, the *hilālī* tax, etc.[3]

[1] Nuwayrī, viii, pp. 200–13; for the term *maḥlūl* cf. ibid., viii, pp. 202, 211, 241; xxvii, fol. 3; Maqrīzī, *Khiṭaṭ*, i, p. 107. The Ottoman use of the term *maḥlūl* is similar, cf. Heyd, *Ottoman documents*, p. 185. For the *tafāwut* cf. Ibn Mammātī, pp. 354–5. The main Ottoman kinds of registers (*mufaṣṣal*, *ijmāl*, *rūznāmche*, and *derdest*) are similar to the Egyptians' registers. The *mufaṣṣal*, which is the most valuable of all, contains a detailed description of the province (*sanjaq*), with its towns, villages, population, revenues, forms of tenure, and list of *tīmār*s; cf. Lewis, 'The Ottoman archives as a source for the history of the Arab land', *JRAS* (1951), pp. 146–9; id., 'Studies in the Ottoman archives', *BSOAS*, xvi (1954), pp. 471, 500–1, and Plate III.

[2] For the officials of the *dīwān al-jaysh*, cf. Qalqashandī, *Ṣubḥ*, iv, pp. 30–1, 34; xi, pp. 321–2; Maqrīzī, *Khiṭaṭ*, ii, p. 227; Suyūṭī, *Ḥusn*, ii, p. 94; Gaudefroy-Demombynes, *La Syrie*, p. lxxii; Popper, *Systematic notes*, i, p. 97; Gottschalk, article 'Dīwān' in *EI*². For the *shāhid* and the *kātib* see below, pp. 158–9.

[3] A detailed discussion of taxes will be found in Chapter III.

The Ayyūbid sultans sometimes granted to the *muqṭa*ʿs some or all of the above-mentioned sultani taxes. This procedure was called *iqṭāʿ khāṣṣ*. According to Professor Cahen, one should distinguish, in Ayyūbid Egypt as well as elsewhere, between the governmental *iqṭā*ʿs (here termed administrative *iqṭā*ʿs), exceptionally established in favour of the 'princes of the blood' or the great amirs who had, besides, under their own jurisdiction, '*des biens propres*' *khāṣṣa*, and the simple *iqṭā*ʿs of ordinary soldiers.[1]

It is probable that the term '*iqṭāʿ khāṣṣ*' signifies that the *muqṭaʿ* had the right to collect the whole revenue of the *iqṭāʿ* (including the share of the sultan) without sharing it with his *ajnād*. This assumption is corroborated by the following evidence. In the year 577/1181–2, the amir Ṣārim al-Dīn Khuṭlubā went to Fayyūm which had been conferred upon him as an *iqṭāʿ khāṣṣ*. Maqrīzī comments that taxes previously imposed on this province were cancelled, leaving Ṣārim al-Dīn the sole beneficiary of the whole revenue of Fayyūm.[2] Presumably, the *iqṭāʿ khāṣṣ* did not imply rights of possession of the *iqṭāʿ*, as Maqrīzī states that in the same year (577/1182) Saladin set aside the province of Fayyūm for himself as domain, after compensating its *muqṭa*ʿs.[3]

After two years (579/1183), Saladin appointed his nephew Taqī al-Dīn ʿUmar ibn Shāhanshāh vice-sultan in Egypt. Quoting Ibn Abī Ṭayy, Abū Shāma states that Saladin conferred upon Taqī al-Dīn Alexandria and Damietta as *iqṭāʿ*, in addition to Buḥayra, Fayyūm, and Būsh as his *khāṣṣa*.[4] Al-Iṣfahānī and other historians provide additional details when they state that Saladin not only conferred upon Taqī al-Dīn—in addition to his Syrian *iqṭāʿ*—Fayyūm with its districts (including all its revenue as well as the *jawālī* tax), but also increased the latter's *iqṭāʿ* by assigning to him Qayāt and Būsh. It is obvious that this special grant permitted Taqī al-Dīn to collect the whole revenue of his *iqṭāʿ khāṣṣ*.[5]

[1] Cahen, 'Évolution', p. 45.

[2] Maqrīzī, *Sulūk*, i, p. 72, tr. Blochet, 'B', p. 539; the Ottoman use of the term *khāṣṣ* is similar. There were *khāṣṣ-i shāhi*—Imperial *Khāṣṣ* or Domain of the Sultan—the revenue of which belonged to the Imperial purse, and *Khāṣṣ-i Mīr-i liwā*—Governor's *Khāṣṣ*—Appanage of the *Mīr-i Liwā* or *Sanjaq-Bey*, cf. Lewis, 'Studies', p. 480.

[3] Maqrīzī, *Sulūk*, i, p. 73, tr. Blochet, 'B', p. 541; Rabīʿ, *Nuẓum*, p. 28.

[4] Abū Shāma, *Rawḍatayn*, ii, p. 53; Gibb, 'The armies of Saladin', p. 75 and p. 86 n. 18; Rabīʿ, *Nuẓum*, pp. 28–9.

[5] Iṣfahānī, *Barq*, v, fol. 120r; Ibn Wāṣil, *Mufarrij*, ii, p. 152; Maqrīzī, *Khiṭaṭ*, ii, p. 364; id., *Sulūk*, i, p. 82, tr. Blochet, 'C', p. 9.

It is in the reign of Sultan al-Kāmil, that the term *iqṭāʿ darbastā* is first encountered in Egypt to denote assignment, to one *muqṭaʿ*, of the right of collecting all taxes in the *iqṭāʿ*, including those collected for the sultan. In this sense, the *iqṭāʿ darbastā* is the antecedent and equivalent of the Ottoman *serbest tīmār* which, in the words of Professor Lewis, 'included certain revenues which in ordinary timars belonged to the Treasury'.[1] Ibn al-ʿAmīd mentions that, in the year 619/1222–3, Sultan al-Kāmil conferred Fayyūm upon the amir Fakhr al-Dīn ʿUthmān ibn Qizil *darbastā*, complete with [stores of] sugar-cane, cows, granaries, and agricultural implements. He also granted him the right to appoint, in this province, governors and other officials.[2]

It is worth mentioning that the term *darbastā* continued to be used with the same meaning during the Mamluk period. It is related, for instance, that, in Shaʿbān 690/August 1291, Sultan Khalīl ibn Qalāwūn released the amir Baysarā al-Shamsī, and conferred upon him Minyat banī Khaṣīb as a *darbastā iqṭāʿ*. Commenting on this, some chroniclers say that it included the *jawālī* tax and the *mawārīth ḥashriyya*.[3]

The right of collecting some non-agricultural taxes was frequently conferred in the form of *iqṭāʿ*s from the reign of Saladin onwards until the Nāṣirī *rawk* of 715/1315.[4] It appears that this type of *iqṭāʿ* was conferred, during the reign of Saladin, mainly upon some members of the Ayyūbid family. Thus, Saladin conferred, in 565/1169–70, Alexandria, Damietta, and Buḥayra as an *iqṭāʿ* upon his father Najm al-Dīn Ayyūb. About the same time he assigned Qūṣ, Aswān, and ʿAydhāb to his brother Tūrānshāh.[5] In the following year, Saladin increased his brother's *iqṭāʿ* by conferring upon him Būsh, Jīza, Samannūd, and other

[1] Lewis, 'Studies', p. 483; *darbast* is a Persian word which signifies 'completely or wholly', cf. Steingass, *Persian–English dictionary*; Qalqashandī (*Ṣubḥ*, xiii, p. 156) interprets the word *darbastā* in the same way, but the editor reads *karbastā*.

[2] Ibn al-ʿAmīd, *Akhbār*, p. 135.

[3] Baybars al-Manṣūrī, *Zubda*, fol. 178ᵛ; Nuwayrī, xxix, fol. 61; Ibn al-Furāt, viii, p. 123; Maqrīzī, *Sulūk*, i, p. 770, tr. Quatremère, ii. i, pp. 131–2.

[4] Maqrīzī, *Khiṭaṭ*, ii, p. 218; Qalqashandī, *Ṣubḥ*, iv, p. 50; Prof. Poliak stated thirty years ago that the word *jiha* denoted under the Mamluks both 'every village named in the *manshūr* of the *iqṭāʿ* holder' and 'a source of monetary income such as tax, a customs duty, a fixed monopoly' (Poliak, 'La féodalité islamique', *REI*, x (1936), p. 258; id., *Feudalism*, p. 18).

[5] Ibn Abī al-Hayjā', fol. 166ᵛ; Ḥanbalī, *Shifā'*, fol. 11ᵛ; Abū Shāma, *Rawḍatayn*, i. ii, p. 466; Maqrīzī, *Khiṭaṭ*, ii, pp. 37, 412; id., *Dhahab*, pp. 70–1.

districts,[1] and in 574/1179 Alexandria was conferred as an *iqṭā'* upon Tūrānshāh, who lived there until his death in 576/1180.[2]

The important question arising here is whether the Ayyūbid *muqṭa'* enjoyed the whole revenue of his *iqṭā'*, which could be a port such as Alexandria, Damietta, and 'Aydhāb, or an inland city such as Qūṣ. It would seem that unless the sultan particularly conferred the *iqṭā'* in the form of *khāṣṣ* or *darbastā*, the *muqṭa'* was only entitled to the collection of certain amounts and kinds of taxes in the port or city mentioned in his *tawqī'* or *manshūr*.[3]

Over the years, the assignment of non-agricultural taxes in the form of *iqṭā'*s became more frequent. This is exemplified by the conferment of the *iqṭā'* of Damietta, after the demolition of the city in 648/1250, upon the amir Baybars al-Badrī who founded a new city on its site. Under al-Badrī Damietta grew fast and developed into a wealthy centre of trade and commerce.[4] After about four years (652/1254–5), it was assigned, by Sultan Aybak, to the amir 'Alā' al-Dīn Aydughdī al-'Azīzī. The size of its revenue, said to have equalled at that time 30,000 *dīnār*s, appears to be exaggerated by the sources. Nor do we know if the amir 'Alā' al-Dīn enjoyed the whole amount or only a certain portion.[5] Nothing is mentioned concerning the extent to which Fāris al-Dīn Aqṭāy, the Baḥriyya chief, had the right to collect taxes in Alexandria which had been conferred upon him, by Sultan Aybak, in the form of *iqṭā'* in 650/1252–3.[6]

It also appears that, from the reign of Sultan Baybars onwards, the Mamluk sultans frequently assigned to some, but by no means all, *muqṭa'*s the right of collecting taxes on vice such as taxes on *mizr* (a kind of beer), *khumūr* (wine), and prostitution.[7] However,

[1] 'Aynī, *'Iqd*, 'A', xii, fol. 165^r; Abū Shāma, *Rawḍatayn*, i. ii, p. 488; Ibn al-Furāt, iv. i, p. 130.

[2] Ibn Abī al-Hayjā', fol. 177^r–v; 'Umarī, *Masālik* (MS. P.), fol. 24^v; Maqrīzī, *Khiṭaṭ*, ii, p. 38.

[3] See above, pp. 42–3.

[4] Ibn Duqmāq, *Intiṣār*, v, p. 81; for the demolition of Damietta in 648/1250, cf. Ibn Wāṣil, *Mufarrij*, fols. 377^v–8^r; 'Umarī, *Masālik* (MS. P.), fol. 94^r; Maqrīzī, *Sulūk*, i, p. 372, tr. Quatremère, i. i, p. 15.

[5] Jazarī, *Tārīkh*, fol. 75^r; Dawādārī, *Durra zakiyya*, fol. 11^r–v; Nuwayrī, xxvii, fol. 115; Dhahabī, *Tārīkh*, (MS. Bodleian Laud. Or. 305), fol. 243^r; Maqrīzī, *Sulūk*, i, p. 394, tr. Quatremère, i. i, p. 55.

[6] Baybars al-Manṣūrī, *Tuḥfa*, fol. 5^v; Nuwayrī, xxvii, fol. 115; Ibn Taghrī Birdī, *Manhal*, i, fol. 209^r; Ibn Duqmāq, *Jawhar*, fol. 93^v; Ibn al-'Amīd, *Akhbār*, p. 164; Maqrīzī, *Sulūk*, i, p. 384, tr. Quatremère, i. i, p. 37.

[7] See below, pp. 120–1.

the *rawk* of 715/1315 ordered by Sultan al-Nāṣir ibn Qalāwūn abolished certain taxes, some of which had formed part of *iqṭāʿ*s. The most important of them were *muqarrar ṭarḥ al-farārīj* or *al-farrūj*, *maks sāḥil al-ghalla*, and *muqarrar al-sujūn*.[1]

D. *Size and value of the* iqṭāʿ

Maqrīzī, who states that from Saladin's time onwards all Egyptian cultivated land had been assigned in the form of *iqṭāʿ*s to the sultan, his *ajnād*, and his amirs, does not specify the method by which the individual shares were allotted, at that time, to the respective beneficiaries.[2] Nor is any mention made of this point by other historians, probably owing to a lack of information about the Ṣalāḥī *rawk* ordered by Saladin in 572/1176.[3] It is also possible that the Ayyūbid sultans prevented the officials of *dīwān al-jaysh* from divulging this secret. The gist of the available information is that, when Sultan Lājīn came to power in the year 696/1296, he found that, of the twenty-four *qīrāṭ*s (*qīrāṭ* means a twenty-fourth part) constituting the cultivated land of Egypt, four were in the hands of the sultan (including the royal mamluks), ten in the hands of the amirs, and the last ten in the hands of the *ajnād al-ḥalqa*.[4] These proportions were changed as a result of the Ḥusāmī *rawk* in 697/1298, and the Nāṣirī *rawk* in 715/1315.[5]

Relying on *Ṣubḥ al-aʿshā*, it can be said that the sultans used to distinguish three kinds of cultivated land conferred in the form of *iqṭāʿ*s in terms of their yield in revenue. Land with the highest yield was offered in the form of *iqṭāʿ*s to the amirs according to their rank, each receiving an *iqṭāʿ* consisting of one to ten villages. Land of the second category was conferred upon the sultani mamluks. In rare cases, sultani mamluks had entire villages to themselves; in most cases there were two or more *muqṭaʿ*s to one village. Land yielding least revenue was assigned to the *ajnād al-ḥalqa*, Bedouin tribes and others, each of the groups sharing a village. Unfortunately,

[1] See below, pp. 103–4, 113.

[2] See above, p. 26.

[3] For the Ṣalāḥī *rawk* see below, pp. 51–2.

[4] Maqrīzī, *Khiṭaṭ*, i, p. 88; id., *Sulūk*, i, pp. 841–2, tr. Quatremère, ii. ii, pp. 65–6; Ibn Taghrī Birdī, *Nujūm*, viii, p. 92; Ibn Iyās, *Badāʾiʿ*, i, p. 137; Gaudefroy-Demombynes, *La Syrie*, p. xl; Poliak, *Feudalism*, p. 24; Ayalon, 'Studies', ii, p. 452.

[5] See below, pp. 52, 54.

there is no other evidence to support Qalqashandī's statement, which appears to point back to the Ayyūbid era[1].

However, the size of a particular *iqṭāʿ* was dictated by the fact that *iqṭāʿ*s of particular holders were scattered in different places and over large areas. It seems that it was the sultan's purpose to reduce the influence of the *muqṭaʿ* in his *iqṭāʿ*, lest he should proclaim independence or rebel. In five cases, there is evidence to prove that it was an Ayyūbid tradition, later taken over by the Mamluks, to scatter particular *iqṭāʿ*s in this way:[2]

(*a*) The *iqṭāʿ* of Tūrānshāh consisted of many cities and villages in Upper and Lower Egypt.[3]

(*b*) The *iqṭāʿ* of Taqī al-Dīn ʿUmar was scattered in many places in Syria and Egypt in 579/1183.[4]

(*c*) The *tawqīʿ* of al-ʿĀdil, Saladin's brother (dated 580/1184–5), preserved by Qalqashandī, indicates that his *iqṭāʿ* consisted of many villages in Egypt, Syria, Jazīra, and Diyār Bakr.[5]

(*d*) Ibn Wāṣil states that while going to Damietta, in Muḥarram 648/May 1250, to see the Muslims entering the city after the defeat of Louis IX, he passed Marṣafā, which he described as 'one of the farms (*ḍayʿa*) forming part of the *iqṭāʿ* of Ḥusām al-Dīn Muḥammad ibn abī ʿAlī [al-Hadhabānī]'.[6]

(*e*) In his written *waṣiyya* to Tūrānshāh, Sultan al-Ṣāliḥ Najm al-Dīn Ayyūb accused the Copts of the intention of weakening the army and ruining the country. More details are found in the statement of Sultan al-Ṣāliḥ to the effect that the Copts would scatter the 1,000 *dīnār* (*jayshī*) *iqṭāʿ* of a *jundī* in five or six places, e.g. in Qūṣ in Upper Egypt, and Sharqiyya and Gharbiyya in Lower Egypt. In such a case the *muqṭaʿ* had to employ four or more *wakīl*s (agents), so that no revenue was left to him, especially if he was absent at war. The sultan advised his son to grant *iqṭāʿ*s in one place or two adjacent places.[7]

[1] Qalqashandī, *Ṣubḥ*, iii, pp. 457–8.

[2] This tradition continued in Syria under the Ottomans. Thus, though *tīmār*s usually fall within a single *nāḥiye*, there are a few which are made up of villages in different *nāḥiyes*. Cf. Lewis, 'Studies', p. 482.

[3] See above, pp. 43–4.

[4] See above, p. 42.

[5] Qalqashandī, *Ṣubḥ*, xiii, pp. 146–7; Rabīʿ, *Nuẓum*, p. 36.

[6] Ibn Wāṣil, *Mufarrij*, fol. 372r; Rabīʿ, *Nuẓum*, p. 36; Marṣafā is now in Banhā district.

[7] Nuwayrī, xxvii, fols. 91–2. It is worth mentioning that there was a prejudice against Coptic clerks on the part of Muslim jurists and writers, probably because they resented their superior experience in financial matters, cf. Cahen, 'Histoires

Unfortunately, Sultan Tūrānshāh, al-Ṣāliḥ's son, ruled only seventy-one days, and was supplanted by the Mamluk sultanate. An increase of the scattering of individual *iqṭāʿ*s in Egypt and Syria over widely separated areas is observable in the Mamluk period.[1]

An alternative explanation of this phenomenon is that *iqṭāʿ*s were allocated as they fell vacant, since they obviously would not fall vacant in territorial blocks, but at random in different parts of the country.

The evaluation of the *iqṭāʿ* was based on what was called the *ʿibra*. Professor Cahen suggests that the *ʿibra* had existed since the advent of Islam and went back even further, perhaps, to Roman antecedents.[2] He also states that the term *ʿibra* used to be applied, in Muslim medieval administration, to the assessment of the fiscal value of a territory. But it is not always easy to see how it was established and what its connection was with the taxes actually levied.[3]

A description of the method by which the *ʿibra* was generally estimated can be found in the *Kitāb mafātīḥ al-ʿulūm* by Khwārizmī. It was based on the average revenue arrived at by calculating the revenue of the best and the worst year, adding the amounts and dividing the resultant sum total by two, after considering changes in price and occasional events such as wars or epidemics.[4] Consequently, the *ʿibra* of the *iqṭāʿ* was—in theory at least—the average yearly revenue from the *iqṭāʿ*. In practice, the *ʿibra* and the actual annual revenue from the *iqṭāʿ* had long ceased to coincide, a discrepancy which may have been quite considerable by the end of the period.[5] This can be easily shown, as Qalqashandī states that the *ʿibra* was useless because the actual revenue of one *iqṭāʿ*, estimated at 100 *dīnār*s *jayshī*, may have been higher than that of another

coptes d'un cadi médiéval. Extraits du *Kitāb tadjrīd saïf al-himma li'stikhrādj mā fī dhimmat al-dhimma* de 'Uthmān b. Ibrāhīm an-Nābulusī', *BIFAO*, lix (1960), pp. 133–50; Asnāwī, *Kalimāt*, fols. 6–14; Perlmann, 'Asnawī's tract against Christian officials', *Goldziher Memor.* ii (1958), pp. 172–208; id. 'Notes on anti-Christian propaganda in the Mamlūk Empire', *BSOAS*, x (1940–2), pp. 843–61.

[1] Ibn Wāṣil, *Mufarrij*, fol. 400r; Ibn Iyās, *Badāʾiʿ*, i, p. 154; Popper, *Systematic notes*, ii, p. 109.

[2] Cahen, 'Évolution', p. 46 n. 3.

[3] Id., 'Le régime des impôts dans le Fayyūm Ayyūbide', *Arabica*, iii (1956), p. 12.

[4] Khwārizmī, *Mafātīḥ*, pp. 60–1.

[5] Cf. Cahen, 'Évolution', p. 46.

*iqṭā*ʿ estimated at 200 *dīnārs jayshī* or more.[1] Ibn al-Jīʿān also states that long intervals of time, the devastation of most villages, the reconstruction of others, and changes in the rate of exchange of the *dīnār* had made nonsense of the ʿ*ibra*.[2]

The unit of calculation of the ʿ*ibra* was not the ordinary *dīnār*, but the *jayshī dīnār* (the army *dīnār*). Qalqashandī states that the *jayshī dīnār* was an arbitrary monetary unit, used by the officials of the *dīwān al-jaysh* in evaluating different *iqṭā*ʿs.[3] It is worth mentioning that even before Qalqashandī, Ibn Mammātī described the *jayshī dīnār* as a fictitious *dīnār*, whose value varied from one group of *ajnād* to another. In Ibn Mammātī's lifetime—before 606/1209—the *jayshī dīnār* used to be assessed as follows: for Turkish, Kurdish, and Turkoman regulars at one gold *dīnār*; for the Kināniya, the ʿAsāqila (from Ascalon), and other similar *ajnād* at ½ gold *dīnār*; for naval service commanders and similar ranks at ¼ gold *dīnār*; for Arab auxiliaries, with certain exceptions, at ⅛ gold *dīnār*.[4]

Ibn Mammātī also states the value of the *jayshī dīnār*, which consisted of a specific combination of payments in cash and kind, namely: ¼ gold *dīnār* and one *ardabb* of crops (consisting of ⅓ *ardabb* of barley and ⅔ *ardabb* of wheat). That is to say, the *iqṭā*ʿ whose ʿ*ibra* amounted to 100 *dīnārs jayshī*, was supposed to yield an average revenue of 25 gold *dīnārs* and 100 *ardabbs*, one third of which was barley and two thirds wheat.[5]

Qalqashandī, Ibn al-Jīʿān, and Suyūṭī state that the value of the *jayshī dīnār* equalled 13⅓ *dirhams* in ordinary currency.[6] Professor Cahen suggests that, since wheat was probably worth about ½ gold *dīnār* an *ardabb* in the Ayyūbid period, and the *ardabb* of barley was half this price, one *ardabb* of corn in the above proportion was worth about ⅖ of the ordinary *dīnār*, so that the *jayshī dīnār* was, all in all, worth about two thirds of the ordinary gold *dīnār*. Professor Cahen insists that, as there seems to be little connection between the figures in the *Kitāb tārīkh al-Fayyūm* and this theoretical calculation, these figures are only approximate and that, in

[1] Qalqashandī, *Ṣubḥ*, iii, p. 442.

[2] Ibn al-Jīʿān, *Tuḥfa*, p. 3.

[3] Qalqashandī, *Ṣubḥ*, iii, p. 442.

[4] Ibn Mammātī, p. 369; Qalqashandī, *Ṣubḥ*, iii, p. 442; for the Kināniya and the ʿAsāqila, cf. Gibb, 'The armies of Saladin', p. 86 nn. 25 and 26.

[5] Ibn Mammātī, p. 369 n. 9; Cahen, 'Évolution', p. 46; id., 'Régime', p. 12.

[6] Qalqashandī, *Ṣubḥ*, iii, pp. 442–3; Ibn al-Jīʿān, *Tuḥfa*, p. 3; Suyūṭī, *Ḥusn*, ii, p. 191.

the Mamluk era, the actual financial revenue diverged ever further from the initial estimate.[1] Professors Poliak and Popper, relying on Maqrīzī's *Khiṭaṭ*, state that the *jayshī dīnār* varied, at the time of the Nāṣirī *rawk* in 715/1315, from 10 to 7 *dirhams*, according to the *muqṭa'*'s rank.[2]

There are three reasons why these attempts to find a relationship between the *jayshī dīnār* and the ordinary *dīnār* can neither be confirmed nor refuted:

(*a*) The *jayshī dīnār* was a fictitious monetary unit, similar to the *qīrāṭ*, which is still in use in Egypt, especially among small landed proprietors. The value of the *qīrāṭ* (*qīrāṭ* means one twenty-fourth part) varies according to time, area, and the condition of the property. Thus, the real value of the *jayshī dīnār* differed from one year to another, and from one *iqṭā'* to another. As has already been pointed out, the value of the *jayshī dīnār* was indeterminate and varied for different people, according to their grades in the army.

(*b*) The rate of exchange of the gold *dīnār*, which was a component part of the *jayshī dīnār*, not only changed from one sultan's reign to another, but also, as will be seen, several times during the reign of a particular sultan.[3]

(*c*) The prices of barley and wheat varied for many reasons, such as high or low floods of the Nile, wars, epidemics, and even transport—i.e. grain could be dear or cheap, according to circumstances. Thus the value of the *jayshī dīnār* in terms of real money could be higher in a bad year or a year of famine when the prices of wheat and barley were high, than in a year of plenty, when they were low.

The reassignment of the *iqṭā'*s took place after every *rawk*, i.e. cadastral survey of Egyptian cultivated land. Professor Poliak has suggested that the concept of the *rawk* was of Mongol origin.[4] One might accept this as correct in the sense that the Mamluk sultans imitated the Mongols in reassigning the *iqṭā'*s after each cadastral survey of land under cultivation. But the opinion that the *rawk* as

[1] Cahen, 'Régime', pp. 12–13.

[2] Maqrīzī, *Khiṭaṭ*, ii, pp. 218–19; Poliak, 'The feudal system of the Mamlūks', pp. 99–100; id., *Feudalism*, p. 21; Popper, *Systematic notes*, ii, p. 109.

[3] See below, Chapter V.

[4] Poliak, 'Le caractère colonial de l'état Mamelouk dans ses rapports avec la Horde d'Or', *REI*, ix (1935), pp. 239–41; id., *Feudalism*, p. 23.

a method of surveying land and estimating taxes was introduced into Egypt by the Mongols does not seem acceptable for two reasons:

(*a*) Etymologically, the word *rawk* comes from the Coptic word ⲣⲱϣ *rōsh*, which means to measure the land by means of a rope. This Coptic word is possibly derived from the Demotic word rḫ *rukh*, which denotes land distribution.[1]

(*b*) It was an old-established Egyptian custom, possibly going back to the days of the Pharaohs, to survey the land to assess the increase and decrease of cultivated land in order to adjust the taxes to be levied. The term *mukallafa* has long been used in Egypt to denote a 'register of landed property'. The *māsiḥ* (surveyor) was the official who drew up the *mukallafāt*, arranged—as Grohmann states—according to the different villages.[2] In corroboration of the above contention, it may not be amiss to give a few data which provide information on the main three *rawk*s held in Egypt previous to the Mongol invasion, although these precede the period under consideration.

In the Caliphate of Hishām ibn ʿAbd al-Malik, ʿUbayd Allāh ibn al-Ḥabḥāb, the then financial director of Egypt, initiated, subsequent to his arrival in Egypt in 105/724, a new land survey, references to which are found in a papyrus recently published by Dr. Nabia Abbott, and dated 23 Rabīʿ I 106/19 August 724. When Walīd ibn Rifāʿa became governor of Egypt in 109/727, both participated in the land survey and population census which had already been initiated by Ibn al-Ḥabḥāb.[3]

[1] Crum, *Coptic dictionary*, p. 308; Gardiner, *Theban ostraca*, p. 44 n. 1; Mattha, *Demotic ostraka*, p. 23; Lichtheim, *Demotic ostraca from Medinet Habu*, p. 53.

[2] Ibn Mammātī, p. 305; Maqrīzī, *Khiṭaṭ*, i, pp. 86, 88; Qalqashandī, *Ṣubḥ*, iii, p. 458; Grohmann, 'New discoveries in Arabic papyri. An Arabic tax-account book' 'I', *BIE*, xxxii (1949–50), p. 163. Dietrich published (*Arabische Papyri*, pp. 81–4) a 3rd/9th century papyrus which he described as a land-tax register. He suggested that the columns of the latter represented, not tax totals in *dīnārs*, but the number of *faddān*s planted with wheat or clover at successive dates, obviously i.e. a fragment of *mukallafa*. It is worth noting that the eastern equivalent of the *mukallafa* in Egypt was termed *qānūn al-kharāj*; cf. Lewis, article 'Daftar' in *EI*²; the *rawk* is denoted in Egypt today by the term *fakk al-zimām*.

[3] Ibn ʿAbd al-Ḥakam, p. 156; Kindī, *Wulā*, pp. 75–9; Abū Ṣāliḥ the Armenian, pp. 30, 35; Maqrīzī, *Khiṭaṭ*, i, pp. 74–5, 98–9; Suyūṭī, *Ḥusn*, i, p. 87; Nabia Abbot, 'A new papyrus and a review of the administration of ʿUbaid Allāh B. al-Ḥabḥāb', in Makdisi, ed., *Arabic and Islamic studies*, pp. 27–9.

During the Caliphate of al-Muʿtazz, the director of finance, Aḥmad ibn Muḥammad ibn al-Mudabbir, personally supervised, in about 253/867–8, a survey of Egyptian cultivated land, after which Ibn al-Mudabbir increased the *kharājī* tax from 1 *dīnār* for each *faddān* to as much as 4 *dīnārs*.[1]

In the year 501/1107–8, both military and civilian *muqṭaʿ*s suffered badly from the decrease in revenue from *iqṭāʿ*s. Following al-Ma'mūn al-Baṭā'iḥī's advice, al-Afḍal ibn Badr al-Jamālī tried to solve the problem by a cadastral survey of the Egyptian land and a consequent reassignment of the *iqṭāʿ*s.[2] Abū Ṣāliḥ, the Armenian, seems to have preserved in his book the data provided by the Afḍalī *rawk*. He states the number of Egyptian *nawāḥī* (districts) and *kufūr* (hamlets) in the provinces under the Fāṭimids, and also the revenue derived from their *iqṭāʿ*s, excluding Alexandria, Damietta, Tinnīs, Qifṭ, Naqāda, and Birkat al-Ḥabash.[3] These data seem to have been of considerable assistance to Saladin in holding his Ṣalāḥī *rawk*, the first of three *rawk*s which took place in the period under consideration.[4]

The Ṣalāḥī *rawk* was ordered by Saladin in the year 572/1176. It seems that Saladin intended this *rawk* to open a new era in the reassignment of the *iqṭāʿ*s and the financial administration of Egypt. He chose Bahā' al-Dīn Qarāqūsh to supervise the work on the Ṣalāḥī *rawk*, the duration of which is not specified by the known sources.[5] One might infer from al-Fāḍil's *Mutajaddidāt* of Rajab 577/November–December 1181, and from what is quoted from al-Iṣfahānī in *al-Rawḍatayn* relating to the year 581/1185, that the Ṣalāḥī *rawk* directly influenced the reassignment of the *iqṭāʿ*s for a period of ten years or more.[6]

It seems that the Ṣalāḥī *rawk* was the only *rawk* of the Ayyūbid period. This assumption might be confirmed by the fact that, in his *waṣiyya* to his son Tūrānshāh, Sultan al-Ṣāliḥ Ayyūb advised him to base his estimation of the *ʿibra* on 'what it had been in

[1] Ibn Taghrī Birdī, *Nujūm*, i, p. 47; Maqrīzī, *Khiṭaṭ*, i, pp. 99, 103, 314; Dietrich, *Arabische Papyri*, p. 84.

[2] See above, pp. 27–8.

[3] Abū Ṣāliḥ the Armenian, pp. 10–12 (English tr., pp. 15–18).

[4] The other two are the Ḥusāmī *rawk* and the Nāṣirī *rawk*.

[5] Dawādārī, *Durr maṭlūb*, fols. 17^r, 39^r; Maqrīzī, *Khiṭaṭ*, i, p. 101; Qalqashandī, *Ṣubḥ*, iii, pp. 452–3; Rabīʿ, *Nuẓum*, pp. 42–3; Saladin also depended upon Qarāqūsh in building the citadel of Cairo, cf. *RCEA*, ix, pp. 123–4; *CIA*, i, pp. 80–1.

[6] Maqrīzī, *Khiṭaṭ*, i, pp. 86–7; Abū Shāma, *Rawḍatayn*, ii, p. 62.

Saladin's time'. It can therefore be assumed that the evaluation of the *iqṭā*ʿs in the Ṣalāḥī *rawk* became the model for Saladin's successors.[1]

The Ḥusāmī *rawk*, held in the Mamluk period in 697/1298 was instituted by Sultan Ḥusām al-Dīn Lājīn, not only to reassign the *iqṭā*ʿs, but also to investigate the deplorable condition of the mamluks of those amirs who had appropriated the *iqṭā*ʿs of the *ajnād* under the pretext of *ḥimāya* (protection), so that confusion, disorder, and looting in the *iqṭā*ʿs could be prevented.[2]

The Ḥusāmī *rawk* was completed in less than eight months from Jumādā I to Dhū al-Ḥijja 697/March to October 1298, under the supervision of Mankūtamur, the vice-sultan, and other high officials.[3] The two main principles of that *rawk* were that *ḥimāya* was to be abolished, and the Egyptian land to be divided into four *qīrāṭ*s for the sultan's *iqṭā*ʿ *khāṣṣ*; ten *qīrāṭ*s for both the amirs and the *ajnād al-ḥalqa*; one *qīrāṭ* to satisfy the complainants, and the remaining nine *qīrāṭ*s to be conferred in the form of *iqṭā*ʿs upon new troops.[4]

The Ḥusāmī *rawk* assigned the *iqṭā*ʿs *darbastā*, excluding the *jawālī* tax and the *mawārīth ḥashriyya*, which were collected for the sultan, and *al-rizaq al-aḥbāsiyya*, collected from the *waqf* land for religious and charitable purposes.[5] The majority of the *muqṭa*ʿs were dissatisfied with the provisions of the *rawk*. The contemporary historian Baybars al-Manṣūrī states that the Sultan Lājīn and his subordinates urged the *rawk* staff to bring it to a rapid conclusion. They actually surveyed only a part of the land, and the rest only symbolically.[6]

Al-Manṣūrī's statement is significant, because it is well known

[1] Nuwayrī, xxvii, fol. 92.

[2] Baybars al-Manṣūrī, *Tuḥfa*, fols. 69ᵛ–70ʳ; Maqrīzī, *Khiṭaṭ*, i, pp. 87–8; for the *ḥimāya* cf. Cahen, 'Notes pour l'histoire de la ḥimāya', *Mél. L. Massignon*, i (1956), pp. 287–303; id., articles 'Ḍarība' and 'Ḥimāya' in *EI*².

[3] Nuwayrī, xxix, fol. 100; Ṣafadī, *Nuzha*, fol. 58ʳ; Ibn Abī al-Faḍā'il, p. 437; Ibn Taghrī Birdī, *Manhal*, v, fol. 55ʳ; id., *Nujūm*, viii, p. 92; id., *Mawrid*, p. 49.

[4] Maqrīzī, *Khiṭaṭ*, i, p. 88; id; *Sulūk*, i, pp. 841–4, tr. Quatremère, ii. ii, pp. 65–8; Gaudefroy-Demombynes, *La Syrie*, p. xl; Ibn Taghrī Birdī (*Nujūm*, viii, pp. 92–3), quoting from an unknown source, states that 14 *qīrāṭ*s were divided among the troops, 4 *qīrāṭ*s went to the sultan, 2 *qīrāṭ*s to the complainants, and 4 *qīrāṭ*s to the newly recruited troops. For other divisions cf. Ibn Duqmāq, *Jawhar*, fols. 120ᵛ–1ʳ; Anonymous, *Tārīkh*, fol. 21ʳ; Ibn Iyās, *Badā'i*ʿ, i, p. 137.

[5] Nuwayrī, xxix, fol. 100; Maqrīzī, *Sulūk*, pp. 844–5; tr. Quatremère, ii. ii, p. 68.

[6] Baybars al-Manṣūrī, *Zubda*, fol. 198ᵛ.

that the *ajnād al-ḥalqa* rebelled against the Ḥusāmī *rawk* which gave them only half of what they had had before. Besides, the revenue of each new *iqṭāʿ* was insufficient to meet the expenses or duties of the *muqṭaʿ*. Some *ajnād* went in a body to Mankūtamur, asking him to increase their *iqṭāʿ*s or to tranfer them to the amirs' service or to release them entirely from military service. As the vice-sultan was severe, he imprisoned them, and threatened the amirs. The reaction was that both the sultan and Mankūtamur were killed and, in the words of Maqrīzī, 'that *rawk* was the main reason of the collapse of [Lājīn's] regime'.[1] The anonymous contemporary historian points to the Ḥusāmī *rawk* as the prime cause of the weakness of the Mamluk army, especially the *ḥalqa*.[2] Ibn Taghrī Birdī ascribes it to the fact that no one obtained a satisfactory quantity. In reality, the injustice was even worse as, after Lājīn's murder, the nine *qīrāṭ*s saved by the *rawk* were assigned to the amirs only, disregarding the claims of most *muqṭaʿ*s, which resulted in a deterioration of the position of the *ḥalqa*.[3]

The only evidence that there was no *rawk* in the period between the Ḥusāmī *rawk* and the Nāṣirī *rawk* comes from the later historian Ibn Iyās, who states that the Nāṣirī *rawk* followed the Ḥusāmī *rawk*.[4] The Nāṣirī *rawk* took place during the reign of al-Nāṣir Muḥammad ibn Qalāwūn.

In ordering an Egyptian *rawk*[5] in Shaʿbān 715/November 1315, al-Nāṣir seems to have had several ends in view:

(*a*) to survey the Egyptian land to estimate what was cultivated and what uncultivated, and determine the yield of different kinds of taxes;
(*b*) to abolish the taxes conferred in the form of *iqṭāʿ*s upon *muqṭaʿ*s;
(*c*) to cancel or decrease large *iqṭāʿ*s.
(*d*) to increase the sultan's *khāṣṣ*.

[1] Maqrīzī, *Khiṭaṭ*, ii, p. 387; id., *Sulūk*, i, p. 846, tr. Quatremère, ii. ii, p. 69.

[2] Zettersteen, p. 45.

[3] Ibn Taghrī Birdī, *Nujūm*, viii, p. 95; Ayalon, 'Studies', ii, p. 452.

[4] Ibn Iyās, *Badāʾiʿ*, i, p. 159.

[5] The *Shāmī rawk* took place by order of Sultan al-Nāṣir ibn Qalāwūn in various parts of Syria in the year 713/1313–14. Subsequently there were *rawk*s in Tripoli in 717/1317, and in Aleppo in 725/1325. Cf. Nuwayrī, xxx, fols. 81, 105; 'Aynī, *'Iqd*, 'A', xvii, fol. 16ᵛ; id., *Badr*, fols, 5ʳ, 16ᵛ; Ṣāliḥ ibn Yaḥyā, pp. 125–31; Zettersteen, pp. 160–1; Ibn Abī al-Faḍā'il, p. 742; Maqrīzī, *Sulūk*, ii, pp. 127, 264; Ibn Ḥajar, *Durar*, ii, pp. 170–1, iv, pp. 354–5; Ibn Iyās, *Badāʾiʿ*, i, pp. 159, 164.

After Fakhr al-Dīn Muḥammad ibn Faḍl Allāh, the *nāẓir al-jaysh*, had prepared lists, stating the area and *ʿibra* of each district, the sultan sent amirs, clerks, and land surveyors to all Egyptian provinces and districts. In order to be in touch with these amirs, Sultan al-Nāṣir himself went to Upper Egypt and spent about two months there. When each of the amirs had completed his survey, he summoned the *shaykhs*, *dalīls*, and qadis of each village to examine the registers as well as the financial resources of the village surveyed both in money and crops, its cultivated and uncultivated areas, its *ʿibra* and the *ḍiyāfa* (gifts) which were collected for the *muqṭaʿ*. Almost all the amirs and their assistants carried out such a survey of the village lands to differentiate between the *khāṣṣ* of the sultan, those of the amirs, and the *ajnād* as well as the *rizaq al-aḥbāsiyya*.[1] After the completion of the *rawk*, Sultan al-Nāṣir turned to the *muqṭaʿ*s. Having ascertained the name, origin, and experience of each *muqṭaʿ*, he proceeded to the reassignment of the *iqṭāʿ*s. It is to be ascribed to al-Nāṣir's personal merits that no *muqṭaʿ* returned the *mithāl* handed to him by the sultan, whose sense of justice is also proved by the fact that he forbade a *muqṭaʿ* to be recommended to him by any amir in order to prevent favouritism.[2]

The changes made in the *iqṭāʿ* system and taxation by the Nāṣirī *rawk* were as follows:

1. Ten *qīrāṭ*s of Egyptian land were set aside as *iqṭāʿ khāṣṣ* for the sultan, while the other 14 *qīrāṭ*s were reassigned to the amirs and the *ajnād* in the form of *iqṭāʿ*s.[3]
2. Old and disabled *ajnād* were excluded from *iqṭāʿ* grants, the sultan allotting to each of them a pension of about 3,000 *dirhams* yearly.[4]
3. The *hadiyya* and the *ḍiyāfa* imposed on the *fallāḥīn*, and the *jawālī* tax, were calculated in the *ʿibra* of each *iqṭāʿ*.[5]

[1] Nuwayrī, xxx, fols. 90–1; Ṣafadī, *Nuzha*, fols. 79ᵛ–80ʳ; Maqrīzī, *Khiṭaṭ*, i, p. 88; id., *Sulūk*, ii, pp. 146–7; Ibn Taghrī Birdī, *Nujūm*, ix, pp. 42–4; for the *dalīl*, see below, pp. 73, 135, 160.

[2] Zetterstéen, p. 164; Ibn Abī al-Faḍā'il, pp. 761–2; Ibn Kathīr, xiv, p. 75; Maqrīzī, *Khiṭaṭ*, i, pp. 90–1; id., *Sulūk*, ii, pp. 154–7; Ibn Taghrī Birdī, *Nujūm*, ix, pp. 51–5.

[3] Maqrīzī, *Khiṭaṭ*, i, p. 90; Gaudefroy-Demombynes, *La Syrie*, p. xli.

[4] Maqrīzī, *Sulūk*, ii, p. 156; id., *Khiṭaṭ*, i, p. 90.

[5] Id., *Khiṭaṭ*, i, pp. 88–90; id., *Sulūk*, ii, pp. 150–3; Ibn Taghrī Birdī, *Nujūm*, ix, pp. 43–4, 50.

4. All districts were exempted from arrears until the end of 714/1315.[1]
5. *Al-taqāwī al-sulṭāniyya* (seeds from the sultan), which were given to every *muqṭaʿ* on conferment of the *iqṭāʿ* and were returnable in case of his transfer, remained the permanent property of the *iqṭāʿ* from which they could not be removed.[2]
6. Some villages were set aside to cover the costs of maintenance of the sultan's retinue, while the pay of the civil officials came from other financial sources.[3]
7. Taxes assigned in the form of *iqṭāʿ*s were abolished.[4]
8. The financial administration of the *iqṭāʿ*s was affected by this *rawk* in a manner which will be discussed elsewhere.[5]

The Nāṣirī *rawk* had its advantages and disadvantages. First of all, it modified the very principle of the *iqṭāʿ* system in Egypt, limiting the *iqṭāʿ*s to cultivated land only. It affected also the financial administration of Egypt, not only within the first Mamluk period, but also under the Circassians.[6] Figures found in the *Kitāb al-tuḥfa al-saniyya* by Ibn al-Jīʿān indicate that the data provided by the Nāṣirī *rawk* were copied, without modification, from its registers until the end of the fifteenth century or even later.[7] Secondly, the Nāṣirī *rawk* minimized the influence of the great amirs by decreasing and changing their *iqṭāʿ*s. Thirdly, it afforded comfort to inhabitants of the *iqṭāʿ*s by abolishing heavy taxes.

As to the disadvantages of the Nāṣirī *rawk*, it may be said that it had two. First, the addition of the *jawālī* tax to the *ʿibra* of the *iqṭāʿ* was a grave mistake since, by making it a local tax, it gave Copts an opportunity to evade payment by moving from one village to another. Whenever the *muqṭaʿ* or his clerks demanded payment of this tax, they refused under the pretext that they were not permanent residents of the village. Naturally, the *muqṭaʿ* preferred to accept a part of the *jawālī* tax instead of nothing.[8]

[1] Nuwayrī, xxx, fol. 91; ʿAynī, *ʿIqd*, 'C', xxiii. i, fol. 55; Maqrīzī, *Sulūk*, ii, p. 153; Ibn Taghrī Birdī, *Nujūm*, ix, p. 49; for the arrears cf. Grohmann, 'New discoveries', i, pp. 164, 167.

[2] Maqrīzī, *Khiṭaṭ*, i, p. 91; see below, p. 68.

[3] Nuwayrī, xxx, fol. 91; ʿAynī, *ʿIqd*, 'C', xxiii. i, fol. 54; Ibn Ḥajar, *Durar*, i, p. 359.

[4] See below, pp. 103–5, 113.

[5] See below, p. 64.

[6] Maqrīzī, *Khiṭaṭ*, i, p. 91; Ibn Taghrī Birdī, *Nujūm*, ix, p. 51.

[7] Ibn al-Jīʿān, *Tuḥfa*, pp. 5, 6, 27, 39, 99, 106, 117, 125, 127, 129, 135, 138, 139; Poliak, *Feudalism*, pp. 22–3.

[8] Nuwayrī, xxx, fol. 91; Maqrīzī, *Khiṭaṭ*, i, p. 90.

Secondly, the Mamluk army was weakened by the increase of the expenses of tax collection which grew constantly parallel with the scattering of particular *iqṭā*ʿs over many provinces of Lower and Upper Egypt.[1] This increase appears to have been caused by the need to employ a separate agent and staff of clerks in each part of the *muqṭa*ʿs scattered *iqṭā*ʿ. The cost of their salaries, as well as frequent dishonesty, decreased the revenue derived from the *iqṭā*ʿ. Hence the *muqṭa*ʿ's difficulties in fulfilling his military obligations, which were so great that, under al-Nāṣir's successors, the *ajnād al-ḥalqa* resorted to *nuzūl* to have their *iqṭā*ʿs changed to pay, or else accepted compensation. The prestige of the Mamluk army suffered because so many non-military persons, such as pedlars and common people, held *iqṭā*ʿs.[2]

E. *Rights of the* muqṭaʿ

The sultan, being the original source of the *iqṭā*ʿs, could cancel them at any time.[3] It appears that, to legalize the *iqṭā*ʿs, each new sultan in Egypt had to issue new brevets to his *muqṭa*ʿs when he came to power. The historical sources mention two examples which can be quoted in support of this assumption. After the death of Sultan al-Ṣāliḥ Ayyūb in Dhū al-Qaʿda 647/February 1250, the ambitious amir Fakhr al-Dīn Yūsuf ibn al-Shaykh, who was aiming at the sultanate, issued brevets to the *muqṭa*ʿs in his own name.[4] Nuwayrī states that when Shajar al-Durr was saluted as ruler in 648/1250, she issued new *iqṭā*ʿ brevets with her own signature.[5] These two reports prove that the signing of *iqṭā*ʿ brevets was thought to enhance the sultan's authority. However, it would seem that, during the Mamluk period, the issuing of new brevets at the

[1] Maqrīzī, *Khiṭaṭ*, i, p. 90.

[2] Ibid., ii, p. 219; Gaudefroy-Demombynes, *La Syrie*, pp. xliv–xlv; Ayalon, 'Studies', ii, p. 453; id., 'The system of payment', p. 45.

[3] Qalqashandī, *Ṣubḥ*, iii, p. 279; Maqrīzī, *Khiṭaṭ*, ii, p. 217; Subkī, *Muʿid*, p. 28; sometimes the vice-sultan was authorized to grant a small *iqṭā*ʿ, cf. Nuwayrī, xxviii, fol. 13; Qalqashandī, *Ṣubḥ*, iv, pp. 16–17, xi, p. 134; Maqrīzī, *Khiṭaṭ*, ii, p. 215; Suyūṭī, *Ḥusn*, ii, p. 93; Ayalon, 'Studies', iii, p. 57; Poliak, *Feudalism*, p. 8.

[4] Nuwayrī, xxvii, fol. 89; Ibn al-ʿAmīd, *Akhbār*, p. 159; Maqrīzī, *Sulūk*, i, p. 343, tr. Blochet, 'E', p. 213; Rabīʿ, *Nuẓum*, pp. 37–8; with regard to the amir Fakhr al-Dīn's aspirations to the sultanate cf. Ibn Wāṣil, *Mufarrij*, fols. 362v, 366r; ibid., (MS. Bibliothèque Nat., 1703 Arabe), fol. 78r; Maqrīzī, *Sulūk*, i, p. 345, tr. Blochet, 'E', p. 214; for Fakhr al-Dīn's family see Gottschalk, article 'Awlād al-Shaykh' in *EI*2.

[5] Nuwayrī, xxvii, fol. 122.

beginning of the reign of each successive sultan was mostly done automatically by officials of the *dīwān al-jaysh*.

It is worth mentioning that the assignment of an *iqṭāʿ* by the sultan did not imply ownership of the cultivated land of the *iqṭāʿ*. Nor did it imply long-term enjoyment of the revenue from the *iqṭāʿ*, although, in one particular case mentioned in an undated fragment found in the Vienna papers, this extended to thirty-six years. The assignment of the *iqṭāʿ* gave the *muqṭaʿ* merely the right to collect, for himself and his *ajnād*, a limited group of taxes in return for his military and non-military services. They were, however, probably unlimited in *darbastā iqṭāʿ*s.[1]

The *muqṭaʿ* had apparently the right to relinquish his *iqṭāʿ*, especially when its revenue failed to cover his expenses, or for political reasons. In a fragment of a petition from Saladin's time, definitely written before 578/1182, which is found in the Geniza collection, the petitioners state that the amir ʿAlī al-Mahrānī had relinquished his *iqṭāʿ* consisting of the village of Minyat Khalaf, and ask the amir Sayf al-Islām (Ṭughtegīn), Saladin's brother, to confer this vacant *iqṭāʿ* upon themselves, in order to enable them to serve the sultan. There is no mention, in the sources, of the amir Mahrānī's reasons for renouncing his *iqṭāʿ*, but it seems that it was due to the decreasing revenue of the *iqṭāʿ* which did not suffice to cover the expenses of participation in Saladin's protracted wars.[2] More evidence to the effect that a *muqṭaʿ* had the right to

[1] A.Ch. 10218; see Ibn Nujaym, *Risāla fī bayān al-Iqṭāʿāt*, fol. 134ᵛ.

[2] T.–S. B. 42, F. 94. There are three main reasons for the attribution of this fragment to Saladin's time: (*a*) the style and the formula differ from those current in the Fāṭimid and Mamluk eras; (*b*) the top right-hand corner contains the word al-Nāṣiriyya which was probably preceded by the word *al-umarāʾ* meaning together the Nāṣirī amirs; (*c*) the *laqab* sayf al-Islām mentioned in it used to be given to Ṭughtegīn, Saladin's brother. In 577/1182, Saladin ordered Ṭughtegīn to settle in the Yemen where he lived until his death in 593/1197. Cf. Iṣfahānī, *Sanā*, fol. 205ʳ; Ibn Abī al-Hayjāʾ, fols. 169ʳ, 178ʳ, 184ʳ; Ibn Wāṣil, *Ṣāliḥī*, fols. 201ʳ, 216ʳ; Dawādārī, *Durar*, fol. 188ʳ; id., *Durr maṭlūb*, fol. 26ᵛ; ʿAynī, *ʿIqd*, 'A', xii, fol. 222ʳ, 'B' xiii, fol. 108ᵛ; Ibn Khallikān, i, pp. 424–6; Qalqashandī, *Maʾāthir*, ii, p. 68; Bāshā, *Alqāb*, p. 341; Ibn Shaddād (*Nawādir*, p. 110) refers to the presence of al-Mahrāniyya among warriors at Acre in Shaʿbān 585/October 1189, while Ibn al-Furāt (MS. AF. 120, fol. 151ᵛ) mentions them among the troops who deserted Sultan al-ʿAzīz ʿUthmān in 591/1194–5. It is also said that the name of an amir, Muʿīn al-Dīn Ibrāhīm al-Mahrānī, occurs in an inscription on a tombstone from 599/1203; cf. *RCEA*, ix, p. 240; Bāshā, *Funūn*, i, p. 156. For Minyat Khalaf which is in the Manūfiyya province, cf. Ibn Mammātī, p. 188; Ibn al-Jīʿān, *Tuḥfa*, p. 111; ʿAlī Mubārak, *Khiṭaṭ*, xvi, p. 63; Ramzī, *Qāmūs*, ii. ii, p. 195. This fragment was kindly put at my disposal by the late Dr. S. M. Stern.

renounce his *iqṭāʿ* stems from the year 707/1307. Several historians relate that the amir Karāy al-Manṣūrī asked Sultan al-Nāṣir to cancel his *iqṭāʿ* and let him live in Jerusalem. One of the historians in question, Ibn Ḥajar, states that Karāy was dissatisfied with the influence the amirs Baybars and Salār exerted on Sultan al-Nāṣir.[1]

There is a difference of opinion on whether the *iqṭāʿ* was cancelled on the death of a *muqṭaʿ*. Professor Poliak's ideas are somewhat contradictory. He states that the Mamluk *iqṭāʿ*s were hereditary 'on the condition of loyal behaviour of their holders'.[2] Later Professor Poliak also puts forward an idea which is accepted by Professor Ayalon that, as a result of the influence of the Latin and Ayyūbid feudal systems at the beginning of the Mamluk era, the *muqṭaʿ*s became 'hereditary rulers of their respective regions'.[3] Furthermore, Professor Poliak is of the opinion that 'whereas the Mamluk fiefs, after the downfall of the Latin states, were as a rule not hereditary, the Ayyūbids imitated the hereditary feudal system of the Zangid State'.[4] Professor Gibb agrees with this when he states that Saladin's *iqṭāʿ* system seems to have been identical with Nūr al-Dīn's *iqṭāʿ* system, which was also hereditary.[5]

According to Gaudefroy-Demombynes and Michel, *iqṭāʿ*s were granted either for life or for a fixed period; but could, within these limits, be revoked, changed, or increased by the whim of the sultan, or at the request of the *muqṭaʿ*.[6] Gaudefroy-Demombynes states that when the *iqṭāʿ* was conferred for a number of years, and the holder died before this time had expired, it was stipulated that it should not pass to his heirs, but be returned to the *bayt al-māl*. He also suggests that the hereditary principle was put forward by the amirs in the fourteenth century.[7] Also Professor Cahen says that the frequency of changes shows that the *iqṭāʿ* was not necessarily lifelong, *a fortiori* it was not hereditary.[8]

[1] Baybars al-Manṣūrī, *Zubda*, fols. 257ᵛ–8ʳ; Nuwayrī, xxx, fol. 44; Ṣafadī, *Aʿyān*, (MS. A.S. 2967), fol. 50ʳ; Maqrīzī, *Sulūk*, ii, pp. 36–7, tr. Quatremère, ii. ii, p. 278; Ibn Ḥajar, *Durar*, iii, p. 266.

[2] Poliak, 'The feudal system of the Mamlūks', p. 98.

[3] Poliak, *Feudalism*, pp. 23, 28; Ayalon, 'Studies', ii, p. 452.

[4] Poliak, 'The Ayyūbid feudalism', *JRAS* (1939), p. 431.

[5] Gibb, 'The armies of Saladin', p. 75.

[6] Gaudefroy-Demombynes, *La Syrie*, p. xliv; Michel, 'L'organisation financière de l'Égypte sous les sultans mamelouks d'après Qalqachandi', *BIE*, vii (1924–5), p. 142.

[7] Gaudefroy-Demombynes, *La Syrie*, p. xlvi.

[8] Cahen, 'Évolution', p. 48.

A comparison of the above assumptions with information provided by the original sources cannot but lead to the conclusion that the concept of the hereditary *iqṭāʿ* must be rejected for two reasons:

First of all, neither the very nature of the *iqṭāʿ* nor the sultan's endeavour to improve the efficiency of this system, admits of the hereditary principle. The sultans were sure that a hereditary *iqṭāʿ* would have an adverse influence on military service in cases where the *muqṭaʿ* had an infant son or, which was even worse, a number of children, since an *iqṭāʿ*-holder, who was not yet of the age to bear arms, could not participate in military expeditions, and the distribution of the *iqṭāʿ* among many children was likely to cause confusion in the *iqṭāʿ*. In the Mamluk era, the sons of the amirs were, in any case, excluded from the Mamluk corps and assigned to the *ḥalqa*, a much lower unit. They were known as *awlād al-nās* 'children of the people', that is 'of the best people, of the gentry'.[1]

Secondly, only five cases of actual inheritance of an *iqṭāʿ* are found recorded in the available sources for the whole period under observation. Three of them took place in the reign of Saladin, and the other two during the sultanates of al-Ẓāhir Baybars and al-Nāṣir Muḥammad:

1. In the year 581/1186, after the death of Nāṣir al-Dīn Muḥammad ibn Shīrkūh, Saladin conferred his *iqṭāʿ* upon Nāṣir's son Shīrkūh.[2]
2. In the year 583/1187–8, Saladin granted the *iqṭāʿ* and the office of Shams al-Dīn ibn al-Muqaddam, *amīr al-ḥājj al-Shāmī*, leader of the Syrian caravan of pilgrims to Mecca, to the latter's son ʿIzz al-Dīn.[3]
3. In the year 588/1192, Saladin conferred two thirds of the *iqṭāʿ* of the amir Sayf al-Dīn ʿAlī ibn Aḥmad al-Mashṭūb upon his son ʿImād al-Dīn and two other amirs.[4]
4. In the year 662/1264, after the death of the amir Shihāb al-Dīn

[1] ʿAynī, *ʿIqd*, 'A', xvii, fol. 94ʳ; Maqrīzī, *Sulūk*, ii, p. 228; Ayalon, 'Studies', ii, p. 456; id., 'The system of payment', p. 45; id., article 'Awlād al-Nās', in *EI²*.

[2] Iṣfahānī, *Sanā*, fol. 226ᵛ; Ibn Abī al-Hayjāʾ, fol. 183ʳ; Ibn Wāṣil, *Ṣāliḥī*, fol. 202ᵛ; id., *Mufarrij*, ii, p. 174; ʿUmarī, *Masālik* (MS. P.) fol. 29ᵛ; Dhahabī, *Tārīkh* (MS. Bodleian Laud. Or. 305), fol. 129ʳ⁻ᵛ; ʿAynī, *ʿIqd*, 'B', xiii, fol. 11ᵛ; Ibn al-Athīr, *Kāmil*, xi, p. 341; Ibn Khallikān, i, p. 406; Rabīʿ, *Nuẓum*, p. 37.

[3] Ibn Wāṣil, *Mufarrij*, ii, p. 252.

[4] Ibn Wāṣil, *Mufarrij*, ii, pp. 410–11; Ibn Khallikān states (*Wafayāt*, i, p. 72), that Saladin conferred two-thirds of the *iqṭāʿ* upon ʿImād al-Dīn alone; Rabīʿ *Nuẓum*, p. 37.

al-Qaymarī, Sultan Baybars transferred his *iqṭā'* to the former's son.[1]

5. In the year 711/1311–12, Sultan al-Nāṣir Muḥammad cancelled the *iqṭā'*s of old and disabled amirs, and if one of them had a son who was fit for military service, he transferred the father's *iqṭā'* to the son.[2]

These five cases, however, are no actual proof of the hereditary character of the *iqṭā'*, because the cases of *iqṭā'* cancellation after the death of *muqṭa'*s under Saladin and later sultans are more numerous.[3]

In Egypt, however, in the period under review, the *iqṭā'* had no stipulated length of tenure. It seems that the *muqṭā'* enjoyed the benefits derived from the *iqṭā'* while he fulfilled his military obligations and remained in good health.

Because an *iqṭā'* grant was intended to ensure the provision of adequate military service, the sultans cancelled the *iqṭā'* of any amir who neglected his military duties. This was a Zankid tradition adopted by the Ayyūbids.[4] There is ample evidence from the period under study to show the truth of this statement. In Jumādā II 573/November 1177, Saladin cancelled the *iqṭā'*s of a group of Kurds, because they were the cause of his army's defeat in Ramla.[5] During the war between Saladin and the third Crusade, Saladin cancelled and reassigned, in Jumādā II 587/July 1191, the *iqṭā'*s of some fugitive amirs.[6] Saladin's son, Sultan al-'Azīz 'Uthmān, had the courage to cancel the *iqṭā'*s of those amirs who preferred to settle in Syria and refused to participate in military service; so did al-'Azīz in 590/1193–4.[7] There is evidence to show that there were similar cancellations during the reign of Sultan Lājīn in the Mamluk era. In 697/1298, the Sultan warned the amirs, headed by

1 Ibn 'Abd al-Ẓāhir, *Rawḍ*, p. 1015.

2 Dawādārī, *Durr fākhir*, p. 238.

3 Cf. Nuwayrī, xxvii, fol. 6; xxix, fols. 101, 118, 121; xxx, fols. 3, 43; 'Aynī, *'Iqd*, 'A', xvii, fol. 77r; id., *Badr*, fols. 6r, 17r, 23r; Ibn Kathīr, xiii, p. 31; Ibn al-Furāt, vii, p. 258; Maqrīzī, *Khiṭaṭ*, ii, pp. 50, 93; id., *Sulūk*, i, pp. 75, 909, 927; ii, pp. 177, 269, 327, tr. Blochet, 'B', p. 543, Quatremère, ii. ii, pp. 177, 194; Ibn Taghrī Birdī, *Nujūm*, ix, pp. 232, 241, 277, 287; Ibn Nujaym, *Risāla fī bayān al-Iqṭā'āt*, fol. 134v; Suyūṭī, *Ḥāwī*, i, p. 125.

4 See above, p. 29.

5 Maqrīzī, *Sulūk*, i, pp. 64–5, tr. Blochet, 'B', p. 527; Rabī', *Nuẓum*, p. 35.

6 Iṣfahānī, *Fatḥ*, pp. 352–3; Rabī', *Nuẓum*, p. 35.

7 Iṣfahānī, *Fatḥ*, pp. 457; Maqrīzī, *Sulūk*, i, p. 119 (Blochet 'C', p. 74 incorrectly translates the term *khubz* as 'pension'; it has here the sense of *iqṭā'*).

the amir Baktāsh al-Fakhrī, that they would lose their *iqṭāʿ*s in Egypt if they failed to capture Tall-Ḥamdūn, and they dared not disregard that warning.[1]

As illness prevented the amir from participating in military expeditions, it was obviously a reason for the cancellation of the *iqṭāʿ*. When the famous amir Baktāsh al-Fakhrī fell ill in 705/1306, at over seventy years of age, Sultan al-Nāṣir ibn Qalāwūn cancelled his *iqṭāʿ* and ordered five thousand *dirhams* to be paid to him monthly, as *ṭarkhān*, in spite of Baktāsh's wish to keep his *iqṭāʿ*.[2]

The term *ṭarkhān*, which occurs in the Great *Yāsa* where it refers to a person exempted from state service or tax and has more or less the same meaning in other sources, was introduced by the Mamluks who applied it to an amir whose *iqṭāʿ* was cancelled due to old age or illness.[3]

During the Mamluk era, a *ṭarkhān* had the right to be exempted from military service and other obligations, to dwell wherever he liked, and to move whenever he desired. Sometimes the *ṭarkhān* received a free pension, as in the case of the amir Baktāsh.[4]

It appears that the amount of pension depended on the whim of the sultan. When, for instance, Sultan al-Nāṣir Muḥammad permitted the Qadi Quṭb al-Dīn ibn al-Mukarram to be considered as *ṭarkhān*, with half his salary as a pension, he allowed it to be transferred after his death to his sons and grandsons.[5] As Quṭb

[1] Nuwayrī, xxix, fols. 97–9; Maqrīzī, *Sulūk*, i, pp. 838–9, tr. Quatremère, ii. ii, p. 62.

[2] Baybars al-Manṣūrī, *Tuḥfa*, fol. 85v; id., *Zubda*, fol. 251v; Nuwayrī, xxx, fol. 38; Ibn Ḥabīb, *Durra* (MS. Marsh 591), i, fol. 75v; Ibn Taghrī Birdī, *Manhal*, ii, fol. 84v; Zetterstéen, p. 132; Dawādārī, *Durr fākhir*, pp. 146–7; Maqrīzī, *Sulūk*, ii, pp. 18–20; 30–1, tr. Quatremère, ii. ii, pp. 256–7, 271; it emerges from one of al-Fāḍil's letters to Saladin that the cancellation of the *iqṭāʿ* was considered an insult even during the Ayyūbid period, see *Rasāʾil al-Qāḍī al-Fāḍil* (MS. Brit. Mus., Add. 25757), fol. 73r–v.

[3] Rashīd al-Dīn, *Taʾrīḫ-i-Mubārak-i-Ġāzānī (1265–1295)*, p. 10; Vernadsky, *O sostave velikoi Yasui Chingis Khana*, pp. 18–19; Minovi and Minorsky, 'Naṣīr al-Dīn Ṭūsī on finance', *BSOAS*, x (1940–2), pp. 776, 781, 789; Poliak, 'The influence of Čhingiz-Khān's Yasa', p. 870. The term *ṭarkhān* occurs in various forms in different languages, e.g. Frye, 'Ṭarxūn-Türxūn and Central Asian history', *HJAS*, xiv (1951), pp. 124–5, states that *Ṭarxūn* not *Türxūn*, which appears as a personal name in Islamic sources, is an Altaic word; for the Chinese usage of the word *ṭarkhān* cf. Bailey, 'Indo-Turcica', *BSOAS*, ix (1937–9), p. 300; id., 'Turks in Khotanese texts', *JRAS* (1939), p. 91; for use of the word in Arabic in earlier periods cf. Khwārizmī, *Mafātīḥ*, pp. 120, 129.

[4] Qalqashandī, *Ṣubḥ*, xiii, pp. 48, 51–2.

[5] Ibid., xiii, pp. 52–3. For pensions in the early Islamic era until 235/850

al-Dīn had been a civil official working in the *dīwān al-inshā'*, one may assume that a similar principle of assessment underlay the pensions of the amirs who became *ṭarkhān*s, with the *iqṭā'* revenue as the basis of assessment. No other evidence besides the pension of the amir Baktāsh can be found to support this assumption.

An amir dismissed from military service, and deprived of his *iqṭā'* and office if he had any, was, in the period under review, given the name '*baṭṭāl*'. In Egypt, this term appeared for the first time in the year 568/1172–3, when Tūrānshāh, Saladin's brother, conferred Ibrīm as *iqṭā'* upon the amir Ibrāhīm al-Kurdī. Quoting Ibn Abī Ṭayy, Abū Shāma states that Tūrānshāh sent with him a group of *baṭṭālīn*.[1]

There is no evidence that a *baṭṭāl* had a pension after the cancellation of his *iqṭā'*. He probably only received a salary if the sultan employed him in another capacity. Thus, for instance, Saladin employed, in 577/1182, the *baṭṭālīn* for 33 *dīnār*s monthly per person and sent them to the Yemen.[2] During the siege of Acre in 586/1190, there were large numbers of *baṭṭālīn* receiving pay; al-Iṣfahānī calls them *al-abṭāl al-baṭṭālūn*, 'the brave *baṭṭālīn*'.[3]

During the Mamluk period, the sultans frequently employed *baṭṭālīn*, but let them enter their services and paid them salaries, not pensions.[4] As Gaudefroy-Demombynes states, the amir was not only *baṭṭāl* because he had lost the favour of the prince or had become too old. He may have wished to disappear to save his head or to prepare a coup or a rebellion. Sometimes the sultan himself advised an amir to hide until the storm had passed.[5]

The question arises here whether the *muqṭa'* had any other than financial rights over the population of the *iqṭā'*. In theory, the sultan granted him merely certain financial rights. The Egyptian *iqṭā'* system—perhaps influenced by the theory of Niẓām al-Mulk

cf. Tritton, 'Notes on the Muslim system of pensions', *BSOAS*, xvi (1954), pp. 170–2; for the *ṭarkhāniyyāt* cf. Björkman, article 'Diplomatic', in *EI*².

[1] Abū Shāma, *Rawḍatayn*, i. ii, p. 532; Gibb, 'The armies of Saladin', p. 75, states that the *baṭṭālīn* were soldiers not on regimental payrolls.

[2] Maqrīzī, *Sulūk*, i, pp. 75–6, tr. Blochet, 'B', p. 544, Sa'dāwī, *al-Tārīkh al-ḥarbī*, pp. 128–9.

[3] Iṣfahānī, *Fatḥ*, pp. 313–14.

[4] Ṣafadī, *Nuzha*, fol. 69ᵛ; Anonymous, *Tārīkh*, fol. 7ʳ; Dawādārī, *Durr fakhīr*, p. 245; Maqrīzī, *Sulūk*, i, p. 897, tr. Quatremère, ii. ii, p. 166.

[5] Gaudefroy-Demombynes, *La Syrie*, pp. xlvii–xlviii, note 3; see also Poliak, *Feudalism*, p. 32 n. 7; the word *baṭṭāl* in Arabic denotes an unemployed person, cf. *Muḥīṭ al-muḥīṭ*, i, p. 102.

—seems to emphasize the exclusively financial nature of the rights of the *muqṭaʿ* over the inhabitants of his *iqṭāʿ*. After the expected amount of revenue had been collected, the personal security and financial security of the *fallāḥīn* and their wives and children was inviolable.[1]

In practice, however, the *muqṭaʿ*s often exercised coercion. Nuwayrī designates the *fallāḥīn* by the term '*al-fallāḥūn al-qarāriyya*', which means that they had to remain in the village until death.[2] As they could not leave their village they were, to all intents and purposes, attached to the soil. It is interesting to note that Maqrīzī describes the *fallāḥ* who lived in the *iqṭāʿ*s by the term '*qinn*' (serf).[3] If a *fallāḥ* fled from tyranny and cruelty, the *muqṭaʿ* or his clerks had the authority of the state to oblige him to return.[4] Consequently, the *muqṭaʿ* exploited the *fallāḥīn* by putting them to work which he himself was obliged to perform under the terms of his *iqṭāʿ*. Obviously, it was only a question of non-military functions.[5]

Concerning the residence of the *muqṭaʿ*, it would seem that it depended upon his status, both in the state and the army. The amirs of high rank usually lived far from their *iqṭāʿ*s, generally in the capital and in the proximity of the sultan. If they were provincial governors, they would live in their provincial residences, and leave the administration of their *iqṭāʿ*s to their clerks.

In Saladin's lifetime, it seems that even the ordinary *muqṭaʿ* frequently lived far away from his *iqṭāʿ*. The contemporary historian Ibn Abī al-Hayjā' mentions that, in 581/1185–6, a Kurdish soldier from the *ḥalqa* sent some verses to Saladin complaining that his *iqṭāʿ* was in Qūṣ in Upper Egypt, while he himself served in Mosul. Saladin cancelled the *iqṭāʿ* for which he substituted a *nafaqa*. However, this is the only example of its kind from the Ayyūbid period.[6]

It also appears that, in the Mamluk era, high-ranking amirs gathered in Cairo in peacetime, a fact which the sultans, who

[1] See Subkī, *Muʿid*, p. 48; for the status of the peasant in the Saljūqid *iqṭāʿ* system cf. Niẓām al-Mulk, *Siyāsat Nāma*, English translation, Chapter V, p. 33; Lambton, *Contributions*, pp. 258–9; id., *Landlord and Peasant*, p. 66; Cahen, 'Évolution', p. 39.

[2] Nuwayrī, viii, p. 248.

[3] Maqrīzī, *Khiṭaṭ*, i, p. 85.

[4] Nuwayrī, viii, p. 298; Poliak, *Feudalism*, p. 64. The *sukhra* (corvée) continued even after the collapse of the Mamluk sultanate; al-Shirbīnī states that, during the Ottoman period, few *fallāḥīn* dared to visit the city, lest they should be put into corvée, cf. Shirbīnī, p. 45.

[5] See below, pp. 66, 71–2.

[6] Ibn Abī al-Hayjā', fol. 182ᵛ.

endeavoured, as far as possible, to prevent the *muqṭa*ʿs from fomenting rebellion, did not welcome, especially during their own absence from the capital. Ibn ʿAbd al-Ẓāhir mentions in the *Kitāb al-alṭāf al-khafiyya*, that high-ranking amirs accompanied the Sultan Khalīl ibn Qalāwūn when he visited Alexandria in 690/1291. Only when they arrived in Alexandria did the sultan give them permission to visit their *iqṭā*ʿs.[1] Sultan al-Nāṣir Muḥammad went even further. When he went on his pilgrimages in the years 719/1320 and 732/1332, he ordered all the *muqṭa*ʿs, living in Cairo, to go to their *iqṭā*ʿs and stay there until he came back.[2] These two reports prove, indirectly, that the majority of the *muqṭa*ʿs lived far away from their *iqṭā*ʿs. Since the *muqṭa*ʿ did not reside in his *iqṭā*ʿ, it had to be administered by someone else, living on the spot. It would seem that the clerks who administered the *iqṭā*ʿ were divided in two groups: those subordinated to the sultan, and those under the direct order of the *muqṭa*ʿ.

Concerning the first group, the sources only mention that, before the Nāṣirī *rawk* in 715/1315, there was always a staff of sultani clerks in every large or small village. This staff consisted of a *nāẓir*, a *mustawfī*, and a number of subordinate clerks. It appears that some of them worked in the *iqṭā*ʿ from the Ayyūbid period. However, after the above-mentioned *rawk*, these staffs were of little use, and disappeared from most villages. A rudimentary staff survived only in a group of villages where the taxes were collected for the sultan, and where, according to Nuwayrī, only one *shāhid* and one ʿ*āmil* (or, to judge by Maqrīzī and Ibn Taghrī Birdī, one *nāẓir* and one *amīn*) remained in function in each village of the *khāṣṣ*.[3]

The clerks directly subordinated to the *muqṭa*ʿ formed, during the Mamluk period, what has been termed *dīwān al-amīr*.[4] This term occurs in a document from the Vienna papers dated 5 Ramaḍān 728/15 July 1328 in which a certain Aḥmad ibn al-Ḥājj undertakes to deliver to the *dīwān* of the amir Balabān al-Nāṣirī 2,000 stalks of the alfalfa plant for the protection of fields from the

[1] Ibn ʿAbd al-Ẓāhir, *Alṭāf*, pp. 25–6.

[2] Nuwayrī, xxx, vols. 127–8; Maqrīzī, *Sulūk*, ii, p. 351; Ibn Taghrī Birdī, *Nujūm*, ix, p. 102.

[3] Nuwayrī, xxx, fol. 91; Maqrīzī, *Sulūk*, ii, p. 153. Ibn Taghrī Birdī, *Nujūm*, ix, p. 48; for the *nāẓir*, the *mustawfī*, the *shāhid*, the ʿ*āmil*, and the *amīn*, see below, Chapter IV.

[4] Qalqashandī, *Ṣubḥ*, iv, p. 62; Subkī, *Muʿīd*, pp. 42–3; Ibn Ḥajar, *Durar*, i, p. 82.

impending Nile flood.[1] As a matter of course, a *muqṭaʿ* relied on his clerks for the collection of taxes, the improvement of cultivation, irrigation, and the preservation of peace in the *iqṭāʿ*. Unfortunately, there is no list in the known sources, not even in the Geniza, which would contain the names of these clerks of the *iqṭāʿ*, but it can be assumed, on the basis of scattered evidence, that each *iqṭāʿ* had a *wakīl* and a number of subordinate clerks.

It seems that the *wakīl* (agent) was an important figure in the *iqṭāʿ*. Two documents from the Geniza collection throw some light on this office. The first is a flimsy fragment of an undated letter which most probably originates from the period under study. It comes from a *muqṭaʿ*, and contains praise of his *wakīl* for informing the *wālī* (province governor) that most of the sugar-cane had been distributed among the peasants, and only a minor part had gone to the *muqṭaʿ*. The *muqṭaʿ* urges his *wakīl* to deliver what he had gradually collected from the *iqṭāʿ*, because they were going to fight a long war. This fragment indicates that the *muqṭaʿ*'s *wakīl* had a great deal of influence and authority in the *iqṭāʿ*.[2]

The second document is a fragment from a letter dated Monday, 7 Rabīʿ I 644/23 July 1246, and addressed to the village of Minyat Bāsik, which is now known as al-Minya in the district of al-Ṣaff in the province of Jīza. The sender asks the help of the Shaykh Musallam or Musallama Abū ʿAlī, the *wakīl* of Shams al-Dīn Ildakiz al-Birṭāsī, because, as everything is so expensive, he has contracted debts, and himself eats only bread and onions. Presumably, there was a *wakīl* in every *iqṭāʿ*, and each of them enjoyed prestige and wealth, similar to that of the Shaykh Musallam.[3]

Furthermore, one might infer from the written *waṣiyya* of Sultan al-Ṣāliḥ Ayyūb to Tūrānshāh that, even in the Ayyūbid period, four or five *wakīl*s might be employed in the scattered *iqṭāʿ* of one *muqṭaʿ*.[4]

[1] A.Ch. 12479.

[2] T.-S. B.39, fol. 118.

[3] T.-S. B.39, fol. 386; the document states that the village of Minyat Bāsik is in '*ʿamal* al-Sharqiyya'. It is worth mentioning that the Aṭfīḥiyya province, which now comprises a part of Jīza province, was known as al-Sharqiyya because its villages lay east of the Nile. There is also another province in Lower Egypt which still bears the name Sharqiyya. However, Minyat Bāsik was attributed to Bāsik, the brother of Bahrām, the Armenian Fāṭimid vizier, cf. Ibn Mammātī, p. 191; Ibn al-Jīʿān, *Tuḥfa*, p. 150; Dawādārī, *Durra muḍiyya*, p. 518; ʿAlī Mubārak, *Khiṭaṭ*, xvi, p. 59; Ramzī, *Qāmūs*, ii. iii, introduction, p. 7 and p. 31; Maqrīzī (*Khiṭaṭ*, i, p. 205), refers to it as Minyat al-Nāsik.

[4] Nuwayrī, xxvii, fols. 91–2; see above, p. 46.

During the Mamluk period, at least until the year 679/1281, each *muqṭaʿ* employed one *wakīl* or more. From a *tadhkira* (memorandum) addressed to Kitbughā, the vice-sultan of Sultan Qalāwūn in Dhū al-Ḥijja 679/March–April 1281, on the occasion of the latter's journey to Syria, one may infer that the *wakīl* was still responsible for collecting the financial revenue of the *iqṭāʿ*, the figures of which he used to enter in a special register. A copy of this register was kept in the sultani *dīwān* to provide the sultan with information about the revenue of the *iqṭāʿ* in question. This information often proved of value when the sultan investigated possible complaints.[1]

After 679/1281, at a date not mentioned by the sources, the *wakīl* seems to have been replaced, as a representative of the *muqṭaʿ*, by another clerk, the *ustādār*. As such, the *ustādār* played an important role. He deputized for the *muqṭaʿ*—when required by sultani *dīwāns*—in matters concerning taxation and some services incumbent on the *muqṭaʿ* in the *iqṭāʿ*.[2] According to Idfuwī—who lived during the reign of al-Nāṣir ibn Qalāwūn—it appears that the frequent visits of the *ustādār* to each village in the amir's *iqṭāʿ* took place mainly for the collection of taxes.[3] He was responsible for the treatment of the *fallāḥīn*. He supervised their work, not only in the *iqṭāʿ*, but also when the amir sent them to participate in one of his non-military functions such as digging a canal, or building stables for the sultan.[4] The function the *ustādār* performed in the *iqṭāʿ* is illustrated by Subkī's advice to him to treat the *fallāḥīn* kindly and to avoid collecting illegal taxes for his amir.[5]

The most important among the lesser clerks of the *iqṭāʿ* was the holder of the *shadd*, called *mushidd* or *shādd*. There were, at times, several *shādds* in one *iqṭāʿ*. Professor Cahen suggests that the

[1] Ibn al-Furāt, vii, pp. 199–200; Qalqashandī (*Ṣubḥ*, xiii, pp. 97–8) mentions the same *tadhkira* but errs in saying that it was written in the year A.H. 799. Another undated memorandum composed by Shāfiʿ ibn ʿAlī (*Faḍl*, fol. 95^{v}) addressed to al-Ṣāliḥ, Qalāwūn's son, contains the advice of the sultan to al-Ṣāliḥ to help the *wukalāʾ* of the *muqṭaʿ*s in collecting the revenue from the *iqṭāʿ*s; for the *tadhkira* (pl. *tadhākīr*) cf. Lewis, article 'Daftar' in *EI*²; Björkman, article 'Diplomatic' in *EI*².

[2] Subkī, *Muʿīd*, p. 39.

[3] Idfuwī, *Ṭāliʿ*, p. 357.

[4] ʿAynī, *ʿIqd*, 'C', xxii. i, fol. 3; Maqrīzī, *Sulūk*, ii, pp. 111, 434; id., *Khiṭaṭ*, ii, p. 229.

[5] Subkī, *Muʿīd*, pp. 39–40; the importance of this office can be judged by the numerous titles of an *ustādār* inscribed on half a copper ball (*demi-sphère en cuivre*) from the year 741/1340, preserved in the Victoria and Albert Museum, *RCEA*, xv, p. 181.

mushidd was an associate, frequently a soldier, who gave support to the native staff which mostly consisted of Copts.[1] As to the description of the *mushidd*'s work given by Nuwayrī and Subkī in *Nihāyat al-arab* and *Muʿīd al-niʿam*, it confirms Professor Cahen's assumption. These two Arabic authors also relate that the *mushidd* enjoyed great authority in the *iqṭāʿ*, as he used to collect the arrears in taxes, especially those due to tax evasion. The *mushidd* was also responsible for the cultivation of the *iqṭāʿ*, and for the apprehension of persons who left the village without permission. He had to keep highwaymen in check and appoint the *khufarāʾ* (watchmen). The *mushidd* also had the power to punish criminals and transgressors.[2] The *shādd* or *mushidd* is referred to in two unpublished and undated fragments from the Mamluk period found among the Vienna papers. The *shādd* mentioned in the first fragment seems to be an important figure concerned with the collection of the taxes of the *iqṭāʿ* in question, while the *mushidd* of the other fragment seems to have been responsible for the irrigation of another *iqṭāʿ*.[3] Consequently, it might be assumed that the name *mushidd al-aḥbās* was applied to the clerk given the task of reinforcing the administration of the *ḥubūs* or *waqf*, and that the *mushidd al-ʿayn* was one attached to the collector of taxes paid in cash (*ʿayn*).[4]

In addition to the *mushidds*, it seems that there were other officials in the *iqṭāʿ* such as: *khawlī al-baḥr* whose task was perhaps to keep the banks of the canals in good order; *khawlīs* who seem to have served as stewards, or supervisors of the affairs of the *fallāḥīn*; *khufarāʾ*, who worked as watchmen in the farms; and *arbāb al-adrāk*, who—to judge by the word '*darak*' which still denotes a 'beat' in Egypt—were possibly employed as watchmen, overseers, or policemen.[5]

It is worth mentioning that a considerable number of the above-named clerks in the *iqṭāʿ* were non-Muslims. Maqrīzī, for example, states that, in Muḥarram 724/January 1324, when the amir Arghūn, the vice-sultan of Sultan al-Nāṣir ibn Qalāwūn, visited his *iqṭāʿ* in

[1] Cahen, 'Régime', p. 19; id., article 'Ayyūbids' in *EI*².

[2] Nuwayrī, viii, p. 298; Subkī, *Muʿīd*, pp. 41–2.

[3] A.Ch. 10219, 12509.

[4] Nābulsī, *Fayyūm*, pp. 33, 59, 62, 73, 77, 87, 89, 104, 109, 123, 124, 127, 156, 163, 171; Cahen, 'Régime', p. 19.

[5] Cf. Nābulsī, *Fayyūm*, pp. 43, 61, 65, 74, 77–9, 89, 95, 105, 123, 126, 129, 133, 156, 159, 170; Ẓāhirī, *Zubda*, p. 130; Quatremère, op. cit., i. i, p. 169 n. 51; Dozy, *Supp. Dict. Ar.*, i, p. 437.

Minyat ibn Khaṣīb, he had some of the inhabitants beaten because they had come to him with complaints about the behaviour of his officials. The citizens retaliated by throwing stones at him. When Arghūn was informed that the majority of them were Copts, he decided not to employ any more Copts in his *dīwān* and to dismiss those already working there.[1] However, most *muqṭa*ʿs, including the vice-sultan, continued to employ Copt clerks. As Professor Ashtor states, 'the feudal aristocracy was ready to dismiss the non-Moslem officials from time to time, but soon they engaged them again since they could not do without their service'.[2]

F. *Non-military functions of the* muqṭaʿ

In addition to his military duties, the *muqṭaʿ* had a number of non-military functions to fulfil. The most important of them were those which dealt with the irrigation and cultivation of the *iqṭāʿ*.

Among the non-military duties of the Ayyūbid or Mamluk *muqṭāʿ* and his clerks was the distribution of *al-taqāwī al-sulṭāniyya* among the *fallāḥīn* in the *iqṭāʿ*. These *taqāwī*, from which every subsequent harvest was grown, were offered by the sultan to the *muqṭaʿ* together with the *iqṭāʿ*, and were of the best quality, considered most conducive to good crops. The outgoing *muqṭaʿ* could not take seeds which guaranteed a good harvest to his successor when he vacated his *iqṭāʿ*.[3]

The *iqṭāʿ* sometimes consisted, wholly or partly, of an area of land reclaimed by means of new canals or *jusūr* (irrigation dams). They were called *zāʾid al-qānūn*, that is additional to the lands already registered in previous surveys. The *muqṭa*ʿs did their best to improve the reclaimed land, which increased particularly during the reign of al-Nāṣir ibn Qalāwūn. It is said that he assigned, to some *muqṭa*ʿs, *iqṭā*ʿs containing reclaimed land in Buḥayra, Jīza, and Sharqiyya provinces, as well as in the Fuwwa district, as early as the year 721/1321.[4]

[1] Maqrīzī, *Sulūk*, ii, pp. 253–4.

[2] Ashtor, 'The social isolation of Ahl-adh-dhimma', *Études orientales à la mémoire de Paul Hirschler* (1949–50), p. 89.

[3] Nābulsī, *Fayyūm*, pp. 36, 44, 52, 65, 71–2, 74, 78, 87, 90, 105, 118, 132–3, 137, 142, 149, 160, 163, 172–3; Ibn ʿAbd al-Ẓāhir, *Alṭāf*, p. 55; Nuwayrī, viii, p. 221; Maqrīzī, *Khiṭaṭ*, ii, p. 429; id., *Sulūk*, i, p. 808, ii, p. 20, tr. Quatremère, ii. ii, pp. 24, 257 and n. 52; Cahen, 'Régime', p. 26.

[4] Maqrīzī, *Sulūk*, ii, p. 231; Ibn Taghrī Birdī, *Nujūm*, ix, pp. 190–1; for the term *qānūn* cf. Lewis, article 'Daftar' in *EI*².

It is interesting to note that the *muqṭa*ʿs sometimes sent their *ajnād* to cultivate land when there was a shortage of *fallāḥīn*. This happened mainly during the epidemics which occurred in Egypt several times during the Ayyūbid and Mamluk eras. Ibn Waṣīf Shāh, Maqrīzī, and Ibn Iyās state that, during the epidemic which occurred in the reign of Sultan al-ʿĀdil the Ayyūbid in 596–99/1200–1203, the *ajnād* went to the *iqṭā*ʿs to cultivate the land, to harvest, and to thresh the crop.[1] It seems that the *ajnād* performed the same task during the epidemic of 694–5/1294–6, in the reign of Sultan Kitbughā.[2]

The extent to which the *muqṭa*ʿs and their *ajnād* were preoccupied with agricultural matters and the collection of taxes is proved by the frequent visits the *muqṭa*ʿs paid to their *iqṭā*ʿs. This occasionally caused difficulties to the sultans who, on their part, tried to avoid seasons in which the crops were harvested, when announcing war. They would even attempt to terminate hostilities without bringing them to a successful conclusion in order to give the *muqṭa*ʿs opportunities to return to their *iqṭā*ʿs and to bring their crops. Thus, while Saladin was in Syria in the year 571/1175, he permitted the Egyptian troops to return to Egypt to take care of the harvest, but ordered them to return to Syria after they had performed their task.[3] Saladin's generous action even resulted in some trouble, because he was attacked by the Zankid army in the absence of his troops. Ibn al-Athīr—pro-Zankid and anti-Saladin—states

[1] Ibn Waṣīf Shāh, *Jawāhir*, fol. 55ᵛ; Maqrīzī, *Ighātha*, p. 31; Ibn Iyās, *Badāʾiʿ*, i, p. 76. The contemporary traveller ʿAbd al-Laṭīf al-Baghdādī (*Ifāda*, pp. 252, 254, 262, tr. de Sacy pp. 376, 412–13) states that as a result of this epidemic, villages were deserted by their Egyptian *fallāḥīn*; see also Nuwayrī, xxvii, fols. 1–2; Maqrīzī, *Ighātha*, pp. 29–32; id., *Sulūk*, i, pp. 156–8, tr. Blochet, 'C', pp. 119–20.

[2] For the epidemic which occurred under the sultanate of Kitbughā, and which resulted in the death of a large proportion of villagers, cf. Muẓaffarī, *Dhayl mufarrij*, fol. 212ᵛ; Nuwayrī, xxix, fol. 84; ʿUmarī, *Masālik* (MS. P.) fol. 133ʳ; Ibn Ḥabīb, *Tadhkira*, fols. 33ᵛ–35ᵛ; id., *Durra* (MS. Marsh 591), i, fol. 60ʳ; Ibn Duqmāq, *Jawhar*, fol. 119ᵛ; Ibn Taghrī Birdī, *Manhal*, v, fol. 40ʳ; Anonymous, *Tārīkh*, fol. 20ʳ; Ibn Iyās, *Nashq*, fol. 213ʳ; Ibn Abī al-Faḍāʾil, pp. 427–8; Ibn Kathīr, xiii, p. 343; Ibn al-Furāt, viii, pp. 199–200, 208–10; Maqrīzī, *Ighātha*, pp. 32–8, tr. Wiet, 'Le traité des famines', *JESHO*, v (1962), pp. 32–41; *Sulūk*, i, pp. 810, 813–15, tr. Quatremère, ii. ii, pp. 25–6, 30–4. For the effect of the epidemics on the Mamluk army in later period, cf. Ayalon, 'The plague and its effects upon the Mamlûk army', *JRAS* (1946), pp. 67–73. For sources dealing with the epidemics from the viewpoint of jurists, cf. Ibn Abī Ḥajala, fols. 141–6; Ḥijāzī, *Juz*', fols. 147–55; Ibn Abī Sharīf, fols. 156–63; Suyūṭī, *Aḥkām al-ṭāʿūn*, fols. 172–95.

[3] Abū Shāma, *Rawḍatayn*, i. ii, p. 643; Ibn Kathīr, xii, p. 291.

that, if the Zankids had seriously fought Saladin, they could have defeated him in these circumstances, but they delayed. Saladin was saved only by the return of his troops and defeated the Zankids at Tall al-Sulṭān in Shawwāl 571/April 1176.[1]

It would seem that the frequent visits of the *muqṭa*ʿs to their *iqṭā*ʿs to supervise the harvest continued at least until the end of the reign of al-Ẓāhir Baybars. Al-Yūnīnī, Shāfiʿ ibn ʿAlī, and al-Mufaḍḍal ibn Abī al-Faḍā'il relate that Sultan Baybars tried, in Shawwāl 663/July 1265, to take the opportunity of Hūlāgū's death to invade Iraq. He failed to take action because the *muqṭa*ʿs' *ajnād* were scattered in the *iqṭā*ʿs. The fact that this happened in July seems to suggest that the failure was due to the absence of the *muqṭa*ʿs and their *ajnād*, who were bringing in the harvest.[2]

A year after these events, in 664/1266, while Sultan Baybars was preparing the troops for the Ṣafad expedition, he ordered the *wālī*s of the provinces to summon the *ajnād* from their *iqṭā*ʿs. When Baybars found that they had delayed summoning the *muqṭa*ʿs, he sent his *silāḥdār*s (armour-bearers) to punish the negligent governors—if the accounts in question are to be credited—by hanging them by their arms for three days![3]

The maintenance of *al-jusūr al-baladiyya* (the small irrigation dams) which were of paramount importance for the irrigation of the *iqṭā*ʿs, was another important non-military function of the *muqṭa*ʿ, under both the Ayyūbids and the Mamluks. It seems that every *muqṭa*ʿ was responsible for the upkeep of these *jusūr* within the confines of his *iqṭā*ʿ. Ibn Mammātī states that—at least before 606/1209—the outgoing *muqṭa*ʿ had the right to be reimbursed by his successor for his expenses for *al-jusūr al-baladiyya* in the year of his transfer. There is no conclusive evidence to prove that this procedure continued until the end of the period under review; Qalqashandī and Maqrīzī merely copy Ibn Mammātī's statement.[4]

As to *al-jusūr al-sulṭāniyya* (the great irrigation dams) which were constructed for the benefit of the provinces, the *muqṭa*ʿ was

[1] Ibn al-Athīr, *Kāmil*, xi, pp. 283–4.

[2] Yūnīnī, *Dhayl*, ii, p. 322; Shāfiʿ ibn ʿAlī, *Ḥusn*, fols. 62^r–3^r; Ibn Abī al-Faḍā'il, p. 145.

[3] Ibn ʿAbd al-Ẓāhir, *Rawḍ*, pp. 1071–2; Nuwayrī, xxviii, fol. 87; Ibn al-Furāt, vi, fol. 98^v; Maqrīzī, *Sulūk*, i, p. 544, tr. Quatremère, i. ii, p. 27.

[4] Ibn Mammātī, pp. 232–3, 344; Qalqashandī, *Ṣubḥ*, iii, p. 449; Maqrīzī, *Khiṭaṭ*, i, p. 101.

not responsible for them, at least in theory.[1] Practically, especially during the Mamluk period, the *muqṭa*ʿs assisted the sultan in the construction of this type of *jusūr* by supplying men, cows, harrows, and tools. Three important *jusūr* were built during the reign of al-Nāṣir ibn Qalāwūn, chiefly with the help of the amirs who participated with their *ajnād* and *fallāḥīn*. The first dam to be built was completed in 713/1313–14, extended from the Nile to Umm Dīnār village, and was intended to improve the irrigation in the Jīza province.[2] The second, built in 723/1323, extended from Būlāq to Minyat al-Shīrij or al-Sīrij, and was constructed to prevent the threat of the high Nile floods to Cairo and its suburbs. Maqrīzī states that the amirs summoned from the *iqṭā*ʿs their *fallāḥīn* who brought cows and harrows as well as tools to assist the progress of the work.[3] The third, completed in 739/1338–9, from Shibīn al-Qaṣr to Banhā al-ʿAsal, was constructed to irrigate the high levels of cultivated land in the Sharqiyya province. All Egyptian *muqṭa*ʿs assisted in the execution of this last project, which took 12,000 men with 200 harrows three months to complete.[4]

In continuation of an Ayyūbid tradition, the *muqṭa*ʿ also participated in the digging and cleaning of some of the Nile canals. In the year 628/1231, Sultan al-Kāmil the Ayyūbid ordered his amirs, *jund*, and others to dig a canal in the territory between Miṣr (the Fusṭāṭ) and the island of al-Rawḍa, to expedite navigation and to help the people to transport water during the dry season of the Nile.[5] The participation of the *muqṭa*ʿs and their *ajnād* in the digging and cleaning of canals became more frequent during the Mamluk era. Thus, for example, Sultan Qalāwūn went in person to the Buḥayra province to supervise the digging of the Ṭayriyya canal in Muḥarram 682/April 1283, dividing the work among his amirs and their men only. It was only after they had completed the entire operation, which had lasted ten days, that Sultan Qalāwūn gave them *dastūr* (permission) to return to their *iqṭā*ʿs.[6]

[1] Ibn Mammātī, p. 232, compares the sultani *jusūr* with the wall of the city which the sultan has to keep in good order. Qalqashandī (*Ṣubḥ*, iii, p. 449) and Maqrīzī (*Khiṭaṭ*, i, p. 101) repeat Ibn Mammātī's statement.

[2] Ṣafadī, *Nuzha*, fol. 73^{r-v}; Dawādārī, *Durr fākhir*, p. 266; Maqrīzī, *Sulūk*, ii, p. 130; Ibn Taghrī Birdī, *Nujūm*, ix, p. 190.

[3] Maqrīzī, *Khiṭaṭ*, ii, p. 166; id., *Sulūk*, ii, p. 251.

[4] Id., *Khiṭaṭ*, ii, p. 170; id., *Sulūk*, ii, pp. 466–7.

[5] Nuwayrī, xxvii, fols. 36–7; Ibn Duqmāq, *Jawhar*, fol. 85^{v}; Maqrīzī, *Khiṭaṭ*, i, pp. 344–5; id., *Sulūk*, i, p. 241, tr. Blochet, 'D', p. 259.

[6] Baybars al-Manṣūrī, *Tuḥfa*, fol. 44^{v}; id., *Zubda*, fols. 139^{v}–40^{r}; Nuwayrī,

Sultan al-Nāṣir ibn Qalāwūn went so far as to employ the *muqṭa*ʿs and their men to dig and clean his famous large-scale canals, especially the Alexandria canal and the Nāṣirī canal. The work on the former began in Rajab 710/November–December 1310, and was executed by about 40,000 men recruited from the Egyptian *iqṭā*ʿs.[1] The work on the Nāṣirī canal lasted two months in 725/1323. Most of the Egyptian *muqṭa*ʿs participated in it, with the *fallāḥīn* from their *iqṭā*ʿs. It is worth mentioning that it was the special purpose of that project to facilitate the transport of crops and materials to the sultan's new palace and *khanqāh* (*ṣūfī* house) of Siryāqaws.[2] The *muqṭa*ʿs and their men contributed to the sultani projects to the extent of building the hippodrome under the Citadel in 713/1313–14,[3] digging the Nāṣirī lake in 721/1321,[4] and constructing the stables of the Citadel in the year 738/1337.[5]

The conclusion therefore appears to be that, as the *muqṭa*ʿs were responsible for a part of the army expenditure, and performed a number of non-military functions on behalf of the sultan and the *dīwān*s, the impact of the Egyptian *iqṭā*ʿ system on army structure, taxation, expenditure, and financial administration was considerable.

xxix, fol. 26; ʿUmarī, *Masālik* (MS. P.), fol. 121ᵛ; Ibn Ḥabīb, *Tadhkira*, fol. 9ʳ⁻ᵛ; id., *Durra* (MS. Marsh 591), fol. 41ʳ⁻ᵛ; Ibn ʿAbd al-Ẓāhir, *Tashrīf*, pp. 25–6; Ibn al-Furāt, vii, p. 260; Maqrīzī, *Sulūk*, i, p. 712, tr. Quatremère, ii. i, p. 59.

[1] Maqrīzī, *Khiṭaṭ*, i, pp. 171–2; id., *Sulūk*, ii, pp. 111–12; Ṭūssūn, *Tārīkh khalīj al-Iskandariyya*, pp. 25–7.

[2] Ibn Ḥabīb, *Durra* (MS. Marsh 591), fol. 97ᵛ; ʿAynī, *Badr*, fol. 16ʳ⁻ᵛ; Ibn Taghrī Birdī, *Manhal*, v, fol. 203ᵛ; id., *Nujūm*, ix, pp. 81–3; Ibn Iyās, *Nashq*, fol. 37ᵛ; Dawādārī, *Durr fākhir*, pp. 315, 319; Maqrīzī, *Khiṭaṭ*, i, p. 145; id., *Sulūk*, ii, pp. 261–2.

[3] Maqrīzī, *Sulūk*, ii, p. 123.

[4] ʿAynī, *Badr*, fol. 12ʳ; Maqrīzī, *Khiṭaṭ*, ii, p. 165.

[5] ʿAynī, ʿ*Iqd*, ʿA', xvii, fol. 124ʳ⁻ᵛ; Maqrīzī, *Khiṭaṭ*, ii, p. 229; id., *Sulūk*, ii, pp. 433–5; Ibn Taghrī Birdī, *Nujūm*, ix, pp. 119–21.

III

TAXATION AND OTHER SOURCES OF REVENUE

In discussing the economic role of taxes and other sources of fiscal revenue in Egypt between 564/1169 and 741/1341, it is imperative to avoid the conventional classification into legal and illegal taxes which had no practical significance in the period under study.

A. *Taxes on production*

1. *Cultivation*

In Egypt, during the period under consideration, the term *kharāj* denoted a tax levied on cultivated land. Theoretically, under both the Ayyūbids and the Mamluks, the sultan had the right to impose the *kharāj* as soon as the Nile flood reached the height of 16 *dhirā'* when all cultivated land was covered by water.[1]

Makhzūmī, who writes at the beginning of the Ayyūbid era, states that when the water receded each *dalīl* (agent) had to prepare the *qānūn al-rayy* of the plots flooded. He had to distinguish between cultivable land at various degrees of fertility, and non-cultivable land. The *dalīl* supervised the yearly assignment (*taḥḍīr*) of the land covered by water to the *fallāḥīn* in accordance with the survey. Once the crops had been planted, the *dalīl* drew up a *qānūn al-zirā'a* which contained the details of the *faddān*s, the taxes in fixed amounts and the names of the cultivators. The next step was

[1] 'Abdarī, fol. 78r, ed., al-Fāsī, pp. 145–6; Jawharī, *Durr*, fol. 31v; Anonymous, *Awrāq*, fols. 21v–22r; Ibn Ẓuhayra, fol. 52r-v; Muqaddasī, p. 206; Baghdādī, pp. 200 ff., tr. S. de Sacy, pp. 329 ff.; Harawī, p. 45; Qazwīnī, *Āthār*, p. 175; Qalqashandī, *Ṣubḥ*, iii, pp. 293–4, 297; Maqrīzī, *Khiṭaṭ*, i, p. 61; for the description of the Nilometer in use during the period under study cf. Iṣfahānī, *Barq*, iii, fol. 112r; id., *Sanā*, fol. 196r; Benjamin of Tudela, pp. 71–2, Arabic tr., pp. 173–4; Ibn Jubayr, pp. 54–5; Ibn al-Wardī, *Kharīda*, pp. 32–3; Qalqashandī, *Ṣubḥ*, iii, p. 298; Ghaleb, 'Le miḳyâs ou Nilomètre de l'Île de Rodah', *MIE*, liv (1951), pp. 1–175; Popper, *The Cairo Nilometer*, pp. 16–47. For the *kharāj* in early Islam cf. Ibn 'Abd al-Ḥakam, pp. 152–3; Abū 'Ubayd, p. 68; Māwardī, pp. 140–1, see also Ibn Nujaym, *Tuḥfa*, fols. 58v–60r; Løkkegaard, *Islamic taxation*, pp. 72 ff.; Rayyis, *Kharāj*, pp. 130–1.

the yearly pre-harvest survey, which was executed by the *māsiḥ* (surveyor) under the supervision of the *ʿāmil* and the *mushārif*. The document drawn up every day by the *māsiḥ* before witnesses was called the *qundāq*, derived through Syriac from the Greek *kontakion* (= 'reglet' or 'small rule' to which a long strip of papyrus or paper was attached). The *qundāq* was supposed to contain the exact geometric description of the plot in question, copies of all the calculations, the names of the cultivators and of the crops, and finally the tax figures given in the *sijillāt*. A *mukallafa* was then sent to each particular cultivator, informing him exactly how much he would have to pay.[1]

According to Makhzūmī, the *kharāj* was divided into two categories: (*a*) *kharāj al-zirāʿa*, that is *kharāj* on cropped land, but not trees, and (*b*) *kharāj al-basātīn wa mā shākalahā*, that is that imposed on orchards, etc.[2] The distinction he makes is of great importance, because these two categories continued in existence, under varying appellations, at least until the end of the period under study.

Kharāj al-zirāʿa was collected in cash, *ʿayn*, in fixed amounts per *faddān*, or in kind.[3] The term *mufādana* used by Makhzūmī and Ibn Mammātī for that collected in cash corresponds to the *kharāj fudun al-zirāʿa* or the *kharāj al-fudun* or the *kharāj al-zirāʿa* of Nābulsī and the *mā yusajjal bi al-naqd* of Nuwayrī.[4] When discussing the cultivation of each crop, the seed required, the dates of

[1] Makhzūmī, fols. 165^{r}–168^{v}; Cahen, Contribution, pp. 258–68. Prof. Cahen (ibid., p. 261) reads *taḥḍīr* as *takhḍīr*, 'making green', with the admission this might be arguable. However, there is no doubt that it is to be read *taḥḍīr*, cf. Nuwayrī, viii, p. 248 and n. 8. The editor of Qalqashandī's *Ṣubḥ* (iii, p. 458) reads *qundāq* as *fundāq*, and this recurs in Gaudefroy-Demombynes, *La Syrie*, p. xliii. For the term *mukallafa* see above, p. 50; for the term *qānūn* see Khwārizmī, *Mafātīḥ*, p. 54; Minovi and Minorsky, Naṣīr al-Dīn, pp. 761, 773, 781; Lewis, article 'Daftar' in *EI*^{2}. A comparison of the information proffered by Makhzūmī (fols. 165^{r}–168^{v}) and Nuwayrī (viii, pp. 246–53) indicates that no substantial change had occurred in the methods of assessment of the *kharāj*.

[2] Makhzūmī, fol. 142^{v}: 'وأما الخراجي فانه على نوعين خراجى الزراعه وأول عامه توت وآخرها مسرى وخراجى البساتين وما شاكلها مما يشرب بالسواقي وما يجرى مجراه . . .'. The term *kharāj al-zarʿ* occurs in two fragments from the Vienna papers (A.Ch. 8, fol. 7113 and fol. 7425).

[3] A fragment from the Vienna papers (A.Ch. fol. 12340) from the reign of al-Mustanṣir proves that this procedure was Fāṭimid in origin.

[4] Makhzūmī, fol. 166^{r-v}; Ibn Mammātī, pp. 336–7; Nābulsī, *Fayyūm*, pp. 28, 32, 60, 108; Nuwayrī, viii, p. 253; see Cahen, 'Régime', p. 16; id., 'Contribution', p. 263.

sowing and harvest, and the yield per *faddān*, Ibn Mammātī includes in his data *kharāj* dues calculated in money. The basic approach to the assessment and collection of these types of *kharāj* is illustrated by the following table:[1]

Kind of crop	*The* kharāj *per* faddān
flax (*kattān*)	differs from place to place: the basic 3 *dīnārs*, equal to 13 *dīnārs* in Dalāṣ and about 5 *dīnārs* in Upper Egypt.
clover (*qurṭ*)	about one *dīnār*.
onions (*baṣal*)	2 *dīnārs*.
garlic (*thūm*)	,,
lupin (*turmus*)	1¼ *dīnārs*.
cumin (*kammūn*)	1 *dīnār*; under the Fāṭimids it was 2 *dīnārs*.
caraway (*karāwiya*)	,, ,, ,, ,, ,,
rape (*saljam*)	,, ,, ,, ,, ,,
water-melon (*biṭṭīkh*)	1–2 *dīnārs*.
kidney beans (*lūbiyā*)	3 *dīnārs*.
sesame (*simsim*)	1 *dīnār*.
cotton (*quṭn*)	,,
sugar-cane (*qaṣab al-sukkar*)	for the first harvesting (*ra's*) 5 *dīnārs*, and for the second (*khilfa*) 2 *dīnārs* and 5 *qīrāṭs*.
colocasia antiquorum (*qulqās*)	4 *dīnārs*; under the Fāṭimids it was 5 *dīnārs*.
aubergines (*bādhinjān*)	3 *dīnārs*.
indigo (*nīla*)	,,
radishes (*fujl*)	1 *dīnār*.
turnip (*lift*)	1 *dīnār*.
lettuce (*khass*)	2 *dīnārs*.
cabbage (*kurunb*)	,,

The *kharāj al-zirā'a* payable in kind at the beginning of the Ayyūbid era, is sometimes referred to as *munājaza*, or *mushāṭara*, or *qabāla*.[2]

[1] Ibn Mammātī, pp. 261–70; see also Qalqashandī, *Ṣubḥ*, iii, pp. 452–3; when he published a 3rd/9th-century papyrus which represents a land-tax register, Prof. Dietrich (*Arabische Papyri*, p. 84) pointed out that the extent of the tax depended on the kind of crop (wheat, clover, flax, etc.), the productivity of the soil, and the type of irrigation.

[2] Relying on Makhzūmī and Ibn Mammātī, Prof. Cahen ('Contribution', pp. 263–5) originally assumed that, since the terms *munājaza* and *qabāla* partly overlapped and were sometimes even interchangeable, Nābulsī's assumption that in *munājaza/mushāṭara* dues per *faddān* were paid in kind and not in ready money was correct. Now, though he still believes that *munājaza/mushāṭara* was assessed by area and had no connection with the dues proportional to the yield

According to Ibn Mammātī, this type of *kharāj* tax was imposed at the following rates:[1]

Kind of crop	*Tax per* faddān *under cultivation*
wheat (*qamḥ*)	before 567 A.H. 3 *ardabbs*; $2\frac{1}{2}$ *ardabbs* after the *rawk* of 572.
barley (*sha'īr*)	before 567 A.H. 3 *ardabbs*; $2\frac{1}{2}$ *ardabbs* after the *rawk* of 572.
beans (*fūl*)	3–$2\frac{1}{2}$ *ardabbs*.
chick peas (*ḥummuṣ*)	$2\frac{1}{2}$ *ardabbs*.
bitter-vetch (*julbān*)	”
lentils (*'adas*)	”

It is worth noting that it was possible in Egypt—at least at the beginning of the Ayyūbid period—for the tax in kind to be paid, not in the plant on which the tax was actually imposed, but in another, their respective values being assessed according to an official scale of equivalents. Ibn Mammātī mentions the rates of exchange between the above agricultural products on which the *kharāj* was levied in kind. This is illustrated by the following table:

Tax paid in kind	Equivalent (in *ardabbs*)				
	wheat	barley	beans	chick peas	bitter-vetch
1 *ardabb* of wheat	—	2	$1\frac{1}{2}$	1	$1\frac{1}{2}$
” ” ” barley	$\frac{1}{2}$	—	$\frac{1}{3}$	$\frac{1}{2}$	$\frac{1}{3}$
” ” ” beans	$\frac{1}{3}$	$1\frac{1}{2}$	—	$\frac{1}{3}$	1
” ” , chick peas	1	2	$1\frac{1}{2}$	—	$1\frac{1}{2}$
” ” ” bitter-vetch	$\frac{1}{3}$	$1\frac{1}{2}$	1	$\frac{1}{3}$	—

Ibn Mammātī says nothing of the rate of exchange of lentils, but states that there was none for sesame, rape, or flax. He mentions that the best way of evaluating the *badal* is on the basis of the prices of the crops in season.[2] It seems that these rates of exchange remained valid for a long period, as Qalqashandī copies Ibn Mammātī when he explains the *badal* in his own lifetime.[3]

so characteristic of the land-tax system in other regions of the Muslim world, and though the tax in kind on cereals and corn in open farming was a common form of *munājaza*, Prof. Cahen inclines to the opinion that the situation was more complex, and that there could have been, besides the *mufādana*, a tax in money, or in any case calculated if not paid in money, but conforming to the *qabāla/munājaza* type and parallel to the taxes of this type which were payable in kind.

[1] Ibn Mammātī, pp. 258–61; see also Qalqashandī, *Ṣubḥ*, iii, pp. 452–3.

[2] Ibn Mammātī, pp. 359–60; Rabī', *Nuẓum*, p. 43 n. 3.

[3] Qalqashandī, *Ṣubḥ*, iii, pp. 454–5.

There is little doubt that the amount of the *kharāj al-zirā'a*, whether payable in money or in kind, underwent several changes, although the sources give little information on this evolution. Maqrīzī says, without stating the date, that the 2½ *ardabb*s of *kharāj* per *faddān* under wheat was reduced to 2 *ardabbs*.[1] Nuwayrī gives some information about the amount of the *kharāj al-zirā'a* at the end of the period under study, when the *kharāj* payable in kind varied according to the *qaṭī'a* and custom from ⅙ to 3 *ardabb*s per *faddān*. There was an additional tax called *ḥuqūq*, of between 2 and 4 *dirham*s per *faddān* imposed on some cultivated land. As to the *kharāj al-zirā'a* payable in money, Nuwayrī says that it varied as well, thc largest sum being 250 *dirham*s per *faddān* in Jīza, where such land was mostly cultivated with flax. He adds that the *kharāj* payable in money used to be paid in two or three instalments.[2] A fragment from the Vienna papers, dated Rajab 724/June–July 1324, apparently a list of arrears of barley, possibly indicates that even the *kharāj* paid in kind was, by the end of the period, payable in instalments, especially in view of the existence of the *badal*.[3]

The tax imposed on vineyards and orchards forms, in the whole period under consideration, the second category of the *kharāj* tax, known as *kharāj al-rātib*.[4] Unlike *mufādana* land, which was measured annually, *rātib* land, which was less subject to sudden changes than land under ordinary crops, was surveyed every three years. Makhzūmī, from whom this information is derived, says that officials kept registers of trees, as taxes varied from kind to kind. Besides, since there was less tax to pay on sapling trees, they had to register all new plantations.[5] According to Ibn Mammātī, this tax amounted in his time to ¼ *dīnār* on each *faddān* in the first year of cultivation, and would increase in the fourth year to 3 *dīnār*s per *faddān*. The amount was fixed and payable in a lump sum.[6]

[1] Maqrīzī, *Khiṭaṭ*, i, p. 101.

[2] Nuwayrī, viii, pp. 249, 253. It seems that the *ḥuqūq* tax was introduced by the Ayyūbid Sultan al-Kāmil and remained in force until al-Nāṣir's reign, cf. Maqrīzī, *Sulūk*, i, p. 260, tr. Blochet, 'D', p. 293.

[3] A.Ch. 12439.

[4] Makhzūmī, fol. 168ᵛ; Ibn Mammātī, p. 239; Nābulsī, *Fayyūm*, pp. 28, 32, 45, 69, 94, 108; Nuwayrī, viii, p. 253; see also Cahen 'Régime', p. 16.

[5] Makhzūmī, fol. 168ᵛ; Cahen, 'Contribution', p. 267.

[6] Ibn Mammātī, p. 276. It is noteworthy that acacia trees, '*ḥirāj al-sanṭ*', in Upper Egypt were not subject to *kharāj al-rātib*, as they were a state monopoly

In practice, the amount of the *kharāj al-rātib* varied to some extent by the end of the Ayyūbid era. An examination of the data given by Nābulsī in the *Tārīkh al-Fayyūm* for the *kharāj al-rātib* imposed on the villages of al-ʿUdwa, al-Qubarā, Babīj Anshū, Sinnawris, and Fānū, shows that the *rātib* on vineyards was 5⅓ *dīnār*s per *faddān*. In al-ʿUdwa, Babīj Anshū, and Fānū, the *rātib* on trees was payable at a flat rate of 2 *dīnār*s per *faddān*. In al-Qubarā and Sinnawris the *rātib*—not including the *kharāj* on vineyards—was subdivided into two categories, *kāmil* (growing) and *ghars ʿāmayn* (2-year-old plants). By dividing the amount of tax by the numbers of *faddān*s, one finds that the *kāmil* amounted to 2 *dīnār*s and the *rātib* on the *ghars* to 1 *dīnār* per *faddān*. Consequently, it seems that the ¼-*dīnār* tax per *faddān* of 1-year-old trees referred to by Ibn Mammātī was increased to 1 *dīnār* in the second year, and that the 3-*dīnār*s tax per *faddān* of fully-grown trees was reduced by the end of the Ayyūbid era to 2 *dīnār*s.[1] Besides these, there were subsidiary taxes, mainly the *iḍāfa*, referred to by Professor Cahen as taxes destined to cover the cost of assessment and collection of the *kharāj* calculated by *aṣl* (basic tax) and *faddān*.[2]

The *kharāj al-rātib* imposed on orchards and payable in money continued to be collected until the end of the period under study or even longer. Nuwayrī alone gives data on the changes it underwent under the Mamluks. Cultivators contracted (*yuqāṭiʿū* not to be confused with the *iqṭāʿ*) to pay a fixed yearly amount of money at certain times on a certain number of *faddān*s, thus sparing the *dīwān* the trouble of devising a theoretical scheme of taxation. In other words, the *kharāj al-rātib* was no longer under the Mamluks a tax of 3 or 2 or 1 or ¼ *dīnār* imposed on a *faddān*, as it had been under the Ayyūbids, but began to vary from province to province and from village to village. Nuwayrī stresses that the *kharāj al-rātib* used to be paid in instalments at fixed times during the harvest of

for the benefit of the fleet, during the Ayyūbid and possibly the Mamluk eras. The inhabitants of these areas had to pay two taxes, *rasm al-ḥirāj* and *muqarrar al-sanṭ*, the first on the tips cut for fuel and other purposes, the second for the expense of cutting wood for the government. The fruit of the acacia, the *qaraẓ*, was also a state monopoly, as it was prohibited to gather it privately; cf. Ibn Mammātī, pp. 344–7; Nābulsī, *Lumaʿ*, pp. 48–50; Maqrīzī, *Khiṭaṭ*, i, pp. 110–11, ii, p. 194; Rabīʿ, *Nuẓum*, p. 44; see also Ali Bahgat, 'Les forêts en Égypte', *BIE*, 4e sér., no. 1 (1900), pp. 141–58. According to Ibn ʿAbd al-Ẓāhir (*Rawḍ*, p. 919) Baybars valued the *ḥirāj* so much that he forbade the sale of the wood.

[1] Nābulsī, *Fayyūm*, pp. 32, 40–1, 73, 108, 134–5.

[2] Cahen, 'Régime', p. 17.

fruit and grapes whether the land was irrigated or not, cultivated or not. The *muqāṭiʿ* 's death did not annul the obligation to pay the *kharāj al-rātib*. Only when the *baḥr* (the Nile) permanently flooded the cultivated land was the *kharāj al-rātib* waived.[1]

2. *Pasturage*

A tax on pasture-land was introduced in Egypt, according to Maqrīzī and Ibn Iyās, by Ibn al-Mudabbir in the second half of the 3rd/9th century, and seems to have remained in force through the whole period under consideration.[2] From the study of Nābulsī's *Tārīkh al-Fayyūm*, Professor Cahen has deduced that—at least in Fayyūm itself under the Ayyūbids—the term *marāʿī* applied to two different taxes, one on pasture-land, and the other on livestock. The latter was calculated per head of unspecified larger animals, at 2¼ *dirhams* per head, and at 20, 30, 50, 70, and 100 *dirhams* per 100 head of poultry. Professor Cahen could find no other text to throw light on this subject.[3] There is in fact another text dealing with this matter for the Mamluk period in Nuwayrī's *Nihāyat al-arab*. Nuwayrī says that the *marāʿī*, which remained in force until his time, was a tax levied in one of two ways, either as a fixed tax (*ḍarība muqarrara*) payable annually, often in instalments, or as a variable tax collected every year after the Nile flood had receded, and calculated according to the number of grazing animals. The variable tax was subject to increase or reduction according to the size of the livestock, and the assessment varied from one place to another. It seems, therefore, that only the second was a *per capita* tax, while the first was a kind of rate imposed, as the term *marāʿī* indicates, on pasture-land. This later authority seems to corroborate Professor Cahen's assumption.[4]

[1] Nuwayrī, viii, pp. 253–5; for *muqāṭaʿa* cf. Cahen article 'Bayt al-Māl' in *EI*². For the *kharāj* in Iraq and the East in 13th and 14th centuries cf. Minovi and Minorsky, 'Naṣīr al-Dīn', pp. 759–60, 771–3, 781.

[2] Maqrīzī, *Khiṭaṭ*, i, p. 103; Ibn Iyās, *Nashq*, fol. 30ʳ.

[3] Cahen, 'Régime', pp. 15, 19–20, and p. 20 n. 1; id. 'Contribution', p. 267.

[4] Nuwayrī, viii, p. 262. It is noteworthy that the papyri mention two taxes, a tax on meadows (*murūj*) and a pasture-tax (*marāʿī*); cf. Grohmann, 'New discoveries', II, *BIE*, xxxv (1952–3), pp. 160, 161, 163; id., *Arabic papyri*, iii, pp. 173, 222–3, iv, pp. 73–4, 81, 96–7. The *marāʿī* mentioned by Ṭūsī was a levy collected per number of animals capable of reproduction and grazing. The Mongol equivalent of the term was *qopchur*; cf. Minovi and Minorsky, 'Naṣīr al-Dīn', pp. 761, 773–4, 782. In Ottoman Syria, most villages and several towns paid taxes in money on livestock (sheep, goats, buffaloes, and bees are named). The rate of taxation was ½ *asper* per goat, 1 *asper* per beehive, and 6 *aspers* per

Nuwayrī's data are also important, in that they help us to understand Nābulsī's information concerning the *marāʿī* tax in his time. It is very probable that what Nābulsī refers to as *rātib* is identical with the fixed 2¼ *dirhams per capita* tax on the livestock of residents grazing the whole year, and what he refers to as *ṭārī*', was the *per capita* tax of 70, 50, 30, or 25 *dirhams* per 100 head imposed on the livestock on newcomers which came to graze for a limited time, probably after the Nile flood. It seems that the second category of the tax varied according to the age and size of the livestock. However, Nābulsī mentions an additional tax called *rasm al-mustakhdamīn*, seemingly levied to cover the costs of collection. By dividing the amount of this *rasm* in every village by the whole number of the taxed livestock, both *rātib* and *ṭārī*', one finds that it was a fixed additional tax of 6¼ *dirhams* per 100 head.[1] Unfortunately, the sources do not provide information to show whether that was the case in every Egyptian province during the period under study.

3. *Industry*

A tax on oil-presses referred to in a papyrus fragment indicates that industrial taxes were collected relatively early in Islamic Egypt.[2] Muqaddasī, writing about the second half of the 4th/10th century, states that taxation was heavy in Egypt, especially in Tinnīs, Damietta, and on the banks of the Nile, and that the *qabāla* of Tinnīs was 1,000 *dīnār*s daily.[3] Nāṣir-i Khusraw also mentions that the revenue derived from Tinnīs alone amounted to 1,000 Maghribī *dīnār*s daily.[4] As Tinnīs and Damietta are known, at least in the heyday of the Fāṭimids, to have been concerned in the manufacture of textiles, these figures, though possibly exaggerated, imply that the Fāṭimids imposed heavy taxes on the textile industry.[5]

buffalo; cf. Lewis, *Notes and documents from the Turkish archives*, pp. 18–19; id., 'Studies', pp. 484, 491.

[1] Nābulsī, *Fayyūm*, pp. 30–1, 33–4, 36, 41–2, 70, 95, 99, 104–5, 109, 173.

[2] Grohmann, 'New discoveries', ii, p. 160.

[3] Muqaddasī, p. 213.

[4] Nāṣir-i Khusraw, p. 40.

[5] Tinnīs and Damietta were famous for their textile industry in the Fāṭimid period; cf. Muqaddasī, p. 203; Ibn Ḥawqal, *Ṣifa*, fol. 73; Anonymous, *Awrāq*, fol. 26^{r-v}; Anonymous, *Istibṣār*, pp. 87–8; Ibn Ẓuhayra, fol. 16^{r}; Maqrīzī, *Dimyāṭ*, fol. 61^{v}; see also A. Bahgat, 'Les manufactures d'étoffe en Égypte', *BIE*, 4e sér., no. 4 (1903), pp. 351–61; R. B. Serjeant, 'Material for a history of Islamic textiles', *AI*, xiii–xiv (1948), pp. 110–13.

There were probably also taxes on other products, though Nāṣir-i Khusraw does not mention any on the manufacture of pottery, glassware, and oils in Fusṭāṭ or on the wool industry in Asyūṭ, these being places where such industries flourished.[1] This assumption is supported by the fact that, among the Fāṭimid taxes levied in Cairo and Fusṭāṭ which Saladin abolished when he came to power, were: 3,108 *dīnār*s from the *dār al-qand* where candy was manufactured, 135 *dīnār*s derived from a *maks* of ½ a pound on sugar products, 400 *dīnār*s on acid vinegar and its derivatives, 84 *dīnār*s on *mizr* (a kind of beer), 500 *dīnār*s collected from the fat shop and sesame-oil and vinegar press, 236 *dīnār*s from the potteries, and 350 *dīnār*s from the spinning workshops. The tax on the dyeing, spinning, and weaving of silk amounted to 334 *dīnār*s per annum. Moreover, Maqrīzī mentions an important industrial tax, the revenue of which amounted to 1,500 *dīnār*s. It was called *khātam al-sharb*, 'the seal on fine linen', which indicates that the finished products bore the seal of the tax-collector. On the basis of a document from the Geniza written around 1100, Professor Goitein suggests that it was done to make fabrics woven or dyed in private homes (which was prohibited) or manufactured without payment of the tax, immediately recognizable as such by the absence of the stamp.[2]

The lack of information about industrial taxes under the Ayyūbids is total. While Baghdādī states that, before the epidemic of 596/1200, there were 900 factories of rush mats, and Ibn Sa'īd al-Andalusī mentions the existence of sugar and soap *maṭābikh* (literally: places of cooking) in Fusṭāṭ under al-Ṣāliḥ Ayyūb, neither speaks of taxation.[3] But, relying on Nābulsī's *Tārīkh al-Fayyūm*, it can be assumed that the *hilālī* tax collected from wax-makers, potteries, tanneries, perfume shops, etc.—though actually not in any way a tax on industry, in the sense of one which increased or decreased in proportion to the amount manufactured—constituted a tax on production. However, this is only an assumption which requires justification by further research.[4]

[1] Nāṣir-i Khusraw, pp. 60–1, 70–1; for other industries cf. Goitein, 'The main industries of the Mediterranean area', *JESHO*, iv (1961), pp. 168–97; id., *Med. Soc.*, i, pp. 99–116; Canard, article 'Fāṭimids' in *EI*².

[2] Maqrīzī, *Khiṭaṭ*, i, pp. 104–5; Goitein, *Med. Soc.*, i, p. 116.

[3] Baghdādī, p. 256, tr. S. de Sacy, p. 409; Ibn Sa'īd, *Mughrib*, i, p. 11; see also Maqrīzī, *Khiṭaṭ*, i, pp. 342, 367. *Maṭābikh al-sukkar* are often referred to in the Geniza; cf. Worman, 'Notes on the Jews in Fustāt', *JQR*, xviii (1905–6), p. 18; Goitein, *Med. Soc.*, i, pp. 81, 126.

[4] See below, pp. 105–6.

The tax on sugar manufacture, Fāṭimid in origin, was abolished by Saladin and reintroduced at an unknown date. Egyptian cane-sugar constituted an important item of export to Asia and the Mediterranean until the end of the 14th century, when Sicilian competition threatened Egypt's supremacy in the European sugar markets.[1] There is a lack of evidence about the amount of the tax collected from sugar presses, which was not abolished until the Nāṣirī *rawk*.[2] It seems, however, that it was reintroduced before the end of the period under study. In 733/1333, al-Nashw, the then *nāẓir al-khāṣṣ*, checked the amount of the candy delivered by the sugar presses to the *dār al-qand* on behalf of the amirs. Although candy manufactured by the amirs had been exempted from tax by Sultan al-Nāṣir, al-Nashw reimposed the tax, and its subsequent yield reached in one day the amount of 6,000 *dīnār*s, which encouraged al-Nāṣir to abandon his previous policy of exemption.[3] Al-Nashw went so far as to send inspectors to supervise the candy factories in 738/1337–8. The latter having discovered that the Awlād Fuḍayl in Mallawī in Upper Egypt had manufactured about 14,000 *qinṭār*s of candy in one year, but paid tax only on 1,000 *qinṭār*s, al-Nashw declared all the candy in question, plus an additional 8,000 *qinṭār*s, confiscated on behalf of the sultan.[4]

4. *Mines*

The gold-mines of al-ʿAllāqī having been exhausted before the advent of the Ayyūbids, only alum, natron, salt, and emeralds continued to be mined.[5]

The exploitation of alum—known since the Pharaonic period—

[1] Mazuel, *Le sucre en Égypte*, pp. 12–20; Heyd, *Histoire du commerce*, ii, pp. 687–9; for export sugar to Syria cf. Maqrīzī, *Sulūk*, i, pp. 344, 353, tr. Blochet, 'E', pp. 213, 223. In 650/1252–3, 600 *ḥiml*s of Egyptian sugar were among the load of a Baghdad-bound caravan seized by the Mongols; cf. Maqrīzī, *Sulūk*, i, pp. 383–4, tr. Quatremère, i. i, pp. 36–7; for the *ḥiml* see below, p. 192 n. 1.

[2] Maqrīzī, *Khiṭaṭ*, i, p. 89; id., *Sulūk*, ii, p. 151; Ibn Taghrī Birdī, *Nujūm*, ix, p. 47; Labib, *Handelsgeschichte*, p. 251.

[3] ʿUmarī, *Masālik* (MS. A.S. 3434), fol. 7r; Maqrīzī, *Sulūk*, ii, pp. 360–1; for the *nāẓir al-khāṣṣ* see below, pp. 143–4.

[4] Maqrīzī, *Sulūk*, ii, p. 431; id., *Khiṭaṭ*, i, p. 204; Ibn Iyās, *Nashq*, fol. 48r; id., Badā'iʿ, i, p. 169. For the manufacture of candy and sugar cf. Nuwayrī, viii, pp. 267–72; for *maṭābikh al-sukkar* in later period, cf. Ibn Duqmāq, *Intiṣār*, iv, pp. 41–6; Shayyāl, *Miṣr al-Islāmiyya*, i, pp. 107–9; Udovitch, 'England to Egypt', in Cook, ed., *Studies*, p. 116.

[5] See below, p. 169.

was of great importance for Egypt in the period under study, not only because it was put to domestic use in the manufacture of felt and dyes, but also because of the demand from Europe, where it was needed for dyeing and preparation of textiles, skins, and leather, enabling Egypt to balance her payments without exhausting her store of gold.[1]

The importance of alum as a source of revenue is evident before the Ayyūbid era. Maqrīzī states that, in 515/1121, when the Fāṭimid vizier al-Baṭā'iḥī renounced the collection of arrears in taxes until the end of 510/1117, there were, among the items concerned, 913½ *qinṭār*s of alum, which implies that a quite considerable part of the Egyptian revenue came from alum.[2] It can be inferred from Makhzūmī's *Minhāj* that alum was a state monopoly, compulsorily delivered to a government distribution centre, the *matjar*, where alone it was sold.[3] This is confirmed by evidence in Ibn Mammātī, who stresses that nobody dared buy the alum from the Bedouin Arabs without the intermediary of the *dīwān*.[4] Mention of the exploitation of alum is found in a European source from A.D. 1175, where Burchard (or Gerard), vice-dominus of Strasburg, reporting to Frederick Barbarossa on his mission to Saladin, states that alum, mined at six days distance from Cairo, 'is collected for the use of the king'.[5]

Ibn Mammātī describes the method of exploitation of the beds of alum in the desert of Upper Egypt from where it was transported to the banks of the Nile at Qūṣ, Akhmīm, Asyūṭ, and Bahnasā and to Alexandria during the Nile flood. 13,000 *qinṭār*s were sold in 588/1192, when Ibn Mammātī controlled the *dīwān*. The last sale

[1] Cf. Cahen, 'L'Alun avant Phocée', *RHES*, xli (1963), pp. 436–7, 440; id., 'Quelques problèmes concernant l'expansion économique Musulmane au haut moyen âge', *Settimane di studio del Centro Italiano di Studi sull'Alto Medioevo*, xii (1965), i, p. 431. References to alum occur already in ancient Egyptian texts. It was used in tanning leather, as a mordant in dyeing, for medicinal purposes, and in mummification; cf. Lucas, *Ancient Egyptian materials*, pp. 257–9, 303; Singer, *The earliest chemical industry*, pp. 1–6. Abū Dulaf (4th/10th century) states that there was a mine of red alum in Badhdhan in Iran. This alum used to be transported to the Yemen and Wāsiṭ, and was stronger than the Egyptian kind; cf. Abū Dulaf, *al-Risāla al-thāniya*, p. 6, tr. Minorsky, p. 35.

[2] Maqrīzī, *Khiṭaṭ*, i, p. 83.

[3] Makhzūmī, fols. 156^{r-v}, 163^{v}–164^{r}; for the *matjar* see below, pp. 92–4.

[4] Ibn Mammātī, ed. Atiya, p. 329, ed. Najjār, pp. 23–4.

[5] *Arnoldi Chronica Slavorum*, Lib. vii. 8, p. 271; see also Cahen, 'Alun', p. 437; for Burchard (or Gerard), see above, p. 21. Sometimes Saladin permitted certain members of his family to sell in Europe certain quantities of alum for their own benefit; cf. Amari, *Diplomi Arabi*, no. 9, p. 263.

to *tujjār al-Rūm*, that is merchants from Byzantium or the European Christian countries in general, amounted to 12,000 *qinṭārs*. The *dīwān* used to pay 30 *dirhams* and sometimes less for a *qinṭār laythī* of alum, while the selling price fluctuated between 4 and 6 *dīnārs*, and—according to another passage—between $5\frac{5}{12}$ *dīnārs* and 5 *dīnārs* per *qinṭār jarwī*. 80 *qinṭārs jarwī* used to be sold yearly to Cairo felt makers, dyers, and to rush-mat makers at the price of $7\frac{1}{2}$ *dīnārs* per *qinṭār*. There was a type of alum from the oases in the Western desert (al-Wāḥāt) called *kawārī*, which was priced at 1 *dīnār* and 2 *qīrāṭs*, but for which there was little demand.[1]

Alum was important in that it was used in the Ayyūbid period as currency to pay for imports of merchandise such as timber and iron purchased from private merchants by the *matjar*. It was, however, not a question of straight barter, as a minor part of the purchase price was always settled in gold. The procedure, which was quite complicated, was as follows: when the value of the total merchandise purchased by the state from a merchant exceeded the *khums* tax levied on his goods, he was paid two thirds of the difference between the sum credited to him and the tax due from him in alum, and only one third of it in gold.[2] It seems that Saladin valued the revenue from alum to such an extent that, in the year 577/1181, he sent cavalry to Upper Egypt to guard the route by which alum was transported on its way 'to the Franks'.[3]

The revival of the alum trade of Asia Minor, where the Venetians began to exploit ancient Byzantine alum beds, in no way affected Egyptian mining activity.[4] Maqrīzī states that under Sultan al-Kāmil and his son al-Ṣāliḥ, the *muqṭa*'s of al-Wāḥāt were obliged to deliver to Cairo 1,000 *qinṭārs* of white alum per year in payment of the *jawālī* imposed on the *dhimmīs* of al-Wāḥāt.[5] Moreover, there is evidence to show that, in 1248, the Genoese were expecting the arrival of a cargo of Alexandrian alum, which subsequently figures,

[1] Ibn Mammātī, ed. Atiya, pp. 328–9, ed. Najjār, pp. 23–4; Becker, *Islamstudien*, i, p. 188; id., article 'Egypt' in *EI*[1]; Cahen, 'Alun', pp. 434–5; Rabī', *Nuẓum*, p. 45; see also Maqrīzī, *Khiṭaṭ*, i, p. 109, Qalqashandī, *Ṣubḥ*, iii, pp. 288, 459–60. The *qinṭār laythī* was equivalent to 62 kg., the *jarwī* to 96·7 kg.; cf. Hinz, p. 25; Cahen, 'Alun', p. 434 n. 8. The *qīrāṭ* = $\frac{1}{24}$ *dīnār*.

[2] Ibn Mammātī, ed. Najjār, p. 23, ed. Atiya, p. 327; Cahen, 'Alun', p. 435; id., 'Douanes', p. 260; for the *khums* see below, pp. 90 ff.

[3] Maqrīzī, *Sulūk*, i, p. 72, tr. Blochet, 'B', pp. 539–40; Cahen, 'Alun', p. 436.

[4] Cahen, 'Alun', p. 444. For the exploitation of alum mines in Asia Minor in the 13th century cf. id., *Pre-Ottoman Turkey*, pp. 160–1, 318–19.

[5] Maqrīzī, *Khiṭaṭ*, i, p. 236.

with a full statement of its provenance, in the Venetian tariff of 1255. Mention of significant amounts of Egyptian alum can still be found up to the middle of the thirteenth century, not so much in Genoese documents—Genoa derived its alum from Asia Minor—but in those of Venice and Crete. In later times, however, Egyptian alum practically disappeared, so that it was, in Maqrīzī's time, hardly more than a memory.[1]

Natron (which is a naturally occurring compound of sodium carbonate and sodium bicarbonate) was mined in ancient Egypt and used in purification ceremonies, in the manufacture of incense, glass, glaze, in cookery, in medicine, in bleaching linen, and in mummification.[2] It is said that the exploitation of natron was unrestricted until Ibn al-Mudabbir introduced a state monopoly, which was still in force long after Maqrīzī's time.[3] Nābulsī speaks of a special Fāṭimid *dīwān* set up to deal exclusively with natron.[4] Ibn Mammātī states that natron was mined in al-Ṭarrāna in the Buḥayra province, and in al-Fāqūsiyya in the Sharqiyya province. The cost of production was only 2 *dirhams* per *qinṭār*, while its selling price in Cairo and Alexandria amounted to 70 *dirhams*. As there was a demand for 30,000 *qinṭār*s every year, one can imagine that much revenue was derived from natron. The *ḍāmin*s, who were apparently entrusted with its sale, were obliged to collect the natron from the store in al-Ṭarrāna, and any subsequent loss in weight was their responsibility. There was no lack of corruption. This is illustrated by Ibn Mammātī's account of *ḍāmin*s who delayed the delivery of natron from the store to Cairo, substituting for it cheap natron purchased illicitly from Bedouin Arabs. In the early Ayyūbid era, the revenue from natron was spent on the equipment of the army and navy and on charities for the poor, the needy, and wayfarers.[5]

[1] Maqrīzī, *Khiṭaṭ*, i, p. 109; Cahen, 'Alun', pp. 444–5 and n. 62; see also Qalqashandī, *Ṣubḥ*, iii, pp. 459–60; for the alum trade in later middle ages, cf. Marie-Louise Heers, 'Les Génois et le commerce de l'alun', *RHES*, xxxii (1954), i, pp. 31–53; L. Liagre, 'Le commerce de l'alun en Flandre au moyen-âge', *Le Moyen Âge*, lxi (1955), pp. 177–266.

[2] Lucas, *Ancient Egyptian materials*, pp. 263–7, 278 ff. The mention of a pound of *naṭrūn* in diminutive fragment found in the Vienna papers (A.Ch. 8, fol. 7133) implies that in medieval Egypt it was used by copper-polishers, tinners, bleachers, fullers, weavers, and knitters; see Ibn Mammātī, p. 335.

[3] Maqrīzī, *Khiṭaṭ*, i, p. 109; Ibn Iyās, *Nashq*, fol. 30r.

[4] Nābulsī, *Luma'*, p. 36, tr. Cahen, 'Quelques aspects', p. 104.

[5] Ibn Mammātī, ed. Atiya, pp. 248, 334–6, and 336 n. 4; ed. Najjār, p. 24; Becker, *Islamstudien*, i, pp. 188–9; Rabī', *Nuẓum*, p. 45.

In 577/1181, Saladin established a special *dīwān* to deal with the affairs of the fleet. Among the revenues transferred to it were the proceeds from the sale of natron, the *ḍamān* of which in that year amounted to 8,000 *dīnār*s.[1] In 585/1190, the *ḍamān* of natron reached, according to al-Qāḍī al-Fāḍil in Khiṭaṭ, the amount of 15,500 *dīnār*s, and the following year 7,800 *dīnār*s.[2]

The exploitation of natron in Egypt continued without decline until at least the first half of the fifteenth century. Nābulsī, who wrote at the end of the Ayyūbid era, states that the *dīwān al-māl* (treasury) in the capital had a special *mutawallī* (administrator) for the affairs of natron.[3] Qazwīnī (died 682/1283) mentions a natron mine in the city of Abyār.[4] Moreover, al-ʿUmarī, who was al-Nāṣir's contemporary, states in the *Taʿrīf* that the natron exploited in the 100 *faddān*s *birkat al-naṭrūn* in the Buḥayra province yielded a revenue of about 100,000 *dīnār*s. Granted that this figure is exaggerated, there is no doubt that natron provided al-Nāṣir with a considerable amount of money, especially as Qalqashandī says that, in his lifetime, the value of natron had greatly increased, so that the price of a *qinṭār* reached about 300 *dirhams*.[5]

The first mention of a tax on salt in the available sources goes back to the advent of Saladin, who is said to have abolished, among other Fāṭimid taxes, a tax on salt. This indicates that a tax on salt was known in the Fāṭimid period and even earlier.[6] The tax on salt seems to have been reintroduced by al-ʿAzīz ʿUthmān. According to Maqrīzī, tax was collected from a certain salt-seller for the salt he carried in a basket on his head. The tax-gatherers referred to the salt-tax as *zakāt*, which was probably just a device of the usual kind, to find a *sharʿī* justification for a non-*sharʿī* tax.[7] Soon, however, at a date not mentioned in the sources, an official salt-tax was introduced. Described as *maks al-milḥ*, it remained in force until it was abolished by al-Nāṣir in 720/1320. The sultani decree of abolition was read in the mosques, and letters of instruction were sent to officials in the provinces, proclaiming that no one should be

[1] Maqrīzī, Khiṭaṭ, ii, p. 194; id., *Sulūk*, i, pp. 73, 107, tr. Blochet, 'C', p. 57; for *ḍamān* and *ḍāmin* see below, pp. 136–7.

[2] Maqrīzī, Khiṭaṭ, i, pp. 109–110; Rabīʿ, *Nuẓum*, p. 45.

[3] Nābulsī, *Lumaʿ*, p. 29, tr. Cahen, 'Quelques aspects', p. 103.

[4] Qazwīnī, *Āthār*, p. 93.

[5] ʿUmarī, *Taʿrīf*, p. 175; Qalqashandī, *Ṣubḥ*, iii, pp. 287–8, 460–1; for the later period cf. Ẓāhirī, *Zubda*, pp. 35–6; Ibn Iyās, *Nashq*, fol. 278r.

[6] Maqrīzī, Khiṭaṭ, i, p. 104.

[7] Ibid., i, p. 108.

prevented from obtaining free salt from the salt mines (*mallāḥāt*). What a heavy burden on the inhabitants the salt-tax was may be inferred from the fact that, after its abolition the price of an *ardabb* of salt fell from 10 to as little as 3 *dirhams*.[1]

Concerning emeralds, there is ample evidence in Mas'ūdī's *Murūj al-dhahab* to show that the emerald mines east of the Nile in Upper Egypt prospered in the 4th/10th century, because of the heavy demand for these gems outside Egypt for the crowns, rings, and bracelets of foreign sovereigns.[2] Ibn Ḥawqal also describes the emerald mine in Egypt as unique.[3]

Although there is no information on emerald mining under the Ayyūbids and in the first 57 years of the Mamluk period, emeralds were actively mined until the reign of al-Nāṣir Muḥammad according to Qalqashandī, or the reign of his son Ḥasan according to Maqrīzī.[4]

It would seem that the Ayyūbid and Mamluk sultans often appointed *ḍāmins* to mine emeralds. In 705/1306, for example, Sanjar al-Zumurrudī, *ḍāmin al-zumurrud*, found an emerald which weighed 145 *mithqāls*, and which he sold to Ibn 'Afāna al-Kārimī for about 600 or 900 *dīnārs*. Ibn 'Afāna went to the Yemen, where he refused to sell this precious stone for 3,000 *dīnārs*. Unfortunately, he brought it back to Egypt at a time when the *ḥiml* to the sultan fell due. Sanjar, who was unable to acquit himself of it, told the sultan that he had given Ibn 'Afāna the stone in security for a debt. As a result, the emerald was taken from Ibn 'Afāna and sent to the treasury.[5]

It seems that Sultan al-Nāṣir, not satisfied with the yearly *ḥiml* of emeralds, decided to appoint a *wakīl* (agent) to supervise emerald exploitation and send the whole production to the treasury. This assumption is confirmed by another episode narrated

[1] Nuwayrī, xxx, fol. 139; 'Aynī, *'Iqd*, 'C', xxiii. ii, fol. 303; id., *Badr*, fol. 12[v]; Maqrīzī, *Sulūk*, ii, p. 203; Ibn Taghrī Birdī, *Nujūm*, ix, p. 62; Labib, *Handelsgeschichte*, p. 251.

[2] Mas'ūdī, *Murūj*, ii, pp. 23–5; see also Kindī, *Faḍā'il*, fol. 20[r].

[3] Ibn Ḥawqal, *Ṣifa*, fol. 71.

[4] Qalqashandī, *Ṣubḥ*, iii, pp. 286, 309, 459; Maqrīzī, *Khiṭaṭ*, i, p. 233; cf. Anonymous, *Istibṣār*, pp. 85–6; Ibn al-Wardī, *Kharīda*, p. 36; Becker (*Islamstudien*, i, p. 189; id., article 'Egypt' in *EI*[1]) states that the emerald mines in Egypt were exploited by the state, which paid the workers and supplied the instruments. Unfortunately he gives no examples.

[5] Ṣafadī, *Nuzha*, fol. 63[r]; Dawādārī, *Durr fākhir*, p. 133; Ibn Abī al-Faḍā'il, pp. 620–2; Yūnīnī (*Dhayl*, MS. iv, fol. 138[r]) states that an emerald of unique shape, weighing 245 *mithqāl*, was found in *ma'dan al-zumurrud* in 707/1307–8.

by ʿAynī. After the imprisonment of al-Nas͟hw in 740/1339–40, a man who had been employed as a *wakīl* in an emerald mine accused al-Nas͟hw of having appropriated an emerald of unusual beauty and size, an accusation which was confirmed by the then *mus͟hidd* of the *zumurrud*.[1] However, Ibn al-Akfānī, who died in Egypt in 749/1348, mentions some important contemporary emerald finds in Egypt. This indicates that the successful exploitation of the Egyptian emerald mine continued in his time.[2]

5. *Fisheries*

A tax on fisheries was introduced in Egypt by Ibn al-Mudabbir who, as Maqrīzī says, was so ashamed of it that he called it *k͟harāj maḍārib al-awtār wa mag͟hāris al-s͟hibāk* (*k͟harāj* on nets).[3] From that time onward this tax remained in force, and appears in the papyri as well as in the Vienna papers as *maṣāyid* (fishing-licence).[4] Ibn Ḥawqal states that Nastarū, a place situated between the Burullus lake and the Mediterranean, and known for its fisheries, used to pay a huge *qabāla* to the Fāṭimids.[5] In the reign of Saladin, the *ʿibra* of Nastarū reached the amount of 17,500 *dīnār*s, mainly from fisheries. Saladin assigned Nastarū as *waqf* for the benefit of widows and orphans.[6] Later the *waqf* seems to have been revoked and all Egyptian fisheries conferred on *ḍāmin*s. During the reign of al-Ṣāliḥ Ayyūb, the *ḍamān* of Nastarū lake alone amounted to 25,000 Egyptian *dīnār*s, while the *ḍamān* of the remaining Egyptian lakes was only 7,000 *dīnār*s. If these figures are correct, the fisheries provided the Ayyūbid sultan with a considerable income.[7]

Information concerning taxes on fisheries under the Mamluks

[1] ʿAynī, *ʿIqd*, ʿA', xvii, fol. 150^r.

[2] Ibn al-Akfānī, *Nuk͟hab*, pp. 50–1; for Ibn al-Akfānī, cf. Ibn Ḥajar, *Durar*, iii, pp. 279–80.

[3] Maqrīzī, *K͟hiṭaṭ*, i, pp. 107–8; see also Ibn Iyās, *Nas͟hq*, fol. 30^r.

[4] Grohmann, 'New discoveries', ii, p. 160; id., *Arabic Papyri*, iv, pp. 73–6. One fragment from the Vienna papers (A.Ch. 8, fol. 7277) refers to *al-maṣāyid bi* al-Us͟hmūnayn, 'the fisheries at Us͟hmūnayn', while another (A.Ch. 10, fol. 8052) mentions the assignment of the *ḍamān* of *al-maṣāyid bi* Darūṭ, 'the fisheries at Darūṭ', to two men. For fishery as referred to in the Geniza see Goitein, *Med. Soc.*, i, pp. 126–7.

[5] Ibn Ḥawqal, *Ṣūra*, i, pp. 138–9.

[6] Ibn Duqmāq, *Intiṣār*, v, p. 113; Rabīʿ, *Nuẓum*, p. 52; for the *ʿibra* see above, pp. 47–8.

[7] Ibn Saʿīd, *Basṭ*, p. 82; in the text *buḥayrat* Yastarā'. It appears from the description of its location, that it is a question of Nastarū lake or al-Burullus; cf. Ramzī, *Qāmūs*, i, pp. 459–60. The fisheries of Nastarū continued to yield revenue until Qalqas͟handī's time; cf. *Ṣubḥ*, iii, p. 308.

is available only for the reign of al-Nāṣir ibn Qalāwūn. Nuwayrī divides the taxes on fisheries into two types: (*a*) permanent taxes collected in places where the fisheries were active all through the year, such as Damietta, Burullus, and Aswān; (*b*) taxes collected on temporary fishing activities, mainly when the Nile flood receded after the nets had been spread at the exits from the canals whence the water flowed back into the Nile.[1]

There is only one piece of evidence mentioned by ʿUmarī in *Masālik al-abṣār* to prove that there was a tax on fishing in the Nile, excluding the canals. In 737/1336–7 some *mansar*s (house-breakers) who had arrived by way of the Nile robbed the house of the chief qadi Jalāl al-Dīn and killed a watchman. Sultan al-Nāṣir ordered the *wālī* to arrest the criminals. As a result, fishermen fishing in the Nile were arrested in the whole of Upper Egypt. It is said that the sultani officials agreed with the fishermen that they would be exempted from a quarter of the sultani *dīwān*'s due on their catch if they kept watch for the robbers on the Nile. After a few days those guilty of the robbery were caught and crucified. This episode proves that, as a rule, those fishing in the Nile had to pay a tax on their catch to the sultan.[2] This tax seems to have been replaced—in later years—by a tax imposed on the sale of the Nile fish in the fish-markets of Cairo.[3]

B. *Taxes on trade and transactions*

In *Kitāb al-minhāj* Makhzūmī does not distinguish between customs duties proper, remuneration for services or protection, and taxes on commercial transactions. According to Professor Cahen the only distinct demarcation line is between *wārid* (imports) and *ṣādir* (exports).[4]

Taxes at auction sales (*ḥalqa*; plural *ḥilāq*) were payable only when a sale was made. More detailed information on *ḥalqa* dues is found in the *Minhāj*. At Tinnīs the *rasm al-ḥalqa* was 1 *dīnār* per large ship, $\frac{1}{2}$ *dīnār* per small ship, and $\frac{3}{4}$ *dīnār* for distribution among agents such as the weigher, the broker, and the announcer.

[1] Nuwayrī, viii, pp. 262–4.
[2] ʿUmarī, *Masālik* (MS. A.S. 3434), fols. 157^{v}–8^{r}.
[3] See below, p. 103; for the revenue from the fisheries in Ottoman Syria, cf. Lewis, 'Studies', p. 491; id., 'Jaffa in the 16th century, according to the Ottoman tahrir registers', *Necati Lugal Armağani*, Ankara, 1969, pp. 437 and n. 10, 441, 443, 445; Heyd, *Ottoman documents*, p. 141 and n. 7.
[4] Cahen, 'Douanes', p. 244.

At Damietta the tax for the ship was $\frac{2}{3}+\frac{1}{4}$, i.e. $\frac{11}{12}$ *dīnār*, of which $\frac{1}{4}+\frac{1}{6}+\frac{1}{8}$ *dīnār* (= $21\frac{1}{2}$ *dirhams*) went to the agents. In the case of timber, both the total and the dues of the agents were reduced by $\frac{1}{8}$ *dīnār*. At Alexandria the tax was $1\frac{2}{3}$ *dīnārs*, and the list of agents longer, including inspectors, tent boys, watchmen, and porters.[1] Other taxes (the *khums* = fifth) were collected on the occasion of the sale of merchandise.

Information on the *khums* given by Makhzūmī, who held office under the late Fāṭimids, may be taken as an indication that this tax was of Fāṭimid origin. Nuwayrī states that when Shāwar and the Crusaders besieged Saladin in Alexandria in 562/1167, Shāwar demanded from the city the extradition of Saladin and his men, in return for which he promised to exempt it from the *mukūs* and give it the *akhmās*. However, they refused to comply with his request.[2]

Ibn Mammātī states that the *khums* was a tax collected from the Rūm merchants on their imports to Alexandria, Damietta, and Tinnīs. He emphasizes that the term *khums* encompassed all business relating to foreign merchants, regardless of whether the effective total of duty equalled the theoretical 20 per cent or not. Even if it reached 35 per cent or was less than 20 per cent, it was still described as *khums*.[3]

The complex taxes which were in existence in Alexandria in Makhzūmī's time can be subsumed, though not without reservations, into two main categories, sometimes referred to as the *qūf* and the *ʿarṣa*. The meaning of these terms is by no means clear. Professor Cahen surmises that all the taxes of Alexandria were grouped 'around two general concepts, the *qūf* and the *ʿarṣa*, whose fixed total represents 19 per cent (or, with the approximate difference of 1 per cent, the 'fifth' *khums*) of the value of all imported goods whatever their nature'.

Among the various operations and taxes described by the general term *qūf*, one distinguishes, with some difficulty, three groups: ships taxed 'fully' (*bi al-kāmil*) on 1,000 *dīnārs* of merchandise,

[1] Makhzūmī, fols. 104^{r-v}, 125^{v}, 127^{r-v}, 130^{v}, tr. Cahen, 'Douanes', pp. 283, 290–2, 294. It is very probable that the *ḥalqa* (circle) was formed at auctions in *dār al-wakāla* (the agency house) of *wakīl al-tujjār* (representative of the merchants); cf. Goitein, *Med. Soc.* i, p. 188; for personal transactions and public sales *fī al-ḥalqa* see ibid., pp. 192–3.

[2] Nuwayrī, xxvi, fol. 101.

[3] Ibn Mammātī, pp. 326–7; see also Maqrīzī, *Khiṭaṭ*, i, p. 109; Qalqashandī, *Ṣubḥ*, iii, pp. 463–4; Labib, *Handelsgeschichte*, p. 240; Cahen, 'Douanes', p. 235; Rabīʿ, *Nuẓum*, p. 51.

with a tax of $151\frac{1}{4}$ *dīnārs*; ships taxed at 'two-thirds' on $666\frac{2}{3}$ *dīnārs* with a tax of $100+\frac{1}{2}+\frac{1}{3}$, i.e. $100\frac{5}{6}$ *dīnārs*; and finally ships 'half taxed' on 500 *dīnārs* with a tax of $75+\frac{1}{2}+\frac{1}{8}$, i.e. $75\frac{5}{8}$ *dīnārs*. This classification is somewhat obscure. The revenue from the *qūf*, which brought in a regular total of $15\frac{1}{8}$ per cent, was subsequently broken up into: (*a*) salaries of agents such as tax-collectors, warehouse-keepers, and river porters; (*b*) taxes of many categories such as the *khatma* (not explained), the *ṭuʿma* (food), and payment for the *wilāya* (the local command) payable on arrival and departure.[1] Other taxes mentioned by Makhzūmī were those collected for the *mushārif* and the *ʿāmil*, for *ṣāḥib al-baḥr* (the chief of the river); for the interpreter, for the *kātib al-khums* (secretary), and finally a tax for the *jahbadh*, which was described by the Rūm as *ʿarṣa*. Professor Cahen observes that it is not clear whether the term '*ʿarṣa*' referred only to the tax for the *jahbadh* or denoted the sum of taxes to be specified. The data of the accounts section, as well as the use of the term '*ʿarṣa*', in association with the *qūf* (in what Professor Cahen describes as '*les actes italiens*'), to denote a tax of some importance, points to the latter.[2] Documentary sources such as the Geniza and the Vienna papers may, one day, throw light on the complicated conditions described by Makhzūmī.

One thing emerges clearly from Makhzūmī's account, namely that imported merchandise was taxed, in Tinnīs, according to its nature, which required the value of the commodities to be determined from case to case. Most commodities such as perfume, timber, stones, pottery, pitch, etc., paid 30 per cent *ad valorem*. Mastic was taxed at 20 per cent, precious metals, silk, and woven materials at 10 per cent.[3]

There is only one piece of evidence from Saladin's reign concerning the total revenue from the *khums*. According to al-Qāḍī al-Fāḍil in *Khiṭaṭ*, the revenue from the *khums* in Alexandria

[1] Makhzūmī, fols. 105^{r}–7^{v}; tr. Cahen, 'Douanes', pp. 284–5; also ibid., pp. 245–7.

[2] Makhzūmī, fol. 109^{v}; tr. Cahen, 'Douanes', p. 286; also ibid., p. 248: 'والذى يؤخذ عند محاسبة المراكب الخمسية منسوبا الى رسم الأشراف والعمل ورسم صاحب البحرورسوم الولاية ورسوم الترجمة وكاتب الخمس والجهبذ والمحاسبة وتعرف عند الروم بالعرصة'. For the *mushārif*, the *ʿāmil* and the *jahbadh* see below, pp. 157–9. The Italian documents are presumably treaties and privileges conferred by the Fāṭimids, the Ayyūbids, and the early Mamluks on the Italian merchants.

[3] Makhzūmī, fols. 128^{v}–9^{r}, tr. Cahen, 'Douanes', p. 293; also ibid., p. 244.

reached, in 587/1191–2, 28,613 *dīnārs*, an amount which represents a considerable part of the Egyptian revenue under Saladin.[1] It is noteworthy that the term '*khums*' remained in use at least until Qalqashandī's time.[2] Ibn Shaddād and Kutubī state that, on the occasion of his visit to Alexandria in 673/1274, Baybars heard some complaints against the *wālī* of the city. These must have been financial in origin, since Baybars fined the *wālī* 50,000 *dīnārs*, and transferred the affairs of the *khums* and the *dīwān* to Bahā' al-Dīn Ṣandal.[3] At the time of the dispute between the natives of Alexandria and the European merchants in 727/1327, the *dīwān al-khums* was chosen as a temporary office for the vizier and the *nāẓir al-khāṣṣ*.[4]

Merchandise was purchased privately, or by state monopolies managed by the *matjar* (office of commerce). It is worth noting that the office of *matjar* was Fāṭimid in origin. Before 444/1052–3, corn worth 100,000 *dirhams* used to be stored and offered yearly for sale by the state. In that year, the vizier al-Yāzūrī informed the Caliph al-Mustanṣir that a monopoly of this kind was injurious to the inhabitants. Besides, if the price of corn fell, it could not be offered for sale and decayed. He suggested therefore the establishment of a *matjar* to deal with wood, iron, lead, soap, honey, and other goods which were more profitable and decayed less easily. Such was the origin of the *matjar* in Egypt.[5] This is confirmed by evidence from the Geniza. Professor Goitein shows that the Fāṭimid government was the greatest customer in the country. When the prices for silk in Fusṭāṭ were desperately low, a merchant sold his stock to the government and received payment. A document written when a *qinṭār* of pepper in Alexandria cost 40 *dīnārs*, states: 'at such price one can sell only to a government'. Another aspect of the Fāṭimid's economic policy was their prerogative to take possession of commodities such as silk, lead, wax, and olive oil against the wish of the merchants carrying them.[6]

According to information found in Makhzūmī, Ibn Mammātī, and Nābulsī for the Ayyūbid era, and in Maqrīzī for the later

[1] Maqrīzī, *Khiṭaṭ*, i, p. 109.

[2] Qalqashandī, *Ṣubḥ*, iii, p. 463.

[3] Ibn Shaddād, *Rawḍa*, fol. 56^{r}; Kutubī, '*Uyūn* (MS. Köprülü), fol. 34^{r}.

[4] Maqrīzī, *Sulūk*, ii, pp. 284–6; Ibn Baṭṭūṭa (i, pp. 45–7), who was in Mecca at this time, mentions this dispute; see also 'Umarī, *Masālik* (MS. P.) fol. 145^{r-v}; 'Aynī, *Badr*, fol. 19^{v}.

[5] Maqrīzī, *Khiṭaṭ*, i, pp. 109, 465; id., *Ighātha*, p. 20.

[6] Goitein, *Med. Soc.*, i, pp. 266–8.

period, the *matjar* continued to perform, with regard to certain goods, the function of buying and selling, an operation which was not only fiscally profitable, but also assured a steady supply of rare commodities, such as iron and timber, indispensable for the manufacture of arms and for shipbuilding.[1] One third of the purchase price was paid in cash, the rest in alum.[2]

Concerning taxes payable by the European merchants to the *matjar*, there is only an obscure reference in Makhzūmī to the effect that timber of all kinds, iron, nails, the *siyāla* (broken nails), solid or liquid pitch were bought by the *matjar* of Alexandria, taxed at 10 per cent *ad valorem*, and supplemented by $2+\frac{1}{2}+\frac{1}{4}+2$ *ḥabba*, i.e. $2\frac{7}{9}$ per cent, so that the total tax $12\frac{7}{9}$ per cent was lower than the total of taxes imposed on ordinary commerce as stated under the *khums*. If it so happened that the European merchants retained for the private market some of these commodities, the *maks* levied on them was the *khums* and supplementary taxes, i.e. $31\frac{1}{2}$ per cent on the 'complete', $20\frac{13}{16}$ per cent on the 'two-thirds', and $15\frac{5}{24}$ per cent on the 'half'.[3] It seems that, in Makhzūmī's time, Tinnīs was a free market for commodities of this kind which bore a tax of 30 per cent.[4]

In course of time, the administration of the *matjar* became guilty of negligence, an example of which is quoted by Nābulsī in *Luma'*.

[1] Ibn Mammātī, ed. Atiya, p. 327, ed. Najjār, p. 23; Makhzūmī, fols. 156[r–v], 163[v]–164[r], tr. Cahen, 'Douanes', pp. 301–3, 310–11; Nābulsī, *Luma'*, pp. 45–6, tr. Cahen, 'Quelques aspects', pp. 109–10; Maqrīzī, *Khiṭaṭ*, i, p. 109; Becker, *Islamstudien*, i, p. 188; id., article 'Egypt' in *EI*[1]; Cahen, 'Douanes', pp. 257–60; Rabī', *Nuẓum*, p. 51. Iron and timber were commodities which Egypt had to import, the mention of which, together with pitch, recurs in some commercial contracts with European countries in the Middle Ages; cf. Amari, *Diplomi Arabi*, no. 10, p. 264; Heyd, *Histoire du commerce*, i, pp. 385–7; Becker, *Islamstudien*, i, pp. 187–8; Cahen, 'Quelques problèmes', pp. 415–16, 430–1. A report addressed to the Fāṭimid Caliph al-Āmir which announces the arrival of Rūm merchants with a cargo of timber has been published and commented on by Dr. Stern in *Studi . . . Levi Della Vida*, ii (1956), pp. 529–38; see also Goitein, *Med. Soc.*, i, p. 46. The vigilance of the Venetians prevented the transport of a cargo of timber to Egypt in 1224; cf. Thiriet, *Délibérations*, p. 27 no. IX.

[2] See above, p. 84.

[3] Makhzūmī, fol. 102[r–v]; tr. Cahen, 'Douanes', p. 282. To denote 'customs dues' Makhzūmī uses the term *maks*; cf. fols. 102[v], 105[r], 109[v], 110[r], 122[r], 125[r], 128[r–v], 131[v], 133[r–v], 134[r]. The reason why the *maks* was felt as illegal, even when it was openly collected by state officials, may be the originally pejorative sense of the term; cf. Qudāma, *Kharāj*, fols. 96[v]–97[r], tr. p. 56; Suyūṭī, *Risāla fī dhamm al-maks*, MS. Dār al-Kutub (Cairo), 1416 *Ḥadīth*; Forand, 'Notes on 'ušr and maks', pp. 137–41; for the etymology of the term cf. W. Björkman, article 'Maks' in *EI*[1]. The *ḥabba* $=\frac{1}{72}$ *dīnār*.

[4] See above, p. 91.

The *matjar* continued to purchase timber, iron, and lead imported from overseas and to resell them to internal traders with little profit. When it happened that the state needed them for the construction of a fleet or the manufacture of war equipment, it had to buy the very same goods from private merchants at a high price. Nābulsī's suggestion is that the *matjar* should only offer for sale, and at a high price to boot, what remained after the state had satisfied its needs.[1]

Under al-Nāṣir ibn Qalāwūn the *matjar* became sultani property, so that the revenue went, not to the treasury, but to the sultan. According to ʿAynī in *ʿIqd*, Karīm al-Dīn, who was the *kātib* to al-Nāṣir about 710/1310, suggested to the sultan that he should take the *matjar* into his possession. Al-Nāṣir did so, appointing him the *nāẓir al-k͟hāṣṣ*.[2] The revenue of the *matjar al-k͟hāṣṣ* was considerable. In 727/1327, al-Nāṣir ordered 1,000 *dirhams* to be paid from the *matjar* monthly as a retirement pension to the qadi Muḥammad ibn Jamāʿa.[3] In 737/1336, al-Nāṣir exempted a merchant called al-Ṣawwāf, who bought from him Ṣarg͟hitmis͟h al-Nāṣirī, from the payment of 100,000 *dirhams* on behalf of the *matjar*.[4]

As for export taxes, there is some information in the *Minhāj* where they are enumerated commodity by commodity. They were strictly defined, but not subject to a uniform *ad valorem* tax like imports. As Professor Cahen points out, these fixed amounts were calculated according to their value, which cannot now be specified, but the percentage does not appear to have been regular. Methods of assessment were different on imports and exports. In one case, the value was taken into account when the tax was calculated, in the other, it was assumed *a priori* without regard to market fluctuations.[5] In Mak͟hzūmī's time at Damietta, the tax for one exported *qīrāṭ* of cow-hide was $\frac{3}{4}$ *dīnār*, for 2 *qīrāṭ*s of buffalo and tanned hide $1\frac{1}{2}$ *dīnār*s. If the exports of a particular merchant exceeded his imports, he paid only $\frac{5}{16}$ *dīnār* per piece of cow-hide and $\frac{5}{8}$ *dīnār* per piece of buffalo-hide. When exporting *ḥūt* (a kind of fish without scales), the merchant importing goods taxed at 30 per cent had to pay $\frac{5}{6}$ *dīnār* for every thousand fish. Merchants who imported goods

[1] Nābulsī, *Lumaʿ*, pp. 45–6, tr. Cahen, 'Quelques aspects', pp. 109–10.
[2] ʿAynī, *ʿIqd*, 'C', xxiii. iii, fol. 379; see also Ibn Ḥajar, *Durar*, ii, p. 404.
[3] ʿAynī, *Badr*, fol. 19ᵛ; Maqrīzī, *Sulūk*, ii, p. 283.
[4] Ibn Ḥajar, *Durar*, ii, p. 206; Maqrīzī, *K͟hiṭaṭ*, ii, p. 404.
[5] Cahen, 'Douanes', p. 263.

taxed at 20 per cent paid $\frac{5}{12}$ *dīnār* per thousand, while others whose imports were taxable at only 10 per cent paid $\frac{5}{6}$ *dīnār* per thousand. When what was exported exceeded what was imported, a tax of $1\frac{1}{6}$ *dīnār*s per thousand was payable to the special treasury of the *dīwān*. For the tax on *ḥabas̲h̲ī* chickens, exporters who were also importers were assessed differently from those who brought no imports. The former paid $\frac{1}{2}$ *dīnār* per crate valued at 1 *dīnār* per unit, while the latter paid $\frac{1}{2}$ *dīnār* per crate, the tenth of the value, the *wājib* per unit, and one tenth of the tenth. The export tax on 100 *ardabb*s of corn was 25 *dīnār*s, and $2\frac{2}{3}$ *dīnār*s per 100 *ardabb*s of salt. If the exporter of flax paid on arrival at Tinnīs a tax of 30 per cent on his imports, he paid an export tax of $2\frac{1}{2}$ *dīnār*s per *s̲h̲ikāra* (sack of 390 *raṭl jarwī*). If he paid only 20 per cent on his imports, the export tax was $3\frac{1}{4}$ *dīnār*s; if 10 per cent it amounted to $4\frac{1}{2}$ *dīnār*s. For henna, he paid $\frac{1}{2}$ *dīnār* tax per *'idl* (sack), for carded cotton mats $\frac{1}{2}$ *dīnār* a piece; for exported sugar $\frac{1}{2}$ *dīnār* per *qafaṣ* (basket), or *k̲h̲ays̲h̲a* (sack); $\frac{5}{6}$ *dīnār* tax per 1,000 *ḥūt*; on *saljam* oil, olive oil, sesame oil, dregs of sesame oil, dried dates, compressed dates (*'ajwa*) up to the value of 5 *dīnār*s the tax was $\frac{1}{2}$ *dīnār*. Moreover, $1\frac{2}{3}$ *dīnār*s was imposed per 100 *ardabb*s of exported salt; and $\frac{1}{8}$ *dīnār* per *ardabb* of grain, coriander, caraway, anise, and cumin.[1] The available sources fail to show how long taxes on exports continued to be collected in the above amounts; not do they specify the extent or date of later changes, if any.

The main tax imposed on the merchandise of Muslim merchants was the *zakāt*. In theory, the *zakāt* was a tax on livestock, gold, silver, merchandise, horticultural and agricultural produce, for the benefit of the poor, the needy, the administrators of the *zakāt*, recent converts, slaves who could buy their freedom, insolvent

---

[1] Mak̲h̲zūmī, for Damietta, fols. 122ᵛ–124ᵛ, tr. Cahen, 'Douanes', pp. 288–90; for Tinnīs, fols. 131ᵛ–132ᵛ, tr. pp. 295–6; Labib, *Handelsgeschichte*, pp. 241–3. It seems that Egypt used to export fish in the period under study. Some Italian merchants stated in a petition addressed to Sultan al-Ādil that they had traded the greater part of their merchandise for *būrī* fish (a species of mullet), which had perished, so that they sustained a loss; cf. Amari, *Diplomi Arabi*, no. 23, pp. 70–1; Lopez and Raymond, *Medieval trade*, pp. 335–6; Stern, 'Petitions from the Ayyūbid period', *BSOAS*, xxvii (1964), pp. 1–10. Professor Cahen ('Douanes', p. 289) is somewhat hesitant when rendering *dajāj al-ḥabas̲h̲* as 'Poulets de l'armée (?)', presumably reading *ḥabas̲h̲* as *jays̲h̲*. The term '*ḥabas̲h̲*', chicken, is still used in Syria, but has, in the meantime, come to denote a turkey. He also (ibid., p. 296) translates *al-zayt al-ṭayyib* as 'huile de bonne qualité'. In fact it means 'olive oil'. This term is still known in some parts of Upper Egypt.

debtors, volunteers for the holy war, and wayfarers.[1] It is necessary to distinguish, from a comparatively early time onwards, between the real *shar'ī zakāt* and taxes, such as customs duties, etc., which were referred to as *zakāt* merely to provide them with a cover of *shar'ī* legality.

There is a lack of evidence concerning the *zakāt* in the Fāṭimid period, but it is probable that, according to Egyptian usage in pre-Fāṭimid times, people had the right to pay the *zakāt* directly to the beneficiaries without any interference on the part of the state. This assumption seems to be confirmed by Maqrīzī's statement that Saladin was the first ruler to collect the *zakāt* in Egypt. Maqrīzī quotes al-Fāḍil's *Mutajaddidāt* to the effect that, in Rabī' II 567/November 1171, the revenue from the *zakāt* was distributed among the poor, the needy wayfarers, and the insolvent debtors, and that the shares of the officials administrating the *zakāt*, new converts, warriors, and slaves desirous of emancipation were transferred to the *bayt al-māl*.[2]

It seems that the real *shar'ī zakāt*, which represented an alms tax in the strict sense of the word, continued to be collected by sultani officials for many decades after Saladin. It is said that al-Kāmil was in favour of voluntary payment of the *zakāt*, and permitted part of it to be distributed directly among the poor and needy, the jurists and pious people. The *zakāt* revenue having consequently decreased, some *ḍāmin*s asked to be granted its *ḍamān*. After Ibn Mammātī's failure to reform the *dīwān al-zakāt*, the *zakāt* was assigned to *ḍāmins*.[3] Presumably part of the *zakāt* revenue went towards the expenses of schools, mosques, and religious and charitable institutions. This is illustrated by the account of how Ibn Sa'īd al-Andalusī praised the *ḥalqāt* in the mosque of Fusṭāṭ and was told that teachers and students were maintained by funds from the *zakāt*.[4]

As for the *zakāt* on merchandise which Makhzūmī calls *zakāt*-

[1] Abū Yūsuf, *Kharāj*, pp. 76 ff.; Māwardī, pp. 108–20; Ibn Mammātī, pp. 308–17; J. Schacht, article 'Zakāt' in *EI*[1]; Cahen, article 'Bayt al-Māl' in *EI*[2].

[2] Maqrīzī, *Khiṭaṭ*, i, p. 108; Ziada, 'Dīwān al-zakāt', *al-Thaqāfa*, No. 211 (1943), p. 18; Rabī', *Nuẓum*, p. 54. The distribution of the *zakāt* to the needy under Saladin is often mentioned in al-Fāḍil's correspondence; cf. *Rasā'il al-Qāḍī al-Fāḍil* (MS. Brit. Mus., Add. 25757), fols. 10^v, 118^{r-v}; *al-Fāṣil min kalām al-Fāḍil* (MS. Brit. Mus., Add. 7307 Rich), fol. 14^v.

[3] Ibn Wāṣil, *Mufarrij*, fol. 311^v; Maqrīzī, *Khiṭaṭ*, i, p. 109, ii, p. 378; id., *Sulūk*, i, p. 260, tr. Blochet, 'D', p. 293.

[4] Ibn Sa'īd, *Mughrib*, i, p. 7.

ʿuyūn or *ʿurūḍ al-tijārāt*, he says that it applied to Muslim merchants who specialized in import and export. He exemplifies this by the case of a merchant who imports 200 *ardabb*s of corn worth 40 *dīnār*s, and of another who exports 100 *qinṭār*s of cotton worth 50 *dīnār*s. The former would be liable to a tax of 1 *dīnār*, and the latter to one of 1¼ *dīnār*, i.e. 2½ per cent as defined by the *S͟harīʿa*. The tax-collector had to bear in mind that the *zakāt* was not payable until a year from the date of the acquisition of the taxable goods, and take account of the certificates which referred to previous total or part payment of the *zakāt* in another locality. Mak͟hzūmī also comments on the *zakāt* payable by taxable portion (*niṣāb*); for instance, a man bringing a sack of flax to the value of 15 *dīnār*s (that is below the *niṣāb* of 20 *dīnār*s) would have to aver this fact on oath.[1]

The practice of the *zakāt* on merchandise mostly differed from its theory. Under Saladin, the *zakāt* paid by Muslim merchants usually exceeded the legal 2½ per cent, and was sometimes collected before the year from the date of acquisition of the goods had elapsed. Maqrīzī states that in 577/1181, a group of Kārimī merchants arriving from Aden had to pay the *zakāt* for 4 years.[2] On his

[1] Mak͟hzūmī, fols. 150r–152r; Cahen, 'Contribution', pp. 252–5; id., 'Douanes', pp. 269–70.

[2] Maqrīzī, *Sulūk*, i, pp. 72–3, tr. Blochet, 'B', p. 540; Rabīʿ, *Nuẓum*, p. 51. The first available reference to the Muslim Kārimī merchants relates to the year 456/1063–4 (see Dawādārī, *Durra muḍiyya*, p. 380). At Aden and Egypt, they traded in spices and other commodities and soon attained wealth and influence in all important eastern markets. The origin, the exact nature, the rise, the activities, and the causes of the decline of the *kārimiyya* are still obscure. The following references might prove helpful in further research on the Kārimī merchants: *Rasāʾil al-Qāḍī al-Fāḍil* (MS. Add. 25757), fol. 116r; Baybars al-Manṣūrī, *Zubda*, fol. 143r; Dawādārī, *Durr fāk͟hir*, pp. 57 ff.; Nuwayrī, xxvii, fol. 21, xxix, fol. 28, xxx, fol. 82; ʿUmarī, *Masālik* (MS. P.), fol. 145r–v (MS. A.S. 3434), fol. 138r; Ṣafadī, *Aʿyān* (MS. A.S. 2965) fols. 28v–29r; (A.S. 2966) fol. 147r; Ibn Ḥabīb, *Durra*, i (MS. Marsh 591) fols. 86v–87r; Ibn Tag͟hrī Birdī, *Manhal*, iii, fol. 95v; ʿAynī, *Badr*, fol. 28r; Abū S͟hāma, *Rawḍatayn*, ii, p. 37; Ibn al-Mujāwir ,pp. 147–8; Abū Mak͟hrama, ii, pp. 69, 115–16, 138; Ibn ʿAbd al-Ẓāhir, *Tas͟hrīf*, p. 52; Ibn Abī al-Faḍāʾil, pp. 555 ff., 644; al-Idfuwī, *Ṭāliʿ*, pp. 214, 335; Ibn al-Furāt, vii, p. 261, viii, pp. 62, 66; Ibn Kat͟hīr, xiv, p. 156; Qalqas͟handī, *Ṣubḥ*, iii, pp. 461, 468–9, 524, iv, p. 32, v, p. 281, viii, p. 77; id., *Ḍawʾ*, p. 253; Maqrīzī, *Sulūk*, i, pp. 72–3, 739, 899; ii, p. 340; Ibn Ḥajar, *Durar*, i, pp. 450–1, ii, pp. 143, 383–4, iii, pp. 186, 327, 429, iv, p. 148; Heyd, *Histoire du commerce*, ii, p. 59; Labib, 'al-Tujjār al-Kārimiyya', *MTM*, iv (1952), pp. 5–63; id., *Handelsgeschichte*, pp. 60–3, 112 ff.; id., 'Egyptian commercial policy' in Cook, *Studies*, pp. 66 ff.; Wiet, 'Les marchands d'épices', *CHE*, vii (1955), pp. 86 ff.; Ashtor, 'The Kārimī merchants', *JRAS* (1956), pp. 45–56; Fischel, 'The spice trade', *JESHO*, i (1957–8), pp. 157–74; Goitein, 'The beginnings of the Kārim merchants', in *Studies*, pp. 351–60; id., *Med. Soc.*, i, p. 149; Jacqueline Sublet,

arrival at Alexandria in 578/1183, Ibn Jubayr observed the reprehensible behaviour of tax-officials towards his Muslim fellow passengers, whose merchandise and personal effects were taken to the customs house and examined most carefully to assess the *zakāt*, though most of them were pilgrims. Consequently, they paid the *zakāt* regardless of what had been in their possession for less than one year.[1] Ibn Jubayr was also angered when he saw pilgrims and merchants subjected to bodily search by the *zakāt* collectors in Nile ports in Upper Egypt such as Minyat banī Khaṣīb, Akhmīm, and Qūṣ.[2]

These oppressive levies of the *zakāt* on merchandise provided Saladin with a considerable income. In 587/1191, he transferred the *zakāt* amounting to more than 50,000 *dīnār*s to the *dīwān al-usṭūl* to cover part of the cost of the fleet. The date indicates that it was a temporary measure, taken during the siege of Acre.[3] In the next year (588/1192), one Ibn Ḥamdān, who had been appointed to the *dīwān al-zakāt*, undertook to collect the sum of 52,000 *dīnār*s from the *zakāt* within one year.[4]

Nor was there any improvement in the position of the *zakāt*-payer after Saladin.[5] Some verses insulting Sultan al-ʿAzīz, which were written by the poet Ibn ʿUnayn on his arrival in Egypt from the Yemen, indicate that he was fleeced well in excess of the legal 2½ per cent *zakāt* tax on the merchandise he brought.[6] During the epidemic of 592/1195–6, an official appointed by al-ʿAzīz to the

'ʿAbd al-Laṭīf al-Takrītī et la famille des Banū Kuwayk, Marchands Kārimī', *Arabica*, ix (1962), pp. 193–6; Atiya, *Crusade, commerce*, pp. 197–9; Cahen, articles 'Ayyūbids' and 'Ḍarība' in *EI*²; Rabīʿ, *Nuẓum*, pp. 16, 51.

[1] Ibn Jubayr, pp. 39–40; Cahen, 'Douanes', p. 270; Rabīʿ, *Nuẓum*, p. 55. Ibn al-Mujāwir, writing in the first half of the thirteenth century, refers to the reprehensible treatment of passengers in Aden; cf. Ibn al-Mujāwir, i, pp. 138–9; Abū Makhrama, i, pp. 57–8; for Aden see also Ibn Baṭṭūṭa, ii, pp. 177–8.

[2] Ibn Jubayr, pp. 62–4. For the Nile traffic as reflected in the Geniza collection, cf. Goitein, *Med. Soc.*, i, pp. 295–301.

[3] Maqrīzī, *Khiṭaṭ*, ii, pp. 129, 194; id., *Sulūk*, i, pp. 107–8, tr. Blochet, 'C', p. 57; Rabīʿ, *Nuẓum*, p. 71. For Saladin's fleet, cf. Ehrenkreutz, 'The place of Saladin in the naval history', *JAOS*, lxxv (1955), pp. 100–16.

[4] Maqrīzī, *Khiṭaṭ*, i, p. 108; Rabīʿ, *Nuẓum*, p. 55.

[5] Having quoted Ibn Jubayr, Maqrīzī (*Khiṭaṭ*, i, p. 109) says: 'وكذلك يفعل في جميع أرض مصر منذ عهد السلطان صلاح الدين بن أيوب' 'This has been the practice in all parts of Egypt since the time of the Sultan Ṣalāḥ al-Dīn ibn Ayyūb.'

[6] Ibn ʿUnayn, *Dīwān*, p. 223; Ibn Khallikān, i, p. 298; Maqrīzī, *Khiṭaṭ*, i, p. 108, ii, p. 368; Rabīʿ, *Nuẓum*, p. 55.

dīwān al-zakāt was permitted to collect 52,000 *dīnār*s from the *zakāt* in one year, as much as was paid under Saladin in 588/1192.[1]

The *zakāt* on merchandise was collected not only in Cairo and other main towns, but also in the country. Nābulsī mentions *zakāt al-ṣādir* (which was evidently a *zakāt* on export) collected from Madīnat al-Fayyūm, and *zakāt al-dawlaba* which was collected in this city as well as in other places in Fayyūm such as Abū Kasā, Bamūya, Dhāt al-Ṣafā, and Sinnawris.[2] Makhzūmī is the only author to explain *māl al-dawlaba*, a sub-category of the *zakāt* payable by *arbāb al-ḥawānīt* (shopkeepers), but unfortunately gives no data to distinguish it from the *zakāt* on *'urūḍ al-tijārāt*.[3] It may be assumed that all shopkeepers in Egypt had to pay *zakāt al-dawlaba*, not on their transactions, but on their merchandise, whatever the location of their shops.

The Mamluks continued to collect the *zakāt* on merchandise from Muslim merchants. During financial crises, the *zakāt* was often collected illegally. It is said that Sultan Quṭuz collected the *zakāt* before it fell due, so that the taxpayers paid double *zakāt* in one year. These *maẓālim* were abolished by Baybars, but soon reintroduced and even increased.[4] *Zakāt al-dawlaba* in particular was abolished by Qalāwūn, who realized that it tended to impoverish the merchants.[5]

The abolition of *zakāt al-dawlaba* by Qalāwūn evidently did not include the *zakāt* payable by Muslim merchants arriving in Egyptian ports. Al-'Abdarī, arriving in Alexandria from the Maghrib around 688/1289 during the reign of Qalāwūn, observed—like his predecessor Ibn Jubayr—how tax collectors searched passengers, imposing taxes, and forcing them to swear that they had no hidden goods.[6] When al-Balawī arrived in Alexandria from Spain in 737/1337, he and his colleagues were sent to the *dīwān* for the imposition of taxes, mainly the *zakāt*. After an examination of their

[1] Maqrīzī, *Sulūk*, i, p. 132, tr. Blochet, 'C', p. 88.

[2] Nābulsī, *Fayyūm*, pp. 29, 47, 70, 105, 109; see Cahen, 'Régime', p. 20; id., 'Contribution', p. 253 n. 4.

[3] Makhzūmī, fol. 150^{v}; Cahen, 'Contribution', p. 253 and n. 3, Labib, *Handelsgeschichte*, p. 236.

[4] Ibn 'Abd al-Ẓāhir, *Rawḍ*, p. 907; Ibn Iyās, *Badā'i'*, i, p. 96.

[5] Shāfi' ibn 'Alī, *Faḍl*, fol. 124^{r-v}, Baybars al-Manṣūrī, *Zubda*, fol. 99^{v}; Nuwayrī, xxix, fols. 1, 22; Ṣafadī, *Nuzha*, fol. 54^{v}; Ibn Duqmāq, *Jawhar*, fol. 114^{v}; Khālidī, fol. 69^{r}; 'Aynī, *'Iqd*, 'C', xxi. i, fol. 5; Ibn al-Furāt, vii, p. 152; Maqrīzī, *Sulūk*, i, p. 664, tr. Quatremère, ii. i, p. 2.

[6] 'Abdarī, fol. 50^{r}, ed. al-Fāsī, p. 93.

luggage and strict bodily search, they were taxed 2 *dīnār*s on each 10 *dīnār*s and 2 *dirham*s on each 10 *dirham*s, i.e. 20 per cent. Al-Balawī rightly complains of injustice; the *zakāt* was levied regardless of the time of the acquisition and the *niṣāb*.[1] There is a reference in Qalqashandī's *Ṣubḥ* which may—in view of the continuity of tax usage—throw some light on the *zakāt* in the period under consideration. Qalqashandī says that merchants and others had to pay 5 *dirham*s on each 200 on entering the city, but were otherwise unhampered in the pursuit of their trade there, and not further taxed if they returned within the tax year—which was 10 months—with the same amounts of goods. However, the number of tax-free visits was restricted to four. The Kārimī merchants had to pay a yearly *zakāt* in every city they traded in.[2]

The tax imposed on the imports of *dhimmī* merchants was called *wājib al-dhimma*. Ibn Mammātī states that it was a tax in the form of an internal toll in three cities, Miṣr (Fusṭāṭ), Alexandria, and Akhmīm. It was based on the mutual agreement of the *dhimmī*s of these cities who, as a result, were liable only to one half of the previous dues.[3] There is a piece of evidence in Maqrīzī to the effect that ʿUmar ibn al-Khaṭṭāb ordered Abā Mūsā al-Ashʿarī, the *wālī* of Basra, to collect from *dhimmī* merchants 1 *dirham* per 20. Relying on this information, Dr. Labib states that the tax payable by *dhimmī* merchants was generally 10 per cent, increased to practically 15 per cent by the unavoidable bribes.[4] Dr. Labib's statement is implausible, as more than 500 years divide Ibn al-Khaṭṭāb's caliphate from Ibn Mammātī's time, enough for a tax to undergo many changes.[5]

According to Ibn Mammātī, the *zakāt* and *wājib al-dhimma* only were collected from merchants in ʿAydhāb, which indicates that only Muslim and *dhimmī* merchants (from Islamic territories) were engaged in Red Sea trade at the beginning of the Ayyūbid era. Obviously it is doubtful whether Italians were ever able to penetrate there, and very probable that no Hindu or Chinese went further than Aden.[6] Until the end of the period under study,

[1] Balawī, *Tāj*, fol. 27v.

[2] Qalqashandī, *Ṣubḥ*, iii, p. 461; Labib, *Handelsgeschichte*, pp. 245–6; id., 'Egyptian commercial policy', p. 74.

[3] Ibn Mammātī, p. 349.

[4] *Khiṭaṭ*, i, p. 103; Labib, *Handelsgeschichte*, p. 246.

[5] *Wājib al-dhimma* had been abolished before the time of Maqrīzī; cf. *Khiṭaṭ*, i, p. 111.

[6] Ibn Mammātī, p. 327; Cahen, 'Douanes', pp. 221–2. Prof. B. Lewis has

'Aydhāb seems to have maintained its status as a port for non-European trade. The Ayyūbid and Mamluk sultans enhanced the prosperity of 'Aydhāb by protecting the land route to Qūṣ.[1]

Under the Mamluks, Qaṭyā in eastern Egypt, which merchants coming from Iraq and Syria by land could not bypass, developed into an important customs station with fixed taxes on various kinds of goods.[2] Describing a trip made by his father to investigate the affairs of the Bedouin tribes in Sharqiyya in 703/1303–4, Dawādārī states that the Badriyya route was guarded by al-'Ā'id trying to prevent merchants from evading sultani dues in Qaṭyā. Dawādārī's remark that merchants exported from Upper Egypt goods not available in Syria such as flax and its derivatives, indicates that both export and import dues were payable in Qaṭyā.[3]

There are reports by travellers in transit through Qaṭyā, who saw the tax-officials examining passengers and merchants, their luggage and merchandise for the purpose of tax assessment. The yield in revenue seems to have been as high as a thousand gold *dīnār*s daily according to Ibn Baṭṭūṭa, who passed through Qaṭyā in transit on his way to Syria in 726/1326–7. This figure seems somewhat exaggerated, unless he refers to the main trading season.[4] Al-Balawī, on his way to Jerusalem in 738/1337, complains of the

suggested that the Fāṭimids aimed at diverting the eastern trade from the Persian Gulf to the Red Sea, strengthening Egypt and weakening Iraq; cf. Lewis, 'The Fatimids and the route to India', *RFSE* Univ. Istanbul, xi (1949–50), pp. 50–4; id., 'Government, society and economic life', *Camb. Med. Hist.*, iv. i, p. 648; for the decline of the once profitable trade with China cf. Lewis, 'Government', p. 649; for the India trade immediately before the period under study, cf. Goitein, 'Letters and documents' in *Studies*, pp. 329–50.

[1] The burden of taxes imposed on the merchants landing or arriving in 'Aydhāb, and the lack of safety on the road between 'Aydhāb and Qūṣ forms the subject of complaint in some letters from the Geniza; cf. T.–S. B.39, fol. 480; B.40, fol. 56; B.42, fol. 70; T.–S. N.S. J., fol. 117, T.–S. N.S. 321 fol. 23r–v; Brit. Mus. Or. 5535, ii. For 'Aydhāb until 1341 cf. Ibn Shaddād, *Rawḍa*, fol. 15v; Dawādārī, *Durr maṭlūb*, fol. 26r; Ibn Taghrī Birdī, *Manhal*, ii, fol. 101r; Ibn Jubayr, pp. 65–9; Ibn Baṭṭūṭa, i, pp. 109–11; Abū al-Fidā, *Taqwīm*, p. 121; Ibn al-Wardī, *Kharīda*, p. 60; Ibn Duqmāq, *Intiṣār*, v, p. 35; Maqrīzī, *Sulūk*, i, p. 700; Ibn Iyās, *Nashq*, fol. 53r–v; id., *Badā'i'*, i, p. 160; Maqrīzī (*Khiṭaṭ*, i, p. 202) states that the road from 'Aydhāb to Qūṣ was still in use until 760/1358–9; Qalqashandī (*Subḥ*, iii, pp. 468–9) mentions 'Aydhāb, Quṣayr, al-Ṭūr, Suez, as four ports where merchandise imported by Kārimī merchants used to be taxed. It seems that the cases described by Qalqashandī occurred in his lifetime.

[2] 'Umarī, *Ta'rīf*, p. 175; Qalqashandī, *Subḥ*, iii, p. 470: Ibn Iyās, *Nashq*, fol. 66v–r. Despite the tension between the Ilkhānids and the Mamluks, the trade between Iraq and Egypt did not come to a halt; cf. Khaṣbāk, 'Aḥwal al-'Irāq', pp. 167–8.

[3] Dawādārī, *Durr fākhir*, pp. 114–15.

[4] Ibn Baṭṭūṭa, i, pp. 112–13.

reprehensible behaviour of tax-officials in Qaṭyā, who literally wrenched taxable goods from passengers' hands.[1]

As for the sales tax, Maqrīzī's list containing different Fāṭimid *mukūs* abolished by Saladin when he came to power, shows that the main items were tolls collected from almost anything on entering or leaving Cairo or Fusṭāṭ, such as spices, cotton, linen, cows, sheep, henna, coal, etc. As Professor Goitein points out, it is not always possible to distinguish between these tolls and the purchase tax, since both were called, among other names, *wājib* (due). According to Maqrīzī's list, market dues provided the Fāṭimids with a considerable amount of money. The Cairo slave market brought a yearly revenue of 500 *dīnār*s, the market for riding animals (donkeys or mules) 400 *dīnār*s and the camel market 250 *dīnār*s yearly. Evidence from the Geniza shows that market dues used to be collected by a tax farmer who was designated either as such, *ḍāmin al-sūq*, or *ṣāḥib al sūq* (the master of the market), obviously at the sale of goods on the spot.[2]

Although there is a lack of information about sales taxes under the Ayyūbids, the reintroduction by Saladin himself or his successors, of taxes previously abolished by Saladin, cannot be doubted. A letter from the Geniza from the early Ayyūbid period shows that a market tax of 2 *dirham*s was payable per donkey and one of 4 *dirham*s per camel. Professor Goitein assumes that, as prices for donkeys fluctuate in the Geniza documents between 2 and 5 *dīnār*s, with 3 as an average, the purchase tax must have amounted to about $1\frac{2}{3}$ per cent.[3] During the reign of al-ʿAzīz ʿUthmān, 5 *dirham*s were collected in *zakāt* on the sale of a camel for 5 *dīnār*s. As the *niṣāb* of the *zakāt* definitely exceeded 5 *dīnār*s, it is probable that this 5 *dirham*s was actually a sales tax.[4]

[1] Balawī, *Tāj*, fol. 72v. For the decline in the revenue from customs at Qaṭyā in later times cf. Lapidus, *Muslim cities*, pp. 30, 39; Udovitch, 'England to Egypt', pp. 116–17.

[2] Maqrīzī, *Khiṭaṭ*, i, pp. 104–5; Goitein, *Med. Soc.*, i, pp. 194, 270–1. *Ṣāḥib al-sūq* is mentioned in a papyrus from about the second or third century A.H., cf. Grohmann, *Arabic papyri*, v, pp. 152–3.

[3] T.–S. 13 J.26, fol. 21 in Goitein, *Med. Soc.*, i, pp. 270–1. Two unpublished and undated fragments from the Geniza (T.–S. B.39, fol. 342; B.42, fol. 209) are obviously lists of clothes, covers, etc., and names of sellers possibly made by market officials. Neither of them contains a mention of tax. Two other fragments from the Vienna papers (A.Ch. 9531, 9533r–v) form part of a report on revenue probably collected at the sheep market (*sūq al-ghanam*) in Cairo. Unfortunately the fragments are too decayed to ascertain whether these transactions were taxed.

[4] Maqrīzī, *Khiṭaṭ*, i, p. 108.

Mentions of a sales tax are quite frequent under the Mamluks. In 648/1250–1, the vizier al-Fā'izī imposed a tax on the sale of domestic animals such as horses, camels, donkeys, etc., as well as on slaves and other sales transactions.[1] Before 661/1263, the inhabitants of Alexandria were taxed ¼ *dīnār* per *qinṭār* (of weighed merchandise). Since it was a heavy burden on the inhabitants of this city, it was abolished by Baybars.[2] Maqrīzī in *Sulūk* mentions, under the year 739/1338–9, a tax called the *qarārīṭ* imposed on property transactions. In K͟hiṭaṭ, he comments that it was a tax on sales of property amounting to 20 *dirhams* per 1,000 *dirhams* (2 per cent). He states that *ḍamān al-qarārīṭ* was abolished in 778/1376–7 by Sultan S͟ha'bān, al-Nāṣir's grandson.[3] Maqrīzī also mentions—without reference to the period—that Nile fish was taxed when offered for sale in the Cairo fish market.[4]

Muqarrar ṭarḥ al-farārīj or *al-farrūj* used to be collected on the compulsory sale of chickens. It appears that, during the Ayyūbid period, the *fallāḥīn* were provided by the state with chickens to rear. At the end of a specific period, the chickens were divided into 3 portions, one of which was claimed by the sultan, one by the *muqṭa'*, and the remainder left to the *fallāḥ* as a consideration (*ujrat al tarbiyya*). In practice, the *muqṭa'* received more than one third.[5] In order to avoid the trouble of collecting their share, the sultans seem to have made the rearing of chickens a kind of state monopoly, and conferred that right in the form of *iqṭā'*s upon *muqṭa'*s. As a result, all chickens had to be bought from the *ḍāmin* and there were heavy fines on the unauthorized sale of chickens. This type of *iqṭā'* was cancelled in the Nāṣirī *rawk* of 715/1315.[6]

The *maks* or *ḥuqūq sāḥil al-g͟halla* was a tax levied on corn brought to Cairo and Fusṭāṭ harbours, where corn was taxed before it was

[1] Ibid., ii, p. 90.

[2] Ibn Wāṣil, *Mufarrij*, fol. 423r–v; Ibn 'Abd al-Ẓāhir, *Rawḍ*, p. 1000; Baybars al-Manṣūrī, *Zubda*, fols. 60v–61r; Ibn al-Furāt, MS., vi, fol. 33r; 'Aynī, *'Iqd*, 'C', xx. iii, fol. 496. The above-mentioned sources do not specify what merchandise was subject to this tax.

[3] Maqrīzī, *Sulūk*, ii, pp. 458–9; id., K͟hiṭaṭ, i, p. 106. This statement refutes that of Ibn Iyās (*Badā'i'*, i, p. 176) to the effect that this 2 per cent tax on the sale of property was abolished by al-Nāṣir Muḥammad.

[4] Maqrīzī, K͟hiṭaṭ, i, p. 108.

[5] Nābulsī, *Fayyūm*, pp. 43, 57, 61–3, 65, 68, 71, 77, 87, 123, 126, 133; see Cahen, 'Régime', p. 22.

[6] Nuwayrī, xxx, fol. 91; Ibn Ḥabīb, *Tad͟hkira*, fol. 67v; 'Aynī, *'Iqd*, 'C', xxiii. i, fol. 55; Maqrīzī, K͟hiṭaṭ, i, p. 89; id., *Sulūk*, ii, p. 151; Ibn Tag͟hrī Birdī, *Nujūm*, ix, pp. 46–7; Labib, *Handelsgeschichte*, p. 251.

sold. It seems that this tax was Fāṭimid or even earlier in origin. Al-Ḥākim abolished the *mukūs* collected from passengers on corn and rice in 398/1007–8, and taxes on corn brought to harbours and markets in 403/1012–13.[1] This measure seems to have been as temporary as the abolition of all taxes on crops in transport by al-Ẓāhir in 415/1024, which caused a fall in the price of bread.[2] Ibn Muyassar's statement that the exemption from the payment of arrears of *maks al-ghalla* was announced in 526/1132, as well as its abolition by Saladin on his accession to power, indicate that it must have been reintroduced in the meantime.[3]

There is a lack of information on the corn tax under the Ayyūbids. The first mention of a tax on corn under the Mamluks occurs in the year 698/1299 when the vizier Sunqur al-Aʿsar imposed one *kharrūba* (that is less than one *dirham*) per *ardabb* of corn, to be paid by the purchaser.[4] This tax seems to have been increased later, especially on corn brought to Cairo and Fusṭāṭ harbours (*sāḥil al-ghalla*). The official tax per *ardabb* grew to 2 *dirhams*, and an additional ½ *dirham* for the sultan. The total was estimated at 4,600,000 *dirhams* a year, and was conferred in the form of *iqṭā*ʿs on four hundred *muqṭa*ʿs, the share of each ranging from approximately 3,000 to 40,000 *dirhams*.[5] This type of *iqṭā*ʿ was cancelled in the Nāṣirī *rawk* of 715/1315.[6] However, al-Nāṣir introduced a tax on flour (*maks al-qamḥ*), which he abolished in 720/1320.[7] He also seems to have reintroduced *maks al-ghalla*, because it was said in 724/1324 that al-Nāṣir abolished *maks al-ghalla* in Egypt and Syria.[8]

As for *niṣf al-samsara* (half the brokerage), which was a tax collected from each *simsār* or *dallāl* (broker), the sources state that it was introduced in Egypt in 699/1299–1300, after the defeat of al-

[1] Maqrīzī, *Ittiʿāẓ*, MS. fol. 62r–v; Ibn Ḥammād, *Akhbār*, p. 54; Dawādārī, *Durra muḍiyya*, p. 286.

[2] Musabbiḥī, xl, fol. 259r–v; Maqrīzī, *Ittiʿāẓ*, fol. 79r.

[3] Ibn Muyassar, ii, p. 75; Maqrīzī, *Khiṭaṭ*, i, p. 104.

[4] Ibn Ḥajar, *Durar*, ii, p. 177; Maqrīzī, *Khiṭaṭ*, ii, p. 84.

[5] Nuwayrī, xxx, fol. 91; ʿAynī, *ʿIqd*, 'C', xxiii. i, fol. 55; Ibn Duqmāq, *Jawhar*, fols. 130v–131r; Dawādārī, *Durr fākhir*, p. 286; Maqrīzī, *Khiṭaṭ*, i, pp. 88–9; ii, p. 131; id., *Sulūk*, ii, p. 150; Ibn Taghrī Birdī, *Nujūm*, ix, pp. 44–5; Labib, *Handelsgeschichte*, pp. 249–50.

[6] Ṣafadī, *Nuzha*, fol. 80r; Anonymous, *Tārikh*, fol. 28r; see above, pp. 53 ff.

[7] Ibn Ḥabīb, *Tadhkira*, fol. 76r.

[8] ʿUmarī, *Masālik* (MS. P.), fol. 144r; Ibn Ḥabīb, *Tadhkira*, fol. 80v; Ibn Kathīr, xiv, p. 111; see Lapidus, 'The grain economy of Mamluk Egypt', *JESHO*, xii (1969), pp. 1–15.

Nāṣir by the Mongols. Before that date, any broker used to receive 2 *dirhams* brokerage on each 100 *dirhams*, that is, 2 per cent. After that date, the *simsār* split the 2 per cent between himself and the *dīwān*.[1] Evidence from the Geniza shows that the average commission for general goods was around 2 per cent, payable by the buyer and more rarely by the seller.[2] As a result of the introduction of *niṣf al-samsara*, the brokers tried dishonest methods to prevent their share from dropping below the 2 per cent mark, which could only be done at the expense of the seller. *Niṣf al-samsara* was abolished by al-Nāṣir in the *rawk* of 715/1315.[3]

Apart from taxes on sales, there were licence fees obligatory on shops, public baths, mills, bakers, etc., and termed by the sources *al-amwāl al-hilāliyya* or *al-māl al-hilālī*. The word *hilālī* implies that they used to be collected according to the lunar calendar, unlike the taxes related to the harvest, which were levied each solar year.[4]

Dr. Labib states that *al-māl al-hilālī* consisted of a series of taxes on merchandise in shops and bazaars, but does not enlarge on his statement or distinguish between the *hilālī* tax and ordinary sales tax.[5] Professor Goitein's elucidation of this type of tax—even without mention of the term *hilālī*—is more helpful. Relying on Geniza documents, he states that each store—workshops, shops for the sale of foodstuffs and other commodities—had to have a licence, for which dues were paid every month of the Muslim year, because stores, like houses and apartments, were hired on monthly leases.[6]

Tārīkh al-Fayyūm by Nābulsī contains valuable information concerning the *hilālī* taxes collected in Fayyūm. In Madīnat

[1] Maqrīzī, *Khiṭaṭ*, ii, p. 84; id., *Sulūk*, i, p. 899; Ibn Ḥajar, *Durar*, ii, p. 177.

[2] Goitein, *Med. Soc.*, i, p. 185; Professor Goitein (ibid., pp. 160–1) points out that the sources mention three types of middlemen: *simsār*, *dallāl*, and *dallāla* 'female broker', although the distinction between them is often vague. The first two seem to be designations of brokers in general, while *dallāla*, still in use in the old districts of Cairo, may refer to women door-to-door pedlars dealing with ladies' clothes. For the *dallāl* see also Bāshā, *Funūn*, ii, pp. 514–16.

[3] Nuwayrī, xxx, fol. 91; Ṣafadī, *Nuzha*, fol. 80r; Ibn Ḥabīb, *Tadhkira*, fol. 76v; 'Aynī, *'Iqd*, 'C', xxiii. i, fol. 55; Maqrīzī, *Khiṭaṭ*, i, p. 89; id., *Sulūk*, ii, pp. 150–1; Ibn Taghrī Birdī, *Nujūm*, ix, pp. 45–6. Both Dimashqī (*Maḥāsin*, pp. 43–4) and Ibn al-Ḥājj (*Madkhal*, iv, pp. 78–9) warn people to beware of brokers and their dishonesty. For the Ottoman brokerage dues (*simsārīye* and *dellālīye*) cf. Lewis, 'Studies', pp. 484, 494 ff.

[4] See Nuwayrī, viii, p. 228; Maqrīzī, *Khiṭaṭ*, i, p. 107.

[5] Labib, *Handelsgeschichte*, p. 246; id., 'Egyptian commercial policy', p. 74.

[6] Goitein, *Med. Soc.*, i, pp. 269–70.

al-Fayyūm for example, the *hilālī* taxes on the *dīwānī* public baths amounted to 170 *dīnār*s, on *maʿmal al-farrūj* (factory-hatched chickens) $347\frac{1}{2}$ *dīnār*s, on the tannery and the sieve factory 205 *dīnār*s, on the fuller's shop $174\frac{1}{4}$ *dīnār*s, and on two wax and silk factories $33\frac{5}{6}$ *dīnār*s. The *hilālī* taxes collected in Sinnawris on the shops, the linen and silk weavers, the mill, and the chicken hatchery, amounted to $341\frac{7}{12}$ *dīnār*s and one *ḥabba*.[1]

By the end of the Ayyūbid era, the right of collection of the *hilālī* taxes seems to have been frequently conferred in the form of *iqṭāʿ*s upon *muqṭaʿ*s. Nuwayrī has preserved, in *Nihāyat al-arab*, a copy of a *manshūr* issued by Shajar al-Durr to the qadi Ibn Bint al-Aʿazz, the *nāẓir* of one of the *dīwān*s, dated 8 Rabīʿ I 648/10 June 1250, by which she conferred upon him, in the form of *iqṭāʿ*, $\frac{2}{3}$ of the *hilālī* taxes collected from certain quarters in Madīnat al-Fayyūm.[2]

There is little information concerning the *hilālī* taxes under the Mamluks, but it is very probable that they were calculated in the *ʿibra* of each *iqṭāʿ*. Sometimes the taxes collected in certain *iqṭāʿ*s came from the *hilālī* taxes on public baths and *funduq*s (hostelries). In the city of al-Manṣūra, for example, most of the revenue came from the *hilālī* taxes assigned to *muqṭaʿ*s.[3] On the basis of a late Geniza document from the Mamluk period Professor Goitein has stated that the due for a store licence was called *ḥisba*, or payment to the *muḥtasib*.[4] This cannot be true, as the *hilālī* taxes continued to be collected under the Mamluks, while the term *ḥisba* seems to have been applied to the monthly tax called *al-mushāhara*, collected for the *muḥtasib* in later Circassian times until its abolition in 922/1516.[5]

[1] Nābulsī, *Fayyūm*, pp. 27–8, 107–8; see also Cahen, 'Régime', p. 15.

[2] Nuwayrī, xxviii, fol. 63; there is an undated fragment of a petition in the Geniza collection signed by 25 persons, presumably merchants, asking permission to enter Egypt. It seems that it was addressed to Shajar al-Durr, as it states 'والسلام على مجلسها السامى ورحمة الله وبركاته' 'Peace and God's mercy and blessings be upon her noble presence.' According to the contemporary historian al-Makīn ibn al-ʿAmīd, Shajar al-Durr enjoyed a certain authority, even during the sultanate of Aybak; cf. T.–S. B.39, fol. 219; Ibn al-ʿAmīd, *Akhbār*, p. 165; for the full titles of Shajar al-Durr cf. *RCEA*, xi, p. 212; *CIA*, i, pp. 111–12.

[3] Ibn Duqmāq, *Intiṣār*, v, p. 71; for *funduq*, cf. R. Le Tourneau, article *Funduk* in *EI*[2]; Goitein, *Med. Soc.*, i, pp. 349–50.

[4] Goitein, *Med. Soc.*, i, pp. 270, 367.

[5] Ibn Iyās, *Badāʾiʿ*, iii, pp. 12–13, 59.

c. *Taxes on property*

There is no evidence in the available sources of taxes on houses under the Ayyūbids. It is said that when al-Fā'izī became vizier to Sultan Aybak in 650/1252, he introduced, for the first time in Egypt, what was called *al-taṣqīʿ wa al-taqwīm*.[1] The only known historian to explain the meaning of the *taṣqīʿ* and the *taqwīm* in economic terms is Ibn Shaddād in *al-Rawḍa al-ẓāhira*. According to him, the *taṣqīʿ* was equivalent to the rent of two months per year, while the *taqwīm* was a tax imposed on the value of the property itself in *dīnār*s, one *dirham waraq* to be levied yearly per *dīnār*.[2]

Both the *taṣqīʿ* and the *taqwīm* seem to have been imposed merely on property in Cairo and Fusṭāṭ, and remained in force after the vizierate of al-Fā'izī. In 653/1255—in the reign of Aybak—Shajar al-Durr exempted the amir Nūr al-Dīn ʿAlī ibn Hāshim from the payment of any *taṣqīʿ* whatever.[3] When Quṭuz came to power in 657/1259 and was preparing troops to meet the Mongols, a property tax based on the rent of one month was levied on property. The tax burden does not seem to have been easy to bear, since Baybars abolished the *taṣqīʿ* and the *taqwīm* for political motives on his accession to the sultanate.[4]

The abolition of the *taṣqīʿ* and the *taqwīm* by Baybars was not final. It appears that, in times of financial trouble, the Mamluk sultans frequently resorted to the imposition of taxes on property. In Muḥarram 700/September 1300, after the defeat of al-Nāṣir by the Mongols, every owner of property had to contribute a certain amount of money to the equipment of the troops.[5] According to Ibn Kathīr, in Damascus at that time the amount was estimated on

[1] Ibn al-ʿAmīd, *Akhbār*, pp. 165–6; Maqrīzī, *Khiṭaṭ*, ii, pp. 90, 188; id., *Sulūk*, i, p. 384, tr. Quatremère, i. i, p. 37. *Al-ṣuqʿ* is a district or tract; cf. *Muḥīṭ al-muḥīṭ*, ii, p. 1195.

[2] Ibn Shaddād, *Rawḍa*, fol. 215r; 'التصقيع وهو أخذ أجرة شهرين من الأملاك فى كل سنة والتقويم وهو أن تقوم الدار فيؤخذ عن كل دينار درهم ورقا'.

[3] Nuwayrī, xxvii, fol. 123.

[4] Shāfiʿ ibn ʿAlī, *Ḥusn*, fol. 11r; Ibn ʿAbd al-Ẓāhir, *Rawḍ*, p. 907; Ibn Shaddād, *Rawḍa*, fol. 215r; Nuwayrī, xxviii, fol. 1. Dawādārī, *Durra zakiyya*, fols. 27v–28r; Dhahabī, *Tārīkh* (MS. Bodl., Laud Or. 305), fol. 254v; Ibn al-Furāt, MS. vi, fol. 33r; Ibn Waṣīf Shāh, fol. 65r; Khālidī, fol. 67r; Maqrīzī, *Khiṭaṭ*, ii, p. 301; id., *Sulūk*, i, p. 437, tr. Quatremère, i. i, p. 117; Ibn Iyās, *Nashq*., fol. 30r; id. *Badāʾiʿ*, i, p. 96.

[5] Maqrīzī, *Sulūk*, i, p. 906, tr. Quatremère, ii. ii, p. 174; Ibn Ḥajar, *Durar*, ii, p. 178.

the basis of four months' rent. It is probable that such was the amount paid by the owners of property in Cairo and Fusṭāṭ.[1]

D. *Taxes on persons*

The *jāliya* (plur. *jawālī*), which the *fiqh* calls more technically *jizya*, is a poll-tax imposed on non-Muslims.[2] According to Ibn Mammātī, the *jawālī* tax was imposed, in theory, on free men only, not on women, children, monks, slaves, or madmen. There seems to have been some controversy on whether to exempt the very old and the poor who had no source of income, and how much tax to collect from a *dhimmī* who was converted to Islam in the course of the year, or from the heirs of a *dhimmī* who died during the year.[3] Both Makhzūmī and Ibn Mammātī agree that—in their time—this tax varied according to the degree of wealth, the highest yearly tax being $4\frac{1}{6}$ *dīnār*s, the medium tax 2 *dīnār*s and 2 *qīrāṭ*s (that is, $2\frac{1}{12}$ *dīnār*s), and the lowest tax about $1\frac{5}{8}$ *dīnār*s. Only Ibn Mammātī mentions the supplementary tax of $2\frac{1}{4}$ *dirham*s for the agents and *mushidd* to cover the cost of collection. Makhzūmī remarks, however, that the wealthy as a class were far from numerous, and the majority of those liable to taxation belonged to the poorest class.[4]

It is very probable that both Makhzūmī and Ibn Mammātī describe a system of Fāṭimid or earlier origin which had been inherited by the Ayyūbids. Two documents from the Vienna papers prove that the Fāṭimids did not always collect the *jawālī* tax at a flat rate. A fragment of a receipt dated 344/955–6 was given to a person from Ushmūnayn who paid less than one *dīnār* in poll-tax.[5]

[1] Ibn Kathīr, xiv, p. 14.

[2] According to the papyri (cf. Grohmann, 'New discoveries', ii, pp. 160–1; id., *Arabic papyri*, iii, pp. 24, 220, 222, iv, pp. 96–7, 121, 142) as well as the Vienna papers (A.Ch. 8, fol. 7140; 10, fol. 8137; A.Ch. 12185) the term *jāliya* or *jawālī* seems to have been in use in Egypt from the early Islamic era. For the semantic development of the term, cf. Abū Yūsuf, *Kharāj*, pp. 3, 49; Khʷārizmī, *Mafātīḥ*, p. 59; Khafājī, *Shifā'*, p. 77; Dozy, op. cit., i, p. 210; Zayyāt, 'al-Jawālī', *al-Mashriq*, xli. ii (1947), pp. 1–2; Løkkegaard, *Islamic taxation*, pp. 140–1; Cahen, articles 'Djawālī' and 'Djjizya' in *EI*².

[3] Ibn Mammātī, pp. 317–18; for the *Sharī'a* viewpoint on the *jizya* cf. Abū Yūsuf, *Kharāj*, pp. 122–8; Qurashī, *Kharāj*, pp. 71–7 tr. Ben Shemesh, *Taxation in Islam*, i, pp. 52–62; Abū 'Ubayd, *Amwāl*, pp. 36–7; Qudāma, *Kharāj*, fols. 89ʳ–90ᵛ, tr. Ben Shemesh, op. cit., ii, pp. 42–4; Māwardī, pp. 135–40; Shayzarī, *Nihāya*, p. 107; Ibn al-Ukhuwwa, p. 45; Nuwayrī, viii, pp. 234–40; Tritton, *The Caliphs*, pp. 216–18, tr. Ḥabashī, *Ahl al-dhimma*, pp. 238–40; Fattal, pp. 264–91.

[4] Makhzūmī, fols. 143ᵛ–144ʳ; Ibn Mammātī, pp. 318–19; Rabī', *Nuẓum*, p. 45.

[5] A.Ch. 12185.

In a complete receipt from the same collection, dated 11 Ramaḍān 416/15 November 1025, Abū Ilyas ibn Mīnā paid the amount of 1 *dīnār*, $\frac{2}{3}$ and $\frac{1}{2}$ *qīrāṭ* in *jizya* for the year 415.[1] Relying on a Geniza document dated A.D. 1182, Professor Goitein states that $4\frac{1}{6}$ *dīnār*s paid by a physician corresponded exactly to the highest yearly rate as specified by Ibn Mammātī, and also found evidence to confirm the exact lowest grade of tax in Saladin's time.[2]

It seems that the *jawālī* provided Saladin with a considerable revenue. This is corroborated by al-Fāḍil's statement in *Mutajaddidāt al-ḥawādith* that the *jawālī* for the year 587/1191 amounted to 130,000 *dīnār*s.[3] Saladin's son, al-ʿAzīz ʿUthmān, relied on the revenue from the *jawālī* to such an extent that he contracted in 592/1196 a considerable loan from his amirs, expecting them to be fully repaid by the *jawālī* of the following year. Transactions of this kind, however, cannot but have imposed a heavy burden on the *dhimmī*s, who probably paid more than the usual amount of poll-tax to repay the sultan's debt.[4]

Nābulsī implies in *Tārīkh al-Fayyūm* that the *jawālī* tax was assessed in every village of Fayyūm at an over-all rate of 2 *dīnār*s a head for non-Muslims. Thus, for example, 343 *dhimmī*s in Madīnat al-Fayyūm had to pay 686 *dīnār*s, 269 residents 538 *dīnār*s, and 74 non-residents 148 *dīnār*s. In Bājah, most of whose inhabitants were Copts, *jawālī* to a total of 204 *dīnār*s was levied on 102 individuals: 90 residents paid 180 *dīnār*s and 24 *dīnār*s were imposed on 12 non-residents in Lower Egypt. Nābulsī also speaks of Bamūya, where the Coptic community had two churches. Of the 160 local *dhimmī*s, 109 residents paid 218 *dīnār*s, and 51 non-residents in Lower and Upper Egypt 102 *dīnār*s.[5]

Proesssor Cahen does not exclude the possibility of a more differentiated usage and a more equitable distribution in the country and the large towns to which Makhzūmī implicitly refers ($4\frac{1}{6}$, $2\frac{1}{12}$, $1\frac{5}{8}$).[6] However, an unpublished fragment from the Geniza, possibly from the same period, which is a list of non-Muslim residents (*min al-qāṭinīn*) of Cairo and Fusṭāṭ, especially such coming

1 A.Ch. 7379.

2 Oxford F.56 (2821), fol. 45, I.7 in Goitein, 'Evidence on the Muslim poll tax from non-Muslim sources', *JESHO*, vi (1963), p. 286.

3 Maqrīzī, *Khiṭaṭ*, i, p. 107; Rabīʿ, *Nuẓum*, p. 46.

4 Maqrīzī, *Sulūk*, i, pp. 133, 134; Rabīʿ, *Nuẓum*, pp. 46–7.

5 Nābulsī, *Fayyūm*, pp. 29, 64, 71.

6 Cahen, 'Contribution', p. 248.

from Alexandria, Sharqiyya, Gharbiyya, etc., mentions 2 *dīnārs* in instalments as the maximum collected from those financially capable of paying the tax. According to this list, there were 300 residents in Cairo and Fusṭāṭ, including those who came from the country, who were financially unable to pay tax, so that it was only worth while to collect the *jāliya* from 200 individuals.[1] Thus it seems that it is Nābulsī's information that is correct, and that there was a uniform rate of *jāliya* of two *dīnārs* per head on all non-Muslims whether in large or small towns, capital or village, at least in so far as the later Ayyūbid era is concerned.

What a heavy burden the *jawālī* tax on non-Muslims represented is illustrated by evidence from the Geniza.[2] In a letter, presumably written in A.D. 1225, a schoolmaster from Qalyūb who had earned some money by copying books complains to a relative in Cairo that his earnings in Qalyūb did not suffice to pay the poll-tax or buy clothes, but only provided food for himself alone. He sends four books copied by himself, expressing, somewhat hesitantly, the hope that the proceeds will free him from his predicament.[3] The sender of an unpublished and undated letter of recommendation found in the same collection and perhaps coming from the period under consideration, informs the correspondent that if he were not too busy with his work in the country, he would accompany the bearer of the letter to help him obtain exemption from the *jawālī* tax. He adds that the latter had been ill-treated when he could not acquit himself of the *jāliya* and had gone to the capital as *ṭārī'* (a stranger in transit).[4] There is further evidence from the Geniza to show that any *dhimmī* leaving his domicile even for a short period had to carry with him a *barā'a* (receipt), showing that he had paid his *jāliya* for the current year.[5]

There are few data on the *jawālī* tax under the Mamluks, but it

[1] T.–S. B.38, fol. 95. The payment of the *jāliya* in instalments is sometimes referred to in the Geniza documents; cf. Goitein, 'Evidence', p. 289; id., 'Bankers' accounts from the eleventh century A.D.', *JESHO*, ix (1966), p. 66 and n. 1.

[2] From Fāṭimid times, there is a letter to Ephraim ibn Shemariah from his friend Isaac, who asks for money to pay the tax-collector to save him from prison (T.–S. 8 J21, fol. 6 in Mann, *Jews*, i, p. 102, ii, pp. 109–10); see also Goitein, *Med. Soc.*, i, p. 300.

[3] T.–S. 13 J22, fol. 9 in Goitein, 'Evidence', pp. 279–80.

[4] T.–S. B.41, fol. 109.

[5] Goitein, 'The Cairo Geniza', *SI*, iii (1955), pp. 85–6; id., 'Evidence', p. 283; for the *barā'a*, cf. Khwārizmī, *Mafātiḥ*, pp. 55–6; Grohmann, 'New discoveries', ii, pp. 161, 162; Lewis, article 'Daftar', in *EI*².

seems that it weighed heavily on the *dhimmīs* who were frequently obliged to pay double the legal amount of the *jawālī* tax as, for instance, ordered by the vizier al-Fā'izī in 650/1252.[1] It seems that this unfair treatment of the *dhimmīs*, who often paid double *jāliya* under Baybars, continued for many years.[2] In 682/1283, Qalāwūn tried to relieve this burden, not so much by decreasing the amount of the tax in question, but by deferring the date of payment from Ramaḍān to Muḥarram. According to Ibn Mammātī, the *jawālī* used to be collected yearly at the beginning of Muḥarram, but in early Ayyūbid times in Dhū al-Ḥijja. Possibly owing to a financial crisis, this date had been shifted to Ramaḍān at a date not mentioned in the sources. It seems therefore that Qalāwūn merely attempted to right a previous wrong.[3] Qalāwūn's generous gesture must have been temporary, as the month of Ramaḍān continues to figure in Qalqashandī's *Ṣubḥ* as the date of payment of the *jawālī* tax.[4]

Before 715/1315, the revenue from the *jawālī* tax went directly to the treasury, and was not conferred in the form of *iqṭā*'s. After the Nāṣirī *rawk*, the *jawālī* tax was calculated in the *'ibra* of each *iqṭā'* and collected by the *muqṭa*'s for themselves and their *ajnād* exactly as other kinds of revenues in the *iqṭā'*.[5] However, the new local character of the *jawālī* tax gave Copts the opportunity to evade payment by moving from one village to another. Whenever the *muqṭa'* or his clerks demanded payment, they refused under the pretext that they were only temporary residents of the village. Naturally, the *muqṭa'* preferred to accept a part of the *jawālī* tax instead of nothing. According to the contemporary historian Nuwayrī, some clerks in amirs' *dīwāns* began to collect the *jāliya* in amounts of about 4 *dirhams* per head instead of the actual dues of 56 *dirhams*. Nuwayrī adds that, before the Nāṣirī *rawk*, the *ḥushshār* (the *jawālī* gatherers) used to travel all over the country

[1] Ibn al-'Amīd, *Akhbār*, p. 165; Maqrīzī, Khiṭaṭ, ii, p. 497; id., *Sulūk*, i, p. 384; tr. Quatremère, i. i, p. 37.

[2] Maqrīzī, *Sulūk*, i, p. 640; tr. Quatremère, i. ii, p. 154; id. Khiṭaṭ, ii, p. 370; Zayyāt, 'al-Jawālī', p. 5.

[3] Ibn Mammātī, p. 319; Ibn al-Furāt, vii, p. 259; Maqrīzī, *Sulūk*, i, p. 712; tr. Quatremère, ii. i, p. 59. According to a document from the Vienna papers (see above, p. 109) the *jawālī* tax under the Fāṭimid Caliph al-Ẓāhir was payable in Ramaḍān.

[4] Qalqashandī, *Ṣubḥ*, iii, p. 462.

[5] Maqrīzī, Khiṭaṭ, i, p. 88; id., *Sulūk*, ii, pp. 153, 169; Ibn Taghrī Birdī, *Nujūm*, ix, pp. 43–4, 50; see above, pp. 54–5.

collecting the tax from the individual taxpayer wherever he was, giving him a *barā'a* which would be accepted in his village.[1]

Documentary evidence seems to confirm Nuwayrī's statement. It emerges from the fragment of a document in the Vienna papers, possibly written during the reign of al-Nāṣir after 715/1315, that a taxpayer refused to pay the *jawālī* tax to the officials of an amir and even dared to put up resistance.[2]

Sultan al-Nāṣir seems to have realized the danger of considering the *jawālī* a local tax, especially since part of it was used towards the salaries of qadis and other religious men. As soon as al-Nashw was appointed the *nāẓir al-khāṣṣ*, with the purpose of introducing economies, he ordered the officials of the *jawālī* to cease paying the qadis, *shuhūd*, and jurists from the *jawālī* revenue. Instead, the entire proceeds of the *jawālī* were handed over to *khizānat al-khāṣṣ* (the sultan's 'private' treasury).[3]

Another tax on the *dhimmī*s in Egypt was *muqarrar al-Naṣāra*. There is no mention of this tax in the sources from the Ayyūbid era. In the Mamluk period, Ibn al-Furāt and Maqrīzī state that, when Qalāwūn came to power in 678/1279, he abolished this tax which had been in force for the last eighteen years. This is conclusive evidence that it had been introduced by Sultan Baybars in 660/1261–2.[4] Despite its name which implies that it was limited to Copts, this tax of one *dīnār* per head was collected yearly from both Copts and Jews in Egypt. The revenue from this source was spent on military purposes.[5]

A tax on the income of registrars and witnesses was introduced in 700/1300 after the defeat of al-Nāṣir's army by the Mongols, for

[1] Nuwayrī, xxx, fol. 91; Maqrīzī, *Khiṭaṭ*, i, p. 90.

[2] A.Ch. 3, fol. 2007: '. . . فراحوا يطلبوا منه الجوالى امتنع عن دفع الجوالى وتقوا (*sic*) على المماليك وهو مخا . . .' 'They demanded the *jawālī* from him. He refused to pay the *jawālī* and adopted an intransigent attitude towards the mamluks although he was trans-[gressing the law].'

[3] 'Aynī, *'Iqd*, 'A', xvii, fol. 146^r; Maqrīzī, *Sulūk*, ii, p. 475; for the methods of collection of the *jawālī* tax, see below, pp. 134–6. For the poll-tax in Iraq under the Mongols cf. Minovi and Minorsky, 'Naṣīr al-Dīn', pp. 763, 776, 780, 783–5. For the *jizye* levied on non-Muslims under the Ottomans, cf. Lewis, '*Notes and documents*', pp. 2, 10–11; id., 'Studies', pp. 484–5; Heyd, *Ottoman documents*, pp. 121–2, 163, 167–8, 170.

[4] Ibn al-Furāt, vii, p. 152; Maqrīzī, *Sulūk*, i, p. 664; tr. Quatremère, ii. i, pp. 2–3.

[5] 'Aynī, *'Iqd*, 'C', xxi. i, fol. 5; Ibn Taghrī Birdī, *Manhal*, v, fol. 33^v; Ibn Duqmāq, *Jawhar*, fol. 114^v; Khālidī, fol. 69^r; Maqrīzī, *Khiṭaṭ*, i, p. 106.

the consequent preparation of a military campaign. The vizier Sunqur al-Aʿsar imposed a 40-*dīnār*s tax on every registrar, and 20 *dīnār*s on every witness in the capital. Led by the Mālikī chief qadi Ibn Makhlūf, the registrars and witnesses objected to this heavy burden and succeeded in having this tax removed in the same year.[1]

As to *rusūm al-afrāḥ* (the wedding taxes), neither their date of introduction nor the amount are mentioned in the sources. The only information available is that they were collected all over the country by *ḍāmin*s, and were abolished by al-Nāṣir during the *rawk* of 715/1315.[2]

Little is known of the tax on prisoners, which is seemingly of Mamluk origin, and appears to have amounted to 6 *dirham*s payable by each prisoner per day, even if he spent only a moment in prison. The right of collection of this tax was conferred in the form of *iqṭāʿ*s upon some *muqṭaʿ*s who used to employ *ḍāmin*s for the purpose of collection. It was abolished among others by the Nāṣirī *rawk* of 715/1315.[3]

E. *Taxes collected for the maintenance of public services*

These were mainly imposed to cover the expenses of some public services, that is, their proceeds were assigned to purposes such as salaries of certain officials not provided for by *iqṭāʿ* grants, costs of the improvement of irrigation and cultivation of the soil in Egyptian provinces, and the maintenance of mints and the state institution for weights and measures.

Rusūm al-wilāya or *rusūm al-wulā* were collected on behalf of

1 Nuwayrī, xxix, fol. 120; Ibn Ḥajar, *Durar*, ii, p. 178; Maqrīzī, *Sulūk*, i, p. 907, tr. Quatremère, ii. ii, p. 174.

2 ʿAynī, *ʿIqd*, 'C', xxiii. i, fol. 55; Maqrīzī, *Khiṭaṭ*, i, p. 89; id., *Sulūk*, ii, pp. 151–2; Ibn Taghrī Birdī, *Nujūm*, ix, p. 47.

3 Nuwayrī, xxx, fol. 91; Ṣafadī, *Nuzha*, fol. 80v; Maqrīzī, *Khiṭaṭ*, i, p. 89; id., *Sulūk*, ii, p. 151; Ibn Taghrī Birdī (*Nujūm*, ix, p. 46) states that it amounted to 100 *dirhams*. According to a document from *Maḥkama* (*Ḥujjat waqf* Sayf al-Dīn Baktamur dated 14 Muḥarram 707/16 July 1307), prisons in Egypt were of two kinds: (*a*) *sujūn al-ḥukm al-ʿazīz*, under the supervision of qadis, for offenders against the *Sharīʿa*; (*b*) *sujūn al-wulā* for other delinquents. Baktamur was assigned a share from *waqf* revenue to cover the cost of the weekly distribution of bread for prisoners, and for the purchase of 2,000 palm-leaf fans in summer; cf. *Maḥkama*, Box 4, no. 20. For prisons in the period under consideration, cf. Maqrīzī, *Khiṭaṭ*, ii, pp. 188–9; Ziada, 'al-Sujūn fī Miṣr', *al-Thaqāfa*, nos. 260, 262, 279 (1943–4); ʿĀshūr, *al-Mujtamaʿ al-Miṣrī*, pp. 97–100; Bakhīt, *Mamlakat al-Karak fī al-ʿahd al-Mamlūkī* (M.A., The American University of Beirut, 1965), pp. 115–20.

wālīs and *muqaddamīn* in Cairo, Fusṭāṭ, and the Egyptian provinces apparently to finance their salaries and the salaries of their assistants such as the *shurṭa*. There is no evidence in the sources to show whether this tax was of Fāṭimid or even pre-Fāṭimid origin or introduced by Saladin simultaneously with the military *iqṭā'* system. According to Maqrīzī, Saladin exempted the inhabitants of Fusṭāṭ, Cairo, Fayyūm, and Upper Egypt from this tax in 577/1181–2.[1] Maqrīzī specifies neither the amount of this tax nor the reason for this exemption, which seems to have been a temporary measure, as this tax was reintroduced at an unknown date and increased until it reached, in Fusṭāṭ alone, 104,000 *dirhams nuqra* in the reign of Baybars in the Mamluk era. The inhabitants of Fusṭāṭ were exempted from this tax in 662/1264.[2] In Ramaḍān 663/July 1265, Baybars exempted, as a charitable gesture, the inhabitants of the Daqahliyya and the Mirtāḥiyya provinces from *rusūm al-wilāya* to the amount of 24,000 *dirhams nuqra*.[3]

The above evidence suggests that this exemption benefited only certain localities in the year of exemption after the lapse of which the tax was automatically reimposed. It appears that exemptions were frequent, especially at the accession of a new sultan, until *rusūm al-wilāya* was finally abolished in 715/1315 by Sultan al-Nāṣir Muḥammad.[4]

Another tax was levied on the inhabitants of Fusṭāṭ to cover the expenses of roast meat, sweets, and fruit for the Nile flood festival. There is evidence in both Maqrīzī and Qalqashandī to prove that the Fāṭimid caliphs financed this festival, but it is not known whether the Ayyūbid sultans imitated their predecessors in this respect, or resorted to taxation to provide funds for this purpose.[5] Thus evidence is limited to the fact that this tax was collected in the Mamluk era until its abolition by Qalāwūn, who put the responsibility of such expenses on the *bayt al-māl*.[6]

[1] Maqrīzī, *Sulūk*, i, p. 76, tr. Blochet, 'B', p. 545.

[2] Baybars al-Manṣūrī, *Zubda*, fol. 64r; Ibn 'Abd al-Ẓāhir, *Rawḍ*, p. 1025; Nuwayrī, xxviii, fol. 28; Maqrīzī, *Sulūk*, i, p. 514, tr. Quatremère, i. i, p. 240; for *dirham nuqra* see below, p. 174 n. 4.

[3] Nuwayrī, xxviii, fol. 34; Ibn al-Furāt, MS., vi, fol. 78r; Maqrīzī, *Sulūk*, i, p. 538, tr. Quatremère, i. ii, p. 19.

[4] Nuwayrī, xxx, fol. 91; Ṣafadī, *Nuzha*, fol. 80r; 'Aynī, *'Iqd*, 'C', xxiii. i, fol. 55; Maqrīzī, *Khiṭaṭ*, i, p. 89; id., *Sulūk*, ii, p. 151; Ibn Taghrī Birdī, *Nujūm*, ix, p. 46.

[5] Maqrīzī, *Khiṭaṭ*, i, pp. 470–9; Qalqashandī, *Ṣubḥ*, iii, pp. 516–21.

[6] Ibn Iyās, *Badā'i'*, i, pp. 120–1, for the *bayt al-māl* see below, pp. 147–9.

Apart from *al-jusūr al-baladiyya* (the small irrigation dams) whose maintenance was an important function of the *muqṭaʿ*, there were *al jusūr al-sulṭāniyya* (the great irrigation dams) which were of paramount importance for the irrigation of the provinces; their construction and maintenance was financed by the imposition on the *fallāḥīn*, in both the Ayyūbid and the Mamluk eras, of a tax called *muqarrar al-jusūr*. According to Ibn Mammātī, this tax used to be imposed on the inhabitants of districts whose irrigation dams needed improvement or reconstruction, and was payable in kind, that is, by supplying labour, beasts of burden, harrows, hay, in amounts varying according to the cultivated area. Later, in Ibn Mammātī's lifetime, the inhabitants of the districts concerned were given the option of paying a tax of 10 *dīnār*s in place of the above obligations.[1] According to Khiṭaṭ and *Ṣubḥ*, *muqarrar al-jusūr* was collected for a long time after Ibn Mammātī.[2] It seems to have been an Ayyūbid tradition taken over by the Mamluks, that taxes were imposed to finance additional projects for the maintenance of the great irrigation dams. For example, al-Nāṣir found in 740/1339 that the irrigation dam from Shibīn to Banhā al-ʿAsal, which he had constructed in the preceding year, was threatened by the high level of the Nile during the flood. To erect a stockade in the shape of a dam to protect the dam proper, al-Nāṣir imposed on the population of the country a surtax of $\frac{1}{8}$ *dirham* per *dīnār* tax which brought him about 480,000 *dirhams*.[3]

Muqarrar al-mashāʿiliyya was payable on permits for the removal of ordure from mosques, schools, houses, etc. This tax, not mentioned in the sources of the Ayyūbid period, was presumably introduced by the Mamluks. The amount of the tax was assessed, rather arbitrarily, from case to case, by the *ḍāmin* to whom the right of collection was assigned. The *ḍāmin* used to impose very high taxes, as the removal of ordure was conditional on his permission. The tax was abolished by al-Nāṣir in 715/1315.[4]

The revenue of the mint derived from gold and silver coined according to Egyptian regulations on behalf of European as well

[1] Ibn Mammātī, ed. Atiya, pp. 342–4; ed. Najjār, pp. 16–17; for small irrigation dams, see above, p. 70.

[2] Maqrīzī, *Khiṭaṭ*, i, p. 110; Qalqashandī, *Ṣubḥ*, iii, pp. 448–9.

[3] Maqrīzī, *Sulūk*, ii, p. 493. For the irrigation dam between Shibīn and Banhā al-ʿAsal, see above, p. 71.

[4] Maqrīzī, *Khiṭaṭ*, i, p. 89; id., *Sulūk*, ii, p. 152; Ibn Taghrī Birdī, *Nujūm*, ix, p. 48.

as Muslim merchants who came to Egypt to trade. Those who delivered gold or silver to the mint had to pay fees, intended to cover the expenses of the mint. The remainder went to the treasury.[1]

According to Ibn Mammātī, before 586/1191 the charge collected for coining gold *dīnār*s in the Cairo mint, including the *ujra* of the mint workers, amounted to 3·4 per cent of the coined *dīnār*s. After this date, the charge was reduced to 3 per cent, an amount confirmed by Makhzūmī. As for the charge for coining silver *dirhams* in Cairo, it amounted to 1·45 per cent according to Ibn Mammātī, or 1 per cent according to Makhzūmī. Makhzūmī states that they charged 33⅓ *dīnār*s for each 1,000 *dīnār*s, and ½ *dīnār* for each 1,000 *dirhams* in the mint of Alexandria.[2] Ibn Baʿra, who lived under al-Kāmil, stresses, when describing the loss undergone by gold of different types in the refining process required for Egyptian *dīnār*s, that the tax imposed on the coinage of *dīnār*s consisted of a percentage of the gold to be coined. Combined, the tax and mint workers' charge (*rasm wājib al-sikka wa ujrat al-ḍarrābīn*) amounted to 5 *mithqāl*s for every 100 foreign *mithqāl*s.[3]

It seems that the incorporation of the tax in the minting charge, coupled with inadequate supervision of the mint after the reign of al-Kāmil, resulted in a decrease of revenue from the mint. On the evidence of Nābulsī, who describes the mint of al-Ṣāliḥ Ayyūb, the revenue from the mint which had once reached 3,000 *dīnār*s monthly, and had soared, in the years 636–637/1238–40 to the record height of 80,000 *dīnār*s, fell to less than 100 *dīnār*s a month. Nābulsī's explanation is that the staff of the mint intentionally abandoned the custom of registering the names of clients who delivered gold to the mint in order to evade the *zakāt*. In consequence, if a client died in a remote place, mint officials appropriated the money, merely paying an insignificant increase in tax. This obviously deterred merchants from delivering all the gold they possessed to the mint. Another deterrent was that the mint began to refine different types of gold together, to derive increased profit from the difference in the quality of the gold. This suggests

[1] See below, p. 178.

[2] Ibn Mammātī, pp. 331–3; Makhzūmī, fols. 139r–140v; Rabīʿ, *Nuẓum*, p. 49. For the description of the two mints of Cairo and Alexandria, cf. Balog, *The coinage of the Mamluk sultans*, pp. 50–1.

[3] Ibn Baʿra, pp. 58–61; for *mithqāl* see below, p. 193 n. 2.

that more profit went to the staff of the mint than to the treasury by the end of the Ayyūbid era.[1]

The above data prove that the income yielded by the mint varied on the whole, in proportion to the quantities of bullion passing through the mint. It seems that the Ayyūbid sultans found it difficult to confer the mint in the form of *iqṭā*ʿs on *muqṭa*ʿs or even assign the right of the collection to *ḍāmin*s against a fixed sum paid in advance. Prudence dictated that an institution which coined official currency should remain under the control of the sultan. Thus, apart from the salaries and wages of the staff, the revenue from the mint went straight to the treasury. In the course of time, the rapid decrease in the number of coins produced and the consequent decrease in the amount of tax flowing into the mint must have induced the sultans to assign the tax collections from the mint to professional collectors. What seems to support this assumption is that the *ḍāmin*s of the mint petitioned Baybars in 662/1264 to abandon the Nāṣirī *dirhams*. But the sultan merely reduced their *ḍamān* from 250,000 to 200,000 *dirhams*.[2]

The state institution for manufacturing weights and measures was called *dār al-ʿiyār*. Price lists of copper, iron, wood, and staff salaries were supplied by the treasury. Regulations required that all weights and measures should be brought from *dār al-ʿiyār*, where they were also adjusted and repaired against a fixed charge. Saladin assigned the revenue from this institution for the maintenance of the Cairo wall. *Dār al-ʿiyār* continued to perform these functions until and probably beyond the time of Maqrīzī.[3]

F. *War tax*

This type of tax was collected in the Mamluk era whenever the sultan made preparations for a campaign.[4] The Ilkhānid custom of collecting contributions for army equipment from the wealthy in

[1] Nābulsī, *Lumaʿ*, pp. 52–4; tr. Cahen, 'Quelques aspects', pp. 113–14; Rabīʿ, *Nuẓum*, p. 50. For the losses in the refining process of different types of gold, cf. Ibn Baʿra, pp. 58–61.

[2] Ibn ʿAbd al-Ẓāhir, *Rawḍ*, p. 1014; Maqrīzī, *Khiṭaṭ*, ii, p. 206; id., *Sulūk*, i, p. 508, tr. Quatremère, i. i, p. 233.

[3] Ibn Mammātī, pp. 333–4 and notes: Maqrīzī, *Khiṭaṭ*, i, pp. 110, 464; Rabīʿ, *Nuẓum*, p. 50. Ṭūsī mentions tax levied on weights; cf. Minovi and Minorsky, 'Naṣīr al-Dīn', pp. 762, 775 and n. 4.

[4] For mobilization of the Mamluk expeditionary forces on the eve of their move, cf. Ayalon, article 'Ḥarb', in *EI*².

Iraq, and requiring the inhabitants to accommodate and feed troops, seems to point to the *wāfidiyya* as the source for the introduction of a campaign-tax to Egypt.[1] It seems that the revenue from this tax went to the *nafaqa* paid to the amirs on the eve of a campaign.[2] In 658/1259–60, when Quṭuz was calling up his troops to fight the Mongols, he imposed a special war tax of one *dīnār* per person, whether male or female. This tax was abolished when Baybars came to power in the same year,[3] a relief measure which was not permanent, as the tax was repeatedly reimposed during Baybars' reign, though on merchants only, and then abolished by Sultan Qalāwūn on his accession in 678/1279. Both sultans seem to have been prompted by purely political motives.[4] Be this as it may, the war tax was reintroduced in 700/1300–1, in the reign of al-Nāṣir, under the name of *muqarrar al-khayyāla* (cavalry tax), before a campaign against the Mongols. It was imposed on people renowned for their wealth, people who led lives of ease and those who enjoyed an independent income, merchants and those who plied a trade or a craft, in Fusṭāṭ as well as Cairo. Even Copts and Jews contributed to this tax, though they were normally obliged to pay a *dīnār* per person for military expenses in both peace and war.[5]

An additional war tax was levied to provide rewards for heralds of military victories. The sources contain no mention of the origin of this tax, which seems to have been rooted in an Ayyūbid tradition handed down to the Mamluks. This tax also appears to have been confined to Cairo and Fusṭāṭ, as victories were first announced in the capital. The contributions of individuals were assessed according to their social class and wealth. Although this tax was abolished on Qalāwūn's accession to the sultanate in 678/1279, it seems that it was re-established at a date not mentioned in the sources.[6]

[1] Cf. Ibn al-Fuwaṭī, *Ḥawādith*, p. 430; Khaṣbāk, 'Aḥwāl al-'Irāq', p. 138; id., *al-'Irāq*, p. 114.

[2] See above, pp. 33–4.

[3] Shāfi' ibn 'Alī, *Ḥusn*, fol. 11^{r}; Khālidī, fol. 67^{r}; Nuwayrī, xxviii, fol. 2; Dawādārī, *Durra zakiyya*, fols. 27^{v}–28^{r}; Ibn Waṣīf Shāh, fol. 65^{r}; Maqrīzī, *Khiṭaṭ*, ii, p. 301; id., *Sulūk*, i, p. 437, tr. Quatremère, i. i, p. 117; Ibn Iyās, *Badā'i'*, i, p. 96.

[4] Ibn Taghrī Birdī, *Manhal*, v, fol. 33^{v}; Ibn Duqmāq, *Jawhar*, fol. 114^{v}; Anonymous, *Tārīkh*, fol. 17^{r}.

[5] Baybars al-Manṣūrī, *Zubda*, fol. 222^{r}; id., *Tuḥfa*, fol. 75^{r}; Nuwayrī, xxix, fol. 120; Ibn Abī al-Faḍā'il, p. 537; Maqrīzī, *Sūlūk*, i, p. 898, tr. Quatremère, ii. ii, p. 167; see above, p. 112.

[6] 'Aynī, *'Iqd*, 'C', xxi. i, fol. 5; Ibn Duqmāq, *Jawhar*, fols. 114^{v}–115^{r}; Khālidī,

G. *Taxes on vice*

These taxes, some of which seem to go back to pre-Ayyūbid times, were imposed on the production of intoxicants such as *mizr* (a kind of beer), *khumūr* (wine), and hashish, and on prostitution. The jurists often opposed taxation of this kind which, as they felt, was both an infringement of the *Sharīʿa* and an encouragement of sin. A distinct and prolonged conflict is observable, all through the history of the vice taxes, between the desire to combat vice in accordance with religious conscience, and the reluctance of the rulers to renounce the abundant revenue it provided. Successive sultans repeatedly abolished these taxes, but these abolitions were never permanent. When Saladin exterminated the Fāṭimids in 567/1171, he abolished the tax on the *mizr* brewery.[1] He may also have abolished the tax on wine, as Maqrīzī relates that owners of wine shops in Alexandria approached, in 567/1171, Najm al-Dīn Ayyūb, Saladin's father, offering him money. It seems that he was successful in persuading his son to permit the sale of wine in Alexandria.[2] He may have argued that it was impossible to prohibit wine-drinking in Alexandria, where there were numerous foreign merchants. Even during his stay in Syria, Saladin's interest in the suppression of vice in Egypt does not seem to have flagged. In one of his letters to Saladin in 574/1178–9, al-Fāḍil informs him of the efforts of al-ʿĀdil's officials to close brothels and incarcerate prostitutes.[3]

During the monetary crisis which occurred in the reign of al-ʿAzīz ʿUthmān in consequence of the low flood of the Nile of 590/1193, the taxes on vice were reintroduced, obviously to compensate for the lack of revenue, especially as agricultural pursuits were neglected. *Mizr* breweries were taxed in proportion to their production. Some shops had to pay as much as 16 *dīnār*s daily; so did the hashish mill in Ḥārat al-Maḥmūdiyya.[4] The taxes on *mizr* and

fol. 69r; Anonymous, *Tārīkh*, fol. 17r. Maqrīzī (*Ighātha*, pp. 72–5) divides the contemporary population of Egypt into seven categories, the first of which is the ruling class and the last the poor and destitute; see also Popper, *Systematic notes*, ii, pp. 107–18; M. Rodinson, 'Histoire économique et histoire des classes sociales dans le monde musulman', in Cook, ed., *Studies*, pp 139–55. For taxes and other sources of revenue utilized for the maintanance of the navy, cf. above, pp. 77 n. 6, 86, 98.

[1] Maqrīzī, *Khiṭaṭ*, i, p. 105.

[2] Id., *Sulūk*, i, p. 45, tr. Blochet, 'B', p. 502; Rabīʿ, *Nuẓum*, p. 52.

[3] Iṣfahānī, *Barq*, iii, fols. 70v–71r; id., *Sanā*, fol. 194v.

[4] Maqrīzī, *Sulūk*, i, p. 119, tr. Blochet, 'C', pp. 74–5; id., *Khiṭaṭ*, ii, p. 5; Ibn Iyās, *Badāʾiʿ*, i, pp. 73–4.

wine were assigned in the form of a *ḍamān* for 12,000 *dīnār*s in Jumādā II 592/May–June 1196. After two months, the wine *ḍamān* alone amounted to 17,000 *dīnār*s.[1] The wine tax was abolished by al-ʿĀdil I in 612/1215 in Damascus and the rest of his sultanate, which obviously implies Egypt, only to be reimposed by one of al-ʿĀdil's successors at a date not mentioned in the sources.[2] It continued to be collected until the first year of the Mamluk era. According to Ibn Wāṣil and Maqrīzī, the prohibition of wine and the abolition of taxes connected with it was proclaimed on 27 Shawwāl 648/22 January 1251, under Aybak. It is very probable that it was done to raise the morale of the troops as well as of the civilian population of Egypt as al-Nāṣir Yūsuf ibn al-ʿAzīz, the Ayyūbid, the then sultan of Syria, was advancing with his army towards Egypt at that time.[3] This assumption seems to be confirmed by the fact that, after the defeat of al-Nāṣir and the appointment of al-Fā'izī to the vizierate, at the end of the same year, taxes on *khumūr*, *mizr*, hashish, and prostitution were reimposed and the right of their collection assigned to *ḍāmin*s.[4]

Ibn ʿAbd al-Ẓāhir and others state that, in 663/1264–5, Baybars abolished a tax on *mizr* in the whole of Egypt, which had been conferred upon a group of *muqṭa*ʿs, who were given compensation.[5] In 664 or 665/1265–7, Baybars abolished the tax on hashish which yielded 40,000 *dirham*s yearly, ordering addicts to be punished.[6] In 667/1269, taxes on *khumūr* and *khawāṭī* (prostitutes) followed suit. As the right of their collection had been assigned to *muqṭa*ʿs, Baybars compensated them by grants of other *iqṭā*ʿs.[7] Thus the custom of assigning to *muqṭa*ʿs the right to collect vice taxes in the form of *iqṭā*ʿs may have begun under Baybars.

[1] Maqrīzī, *Sulūk*, i, pp. 134, 136; tr. Blochet, 'C', pp. 90, 92.

[2] Nuwayrī, xxvii, fol. 12; Ḥanbalī, *Shifā'*, fol. 54r; Kutubī, *ʿUyūn* (MS. Fatih), fol. 26r; ʿAynī, *ʿIqd*, 'B', xiii, fol. 177r; Ibn Kathīr, xiii, p. 69; Maqrīzī, *Sulūk*, i, p. 182; tr. Blochet, 'C', p. 157; Ibn Taghrī Birdī, *Nujūm*, vi, pp. 169–70; Rabīʿ, *Nuẓum*, p. 52.

[3] Ibn Wāṣil, *Mufarrij*, fol. 381r–v; Maqrīzī, *Khiṭaṭ*, ii, p. 208.

[4] Maqrīzī, *Khiṭaṭ*, ii, p. 90.

[5] Ibn ʿAbd al-Ẓāhir, *Rawḍ*, p. 1052; Nuwayrī, xxviii, fol. 33; Ibn al-Furāt, MS., vi, fol. 65r–v; Maqrīzī, *Sulūk*, i, p. 525, tr. Quatremère, i. ii, pp. 4–6; id., *Khiṭaṭ*, i, pp. 105–6; Labib, *Handelsgeschichte*, p. 248; see above, p. 44.

[6] *Shāfi*ʿ ibn ʿAlī, *Ḥusn*, fol. 90v; Nuwayrī, xxviii, fol. 39; Ibn al-Furāt, MS., vi, fol. 108r; Ibn Waṣīf Shāh, fol. 68r; Ibn Duqmāq, *Jawhar*, fol. 102r; Anonymous, *Tārīkh*, fol. 8r; Maqrīzī, *Khiṭaṭ*, i, p. 106.

[7] Ibn ʿAbd al-Ẓāhir, *Rawḍ*, p. 1160; Dawādārī, *Durra zakiyya*, fol. 64r; Ibn al-Furāt, vi, fol. 156v; Ṣafadī, *Nuzha*, fol. 53r; Ibn Kathīr, xiii, p. 254; Maqrīzī, *Khiṭaṭ*, i, p. 106; id., *Sulūk*, i, p. 578, tr. Quatremère, i. ii, pp. 67–8.

This abolition of the wine tax was not final. After a year or two the right of its collection was assigned, not to *muqṭa*ʿs, but to *ḍāmin*s, perhaps because, at that time, Baybars needed ready money more than service. This tax yielded the incredible figure of a thousand *dīnār*s daily—or possibly yearly. In 669/1271, Baybars again abolished the wine tax and prohibited the drinking of wine in Egypt.[1]

Sultan Qalāwūn reintroduced the wine tax in 678/1280 but abolished it after a few days, alarmed by the sudden increase in drunkenness.[2] Qalāwūn remained faithful to his decision, as he even reminded his son al-Ṣāliḥ in a memorandum dated 681/1282–3 of the necessity to suppress vice and renounce income from this source for the favour of God.[3]

As to the tax on prostitution, it seems to have been reintroduced after Baybars' death at a date not mentioned in the sources, and was not abolished until the Nāṣirī *rawk* of 715/1315. *Ḥuqūq al-qaynāt* was a tax collected from prostitutes. According to Ibn Iyās *ḍamān al-ghawānī*, any would-be prostitute had merely to register her name with a *ḍāmina* and pay her tax, to ply her trade undisturbed.[4]

H. *Casual revenue*

There is in the fiscal usage of the period in question, no collective Arabic term comparable to the Ottoman *bād-i hawā* or Eastern *ṭayyārāt* to denote irregular and occasional revenue from casual sources, most prominent among which were the *muṣādara* and *māl al-mawārīth al-ḥashriyya*.[5]

1. The *muṣādara*

The *muṣādara* (confiscation) was known in Egypt as a source of revenue before the Ayyūbid era.[6] Some Fāṭimid caliphs used to

[1] Ibn Shaddād, *Rawḍa*, fols. 223v–224r; Nuwayrī, xxviii, fol. 56; Dhahabī, *Tārīkh* (MS. Laud. 279), fol. 9r; Ibn al-Furāt, MS., vi, fol. 197r; Yūnīnī, *Dhayl*, ii, p. 454; Ibn Kathīr, xiii, p. 260; Ibn Taghrī Birdī, *Nujūm*, vii, p. 154.

[2] Maqrīzī, *Sulūk*, i, p. 668, tr. Quatremère, ii. i, p. 8.

[3] Shāfiʿ ibn ʿAlī, *Faḍl*, fol. 84r.

[4] Maqrīzī, *Khiṭaṭ*, i, p. 89; id., *Sulūk*, ii, p. 152; Ibn Taghrī Birdī, *Nujūm*, ix, pp. 47–8; Ibn Iyās, *Badāʾiʿ*, i, pp. 175–6.

[5] For Bād-i Hawā cf. Lewis, article 'Bād-i-Hawā', in *EI*²; id., *Notes and documents*, p. 20; id., 'Jaffa', p. 437 and n. 9; Heyd, *Ottoman documents*, p. 59 n. 2; İnalcik, article 'Ḍarība', in *EI*².

[6] The term '*muṣādara*' appears in the papyri; cf. Grohmann, 'New discoveries', i, pp. 165–6; id., *Arabic papyri*, iii, p. 130, iv, p. 202.

confiscate regularly the fortunes of their high officials after their dismissal. For example, in 373/984 al-'Azīz dismissed and imprisoned the vizier Ibn Killis, confiscating 500,000 *dīnār*s, although he employed him again the next year.[1] Many Fāṭimid viziers were known to confiscate the property of the inhabitants. Both Ibn al-Ṣayrafī and Ibn Muyassar state that cases of confiscation increased during the vizierate of al-Jarjarā'ī, which lasted only one year from 440/1049 to 441/1050.[2] Badr al-Jamālī was notorious for his tendency to confiscate. It is said that he built the 'Aṭṭārīn mosque in Alexandria from the money and property he confiscated.[3] Immediately after having been appointed chief collector of revenue by al-Āmir, Abū Najāḥ al-Rāhib confiscated 100,000 *dīnār*s from a group of Copts. This encouraged al-Rāhib to deal in this way with the property of high officials, qadis, clerks, and others. He went so far as to confiscate 20 *dīnār*s, the price of the only camel of a carrier. Al-Rāhib used to sit in 'Amr mosque in Fusṭāṭ and summon the public for confiscation until his death at the order of al-Āmir in 523/1129–30.[4] Moreover, Nuwayrī relates that Ibn Ruzzīk used to look at 'what was in the hands of the people' and confiscate it, even if the victims held no office in the state.[5] The same accusation was made against the Caliph al-'Āḍid.[6]

The Ayyūbids had contracted this habit even before the collapse of the Fāṭimid regime. According to Abū Ṣāliḥ the Armenian, the Kurds (i.e. the Ayyūbids) confiscated in 564/1169 a piece of arable land of about 30 *faddān*s which belonged to the Nahyā monastery in the Jīza province, which had been granted to the monks in perpetuity by al-Āmir. As a result, the monks had nothing left to live on except the fish-pond.[7]

As soon as the Caliph al-'Āḍid died in 567/1171, Saladin confiscated his treasuries and other property, as well as that of the Fāṭimid amirs and prominent persons. He took part of the spoils for himself, distributed another part among the members of his family and the Ayyūbid amirs, and sent a part to Nūr al-Dīn in

[1] Nuwayrī, xxvi, fol. 48. For confiscation in 10th-century Iraq; cf. Dūrī, *Studies*, pp. 304–12; id., *Tārīkh al-'Irāq*, pp. 275–83.

[2] Ibn al-Ṣayrafī, *Ishāra*, pp. 38–9; Ibn Muyassar, ii, p. 5.

[3] Ibn Ẓāfir, fol. 72^{r-v}.

[4] Ibid., fols. 77^{v}–78^{v}; Nuwayrī, xxvi, fols. 86–7.

[5] Nuwayrī, xxvi, fol. 97.

[6] Ibn Ẓāfir, fol. 90^{v}.

[7] Abū Ṣāliḥ the Armenian, pp. 78–9, tr. Evetts, pp. 183–4; for the Nahyā monastery, cf. 'Shābushtī', p. 191

Syria. The remainder was sold, privately or by auction, over about ten years, and much was taken abroad by travellers and merchants.[1] Saladin also confiscated the library of the Fāṭimid palace, which contained more than 125,000 books. Auction sales of these books took place regularly twice a week for many years, and their proceeds are said to have been fabulous.[2] Subsequently, Saladin confiscated *al-manākh al-saʿīd*, which was attached to the palace and contained wood, iron, mills, tools of the fleet, flax, pitch, and other goods.[3] He even went so far as to confiscate the property of the Fāṭimid amirs and their supporters, which he assigned to members of his family and amirs, offering the remainder for sale.[4] It seems that Saladin frequently resorted to confiscation; Maqrīzī states that in 577/1181 Saladin seized the *mustaghallāt* (property) belonging to the Bedouin tribes in the Sharqiyya province, ordering them to move to Buḥayra. This was a punitive as well as preventive action, as they used to smuggle grain to the Franks.[5]

After Saladin's death, confiscation continued to be regarded as a source of revenue, especially during financial crises. In 594/1197 al-ʿAzīz ʿUthmān seized the money and property of a number of wealthy people. A thousand *dīnār*s is said to have been confiscated from a certain Ibn Khālid.[6] In 601/1204–5, Ibn Shukr, the vizier of al-ʿĀdil I, confiscated the property of the chiefs of the *dīwān*s and some state officials, especially wealthy Copts. Threatened by this danger, some of the officials, among them Ibn Mammātī, fled the country.[7] Al-ʿĀdil I even ordered his son al-Kāmil in 613/1216 to confiscate the property of the vizier Ibn Shukr himself, which

[1] Iṣfahānī, *Sanā*, fol. 173ᵛ; Ibn Wāṣil, *Ṣāliḥī*, fol. 196ʳ; id., *Mufarrij*, i, pp. 202–4; Ibn Abī al-Damm, fol. 154ᵛ; Ḥanbalī, *Shifā'*, fol. 19ʳ; Ibn Waṣīf Shāh, fol. 52ᵛ; Dhahabī, *Tārīkh* (MS. Or. 5578), fol. 14ʳ; ʿAynī, *ʿIqd*, 'A', xii, fols. 169ᵛ–170ʳ; Abū Shāma, *Rawḍatayn*, i, pp. 493–5, 508–9; Ibn Kathīr, xii, p. 266; Maqrīzī, *Khiṭaṭ*, i, p. 496; Ibn Taghrī Birdī, *Mawrid*, p. 27; Rabīʿ, *Nuẓum*, p. 53.

[2] Iṣfahānī, *Sanā*, fol. 186ʳ⁻ᵛ; ʿAynī, *ʿIqd*, 'A', xii, fols. 206ᵛ–207ʳ; Abū Shāma, *Rawḍatayn*, i, pp. 507–8, 686–7; Ibn Wāṣil, *Mufarrij*, i, p. 203; Maqrīzī, *Khiṭaṭ*, i, p. 409; Rabīʿ, *Nuẓum*, p. 53.

[3] Ibn Mammātī, p. 353; Maqrīzī, *Khiṭaṭ*, i, p. 444; Rabīʿ, *Nuẓum*, p. 53.

[4] Abū Shāma, *Rawḍatayn*, i, p. 508; Ibn Wāṣil, *Mufarrij*, i, pp. 203–4; Maqrīzī, *Khiṭaṭ*, i, p. 384; Rabīʿ, *Nuẓum*, p. 53.

[5] Maqrīzī, *Sulūk*, i, p. 71, tr. Blochet, 'B', p. 537; Gibb, 'The armies of Saladin', in *Studies*, p. 82.

[6] Maqrīzī, *Sulūk*, i, p. 142, tr. Blochet, 'C', pp. 97–8; Rabīʿ, *Nuẓum*, p. 53.

[7] Nuwayrī, xxvii, fols. 8, 9; Ibn al-Furāt, MS., v, fol. 67ᵛ; Ibn al-ʿAmīd, *Akhbār*, pp. 131–2; Maqrīzī, *Khiṭaṭ*, ii, p. 372.

was estimated at 600,000 *dīnārs*.[1] Summoned by al-Kāmil in 615/1218–19 to help him collect money during the war with the Crusaders, Ibn Shukr confiscated the property of merchants and dignitaries.[2] When Ibn Shukr died in 622/1225, al-Kāmil again confiscated his whole estate.[3]

Al-Ṣāliḥ Ayyūb was not less prone to confiscate than his father. As soon as he became sultan, he seized the money and jewels of his father's wife, the mother of al-ʿĀdil II, as well as the property of amirs who had helped him to overthrow al-ʿĀdil II.[4] In 639/1241, al-Ṣāliḥ confiscated some property on the occasion of the foundation of a school in Bayn al-Qaṣrayn and the Jazīra citadel.[5]

Confiscation continued to represent an important source of revenue under the Mamluks. Baybars al-Manṣūrī and Maqrīzī state that, when the amir Aqṭāy, the head of the Baḥriyya, was killed in 652/1254, and 700 other amirs, his colleagues, fled to Syria, to avoid punishment, Aybak considered it an opportunity to confiscate their property in Egypt to fill his treasury.[6] Most of those affected by these measures in the Mamluk era were state officials who had been dismissed from office.

It cannot be gainsaid that there was some justification for the confiscation of the property of state officials after their dismissal. It would seem that appointment to the vice-sultanate or vizierate, the administration of a *dīwān*, etc., was regarded as a licence to embezzle revenue and increase one's own wealth by hook or by crook. Sources quote a number of instances of this kind. In 655/1257, Quṭuz, the then vice-sultan of ʿAlī ibn Aybak, arrested the vizier al-Fā'izī, confiscating all his wealth.[7] In 677/1279, after the death of the vizier Ibn Ḥannā, Sultan al-Saʿīd ibn Baybars not only confiscated his property, but also imposed a fine of about 300,000 *dīnārs* to be paid by his two grandsons and their cousin.[8]

1 Nuwayrī, xxvii, fol. 14; Rabīʿ, *Nuẓum*, pp. 53–4.

2 Nuwayrī, xxvii, fol. 18; Ibn al-ʿAmīd, *Akhbār*, p. 133; Maqrīzī, *Khiṭaṭ*, i, p. 216.

3 Ibn al-ʿAmīd, *Akhbār*, p. 135; Ḥamawī, *Tārīkh*, fol. 151r.

4 Nuwayrī, xxvii, fol. 88; Maqrīzī, *Sulūk*, i, p. 298, tr. Blochet, 'D', p. 332; Rabīʿ, *Nuẓum*, p. 54.

5 Sibt ibn al-Jawzī, pp. 487–8; Rabīʿ, *Nuẓum*, p. 54.

6 Baybars al-Manṣūrī, *Tuḥfa*, fols. 5v–6r; Maqrīzī, *Khiṭaṭ*, i, p. 383.

7 Ibn Wāṣil, *Mufarrij* (MS. 1703), fols. 121v–122r; Jazarī, *Tārīkh*, fol. 79r; Nuwayrī, xxvii, fol. 123; Ibn Ḥabīb, *Durra* (MS. Marsh 591), i, fol. 8v; Ibn Waṣīf Shāh, fol. 64v; Ibn Kathīr, xiii, p. 199; Ibn Iyās, *Badā'iʿ*, i, p. 93.

8 Dawādārī, *Durra zakiyya*, fol. 101r; Kutubī, *ʿUyūn* (MS. Köprülü) fols.

The next vizier, al-Sinjārī, having been dismissed already in 678/1280, Qalāwūn confiscated all his horses as well as the property of his son, and both their dependants and subordinates. The sultan went so far as to impose on them a fine of 236,000 *dīnār*s.[1] In 687/1288, Qalāwūn dismissed the vizier al-Shujā'ī and confiscated all his belongings and fined him 65,000 *dīnār*s.[2]

Proof of dishonesty on the part of a victim of confiscation was, however, not always forthcoming. Nor was it required by any means. When in 689/1290, Sultan Khalīl ordered the arrest of the amir Ṭurunṭāy, the vice-sultan of his father, everything that had belonged to the vice-sultan—600,000 *dīnār*s, about 170 *qinṭār*s of silver, 200,000 *ardabb*s of corn, mamluks, weapons, livestock, etc.—went to Khalīl's treasury. It is well known that the relations between Khalīl and Ṭurunṭāy had been far from friendly while Khalīl's father was alive. Ṭurunṭāy is said to have been severe with Khalīl, and shown his preference for his brother (al-Ṣāliḥ).[3]

Under Lājīn and during the long reign of al-Nāṣir, cases of confiscation of officials' property were numerous.[4] It is known that al-Nāṣir resorted to confiscation to punish any official or amir who tried to increase his influence in the state. For example, in 710/1310, the imprisonment of the vice-sultan Salār, by al-Nāṣir, was followed by the confiscation of his property. The figure quoted by the sources—300,000,000 *dīnār*s in addition to silver, precious stones, horses, etc.—seems exaggerated. Though the excessive severity in al-Nāṣir's treatment of Salār, to whom he refused food and water until he died, stemmed from long years of resentment and hatred, greed as a secondary motive cannot be denied, for his wealth filled al-Nāṣir's treasuries.[5] Ample details are found in the

85^{v}–86^{r}; Ibn Taghrī Birdī, *Manhal*, iv, fols. 145^{v}–146^{r}; Ibn Abī al-Faḍā'il, pp. 300–1; Maqrīzī, *Sulūk*, i, p. 649, tr. Quatremère, i. ii, p. 166.

[1] Maqrīzī, *Sulūk*, i, p. 666, tr. Quatremère, ii. i, pp. 6–7.

[2] Baybars al-Manṣūrī, *Zubda*, fol. 161^{v}–162^{r}; id., *Tuḥfa*, fol. 50^{r}; Nuwayrī, xxix, fols. 43, 49; Ibn Duqmāq, *Jawhar*, fol. 111^{r}; Anonymous, *Tārīkh*, fol. 14^{v}; Ibn al-Furāt, viii, p. 63; Maqrīzī, *Sulūk*, i, pp. 740–2.

[3] Baybars al-Manṣūrī, *Zubda*, fol. 167^{r-v}; id., *Tuḥfa*, fol. 53^{r}; Dawādārī, *Durra zakiyya*, fols. 134^{v}–135^{r}; 'Aynī, *'Iqd*, 'C', xxi. i, fols. 7–9; Ibn Abī al-Faḍā'il, pp. 370–2; Ibn al-Furāt, viii, p. 101.

[4] For confiscation under Lājīn, cf. Dawādārī, *Durra zakiyya*, fol. 161^{v}; Yūnīnī, Dhayl, MS., iii, fol. 99^{r}; Nuwayrī, xxix, fols. 93, 97; Ibn al-Furāt, viii, pp. 231–2; Ibn Kathīr, xiii, p. 350.

[5] Baybars al-Manṣūrī, *Tuḥfa*, fol. 107^{v}; Yūnīnī, *Dhayl* (MS.), iv, fols. 188^{v}–189^{r}; Nuwayrī, xxx, fol. 60; Ibn Duqmāq, *Jawhar*, fols. 128^{r}–129^{v}; Ibn Taghrī

sources of the huge amount of money, jewels, and property yielded by the confiscation of the property of Karīm al-Dīn al-Kabīr, the *nāẓir al-khāṣṣ*, in 723/1323 and again in 724/1324;[1] of Ibn Faḍl Allāh, the *nāẓir al-jaysh*, in 732/1332;[2] and of the amir Ulmās in 733/1333. According to Dawādārī, the spoils from Ulmās' house alone were estimated at 2,390,000 *dirhams nuqra*. Eighty-one carriers were needed to transport it to the palace.[3]

Al-Nāṣir applied confiscation as an important tool of punishment. In 734/1333–4, he dismissed his *wālī*s for maladministration, confiscating their property.[4] In the next year, 735/1334, he is said to have arrested and replaced 'some officials' of the *dīwān*s, confiscating what they possessed as a matter of course.[5] Not even al-Nashw, the *nāẓir al-khāṣṣ*, known for the tyrannical zeal with which he collected money for the sultan, was spared. The sources are unanimous on the huge amounts of gold *dīnār*s, pearls, and precious stones which were taken from al-Nashw and his family in 740/1339.[6] In 740–1/1340, al-Nāṣir, having conceived doubts as to the loyalty of his vice-sultan in Syria, Tankiz, ordered his arrest and the confiscation of all his property, consisting of more than 330,000 *dīnār*s, 1,500,000 *dirhams*, precious stones, and costly furniture.[7] However, in view of the lack of documentary evidence to confirm the above-mentioned figures, available data must be treated with caution.

It is noteworthy that officials did not shrink from cruelty in enforcing orders of confiscation. In his two biographies of Ala-göz al-Nāṣirī and Lu'lu' al-Fandashī, who both held the office of the *shadd al-dawāwīn* under al-Nāṣir, Ibn Ḥajar states that they used

Birdī, *Manhal*, iii, fols. 93r–94v; Ibn Abī al-Faḍā'il, p. 703; Maqrīzī, *Sulūk*, ii, pp. 97–9; Ibn Iyās, *Badā'i'*, i, pp. 155–6.

[1] 'Aynī, *Badr*, fols. 14r, 15v; Ibn Ḥabīb, *Tadhkira*, fols. 79v–80r; Ibn Ḥajar, *Durar*, i, pp. 403–4.

[2] Ibn Taghrī Birdī, *Manhal*, v, fols. 196v–197r; Ibn Ḥajar, *Durar*, iv, p. 139; Maqrīzī, *Khiṭaṭ*, ii, p. 311.

[3] Dawādārī, *Durr fākhir*, p. 373; see also 'Umarī, *Masālik* (MS. A.S. 3434), fol. 30v; 'Aynī, *Badr*, fol. 31v.

[4] Dawādārī, *Durr fākhir*, p. 378; Ibn Duqmāq, *Jawhar*, fol. 147v.

[5] 'Aynī, *Badr*, fol. 33r; Ibn Bahādir, *Futūḥ*, fol. 134r; Ibn Duqmāq, *Jawhar*, fol. 147v; Dawādārī, *Durr fākhir*, p. 382.

[6] Kutubī, *'Uyūn* (MS. Cambridge), fols. 39v–40r; 'Aynī, *Badr*, fol. 38v; id., *'Iqd*, 'A', xvii, fols. 148v–149v; Ibn Ḥajar, *Durar*, ii, pp. 429–30.

[7] Ṣafadī, *A'yān* (MS. A.S. 2970), fol. 123r-v; Ibn Taghrī Birdī, *Manhal*, ii, fol. 159r-v; Ibn Duqmāq, *Jawhar*, fol. 148v; Anonymous, *Tārīkh*, fol. 30v; Ibn Ḥajar, *Durar*, i, pp. 525–6; Maqrīzī, *Khiṭaṭ*, ii, p. 54.

to punish the owners of confiscated property by beating and torturing them.[1]

2. *Māl al-mawārīth al-ḥashriyya*

The *amān* granted by Jawhar al-Ṣiqillī in Shaʿbān 358/July 969 exempted the Egyptians from the duty of paying contribution to the *bayt al-māl* from the estate of deceased persons.[2] Thus it can be assumed that in pre-Fāṭimid times—according to Sunnī rules of inheritance—all the estate of deceased heirless persons, and part of the estate of those whose heirs were not entitled to the whole inheritance, went to the treasury. This is indirect proof that the Fāṭimids rejected the *mawārīth ḥashriyya* as a source of state revenue. The Fāṭimids introduced the Shīʿite principle according to which descendants on the distaff side (uterine relatives) were given the right to inherit in cases where it was denied to them by Sunnī custom. Such a change in the law of inheritance increased the range of beneficiaries in the estate of deceased persons. The Fāṭimids went so far as to extend the right to inherit to the only daughter, obviously to vindicate the right of Fāṭima to the inheritance of the Prophet.[3]

Despite the theoretical exemption, the Fāṭimids sometimes diverted to the treasury parts of estates whose beneficiaries were absent. This is supported by the statement of Ibn Muyassar to the effect that al-Afḍal ibn Badr al-Jamālī prohibited this practice, ordering the inheritance of an absent heir to be kept in trust by a qadi until it was claimed by the heir. In al-Afḍal's time, as much as 130,000 *dīnār*s was kept in trust for absent heirs.[4]

After the collapse of the Fāṭimid regime, a reversal to pre-Fāṭimid conditions took place, and the *mawārīth ḥashriyya* became again an important part of the financial revenue of the *bayt al-māl*.[5]

Theoretically, according to Ibn Mammātī, the first amount of money to be deducted from an estate after the owner's death was destined for the cost of his funeral, his debts, and legacies, and only the residue was distributed among his heirs. If there were no heirs, or the heir or heirs were not entitled to the whole of the inheritance, the whole estate in the first case, or its residue in the second,

[1] Ibn Ḥajar, *Durar*, i, p. 404, iii, pp. 272–3; for the *shadd al-dawāwīn* see below, pp. 150–3.

[2] Ibn Ḥammād, *Akhbār*, p. 43; see also Maqrīzī, *Ittiʿāẓ*, fol. 16v.

[3] Nuʿmān, *Daʿāʾim*, ii, pp. 363–98; Maqrīzī, *Khiṭaṭ*, i, p. 111.

[4] Ibn Muyassar, ii, p. 59.

[5] Maqrīzī, *Khiṭaṭ*, i, p. 111.

would go to the *bayt al-māl*. As the sole Fāṭimid concession to remain in force, the share of the absent heir would be kept in trust in the treasury until his return. Apparently, to help the officials of the *dīwān al-mawārīth*, Ibn Mammātī attempted to elucidate the position of those who had the right to inherit and those who had none, as well as those who were deprived of the right to hand on their property to their heirs. He also defined the share of each category of heir in every case. How eager the *mawārīth* authorities were to be the first on the spot is proved by a statement of Ibn Mammātī that the undertakers who washed the body of the deceased, wrapped him in his shroud, and carried him to his grave, were obliged to notify the officials of the *mawārīth* before performing these duties. This was obviously done to protect the share of the *dīwān*.[1]

However, it seems that the restrictions enumerated by Ibn Mammātī were hardly ever so stringent in practice, and that the *mawārīth* authorities were already open to corruption under Saladin. There exists a *manshūr* written by al-Fāḍil which reprimands a *mushārif* for his greed, and warns him that the sultan knows of and is worried about the defects of the administration of the *mawārīth*.[2]

In fact, the *mawārīth* authorities were faced with a number of difficulties. Some heirless persons distributed their property before their death, to evade the seizure of their property by the *dīwān al-mawārīth* after their death. For example, Ibn al-Qābiḍ, a wealthy official who had no legal heirs, distributed, in Saladin's reign, most of his wealth among his mamluks before his death in 587/1191.[3] Some others, especially those who had daughters, found in the *waqf* system a means of avoiding the seizure of their property after death by the *dīwān al-mawārīth*. A *ḥujja* of the Qāḍī Sadīd al-Dīn Abī Muḥammad, dated 19 Shaʿbān 649/7 November 1251, and preserved in the *Maḥkama* in Cairo, states that an heirless former slave girl called Khuṭlwā transferred the ownership of her house to the son of her master, the Qāḍī Sadīd al-Dīn, who, in turn, assigned the house as *waqf* to Khuṭlwā to live in and draw benefit from. After her death, the *waqf* of the house was to go to his four daughters and a former slave girl. There is ample evidence

1 Ibn Mammātī, pp. 319–25; Rabīʿ, *Nuẓum*, p. 47.
2 *Rasāʾil al-Qāḍī al-Fāḍil* (MS. Add. 25757), fol. 10^{r-v}.
3 Iṣfahānī, *Fatḥ*, pp. 410–11.

in this document to the effect that the house would remain the endowment of his descendants until they became extinct, and then the revenue would go to poor Muslims.[1]

Injustice in the collection of the *mawārīth ḥashriyya* also prevailed under the Mamluks. When Quṭuz was preparing troops to fight the Mongols, he decided that one-third of the estates belonging to deceased inhabitants (*al-tirak al-ahliyya*) must be collected for the treasury, without considering the number of the heirs or the amount of the estate. This was equivalent to $33\frac{1}{3}$ per cent estate duty. However, Baybars abolished this duty—for political motives—soon after his accession.[2] When the deceased person was an important amir or one of his faithful followers, Baybars often exempted the heirs from the payment of the treasury's share in the estate. For example, in 662/1264, Baybars exempted the daughters of the amir al-ʿAzīzī from the payment of the share of the *dīwān* in the estate of their deceased father to the amount of 400,000 *dirhams*

[1] Rabīʿ, 'Ḥujjat tamlīk wa waqf', *MTM*, xii (1964–5), pp. 191–202. The institution of *waqf* or *ḥabs* played a prominent part in the economy of Egypt and other Muslim countries. The origins and the evolution of the *waqf* system, as well as its impact on the economy of Medieval Egypt, are still obscure. Further research on the *waqf* in Egypt might be facilitated by the following references; cf. *Maḥkama* documents as listed in the bibliography; T.–S. B.306 (N.S.) fol. 1; Musabbiḥī, xl, fol. 252^{r}; *Rasāʾil* al-Qāḍī al-Fāḍil (MS. Add. 25757), fols. 11^{v}–12^{r}; Shāfiʿ ibn ʿAlī, *Ḥusn*, fol. 88^{r}; Nuwayrī, xxvi, fol. 57, xxvii, fol. 92, xxviii, fols. 32, 35–6, 64, 123–4, xxix, fols. 26, 28–31, xxx, fols. 12–18, 20, 22–3, 44–5, 57, 80; Kutubī, *ʿUyūn* (MS. Cambridge), fol. 16^{r}; Ibn Ḥabīb, *Durra*, i (MS. Marsh 391), fol. 79^{v}; ʿAynī, *ʿIqd*, 'A', xii, fol. 207^{r}, 'B', xiii, fol. 119^{r}, 'C', xxi. i, fol. 31; id., *Badr*, fol. 16^{v}; Khālidī, fol. 132^{r}; Suyūṭī, *Risālat al-inṣāf fī tamyīz al-awqāf*, fols. 88^{r}–89^{v}; Ibn Nujaym, *Tuḥfa*, fols. 53^{v}–54^{r}; Kindī, *Wulā*, p. 346; Abū Shāma, *Rawḍatayn*, i, p. 431; Ibn Mammātī, ed. Atiya, pp. 356–7, ed. Najjār, p. 14; Nābulsī, *Lumaʿ*, pp. 25–8, tr. Cahen, 'Quelques aspects', pp. 101–2; id., *Fayyūm*, pp. 59–60; Ibn ʿAbd al-Ẓāhir, *Alṭāf*, pp. 68–70; Zetterstéen, p. 220; Dawādārī, *Durr fākhir*, pp. 311, 391; Ibn Abī al-Faḍāʾil, p. 708; Ibn Kathīr, xiii, p. 250, xiv, pp. 61, 177; Ibn al-Furāt, iv, p. 23; Maqrīzī, *Khiṭaṭ*, ii, pp. 295–6; id., *Ittiʿāẓ*, p. 201; id., *Sulūk*, ii, p. 126; Ibn Ḥajar, *Rafʿ*, i, p. 222, ii, p. 368; id., *Durar*, i, pp. 111, 507, 510, ii, p. 410, iii, pp. 91–2, 358, iv, pp. 202, 338, 413, 605–6; Bāshā, *Funūn*, iii, pp. 1304–8; Bekhit, 'De l'institution du wakf', *EC*, xviii (1927), pp. 403–31; Cahen; 'Réflexions sur le waqf ancien', *SI*, xiv (1961), pp. 37–56; id., 'Régime', pp. 24 ff.; id., articles 'Bayt al-Māl' and 'Ḍarība' in *EI*^{2}; id., *Pre-Ottoman Turkey*, pp. 178–9; Coulson, *A History of Islamic law*, pp. 33, 241; Heffening, article 'Waḳf' in *EI*^{1}; Majid S., 'Wakf as family settlement among the Mohammedans', *JSCL*, N.S., ix (1908), pp. 122–41; Rabīʿ, loc. cit.; Schacht, 'Early doctrines on waqf', *Mél. Köprülü*, 1953, pp. 443–52.

[2] Nuwayrī, xxviii, fol. 1; Dhahabī, *Tārīkh* (MS. Laud. Or. 305) fol. 254^{v}; Khālidī, fol. 67^{r}; Maqrīzī, *Khiṭaṭ*, ii, p. 301; *Sulūk*, i, p. 437; Quatremère, i. i, p. 117, translates '*al-tirak al-ahliyya*' as '*les Turcs domiciliés dans ce pays*', which is erroneous.

nuqra, excluding his property, grain, and horses.[1] In the next year (663/1265), after the death of the amir Baktāsh al-Zāhidī in a campaign to al-Bīra, Baybars ordered that all property should go to his only daughter.[2]

These isolated cases of exemption were, however, not the rule. Ibn ʿAbd al-Ẓāhir and others state that when the amir al-Ḥillī died in 667/1269, the sultan did not take anything from his large estate, which implies that Baybars used to levy a tax on a deceased person's estate even if there were heirs.[3] It is very probable that the officials of the *mawārīth* had to report each deceased case immediately and separately. Evidence of this kind is found in an unpublished fragment from the Geniza, which is a report written on 29 Dhū al-Qaʿda 682/18 February 1284 by some officials reporting the death of a woman called ʿAlā Bint Abū al-ʿAlā who left a father and two sons.[4]

This source of revenue often produced high yields, especially during the frequent epidemics, when numerous heirless persons died suddenly. In the epidemic which occurred during the reign of Kitbughā, there were, in Cairo alone, about 17,500 persons whose property fell to the *mawārīth*, because they had died without heirs in the month of Dhū al-Ḥijja 694/October–November 1295.[5] Ibn Ḥajar puts the figure even higher, at 7,000 persons per day.[6] However, exaggeration cannot be ruled out. This may also be true of another statement by Ibn Ḥajar to the effect that al-Khalīlī, Kitbughā's vizier, decreed that the estate of a deceased person, even if he left an heir, must be transferred to the treasury. As the money was usually already spent by the authorities before the heir could prove his right to his inheritance, he was assigned a share in another [dead] person's estate, but often received nothing in the end.[7] The accession of Lājīn in 696/1296 put an end to what amounted to a seizure of the *mawārīth*.[8]

[1] Ibn ʿAbd al-Ẓāhir, *Rawḍ*, pp. 1014–15; Nuwayrī, xxviii, fol. 27; Ibn al-Furāt, MS., vi, fol. 41ʳ.

[2] Nuwayrī, xxviii, fols. 80–1; Maqrīzī, *Sulūk*, i, pp. 524–5; tr. Quatremère, i. ii, p. 3.

[3] Ibn ʿAbd al-Ẓāhir, *Rawḍ*, p. 1161; Ibn al-Furāt, MS., vi, fol. 160ʳ; Maqrīzī, *Sulūk*, p. 580; tr. Quatremère, i. ii, p. 70.

[4] T.–S. B.39, fol. 189.

[5] Yūnīnī, *Dhayl*, MS., iii, fol. 69ᵛ; Zetterstéen, p. 36; Ibn al-Furāt, viii, p. 199.

[6] Ibn Ḥajar, *Durar*, iii, p. 263.

[7] Ibid., iii, pp. 170–1.

[8] Maqrīzī, *Sulūk*, i, p. 823, tr. Quatremère, ii. ii, p. 42. There is a damaged

Lājīn's humane action had no permanent effect. During the reign of al-Nāṣir, the *mawāri̱th ḥas̱hriyya* was frequently unfairly collected, especially in times of financial crisis. According to Maqrīzī, in 737/1336–7, the sultani mamluks complained that the bestowal of their *kiswa*s (clothing) was delayed. The sultan ordered al-Nas̱hw, the *nāẓir al-ḵhāṣṣ*, to bestow upon them the dresses, together with 20,000 *dīnār*s. Among the measures applied by al-Nas̱hw to procure the money was an order to al-Ṭayyibī, the *nāẓir dīwān al-mawāri̱th*, to collect the amount of 5,000 *dīnār*s from the estates of the deceased, which could only be done illegally. Thus, for example, the whole estate of al-Isʿardī was taken, although he had natural heirs, a wife, a daughter, and a son.[1] Backed by al-Nas̱hw, al-Ṭayyibī instituted a complicated procedure to seize the property of deceased persons on behalf of the *dīwān*. Even if it was a question of a person of some social position who died leaving a son, the *nāẓir* obliged the latter to prove his relationship to the dead person and his claim to a share of the legacy. If he succeeded in that, he had to collect his share from the revenue of the *dīwān* which would procrastinate so long that he finally received nothing. Sultan al-Nāṣir tried in 738/1337–8 to abolish this injustice, forbidding the chief qadis to write reports concerning the inheritance of an estate without the sultan's order. However, he only aggravated it, as the heirs were thus robbed of the opportunity to appeal or state their relationship.[2]

An undated and unpublished letter from the Geniza, possibly derived from the same period, illustrates the injustice of these methods. In this letter a father urges his son to return as soon as possible, as his aunt had died and the *mawāri̱th* officials refused to hand over the inheritance (her house) before he returned. He warns his son that, if his absence was prolonged, 'the *aṣḥāb al-mawāri̱th* would attempt to seize the house'.[3]

It is noteworthy that the unfair seizure of deceased persons'

fragment in the Geniza (T.–S. B.297, N.S., fol. 1) from the reign of Lājīn (697/1298) in which some Egyptian Jews, reporting the death of a woman, state that her father was entitled to inherit her estate.

[1] 'Umarī, *Masālik* (MS. A.S. 3434), fols. 144^{v}–145^{r}; Maqrīzī, *Sulūk*, ii, pp. 413–14. For the bestowal of the *kiswa* in Mamluk military society, cf. Ayalon, 'The system of payment', pp. 257–8.

[2] 'Aynī, *'Iqd*, 'A', xvii, fol. 128^{v}; Maqrīzī, *Sulūk*, ii, pp. 435–6.

[3] T.–S. B.39, fol. 492^{r-v}: '. . . وكلما قعدت قد طمعوا أصحاب المواريث فى الدار . . .'. See also ibid., fol. 25 and T.–S. N.S., J. 383^{r}.

property, in the presence of heirs, was one of the reasons for the growth of the *awqāf*. There is ample evidence in the *Maḥkama* documents to support this assumption. For example, on 17 Rajab 687/17 August 1288, al-Ḥājj Sunbul assigned in the form of *waqf* two-thirds of a house in his possession. Thus he could enjoy the whole income for life without fear of confiscation and, at the same time, be confident that it would be distributed after his death according to the provisions he laid down in the *waqfiyya*, among two traditionalists, three Qur'ān reciters, poor and needy Muslims, etc.[1] In the *ḥujjat waqf* of Sayf al-Dīn Baktamur from the same collection, dated 14 Muḥarram 707/16 July 1307, Baktamur assigns as *waqf* the *qaysāriyya* Jahāraks, which contained 124 shops. He reserved to himself the revenue from this *qaysāriyya* during his life. After his death, $\frac{1}{24}$ of the revenue was to be spent on a mosque, bread for prisoners, etc., the remaining $\frac{23}{24}$ of the revenue being settled on his sons and daughters.[2] In another document from the same collection, dated 14 Rajab 707/9 January 1308, Badr al-Dīn ibn ʿAbd Allāh al-Ḥusaynī, one of the servants of the Prophet's tomb, assigned in the form of *waqf* the income from his house in Cairo after his death to some freed slaves and servants, reserving it for himself for life.[3]

It is worth noting that not all the taxes and other sources of revenue discussed in this chapter were handed over completely to the *bayt al-māl* (treasury). Many non-agricultural taxes used to be conferred upon *muqṭa*ʿs in the form of *iqṭā*ʿs, as each *muqṭa*ʿ had a number of military and non-military obligations to fulfil. Some taxes were imposed when the sultan prepared troops for a campaign. Other taxes went towards the salaries of clerks and officials, financed public services, and even covered the cost of the Nile flood festival. One might say that the cost of all public expenditure is found reflected in tax figures. To direct the financial resources thus obtained into the intended channels was the function of the financial administration, which forms the subject of the next chapter.

[1] *Maḥkama*, Box 3, no. 16.

[2] *Maḥkama*, Box 4, no. 20. For the *qaysāriyya* Jahāraks, cf. ibid., Box 2, no. 13; Maqrīzī, Khiṭaṭ, ii, pp. 87–9. The history of the term '*qaysāriyya*', derived from the word 'Caesar' is not yet known in detail. The *qaysāriyya* was a building devoted specifically to commercial transactions; cf. Goitein, *Med. Soc.*, i, p. 194.

[3] *Maḥkama*, Box 4, no. 21.

IV

FINANCIAL ADMINISTRATION

A. *Methods of tax collection*

1. *Direct collection*

THE study of the *iqṭā'* and tax systems in the two previous chapters has shown that revenue from all sources used to be collected —under both the Ayyūbids and the Mamluks—either by the *muqṭa'*s, if conferred on them in the form of *iqṭā'*s, or by sultani officials to be handed over to the sultan or the *dīwān*. For the *muqṭa'*s and their *ajnād*, taxes—with the exception of those farmed out to *ḍāmins*—were collected by clerks directly subordinated to the *muqṭa'*s.[1]

Tax collection by state officials was one of the functions of a complex system of financial administration. Sultani taxes were collected by farming out in the form of *ḍamān*s, or directly by official tax collectors. Prominent among directly collected taxes were the *kharāj* tax and the *jawālī* tax. The preliminaries of the actual *kharāj* collection have been described in detail in the preceding chapter.[2] The time of the collection of the *kharāj* tax coincided with the harvest. It was estimated according to the *kharājī* year (*al-sana al-kharājiyya*), which was identical with the Coptic solar year. This was a source of administrative difficulties, as the *kharāj* tax was calculated according to the lunar year, which was shorter than the solar year by about $\frac{1}{33}$. To bypass this problem, *kharājī* tax collectors used to disregard, by sultani orders, one solar year every 33 *kharājī* years. This procedure, termed '*taḥwīl al-sana al-kharājiyya al-shamsiyya ilā al-sana al-hilāliyya*', was intended to bring into line the dates of the lunar year and the *kharājī* year.[3]

[1] See above, pp. 64 ff. [2] See above, pp. 73–4.

[3] Makhzūmī, fol. 47^{r-v}; Ibn Mammātī, p. 358; Nuwayrī, i, pp. 164–5; Maqrīzī, *Khiṭaṭ*, i, pp. 273, 275; Qalqashandī, *Ṣubḥ*, xiii, pp. 54–5; Rabī', *Nuẓum*, p. 41; see also Poliak, *Feudalism*, pp. 21–2; Popper, *Systematic notes*, ii, p. 30. The Abbasid Caliph al-Mutawakkil was the first Muslim Caliph to adopt this practice in 243/857, to eliminate the injustice of *kharāj* collection before the crop ripened. The Caliph al-Mu'taḍid followed suit in 282/895; cf. 'Askarī,

The last *taḥwīl* of the Fāṭimid era was one ordered by al-Afḍal ibn Badr al-Jamālī in 501/1107–8, who found that, as a result of the *taḥwīl* having been neglected for about 132 years, the lunar year had overtaken the *kharājī* year by four years. The date implies that al-Afḍal intended the reactivation of this measure to run parallel with the Afḍalī *rawk* which he ordered for the same year.[1] For some reason or other, the Fāṭimids failed to issue a corresponding order when the *taḥwīl* fell due in A.H. 534, which resulted in a two years' gap between the lunar year and the *kharājī* year in 567 after the fall of the Fāṭimid regime. On the personal advice of Makhzūmī, the author of the *Minhāj*, al-Qāḍī al-Fāḍil persuaded Saladin to order a *taḥwīl* for the *kharājī* years 565 and 566 to make them coincide with the lunar year 567. A *manshūr* announcing this *taḥwīl* has been preserved in the *Minhāj* and *Ṣubḥ*.[2]

There is no mention of a *taḥwīl* of the *kharājī* year in the rest of the Ayyūbid era, but its occurrence under the Mamluks implies that the custom was never really discontinued. Baybars al-Manṣūrī and others state that Sultan Lājīn ordered a *taḥwīl* in 697/1298 for the *kharājī* year of 696 to the lunar year of 697 without this affecting the total amount of the *kharāj*.[3] The *taḥwīl* was even performed in Syria, though not simultaneously with the Egyptian *taḥwīl*. In 713/1314, al-Nāṣir ordered the *taḥwīl* of the *kharājī* year A.H. 712 to 713 for Syria alone.[4]

The *jawālī* tax was collected directly by sultani officials. In the *Minhāj*, there is a detailed description of the method of collection of the *jawālī* tax in the first years of the Ayyūbid era. Makhzūmī states that each new *'āmil* and *mushārif* of the *jawālī* obtained from his predecessor a record of the numbers and names of those sub-

Awā'il, fols. 138v–140v; Miskawayh, *Tajārib*, ii, p. 407; Maqrīzī, *Khiṭaṭ*, i, pp. 273–5; Qalqashandī, *Ma'āthir*, i, pp. 264–5; Ibn Iyās, *Nashq*, fol. 279v–280r; al-Rayyis, *Kharāj*, pp. 498–502.

1 Makhzūmī, fol. 49r; Maqrīzī, *Itti'āẓ*, fol. 115r; id., *Khiṭaṭ*, i, pp. 276, 279–81; for the Afḍalī *rawk* see above, p. 51.

2 Makhzūmī, fols. 49r–v, 54r–v; Qalqashandī, *Ṣubḥ*, xiii, pp. 60, 71–4; cf. Maqrīzī, *Itti'āẓ*, fol. 164r; id., *Khiṭaṭ*, i, pp. 276–7, 281–2; Rabī', *Nuẓum*, pp. 41–2 and Appendix no. 2.

3 Baybars al-Manṣūrī, *Zubda*, fol. 199r; Nuwayrī, xxix, fol. 100; Ibn Abī al-Faḍā'il, pp. 436–7; Maqrīzī, *Sulūk*, i, p. 845, tr. Quatremère, ii. ii, p. 68; cf. a list of *taḥwīl* dates in Qalqashandī, *Ṣubḥ*, xiii, pp. 60–2.

4 Nuwayrī, xxx, fol. 81; Maqrīzī, *Sulūk*, ii, p. 127. The Ottomans adopted the dual usage of the lunar year for expenditures and solar year for the collection of revenue, which occasioned financial crises; cf. Halil Sahillioğlu, '*Sıvış* year crises in the Ottoman Empire', in Cook, *Studies*, pp. 230–52.

ject to this tax as well as the names of the *ḥushshār* (pl. of *ḥāshir*). The record also contained the total sum actually collected before the end of the year and the *ʿibra*. Three special categories were the absentees, those deceased during the year, and the converts (*man ihtadā*). Makhzūmī gives a description of the work of the *ḥushshār*, who were assisted in each district by the *adillāʾ* (pl. of *dalīl*). The *aʿmāl* (inventories) of the *ḥushshār* specified the number of those taxable, such as the *rātib* (ordinary *jawālī*-payer), the *nashʾ* (liable to the *jāliya* on attainment of majority), and the *ṭāriʾ* (stranger in transit). When the officials in charge of the *jawālī* in Cairo and Miṣr (Fusṭāṭ) brought their register up to date, they relied on the *taʿrīfāt* (lists) of the dead, converts, and absentees, made out by the *ḥushshār*.

On the other hand, every *mushārif*, *ʿāmil*, and *jahbadh* who collaborated with the *ḥushshār* in collecting the *jawālī* had to keep a *taʿlīq* or *taʿlīq al-muyāwama* (day-book) of the sums daily levied in each district, containing the names of the payers, the year for which the payment was made, and the amount paid. Subsequently, the *jahbadh* drew up a *makhzūma* based on the *taʿlīq* with the joint signature of the *ʿāmil* and the *mushārif*. The revenue for every ten days was entered in the *rūznāmaj*. A similar document for the whole month was called the *khatma*, and one for the whole year the *ʿamal*.[1]

The method of collection of the *jawālī* tax seems to have been less complicated at the end of the period under consideration than at its beginning. According to Nuwayrī, the *mubāshir al-jawālī* (the *jawālī* official) had to compile a *jarīda* (register) which contained names of the non-Muslim *jawālī*-payers. Receipts were issued for the amounts collected, which were also entered, beside the taxpayers' names, in the day-book (*taʿlīq al-muyāwama*), which was

[1] Makhzūmī, fols. 144r–150r; Cahen, 'Contribution', pp. 249–52; for the *ʿāmil*, the *mushārif*, the *dalīl*, and the *jahbadh* see below, pp. 157 ff.; for the *ʿibra* see above, pp. 47–8; for the *ʿamal* and the *khatma* cf. Lewis, article 'Daftar' in *EI*²; for the *taʿlīq*, cf. Makhzūmī, fols. 146r–147v; the frequent occurrence of the term '*makhzūma* (pl. *makhāzim*) in the *Minhāj* indicates that it was reserved for pages edited daily which, as the meaning of the root suggests, were strung up to be filed; cf. Makhzūmī, fols. 155r–156v, 163v–164r; Ibn Mammātī, pp. 304 and 458; Dozy, *Supp. Dict. Ar.*, i, p. 368; Cahen, 'Contribution', p. 251 n. 1; for the *rūznāmaj*, cf. A.Ch. 10, fol. 8137; Lewis, loc. cit.; Grohmann, 'New Discoveries', i, p. 163; id., *Arabic papyri*, vi, pp. 35, 48; Løkkegaard, *Islamic taxation*, p. 149. Makhzūmī, fol. 147v, states that, in his lifetime, the expenses of the army were recorded in a *rūznāmaj*, day by day, though the entries in non-military *rūznāmaj* were usually delayed, possibly for 10 days.

identical with the *rūznāmaj*. So that no one should be able to slip through the net, the chief of the dhimmīs were forced to compile yearly *riqā'* of the *rawātib* (ordinary taxpayers), *ṭawāri'* (strangers in transit), *nawābit* (minors), converts to Islam, emigrants (with mention of their new residence), and the deceased. The last three categories had also to be listed in a separate *mashrūḥ* to be kept in the *mubāshir*'s *jarīda*. In some provinces, the officials of the *jawālī* compelled the chiefs of the *dhimmī*s to inform them daily of every male birth, to enable the *mubāshir* to impose the tax on every boy when he reached 13 years of age. The chiefs of the *dhimmī*s also had to notify the officials of the death of each person.[1]

2. *The* ḍamān

Tax-farming, described above by the term *ḍamān*, was known in the early Islamic era, although it was rejected by the *Sharī'a*. Māwardī mentions that it was illegal, as 'the *'āmil* ought to collect what is imposed and deliver [to the treasury] what he collects', without accepting responsibility for the decrease or credit for the increase in revenue as is usual in the *ḍamān* system.[2] According to Professor Cahen, the *ḍāmin* used to pay, over a period of years, a yearly contracted sum which was less than the calculated revenue from the tax in question, in the expectation that he would be reimbursed with profit. This yearly amount was open to revision. Nor had the *ḍāmin* any certainty that his contract would be renewed. On the other hand, the *ḍāmin* had to manage the tax as defined by the state and had no right to alter it.[3] As Qalqashandī says, the *ḍāmin* conducted the operation at his own peril, benefiting by an eventual surplus but bearing his own losses.[4]

There is evidence in the available sources to prove that the *ḍamān* system was inherited by and in use under the Fāṭimids, and not established by the Ayyūbids.[5] Saladin relied on the *ḍamān*

[1] Nuwayrī, viii, pp. 242–5; for methods of collection in later period cf. Qalqashandī, *Ṣubḥ*, iii, pp. 462–3; for the *jarīda* cf. Lewis, article 'Daftar', in *EI*²; Grohmann, *Arabic papyri*, v, p. 103.

[2] Māwardī, p. 168.

[3] Cahen, article 'Bayt al-Māl', in *EI*²; id., review of Løkkegaard's *Islamic taxation*, pp. 350–1.

[4] Qalqashandī, *Ṣubḥ*, iii, p. 470; see also Løkkegaard, *Islamic taxation*, p. 98.

[5] T.-S. B.40, fol. 37; B.42, fol. 51; Nuwayrī, xxvi, fols. 49, 84; Maqrīzī, *Itti'āẓ*, fol. 122ᵛ; id., *Khiṭaṭ*, i, pp. 83–4, 405; Ibn al-Furāt, iv, pp. 147–8; Ibn al-Ṣayrafī, *Ishāra*, pp. 24, 30; id., *Qānūn*, p. 143; Ibn Muyassar, ii, pp. 45, 82; Dawādārī, *Durra muḍiyya*, p. 229; Sayyida Kāshif, *Miṣr*, p. 341; Barrāwī, *Ḥālat Miṣr*, pp. 322–3.

system to the extent that, in 577/1181–2, the very right to collect the *kharāj* was assigned as a *ḍamān* for 8,000 *dīnārs*.[1] It has been pointed out that the right of selling and possibly even of mining natron was assigned to *ḍāmins*.[2] Some *muqṭa*ʿs, especially those whose *iqṭā*ʿs were composed of non-agricultural taxes, found that the *ḍamān* system guaranteed a stable revenue from their *iqṭā*ʿs, saving them the trouble of tax collection and preventing losses when their military duties kept them away from their *iqṭā*ʿs. It has already been mentioned that taxes imposed on *mizr*, *khumūr*, and hashish under the Ayyūbids used to be collected by *ḍāmin*s under contract to the sultan. The Mamluk sultans frequently conferred such taxes upon *muqṭa*ʿs or assigned the right of their collection to *ḍāmins*.[3]

The *ḍamān* system was invaluable for the collection of taxes from distant provinces, such as the oases in the Western desert. It is related that the *ḍamān* of taxes collected in the oases was once assigned to a certain al-Nāṣiḥ, who was crucified for disloyalty by order of Baybars in 665/1267.[4] By the end of the period under study the *ḍamān* seems to have escaped government control completely, and the *ḍāmins* had become rather unscrupulous in their handling of taxpayers. Both ʿUmarī and Maqrīzī state that in 737/1336–7 the inhabitants of Miṣr (Fusṭāṭ) complained to Sultan al-Nāṣir that al-Fār al-Ḍāmin, who had contracted to collect the taxes of their city in the form of a *ḍamān*, had introduced heavy taxes on sugar-cane, pomegranates, cucumber (possibly in the form of a sales tax), and even on the fruit of the nabk trees offered for sale in a single shop. Al-Nāṣir had the *ḍāmin* imprisoned, and conferred the *ḍamān* on somebody else, after reducing it by 10,000 *dirhams*, in order to ease the burden on the inhabitants of Fusṭāṭ.[5]

B. *Role of the sultan in the financial administration*

In theory, the sultan, being the sovereign, was the head of the *bayt al-māl*, but in practice this was true only of powerful sultans when they resided in the capital. Sultan al-Kāmil, for example, after the

[1] Maqrīzī, *Sulūk*, i, p. 73, tr. Blochet, 'B', p. 541.
[2] See above, p. 85. [3] See above, pp. 119–20.
[4] Nuwayrī, xxviii, fol. 65; Yūnīnī, *Dhayl*, ii, pp. 362–3. For cruel methods of execution under the Mamluks, cf. M. Meyerhof and J. Schacht, *The Theologus Autodidactus of Ibn al-Nafīs*, pp. 81–2.
[5] ʿUmarī, *Masālik* (MS. A.S. 3434) fol. 153r; Maqrīzī, *Sulūk*, ii, p. 420.

death of the vizier Ibn Shukr, supervised the financial administration to such an extent that he kept the accounts in person.[1] The Mamluk Sultan, al-Nāṣir, is said to have ordered the vizier al-Jamālī in 724/1324 to instruct the *nāẓir al-dawla* and the *nāẓir al-khāṣṣ* to send the sultan daily reports on financial revenue and expenditure, which was very unwelcome to the *dīwāns*.[2] However, this was an exception rather than the rule, as the financial administration remained in the hands of the vizier and the officials of the *dīwāns*.

C. *The financial functions of the vizier and the* nāẓir al-khāṣṣ

From the time when Badr al-Jamālī came to Egypt to restore order in the second period of al-Mustanṣir's reign, all the viziers had full powers and often disregarded the authority of the caliphs. Riḍwān, the vizier of al-Ḥāfiẓ in 531/1171, demonstrated his power by taking the title of *al-malik*, which passed to Shīrkūh in 564/1169 and from him to his nephew Saladin.[3]

It is probable that Saladin's experience as the vizier to al-ʿĀḍid made him realize the importance and the dangers of the vizierate. He chose for it al-Qāḍī al-Fāḍil, whom he trusted since he had helped him to overthrow the Fāṭimid caliphate. Al-Fāḍil remained vizier until the death of Saladin and seemingly even for some time under al-ʿAzīz.[4] Maqrīzī mentions that Yūsuf ibn al-Mujāwir served al-ʿAzīz as vizier.[5] Al-ʿĀdil I appointed three viziers, Falak al-Dīn al-Masīrī,[6] Ibn al-Naḥḥāl,[7] and Ibn Shukr, the most important Ayyūbid vizier. Ibn Shukr was vizier under al-ʿĀdil I from 596/1199–1200 to 609/1212, and under al-Kāmil from 615/1219 until his death in 622/1225. An Egyptian from Dumayra, he

[1] Nuwayrī, xxvii, fol. 55; see also, Ibn al-ʿAmīd, *Akhbār*, p. 144; Maqrīzī, *Khiṭaṭ*, ii, p. 377; id., *Sulūk*, i, p. 260, tr. Blochet, 'D', p. 293.

[2] Maqrīzī, *Khiṭaṭ*, ii, p. 393; id., *Sulūk*, ii, p. 258; Ibn Taghrī Birdī, *Nujūm*, ix, pp. 77–8; for the *nāẓir al-dawla* and the *nāẓir al-khāṣṣ* see below, pp. 143–4, 150.

[3] Cf. Canard, article 'Fāṭimids', in *EI*², Dr. Bāshā (*Funūn*, iii, pp. 1332–3) states incorrectly that the vizierate was abolished after Badr al-Jamālī's arrival in Egypt, and that there were no more viziers until the end of the Fāṭimid period.

[4] Khālidī, fol. 14ᵛ; Ibn al-ʿAdīm, *Zubda* (MS. P. 1666 Arabe), fol. 222ʳ; Suyūṭī, *Ḥusn*, ii, p. 138; see above, p. 12.

[5] Maqrīzī, *Khiṭaṭ*, ii, p. 84.

[6] Nuwayrī, xxvii, fol. 83; Maqrīzī, *Khiṭaṭ*, ii, p. 51.

[7] Ibn al-ʿAmīd, *Akhbār*, p. 131; Nuwayrī, xxvii, fol. 8; Maqrīzī, *Sulūk*, i, p. 192, Blochet's ('C', p. 471) rendering of the name is Ibn al-Khāl.

became very powerful owing to his strict control of the financial *dīwān*s, and was well versed in all methods of confiscation, which won him the confidence of al-Kāmil.[1] Another important Ayyūbid vizier was Muʿīn al-Dīn ibn S̲h̲ayk̲h̲ al-S̲h̲uyūk̲h̲, appointed in 637/1240 by al-Ṣāliḥ Ayyūb, who entrusted him with all the affairs of the sultanate, the army, and the treasury.[2]

The Mamluks entrusted the vizier only with the financial administration. ʿUmarī and Qalqas̲h̲andī have preserved the text of an oath Mamluk viziers were made to swear on their appointment to the vizierate. This oath implies that it was the task of the vizier to prevent extravagance, waste, and dishonesty in financial matters, to select only officials known for their ability and honesty, to assign the *ḍamān*s only to honest persons or such who offered to increase the contracted sum, and not to exempt anybody from payment of tax.[3] In the decree appointing the chief qadi Tāj al-Dīn ibn Bint al-Aʿazz to the vizierate issued on 10 Ramaḍān 655/21 September 1257 and preserved by Nuwayrī, the Sultan ʿAlī ibn Aybak reminds the vizier to pay more attention to revenue, and to appoint only honest officials.[4]

What were, then, the characteristics of the vizierate under the Mamluks? First, most of the viziers to Mamluk sultans within the period under consideration had been trained in the work of the *dīwān*s and had held the office of *s̲h̲add al-dawāwīn* or *naẓar al-dawāwīn* before they were promoted to the vizierate. For example, Ḥamza al-Asfūnī, who was nominated vizier by Qalāwūn in 681/1282, had been *nāẓir* in Qūṣ and Ak̲h̲mīm, and had held the office of *naẓar al-dawāwīn* before he was appointed to the vizierate.[5] The vizier al-K̲h̲alīlī, mentioned above as the originator of unfair measures devised for the purpose of the confiscation of the estates

[1] Ibn Wāṣil, *Mufarrij*, fol. 311ᵛ; Nuwayrī, xxvii, fols. 8–9, 14, 25–7; ʿUmarī, *Masālik* (MS. P.) fol. 82ʳ, (MS. A.S. 3439), fol. 120ᵛ; Dhahabī, *Tārīk̲h̲* (MS. Laud. Or. 305) fols. 30ʳ–31ʳ; Ibn al-ʿAmīd, *Ak̲h̲bār*, pp. 127, 131–2, 135; Ibn Kat̲h̲īr, xiii, p. 109; Maqrīzī, K̲h̲iṭaṭ, ii, pp. 371–3; id., *Sulūk*, i, pp. 176, 192–3, tr. Blochet, 'C', pp. 151, 471–2.

[2] Ibn Wāṣil, *Mufarrij* (MS. 1703), fols. 35ʳ, 48ʳ; Nuwayrī, xxvii, fol. 68; Ibn al-ʿAmīd, *Ak̲h̲bār*, p. 151; Maqrīzī, *Sulūk*, i, p. 299, tr. Blochet, 'D', p. 333; Gottschalk, article 'Awlād al-S̲h̲ayk̲h̲', in *EI²*.

[3] ʿUmarī, *Taʿrīf*, pp. 149–50; Qalqas̲h̲andī, Ṣubḥ, xiii, p. 309.

[4] Nuwayrī, xxvii, fols. 124–5; this decree of appointment specifies the composition of the salary of the vizier Ibn Bint al-Aʿazz: 100 *dīnār*s from the revenue of the *jawālī*, 50 *ardabb*s wheat, 30⅓ *ardabb*s barley payable every month, plus a daily *rātib* comprising bread, meat, spices, vegetables, and fodder.

[5] Nuwayrī, xxix, fol. 23; Ibn al-Furāt, vii, p. 247.

of deceased persons, had held the office of *naẓar al-dawāwīn* before being appointed vizier to Kitbughā thanks to his experience in the affairs of the different *dīwāns*.[1] Similarly, the vizier Ḍiyā' al-Dīn ibn al-Nashā'ī was *nāẓir al-dawāwīn* before attaining the vizierate in 706/1306.[2]

Secondly, the tenure of office became increasingly short, with the result that there were six viziers under Qalāwūn,[3] and as many as thirteen viziers under his son al-Nāṣir.[4] Some were appointed more than once. For example, when Qalāwūn became sultan in 678/1279, he confirmed the vizierate of Burhān al-Dīn al-Sinjārī, only to dismiss him in the same year and reappoint him in the following year.[5] Another example is that of the vizier Amīn al-Dīn ibn al-Ghannām, who was nominated vizier three times by al-Nāṣir, the first time in 711/1311 and the third time in 723/1323, but was dismissed in the following year.[6]

Thirdly, the supervision of the activities of the financial *dīwāns* seems to have been too hard a task to be performed by one person, so that the vizier was helped by a vice-vizier. There were sometimes two viziers at the same time, so that one of them (*wazīr al-ṣuḥba*) could accompany the sultan on his campaigns. During the sultanate of Aybak and the vizierate of al-Fā'izī, the qadi Ya'qūb ibn al-Zubayr was appointed vice-vizier, a step which led to a full vizierate under Quṭuz in 657/1259.[7] It is said that Fakhr al-Dīn ibn Ḥannā once acted as vice-vizier to his father Bahā' al-Dīn under Baybars,[8] and that 'Īsā al-Sinjārī was vice-vizier to his father, the vizier Burhān al-Dīn at the beginning of Qalāwūn's sultanate.[9]

[1] Baybars al-Manṣūrī, *Zubda*, fol. 188v; Nuwayrī, xxix, fol. 82; Ibn Taghrī Birdī, *Manhal*, v, fol. 39r; Maqrīzī, *Sulūk*, i, p. 808, tr. Quatremère, ii. ii, p. 24; see above, p. 130.

[2] Yūnīnī, *Dhayl*, MS., iv, fol. 121v; Ibn Abī al-Faḍā'il, p. 622; Ibn Ḥajar, *Durar*, i, p. 444.

[3] Ibn al-Furāt, viii, p. 96; Maqrīzī, *Sulūk*, i, p. 755, tr. Quatremère, ii. i, pp. 110–11.

[4] Kutubī, *'Uyūn* (MS. Cambridge), fol. 51r; Ibn Taghrī Birdī, *Manhal*, v, fol. 205r.

[5] Nuwayrī, xxix, fols. 1, 2, 18; Ibn al-Furāt, vii, pp. 190–209; Maqrīzī, *Sulūk*, i, pp. 664, 666, 682, tr. Quatremère, ii. i, pp. 4, 6–7, 26.

[6] Ṣafadī, *A'yān* (MS. A.S. 2966), fols. 22r–27r; Dawādārī, *Durr fākhir*, pp. 312–14; Ibn Abī al-Faḍā'il, pp. 705–6; Ibn Ḥajar, *Durar*, ii, pp. 251–2; Maqrīzī, *Sulūk*, ii, pp. 124, 248, 256.

[7] Ibn Wāṣil, *Mufarrij* (MS. 1703), fol. 164v; Nuwayrī, xxvii, fol. 126, xxviii, fol. 53; Maqrīzī, *Sulūk*, i, pp. 404, 417, tr. Quatremère, i. i, pp. 73, 86.

[8] Maqrīzī, *Khiṭaṭ*, ii, p. 299.

[9] Dhahabī, *Tārīkh* (MS. Or. 1540), fol. 17v.

The function of the *wazīr al-ṣuḥba*, who accompanied the sultan on his campaigns, was to deal with financial affairs. The first mention of such an office under the Mamluks is made by Maqrīzī who says, without stating the date, that Fakhr al-Dīn ibn Ḥannā was appointed vizier *ṣuḥba* under Baybars.[1] Nuwayrī mentions that, when Baybars was setting out on the campaign of 675/1277, he appointed Fakhr al-Dīn's son, Zayn al-Dīn ibn Ḥannā, *wazīr ṣuḥba*, and that it was the first trip on which the latter accompanied the sultan.[2] The fact that al-Nāṣir appointed ʿIzz al-Dīn ibn Ḥannā to the vizierate *al-ṣuḥba* in 693/1294 indicates that this office continued in existence.[3]

Fourthly, there were many dishonest viziers under the Mamluks. Some of them accumulated enormous wealth while in office, so that it was no wonder that the sultans frequently confiscated the property of viziers who were dismissed or died. Thus the property of the vizier al-Fā'izī was confiscated when Quṭuz dismissed him in 655/1257; that of the vizier ibn Ḥannā after his death in 677/1279 by Sultan al-Saʿīd;[4] and the property of the vizier Saʿd al-Dīn ibn ʿAṭāyā after his dismissal in 706/1306.[5]

Fifthly, the influence of the viziers in the sultanate increased with the passage of time. It is said that Ibn al-Salʿūs, the vizier of Khalīl ibn Qalāwūn, achieved such power that he could order high *dīwānī* officials such as the *nāẓir al-nuẓẓār*, the *shādd al-dawāwīn*, the *wālī*s of Cairo and Miṣr, the *mustawfī*s, the *nāẓir*s of the *dīwān*s, and even the four qadis to accompany him daily on his way to and from the Citadel. After Sultan Khalīl was murdered, Ibn al-Salʿūs' property was confiscated and he was beaten to death in 693/1294.[6]

Finally, Qalāwūn first began to appoint military amirs to the vizierate, which had previously been in the hands of civilian officials, who were deemed more suitable to deal with financial matters. Qalāwūn seems to have desired to strengthen this important office by entrusting it to an amir. The amir Sanjar al-Shujāʿī was the first Mamluk amir to be appointed to the vizierate. His previous

[1] Maqrīzī, *Khiṭaṭ*, ii, p. 299.
[2] Nuwayrī, xxviii, fol. 110; cf. Quatremère, op. cit., i. ii, p. 139 n. 171.
[3] Nuwayrī, xxix, fol. 79; Ibn al-Furāt, viii, p. 183.
[4] See above, p. 124.
[5] Nuwayrī, xxx, fol. 39; Zetterstéen, p. 134.
[6] Baybars al-Manṣūrī, *Zubda*, fol. 184v; Nuwayrī, xxix, fols. 52–4, 78; al-Muẓaffarī, *Dhayl mufarrij*, fol. 209v; Ibn Taghrī Birdī, *Manhal*, v, fols. 168v–169r; Ibn Ḥabīb, *Tadhkira*, fols. 32v–33r; Ibn al-Furāt, viii, pp. 108–9, 176–7; Maqrīzī, *Sulūk*, i, p. 761, tr. Quatremère, ii. i, pp. 117–18.

experience as *shādd al-dawāwīn* seems to have made him severe in his treatment of taxpayers, and his ill treatment of *dīwānī* officials was notorious.[1] When he was dismissed and all his property confiscated in 687/1288, Qalāwūn appointed another amir, Badr al-Dīn Baydarā, who was later promoted to the vice-sultanate by Khalīl.[2]

The Mamluk sultans must have been satisfied with the way Mamluk viziers handled the affairs of the *dīwāns*, for civilian viziers were few and far between in the ensuing period. In 696/1297, Lājīn nominated the amir Sunqur al-Aʿsar vizier as well as *shādd al-dawāwīn*. Although al-Aʿsar was dismissed in the same year, he was reappointed by al-Nāṣir in 698/1299, and was not replaced until 701/1301.[3] His successor was Aybak al-Baghdādī, the fourth amir to hold the vizierate.[4] The fifth was the amir Baktamur al-Ḥājib, who was appointed to the vizierate by al-Nāṣir in 710/1311.[5] The last amir to hold the vizierate during the period under study was Mughulṭāy al-Jamālī, who became vizier in 724/1324 and was dismissed in 729/1329 by al-Nāṣir, who had decided to abolish the vizierate altogether. Consequently, no vizier was appointed during the remaining period of his reign.[6] Al-Nāṣir's motive in taking this step seems to have been alarm at the influence achieved by successive Mamluk viziers who held in their hands all the financial resources of the sultanate, the more so as they flaunted their power.[7]

[1] Ibn Taghrī Birdī, *Manhal*, iii, fols. 108ᵛ–109ʳ; Ibn al-Furāt, viii, p. 96; Maqrīzī, *Sulūk*, i, p. 755, tr. Quatremère, ii. i, p. 110; see above, p. 125.

[2] Baybars al-Manṣūrī, *Zubda*, fol. 162ʳ; Ibn al-Furāt, viii, pp. 63–5; Maqrīzī, *Sulūk*, i, p. 741, tr. Quatremère, ii. i, pp. 95–6.

[3] Nuwayrī, xxix, fols. 108–9, 128; Zetterstéen, p. 43; Dawādārī, *Durr fākhir*, p. 12; Ibn Kathīr, xiii, pp. 349–50; xiv, p. 57; Ibn al-Furāt, viii, pp. 231–2; Maqrīzī, *Sulūk*, i, p. 878, tr. Quatremère, ii. ii, p. 133.

[4] Baybars al-Manṣurī, *Zubda*, fol. 230ᵛ; Nuwayrī, xxx, fol. 1; Ibn Abī al-Faḍā'il, pp. 568–9; Ibn Ḥajar, *Durar*, i, p. 422.

[5] Nuwayrī, xxx, fols. 61–2; Dawādārī, *Durr fākhir*, p. 208, Maqrīzī, *Khiṭaṭ*, ii, p. 64.

[6] ʿAynī, *Badr*, fol. 24ʳ; Ibn Ḥajar, *Durar*, iv, pp. 138, 354–5; Maqrīzī, *Khiṭaṭ*, ii, p. 393; Suyūṭī, *Ḥusn*, ii, p. 142; Prof. Gottschalk (article 'Dīwān', in *EI²*) seems to be mistaken when he states that al-Nāṣir abolished the vizierate in 710/1310. The *ḥujjat waqf* of the amir Mughulṭāy al-Jamālī dated 29 Rabīʿ II 729/1 March 1329 is found in the collection of documents preserved in the Ministry of *Waqf* (Cairo), no. 1666.

[7] Zetterstéen, p. 97; Dawādārī, *Durr fākhir*, pp. 64–5; Ibn Taghrī Birdī, *Nujūm*, viii, pp. 140–1; cf. Ayalon, 'Studies', iii, p. 61; id., 'The system of payment', pp. 279–80.

Qalqashandī quotes 'Umarī's *Masālik* to the effect that, after the abolition of the vizierate by al-Nāṣir, the function of the vizier passed to four lower officials, *nāẓir al-māl*, *shādd al-dawāwīn*, *nāẓir al-khāṣṣ*, and *kātib al-sirr*.[1] However, this division of power seems to have been merely theoretical. In practice, most of it was concentrated in the hands of *nāẓir al-khāṣṣ*, who was the head of *dīwān al-khāṣṣ*, and thus became the most important official in the Mamluk sultanate.[2] However, this development was by no means revolutionary, as *nāẓir al-khāṣṣ* had already dealt with the private financial affairs of the sultan before 729/1329. When the *wakīl al-khāṣṣ* Ibn 'Ubāda died in 710/1310, al-Nāṣir appointed Karīm al-Dīn al-Kabīr to the office of *naẓar al-khāṣṣ*.[3] Karīm al-Dīn's influence as *nāẓir al-khāṣṣ* grew to the extent that he lost the sultan's trust. He was dismissed and his property confiscated in two stages, in 723/1323 and in 724/1324.[4] Subsequently, al-Nāṣir appointed in 723/1323 Tāj al-Dīn Isḥāq, who remained *nāẓir al-khāṣṣ* until his death in 731/1331.[5] He was succeeded by his son Mūsā ibn Isḥāq, who was soon replaced by al-Nashw, who was in his turn dismissed with confiscation of his property in 740/1339.[6]

It was while Isḥāq was *nāẓir al-khāṣṣ* that al-Nāṣir abolished the vizierate, assigning to Isḥāq most of its functions in addition to his original work in the privy purse of the sultan. Thus, the *nāẓir al-khāṣṣ* became, as a result of his close relations with the sultan, the most important official of the sultanate, and seems to have

[1] Qalqashandī, *Ṣubḥ*, iv, pp. 28–9; Gaudefroy-Demombynes, *La Syrie*, p. lxvii; for the first two officials cf. below, pp. 147–53; for *Kātib al-sirr* (secretary of state) cf. Maqrīzī, *Khiṭaṭ*, ii, pp. 225–6; Qalqashandī, *Ṣubḥ*, iv, p. 30.

[2] It seems that the *dīwān al-khāṣṣ* had its origin in the Abbasid *bayt māl al-khāṣṣa*, a concept which first appears in the period of the Caliph al-Mu'taḍid (279–89/892–902); cf. Fischel, 'The bait māl al-khāṣṣa', in *Atti del XIX Congresso Internazionale degli Orientalisti*, 1938, pp. 538–41; Imamuddin, 'Bayt al-mal and banks in the medieval Muslim world', *IC*, xxxv (1961), p. 12; the *Dīwān al-khāṣṣ al-Āmirī* is mentioned in one of the Vienna papers (A.Ch. 10217^{r-v}) dated in 506/1113, representing a list of the costs of repairs to the *ribā'* (tenement-houses) which were the property of this *dīwān*; see also Ibn Muyassar, ii, p. 54; Maqrīzī, *Khiṭaṭ*, i, p. 84, ii, pp. 196, 227; Stern, *Fāṭimid decrees*, pp. 36, 173 and n. 2; Rabī', *Nuẓum*, p. 15. Al-Iṣfahānī (*Barq*, iii, fol. 35^{r}) mentions a person called Ibn Ṣawla, who was *wakīl* (agent) to Saladin and whose function seems to have resembled that of the Fāṭimid *nāẓir al-khāṣṣ*.

[3] Maqrīzī, *Sulūk*, ii, pp. 93, 95; see also Dawādārī, *Durr fākhir*, pp. 296–7.

[4] See above, pp. 125–6.

[5] Ṣafadī, *A'yān*, i (MS. 2962), fols. 179^{v}–180^{r}; 'Aynī, *Badr*, fol. 14^{r}; Ibn Ḥajar, *Durar*, i, p. 357; Ibn Taghrī Birdī, *Nujūm*, ix, p. 289.

[6] 'Aynī, *'Iqd*, 'A', xvii, fol. 59^{r}; Ibn Ḥajar, *Durar*, iv, p. 374; Ibn Taghrī Birdī, *Nujūm*, ix, p. 289; for al-Nashw see above, p. 126.

nominated most of the administrators of the *dīwān*s. All the financial resources which had formerly flowed into *al-khizāna al-kubrā*, that is, *bayt al-māl* (the treasury), were diverted to the *khizānat al-khāṣṣ*, the private sultani treasury controlled by the *nāẓir al-khāṣṣ*, so that only minor financial matters were still subject to the authority of *al-khizāna al-kubrā*.[1] Among other functions of the *nāẓir al-khāṣṣ* was the yearly supply of *kiswa*s (clothing) to the sultani Mamluks, a duty which the *nāẓir*s often neglected.[2]

D. *The financial* dīwāns

The main function of the vizier under both the Ayyūbids and the Mamluks was the administration of the central financial *dīwān*s, which were obviously of Fāṭimid origin. In the period under consideration, it is not easy to draw a clear dividing line between the functions of one financial *dīwān* and another. In any of the available sources, it must be assumed that the term *dīwān* may refer to a branch of another *dīwān*, the more so as it had ceased to apply to particular offices in particular buildings, with numerous clerks and officials, and often denoted merely groups of officials with their registers. Documentary sources such as the Geniza, the Vienna papers, and the *Maḥkama* may one day confirm or refute this assumption.

The function of supervising the financial *dīwān*s seems to have been entrusted, in the late Fāṭimid period, to *dīwān al-majlis*, *dīwān al-naẓar*, and *dīwān al-taḥqīq*. *Dīwān al-majlis*[3] (office of the chamber or council) seems to have been the central administrative office, in which the whole of the financial administration was

[1] Maqrīzī, *Khiṭaṭ*, ii, p. 227; Qalqashandī, *Ṣubḥ*, xi, p. 339; Suyūṭī, *Ḥusn*, ii, pp. 93–4; Popper, *Systematic notes*, i, p. 97.

[2] See above, p. 131; Ayalon, 'The system of payment', p. 286.

[3] *Dīwān al-majlis*, mentioned in a list of houses and their owners or tenants from the Geniza Collection (T.–S. B.38, fol. 137^{r-v}) and in a decree by al-Ḥāfiẓ and al-Afḍal on the subject of the monks of Mount Sinai dated 524/1130, seems to be a new appellation of the *dīwān al-zimām* (office of audit) mentioned in a Fāṭimid decree dated 415/1024; cf. Stern, *Fāṭimid decrees*, pp. 17, 36, 169–70 and n. 3, 173; see also Maqrīzī, *Khiṭaṭ*, i, p. 99. For documents in St. Catherine's Monastery in Mount Sinai, cf. A. S. Atiya, *The Arabic manuscripts of Mount Sinai* (Baltimore, 1955); H. Ernst, *Die mamlukischen Sultansurkunden des Sinai-Klosters* (Wiesbaden, 1960); S. M. Stern, *Fāṭimid decrees*, pp. 5 ff.; B. Lewis, 'Sources for the economic history', p. 80 and n. 5; J. H. Yūsuf, 'Dirāsa fī wathā'iq al-'aṣrayn al-Fāṭimī wa al-Ayyūbī', *BFA*, xviii (1964), pp. 179–208.

concentrated. Nābulsī states that even the affairs of the *zakāt* and the *jawālī*, the estimation of salaries, and the supervision of the accounts of other *dīwāns* such as *dīwān al-kharāj*, *dīwān al-mawārīth*, and *dīwān al-naṭrūn* were in the hands of the officials of this *dīwān*.[1] Qalqashandī and Maqrīzī add that this *dīwān* dealt with the affairs of the *iqṭā*'s and had control over such state expenditure as alms, gifts, uniforms as well as the private purse of the caliph.[2]

The function of *dīwān al-naẓar* or *naẓar al-dawāwīn* (office of supervision) was the supervision of the outstanding accounts of the different financial *dīwāns*.[3] There is evidence to show that this office had been in existence during the reign of al-Ḥākim and remained in force until the late Fāṭimid period. Nor was it abolished by the Ayyūbids or the Mamluks.[4]

Dīwān al-taḥqīq (official inquiry office) was established by al-Afḍal ibn Badr al-Jamālī in 501/1107–8 to keep a check on and organize different *dīwāns*. It continued in existence until the end of the Fāṭimid period, to be abolished by Saladin and reintroduced by al-Kāmil.[5]

As to other Fāṭimid *dīwāns*, there are 14 departments mentioned by Qalqashandī, each called *dīwān*, apparently mostly branches of other *dīwāns*. With the exclusion of the *dīwān khazā'in al-kiswa* (office of the storehouses of clothing) and the *dīwān al-ṭirāz* (office of embroidered-garments factories and storehouses), all these departments are first mentioned by Ibn al-Furāt. It emerges from the lists of both Ibn al-Furāt and Qalqashandī that there was among them a *dīwān al-aḥbās* to deal with the administration of the *aḥbās*; a *dīwān al-rawātib* for wages and salaries; a *dīwān al-Ṣa'īd* (office of Upper Egypt); a *dīwān asfal al-arḍ* (office of Lower Egypt); *dīwān al-jawālī wa al-mawārīth al-ḥashriyya* (poll-tax office also dealing with the estates of the heirless); a *dīwān al-kharāj* for the collection of the *kharāj* tax; and a *dīwān al-hilālī* for the collection

[1] Nābulsī, *Luma'*, p. 36, tr. Cahen, 'Quelques aspects', pp. 103–4.

[2] Qalqashandī, *Ṣubḥ*, iii, pp. 493–4; Maqrīzī, *Khiṭaṭ*, i, pp. 397–8; see also Ibn al-Furāt, iv, p. 142. Musharrafa, pp. 194–5; Rabī', *Nuẓum*, pp. 11–12; Gottschalk, article 'Dīwān', in *EI*².

[3] Maqrīzī, *Khiṭaṭ*, i, pp. 400–1; Qalqashandī, *Ṣubḥ*, iii, p. 493; Barrāwī, *Ḥālat Miṣr*, p. 315; Rabī', *Nuẓum*, p. 15.

[4] Nuwayrī, xxvi, fol. 64; Maqrīzī, *Itti'āẓ*, fol. 140ᵛ; Ibn Muyassar, ii, pp. 86, 87, 95, see below, pp. 149–50.

[5] Maqrīzī, *Itti'āẓ*, fols. 114ᵛ–115ʳ; id., *Khiṭaṭ*, i, p. 401; Ibn al-Furāt, iv, p. 142; Qalqashandī, *Ṣubḥ*, iii, p. 493; Rabī', *Nuẓum*, p. 15. See below, p. 146.

of *al-amwāl al-hilāliyya.*[1] Neither Ibn al-Furāt's nor Qalqashandī's data on the Fāṭimid *dīwāns* seem to be complete. Thus they fail to refer to the *dīwān al-mufrad*, established by al-Ḥākim in 400/1009–10 to deal with the confiscated property of those who had incurred his wrath or had been sent to their death.[2]

By the end of the Fāṭimid era, these Fāṭimid *dīwāns* appear to have been located in the Fāṭimid palace, whence Saladin transferred them in 567/1171 to *dār al-wizāra al-kubrā*, built by Badr al-Jamālī, which he chose for his residence. It remained the seat of the sultanate until 604/1207–8 when al-Kāmil, the then vice-Sultan of his father al-ʿĀdil I, moved to the citadel, which henceforward housed both the sultan and the *dīwāns* until the end of the Mamluk era.[3]

It is also probable that the Ayyūbids replaced *dīwān al-majlis* and *dīwān al-taḥqīq* by conferences of the heads of the *dīwāns* (*majlis aṣḥāb al-dawāwīn*, chamber of the heads of the *dīwāns*) which controlled the functions of different *dīwāns*. Two sessions of this chamber are mentioned in Maqrīzī: one whose object it was to decide whether a certain Ibn Shukr or a certain Ibn ʿUthmān should be made *nāẓir al-dawāwīn* on 10 Ṣafar 580/23 May 1184, and another for an unspecified purpose, headed by Sultan al-ʿAzīz ʿUthmān on Thursday 4 Muḥarram 590/30 December 1193.[4] Sultan al-Kāmil is said to have reintroduced, in 624/1226–7, the Fāṭimid *dīwān al-taḥqīq*, which performed its function of inquiry office for two years until it was abolished in 626/1228–9. There are also mentions of an inquiry office under the reign of Aybak at the beginning of the Mamluk era.[5]

Some other Fāṭimid *dīwāns* such as *dīwān al-jawālī*, *dīwān al-mawārīth*, and *dīwān al-aḥbās* continued to perform their functions

[1] Ibn al-Furāt, iv, pp. 143–5, 147–50; Qalqashandī, *Ṣubḥ*, iii, pp. 493–6; see also Gottschalk, article 'Dīwān', in *EI*². *Dīwān al-kharāj* is mentioned in a decree by al-Ẓāhir dated 415/1024; cf. Stern, *Fāṭimid decrees*, pp. 17, 169.

[2] Maqrīzī, *Ittiʿāẓ*, fol. 63ᵛ; id., *Khiṭaṭ*, ii, pp. 15, 287; Stern, *Fāṭimid decrees*, p. 169, n. 3; Barrāwī, *Ḥalat Miṣr*, pp. 319–20. There was another *dīwān* called '*al-dīwān al-mufrad*' established in 797/1395 to deal with the pay and the *iqṭāʿ*s of the Sultan Barqūq's new mamluks; cf. Maqrīzī, *Khiṭaṭ*, ii, p. 223; Popper, *Systematic notes*, i, pp. 97–8; Ayalon, 'Studies', iii, pp. 61–2; id., 'The system of payment', pp. 280, 283–4; Gottschalk, article 'Dīwān', in *EI*².

[3] Nuwayrī, xxvii, fol. 10; ʿIṣāmī, *Simṭ*, iv, p. 13; Maqrīzī, *Khiṭaṭ*, i, pp. 364, 397, 438, ii, p. 205; id., *Sulūk*, i, p. 169, tr. Blochet, 'C', p. 141; Qalqashandī, *Ṣubḥ*, iii, pp. 372 ff.

[4] Maqrīzī, *Sulūk*, i, pp. 88, 120; Rabīʿ, *Nuẓum*, pp. 83–4.

[5] Nuwayrī, xxvi, fol. 81; Ibn Muyassar, ii, p. 42; Rabīʿ, *Nuẓum*, p. 83.

under the Ayyūbids and the Mamluks. Besides administering the inflow of revenue, they also seem to have directed the flow of expenditure into its proper channels.[1] It is probable that the centre of these *dīwāns*, each of which dealt with a certain definite source of revenue, was *bayt al-māl* or *dīwān al-māl*, the idea of which as a state treasury or fiscus was of early Islamic origin.[2] Nābulsī's somewhat theoretical division distinguishes between two branches of *dīwān al-māl*: *dīwān al-māl bi al-aʿmāl*, dealing with provincial services in the sense that its *nāẓir* was concerned with land taxes, irrigation, and cultivation in the province, and *dīwān al-māl bi al-bāb*, which was subdivided into two branches, one for taxes and sources of revenue destined for the treasury such as the *zakāt*, the *jawālī*, the *mawārīth*, and natron, and the other for *al-naẓar al-ʿāmm*, general central control and supervision. Professor Cahen stresses that there was a special *dīwān* of the *zakāt*, one of the *jawālī*, and one of natron, but that Nābulsī's distinction is not valid for the time of Saladin, nor for the organization of the Mamluk period. It cannot be denied that the services in question existed, but they were by no means officially divided into two groups.[3]

Under both the Ayyūbids and the Mamluks, *bayt al-māl* or *dīwān al-māl* was administered by *nāẓir bayt al-māl*, whose assistants were *wakīl bayt al-māl*, *shuhūd bayt al-māl*, *ṣayrafī bayt al-māl*, and *kātib bayt al-māl*. Some of them were already known in the Fāṭimid era.[4] Relying on data provided by Ibn Shīth al-Qurashī for the Ayyūbid period and by Khālidī, Qalqashandī, and Suyūṭī for the Mamluk era, the *nāẓir bayt al-māl* can be described as a kind of treasurer. His function seems to have consisted in receiving and redistributing the surplus financial revenue of other *dīwāns*. This office used to be offered to men known for their honesty.[5] Nuwayrī says that the chief qadi Ibn Bint al-Aʿazz, the later *nāẓir al-dawāwīn* and vizier, acted as *shāhid bayt al-māl* under al-Kāmil,

[1] For these sources of revenue cf. above, chapter iii.

[2] Abū Yūsuf, *Kharāj*, pp. 45–6; Qudāma, *Kharāj*, fols. 8r–9r; Coulson and Cahen, article 'Bayt al-Māl', in *EI*². *Bayt al-māl al-maʿmūr* or *al-dīwān al-maʿmūr* is frequently referred to in the Geniza; cf. T.-S. B.39, fol. 25 and fol. 133.

[3] Nābulsī, *Lumaʿ*, pp. 28–31 and n. 23, tr. Cahen, 'Quelques aspects', pp. 102–3.

[4] Khālidī, fols. 133v–134r; Maqrīzī, *Khiṭaṭ*, ii, p. 224. *Kātib bayt al-māl*, *al-khāzin fī bayt al-māl*, and *ṣāḥib bayt al-māl* are frequently mentioned by Musabbiḥī, cf. fols. 245r–246v, 248v–249r, 276r; see also Ibn al-Furāt, iv, pp. 143–4.

[5] Ibn Shīth, pp. 29–30; Khālidī, fols. 134v–135r; Qalqashandī, *Ṣubḥ*, iv, p. 31; Suyūṭī, *Ḥusn*, ii, p. 95; see Gaudefroy-Demombynes, *La Syrie*, p. lxxiii.

who so appreciated his ability and honesty that he made him *nāẓir bayt al-māl*.[1] *Naẓar bayt al-māl* was held in 639/1241 by Jamāl al-Dīn ibn Maṭrūḥ, a native of Upper Egypt, who served the later Sultan al-Ṣāliḥ.[2]

The functions of *wakīl bayt al-māl* (the deputy of *bayt al-māl*) are not precisely defined in any source. However, ʿUmarī mentions a piece of advice given to an unmentioned *wakīl bayt al-māl*, which throws light on the duties and activities of an official of this kind. They seem to have corresponded roughly to those of *nāẓir bayt al-māl*.[3] In 590/1194, the qadi Muḥammad al-Anṣārī, *wakīl bayt al-māl* under al-ʿAzīz ʿUthmān, seems to have had sufficient authority to offer for sale—on behalf of *bayt al-māl*—a public bath with grounds belonging to the Fāṭimid palace for 1,200 *dīnārs*.[4] al-Ṣāliḥ Ayyūb appointed Ẓāfir ibn Naṣr to the office of *wikālat bayt al-māl* and trusted him to the extent that he advised his son Tūrānshāh before his death to confirm him in the office, which he held until his death in 677/1278–9. Besides stressing the importance of this office, the above information implies that it was not abolished by the Mamluks.[5]

Both the *naẓar bayt al-māl*, otherwise *naẓar al-khizāna*, and the *wikālat bayt al-māl* continued to be filled by qadis and *fuqahā'* also under the Mamluks. Among the *nāẓirs* were the qadi Aḥmad ibn Shukr, who died in 669/1271,[6] the *faqīh* Sharaf al-Dīn al-Zuhrī, who died in 677/1278–9,[7] and the qadi Burhān al-Dīn al-Burullusī, who died in 708/1308.[8] *Wikālat bayt al-māl* was filled by the qadi Majd al-Dīn al-Khashshāb, who died in 711/1311, succeeded by his son Ṣadr al-Dīn Aḥmad, who remained in office until his death in 714/1314.[9] It seems that under the Mamluks *wakīl bayt al-māl* continued to represent *bayt al-māl* in selling property belonging to *bayt al-māl*. This assumption seems to be confirmed by the statement of Sayf al-Dīn Baktamur in his *ḥujjat waqf* dated 14

[1] Nuwayrī, xxviii, fols. 62–3.
[2] Ibid., xxvii, fol. 113.
[3] ʿUmarī, *Taʿrīf*, pp. 132–4.
[4] Maqrīzī, *Khiṭaṭ*, ii, p. 80.
[5] Ibn Taghrī Birdī, *Manhal*, iv, fol. 10r–v.
[6] Nuwayrī, xxviii, fol. 57.
[7] Kutubī, ʿ*Uyūn* (MS. Köprülü), fol. 108v; for the *faqīh* cf. Macdonald, article 'Faḳīh', in *EI*².
[8] Yūnīnī, *Dhayl*, MS. iv, fol. 150r; Nuwayrī, xxx, fols. 49–50; Maqrīzī, *Sulūk*, ii, p. 50.
[9] Nuwayrī, xxx, fols. 74, 86; Zettersteen, p. 155; Ibn Ḥabīb, *Tadhkira*, fols. 62v, 66r–v; Ibn Ḥajar, *Durar*, i, p. 233, iii, pp. 206–8.

Muḥarram 707/16 July 1307, that he had bought *qaysāriyya* Jahāraks in 706/1307 from *wakīl bayt al-māl al-ma'mūr.*[1]

The abolition of the vizierate and the extension of the authority of *nāẓir al-khāṣṣ* in 729/1329 dealt a heavy blow to the office of *naẓar bayt al-māl*, which lost the rest of its importance after *nāẓir al-khāṣṣ* became the chief treasurer of the sultanate.[2]

E. *The office of* naẓar al-dawāwīn

The Fāṭimid *dīwān al-naẓar* or *dīwān naẓar al-dawāwīn* or *dīwān naẓar al-dawāwīn al-ma'mūra* (office of supervision) continued to control the affairs of different *dīwāns* in both the Ayyūbid and Mamluk eras. Under the Ayyūbids, the office of *naẓar al-dawāwīn* was held by Ibn Mammātī under both Saladin and al-'Azīz 'Uthmān,[3] and by al-A'azz ibn Shukr from 609/1212 until he was dismissed by al-'Ādil I for overspending on the preparations for a campaign to the Yemen in 612/1215–16.[4] Al-Kāmil's *nāẓir al-dawāwīn* was Qayṣar al-Asfūnī, who died in 649/1251.[5] It is said that Tāj al-Dīn ibn Bint al-A'azz was appointed to this office by Tūrānshāh in 647/1250.[6] Ibn Shaddād states—without mentioning the exact date—that when Ya'qūb ibn al-Zubayr was appointed to the office of *naẓar al-dawāwīn* by Baybars, he investigated the arrears in the accounts of the *dīwāns* and found that they amounted to 500,000 *dīnārs*. Consequently he advised Baybars to order that the salaries of the officials should be paid not, as was usual, from the revenue, but from these arrears when their payment was enforced, a cunning measure intended to increase the zeal of the tax-collectors.[7]

As the activities of the *dīwāns* increased, the task of supervision became too heavy to be performed by a single *nāẓir*. Consequently, some Mamluk sultans appointed more than one person to the office of *naẓar al-dawāwīn*. When, in 678/1280, Qalāwūn appointed Sharaf al-Dīn al-Nābulsī to *naẓar al-dawāwīn al-ma'mūra* in place of two *nāẓirs*, Nābulsī was unable to cope with the burden of his

1 *Maḥkama*, Box 4, no. 20.

2 See above, pp. 143–4.

3 See above, p. 14.

4 Nuwayrī, xxvii, fols. 8–9; Ibn al-'Amīd, *Akhbār*, pp. 127–8.

5 Idfuwī, *Ṭāli'*, p. 259.

6 Ibn Wāṣil, *Mufarrij* (MS. 1703), fol. 94^{r-v}; Nuwayrī, xxviii, fol. 63; for *dīwān al-naẓar* under the Ayyūbids see also, Nābulsī, *Luma'*, p. 62; Stern, 'Two Ayyūbid decrees from Sinai' in *Documents from Islamic chanceries*, p. 37.

7 Ibn Shaddād, *Rawḍa*, fol. 215^{v}.

duties, and Qalāwūn had to appoint another *nāẓir* to help him.[1] In 687/1288, Qalāwūn even appointed a third *nāẓir*, Naṣr Allāh ibn Fakhr al-Dīn.[2]

Under al-Nāṣir, *nāẓir al-dawāwīn* is frequently referred to as *nāẓir al-dawla* or *nāẓir al-nuẓẓār*. It emerges from Khālidī's and Qalqashandī's account of the office of *naẓar al-dawla* that its holder had become an important figure in the financial administration who had the authority to supervise the work of the *dīwān*s jointly with the vizier.[3] The tradition of appointing several holders of this office continued under al-Nāṣir. On the death of Tāj al-Dīn al-Ṭawīl, one of the two heads of *dīwān al-naẓar*, in 711/1312, his office was offered to a certain As'ad.[4] In 713/1313 al-Nāṣir appointed Karīm al-Dīn al-Ṣaghīr, the nephew of *nāẓir al-khāṣṣ* Karīm al-Dīn al-Kabīr, to the office of *naẓar al-dawla* as partner to As'ad. Karīm al-Dīn al-Ṣaghīr, known for his honesty in handling sultani revenue, continued in this office until he was dismissed together with his uncle in 723/1323.[5] The office of *naẓar al-dawāwīn* continued in existence after al-Nāṣir, but its heyday was over. The abolition of the vizierate and assignment of new functions to *nāẓir al-khāṣṣ* seem to have reduced the importance of *naẓar al-dawāwīn*.[6]

F. *The office of* shadd al-dawāwīn

The origin of *shadd al-dawāwīn* is still obscure.[7] However, there is a text in Maqrīzī's *Khiṭaṭ* likely to throw some light on the significance of the office of *shadd*. In telling the story of a wronged

[1] Ibn al-Furāt, vii, pp. 158, 279, 281; Maqrīzī, *Sulūk*, i, pp. 667, 713, tr. Quatremère, ii. i, pp. 8, 60.

[2] Ibn al-Furāt, viii, pp. 63–4; Maqrīzī, *Sulūk*, i, p. 741, tr. Quatremère, ii. i, p. 96.

[3] Khālidī, fol. 134^{v}; Qalqashandī, *Ṣubḥ*, iv, p. 29, xi, p. 325; Gaudefroy-Demombynes, *La Syrie*, p. lxviii; Popper, *Systematic notes*, i, p. 98.

[4] Nuwayrī, xxx, fol. 74; Ibn Abī al-Faḍā'il, p. 721; Maqrīzī, *Sulūk*, ii, pp. 106–7.

[5] Cf. Ṣafadī, *A'yān* (MS. A.S. 2962), i, fols. 219^{r}–221^{r}; Ibn Taghrī Birdī, *Manhal*, ii, fol. 7^{r-v}; see also Dawādārī, *Durr fākhir*, p. 312; Maqrīzī, *Sulūk*, ii, pp. 124, 244.

[6] Cf. 'Aynī, *Badr*, fol. 23^{v}; Dawādārī, *Durr fākhir*, pp. 312, 320, 351; Ibn Kathīr, xiv, pp. 112–13, 144, 156; Ibn Ḥajar, *Durar*, i, pp. 53–4, ii, pp. 262–3; Maqrīzī, *Khiṭaṭ*, ii, p. 150; id., *Sulūk*, ii, pp. 247–8, 256, 310, 311–12, 330–1, 334, 468.

[7] Cf. Nābulsī's *Luma'*, ed. Cahen, editor's note 20, p. 14.

taxpayer, he refers to the method of *kharāj* collection under the Fāṭimid Caliph al-Ḥāfiẓ, saying:

'وكانت العادة إذا مضى من السنة الخراجية أربعة أشهرندب من
الجند من فيه حماسة وشدة ومن الكتاب العدول وكاتب نصراني
فيخرجون الى سائر الأعمال لا ستخراج ثلث الخراج على ما تشهد به
المكلفات المذكورة . . . فلما خرج الشاد والكاتب والعدول لا ستخراج
ثلث مال الناحية استدعوا أرباب الزرع على ما تشهد به المكلفة.''

It was the custom that when four months of the *kharājī* year had elapsed, strong and zealous soldiers, *kātib*s of moral integrity, and a Coptic *kātib* were delegated to go to the whole country to collect a third of the *kharāj* according to what is stated in the above-mentioned *mukallafāt* . . . when the *shādd*, the [Coptic] *kātib* and the *kātib*s of moral integrity went to collect the third of the money from the district, they summoned the cultivators as is stated in the *mukallafa*.

In the above text a soldier, who is also given the name *al-shādd*, is mentioned as a member of the tax-collecting team. This supports the assumption that the *mushidd* was a military associate who gave support to the native staff in collecting taxes.[1] Qalqashandī mentions *shadd al-dawāwīn* among the offices held by *arbāb al-suyūf* (the military class), the holder of which assisted the vizier in collecting financial revenue.[2]

The above data suggest that, under the Ayyūbids as well as the Mamluks, the *shādd* or *mushidd al-dawāwīn* was not a clerk or official of a *dīwān*, but an amir, and that it was his function to assist the vizier and probably the *nāẓir* or *nuẓẓār al-dawāwīn* in the financial administration of the *dīwān*s, especially in collecting arrears or punishing tax evaders.

Under the Ayyūbids, the first mention of *shādd al-dawāwīn* comes from Maqrīzī, who states that the amir Sayf al-Dīn ibn Munqidh was appointed *shādd al-dawāwīn* in 586/1190 during Saladin's reign.[3] In 631/1233–4, al-Kāmil appointed to this office

[1] Maqrīzī, *Khiṭaṭ*, i, p. 405; see above, pp. 66–7; for the *mukallafa* see above, p. 50. The same story abridged and with slight alterations appears in Nābulsī's *Tajrīd*, fol. 194^{r-v}; Cahen, 'Histoires coptes d'un cadi médiéval. Extraits du *Kitāb tadjrīd*', pp. 144–5.

[2] Qalqashandī, *Ṣubḥ*, iv, p. 22; Gaudefroy-Demombynes, *La Syrie*, p. lxiii.

[3] Maqrīzī, *Sulūk*, i, p. 105, tr. Blochet, 'C', p. 52; Rabī', *Nuẓum*, p. 82.

the amir Jamāl al-Dīn ibn Yaghmūr, of whom it is said that he dealt with the punishment of officials.[1] At the beginning of al-Ṣāliḥ's reign, the office of *shadd al-dawāwīn* was held by the amir ʿAlam al-Dīn Kurjī, whom al-Ṣāliḥ dismissed in 638/1240, replacing him by the amir Ḥusām al-Dīn Luʾlu'.[2]

The Mamluks continued to appoint only members of the military class to this office in Egypt as well as Syria.[3] It is said that the amir ʿIzz al-Dīn Uzdamur, and the amir ʿAlāʾ al-Dīn al-Ṣuwānī, were the holders of this office under Baybars.[4] In 678/1279, Qalāwūn appointed his Mamluk, the amir Sanjar al-Shujāʿī, *shādd al-dawāwīn*, mainly to assist the vizier in the collection of financial revenue. Subsequently, Sanjar attained high status in Qalāwūn's sultanate.[5]

It seems that lack of financial experience on the part of the holders of *shadd al-dawāwīn*, who were exclusively recruited among amirs trained for military service and not for work in the *dīwān*s, resulted in frequent short-term appointments. This was not conducive to stability. Four amirs, ʿAlāʾ al-Dīn Kushtughdī, Balabān al-Muḥsinī, Sanjar al-Khāzin, and Fakhr al-Dīn Iyāz or Iyās were appointed to the office one after the other in 710/1310–11, one of them (Balabān) holding the office only for a few days.[6] There were cases when the *shādd* had to perform simultaneously the functions of the *shadd* and the vizierate. Thus, for instance, when al-Nāṣir dismissed the vizier Ibn al-Ghannām in 713/1313, the amir Badr al-Dīn al-Turkumānī was appointed to the office of *shadd al-dawāwīn*, and acted successfully as vizier as well as *shādd al-dawāwīn* for about five years, until he asked al-Nāṣir in 718/1318 to be permitted to resign.[7] Another amir, Sanjar al-Ḥummuṣī, summoned by al-Nāṣir from Tripoli in 724/1324 to take over the office of *mushidd al-dawāwīn*, proved so efficient that he was reappointed to

[1] Nuwayrī, xxvii, fol. 48; Nābulsī, *Lumaʿ*, pp. 14, 39, tr. Cahen, 'Quelques aspects', pp. 99, 105; Rabīʿ, *Nuẓum*, p. 82.

[2] Nuwayrī, xxvii, fol. 71; Rabīʿ, *Nuẓum*, p. 82.

[3] For the *shadd al-dawāwīn* in Syria, cf. Nuwayrī, xxx, fols. 41–2; Ibn Ḥabīb, *Tadhkira*, fols. 98v–99v; Ibn al-Furāt, vii, pp. 180–1; Ibn Abī al-Faḍāʾil, pp. 368, 384; Qalqashandī *Ṣubḥ*, iv, p. 186; Bāshā, *Funūn*, ii, pp. 612–13.

[4] Kutubī, *ʿUyūn* (MS. Köprülü), fols. 143v–144r; Maqrīzī, *Khiṭaṭ*, ii, p. 106.

[5] Baybars al-Manṣūrī, *Zubda*, fols. 101v, 109v; Nuwayrī, xxix, fol. 1.

[6] Zetterstéen, pp. 152–3; Maqrīzī, *Sulūk*, ii, pp. 86, 89; for Sanjar al-Khāzin, cf. Ibn Ḥajar, *Durar*, ii, p. 172; Maqrīzī, *Khiṭaṭ*, ii, p. 135.

[7] Nuwayrī, xxx, fol. 117; ʿAynī, *Badr*, fol. 6v; Dawādārī, *Durr fākhir*, pp. 265–6, 293; Zetterstéen, pp. 160, 167; Maqrīzī, *Khiṭaṭ*, ii, p. 313.

this office for a second time in 737/1336, and held it until 740/1340.[1]

The holders of the *shadd al-dawāwīn* seem to have been of great assistance to al-Nāṣir in the execution of orders of confiscation, which by its very nature was subject to the authority of the *shādd*. Some *shādd*s did not shrink from cruelty in enforcing their orders, but their zeal did not protect them from confiscation when they in turn were dismissed from office. Thus in 734/1334 al-Nāṣir dismissed Ibn Hilāl al-Dawla, the then *shādd al-dawāwīn*, and ordered the confiscation of his property.[2]

The sources for the later Mamluk era mention a number of officials, each with the title of *shādd* but in charge of different sources of revenue or expenditure, such as *shādd al-aswāq* (*shādd* of the markets), *shādd al-maʿāṣir* (*shādd* of the presses), *shādd al-khāṣṣ* (associate to the *nāẓir al-khāṣṣ*), etc.[3] In the documents of *Maḥkama*, some *wāqif*s refer in their *waqfiyya*s to the appointment of a *mushidd* to help the agents collecting rents from the tenants of the *waqf* in question. Sultan Baybars al-Jāshnikīr, for example, expresses in his *waqfiyya* the wish that a *mushidd* with a salary of 90 *dirhams nuqra* monthly should be appointed for this purpose.[4] It is to be presumed that the main weapon of the *mushidd*s was physical compulsion or the threat of it.

G. *The employees of the* dīwāns

Conditions in the *dīwān*s, such as the numbers of staff and the demarcation of the functions of individual employees, are illustrated by three lists of civil servants which coincide only to a certain extent. Information for the beginning of the period under study is supplied by Ibn Mammātī in a list of eighteen civil servants of the pen (*min ḥamalat al-aqlām*), clerks, accountants, and secretaries. He does not, however, specify which *dīwān* they were attached to; nor does Nuwayrī at the end of the period under study in his list of eight officials, six of whom (*al-nāẓir*, *al-mutawallī*, *al-mustawfī*, *al-mushārif*, *al-ʿāmil*, and *al-shāhid*) also figure in Ibn

[1] ʿAynī, *Badr*, fol. 15^{r-v}; Kutubī, *ʿUyūn* (MS. Cambridge), fol. 16^{r}; Zettersteen, pp. 193, 209.

[2] Ibn Duqmāq, *Jawhar*, fol. 147^{v}; Zettersteen, p. 188; Ibn Ḥajar, *Durar*, iii, p. 136.

[3] Khālidī, fol. 129^{r}; Quatremère, op. cit., i. i, pp. 110–12 n. 141; Bāshā, *Funūn*, ii, pp. 604 ff.

[4] *Maḥkama*, Box 4, no. 22; for *dirham nuqra* see below, p. 174 n. 4.

Mammātī's list. The two not mentioned by Ibn Mammātī are *ṣāḥib al-dīwān* and *muqābil al-istīfā'*.[1] As to Qalqashandī, his list, though compiled after the period in question, is useful in this context, since it proves that some offices listed by both Ibn Mammātī and Nuwayrī survived far into the 8th/14th century. Qalqashandī enumerates nine employees of the *kuttāb al-amwāl*, including the vizier. The four contained in both Ibn Mammātī's and Nuwayrī's lists are *al-nāẓir*, *al-mustawfī*, *al-'āmil*, and *al-shāhid*; three, *al-mu'īn*, *al-ṣayrafī* (*al-jahbadh*), and *al-māsiḥ* are mentioned by Ibn Mammātī alone, while *ṣāḥib al-dīwān* also figures in Nuwayrī's list.[2]

The above data imply, first, that Nuwayri's list is far from comprehensive and, secondly, that not all eighteen employees mentioned by Ibn Mammātī worked in each financial *dīwān*. The *ḥāshir*, for example, was actually the *jawālī* tax-gatherer of the *dīwān al-jawālī*, and the *māsiḥ* was a land-surveyor, whose work, though important for the estimation of the *kharāj* tax, had no bearing on any other source of revenue.[3] Finally, it must be borne in mind that there was a considerable discrepancy between the duties of these officials as they are described by Ibn Mammātī, Nuwayrī, and Qalqashandī, and as they were performed in actual fact. It was the difference between theory and practice, between the ideal envisaged in regulations or perhaps in court orders and its execution. This is what seems to prevent the chroniclers from providing accurate information on the nature and function of each particular official. Documentary sources such as the Geniza and the Vienna papers may prove very useful one day in the elucidation of these as yet obscure matters.

As the *nāẓir* (controller) was the responsible chief of each *dīwān*, there was a *nāẓir* for the *dīwān al-aḥbās*, a *nāẓir* for the *dīwān al-mawārīth*, etc. It seems that the *nāẓir* was uppermost in the *dīwānī* hierarchy, and that he was responsible for the regularity of acts and deeds issued by another high official, *al-mutawallī*. Ibn Mammātī says that the *nāẓir* had to be watchful lest any official of the *dīwān* should exceed the limits of his authority, and that he was responsible for any shortcomings. Nuwayrī adds that the *nāẓir*

[1] Ibn Mammātī, ed. Najjār, pp. 7–10. However, only 17 employees excluding the *ḍāmin* are mentioned in Atiya's edition of Ibn Mammātī's work, pp. 297–306. Prof. Gottschalk (article 'Dīwān' in *EI*²) follows the latter; Nuwayrī, viii, pp. 298–305.

[2] Qalqashandī, *Ṣubḥ*, v, pp. 465–6.

[3] See above, pp. 134–5; see below, p. 160.

had to keep lists of the estimated revenue and expenditure, of arrears and surplus of financial revenue, and to supervise the financial accounts kept by the employees of his *dīwān*.[1]

The *mutawallī al-dīwān* seems to have been the real technical director of the *dīwān*. Ibn Mammātī states that the *mutawallī* used to be chosen on one of three conditions: (*a*) if he was reputed to be honest, since he had to do his best to eliminate dishonesty from the affairs of the *dīwān* and would be made responsible for any case of dishonesty which occurred there: (*b*) if he pledged or promised to increase the original revenue of the *dīwān*, though he was in danger of being punished or even dismissed in case he failed to fulfil this promise; (*c*) if he paid in advance a contracted sum (*ḍamān*) into the treasury.[2]

The office of the *mutawallī* increased in importance under the Mamluks, and it seems that the status of the *mutawallī* in the *dīwān* was rated higher than that of the *nāẓir*. *Mutawallī*s were recruited from the military class, as Nuwayrī states that they were also called *mushidd*s in his time. According to him, the holder of this office had some police authority, as he had to punish criminals and appoint watchmen, and to force those who left their villages to return.[3]

The function of the *ṣāḥib al-dīwān* overlapped with that of the *nāẓir*. He was a kind of auditor, who had to countersign every account or register signed by the *nāẓir*. If there was no *ṣāḥib al-dīwān*, the *nāẓir* took over his duties. The *ṣāḥib al-dīwān* seems to have become subsequently an important figure in the *dīwān*, and to have replaced the *mutawallī al-dīwān*. That is why Qalqashandī says that the *ṣāḥib al-dīwān* used to be addressed, in earlier days, as the *mutawallī al-dīwān*.[4]

[1] Ibn Mammātī, p. 298; Nābulsī, *Luma'*, pp. 23, 26, 29–30 and n. 23, tr. Cahen, 'Quelques aspects', pp. 100, 101, 103; Nuwayrī, viii, p. 299; Qalqashandī, *Ṣubḥ*, v, p. 465; Rabī', *Nuẓum*, p. 84. The word *nāẓir* was prefixed to a number of titles, cf. Bāshā, *Funūn*, iii, pp. 1177 ff. Every *ḥujja* in the *Maḥkama*'s collection contains a reference to the appointment of a *nāẓir* to deal with the affairs of the *waqf*, i.e. to maintain it in good order, to supervise the collection of its revenue, to direct it to its proper channels according to the provisions of the *waqfiyya*, cf. *Maḥkama*, Box 1, no. 7; Box 3, no. 16; Box 4, nos. 21, 22; Rabī', 'Ḥujjat tamlīk', pp. 198–200.

[2] Ibn Mammātī, ed. Atiya, pp. 298–300, ed. Najjār, pp. 7–8; Labib, *Handelsgeschichte*, pp. 234–5; for the *ḍamān* see above, pp. 136–7.

[3] Nuwayrī, viii, p. 298; for the different uses of the title *mutawallī* as observable in the inscriptions, cf. Bāshā, *Funūn*, iii, pp. 996–1019.

[4] Nuwayrī, viii, p. 300; Qalqashandī, *Ṣubḥ*, v, p. 466.

The office of the *istīfā'*, administered by the *mustawfī*, was known in the East under the Ghaznavids and Saljūqids and was concerned with accountancy.[1] It seems to have been introduced into Egypt by the Fāṭimids, as both Ibn al-Furāt and Qalqashandī mention a *mustawfī* among the employees of *dīwān al-kurā'* for horses and stables.[2] Ibn al-Ṭuwayr—in *Khiṭaṭ*—mentioned that one of the officials of *dīwān al-jaysh* under the Fāṭimids, the *mustawfī*, had to be informed of any case of death or illness among the *ajnād*.[3] The rank of the *mustawfī* seems to have been high under the Ayyūbids, as he was the head of a chamber (*majlis*) in the *dīwān*. He dealt mainly with accounts. It was his task to check and compare the accounts of *dīwānī* officials, and notify the *mutawallī al-dīwān* that it was time to collect the financial revenue.[4] According to Nābulsī, the status of the *mustawfī*s increased when they were entrusted with the preparation of lists of vacant offices under al-Kāmil, which gave them the opportunity and the right to recommend aspirants. Nābulsī claims that when al-Kāmil discussed the affairs of the *dīwān*s, he consulted, besides him, only two *mustawfī*s, to the exclusion of other *dīwānī* officials.[5]

Under the Mamluks the office of *al-istīfā'* remained in the service of accountancy. The function of the *mustawfī* grew in importance, as it was he who checked and adjusted all accounts, including the arrears and unused but available funds.[6] In addition to the *istīfā'*, which was limited to a single *dīwān*, the Mamluks introduced the office of *istīfā' al-dawla*. According to Qalqashandī, its holder had the right to deal with everything within the competence of the vizier and the *nāẓir al-dawla*, mainly controlling the accounts of the financial revenue and expenditure of the *dīwān*s.[7]

Since the office of *istīfā' al-dawla* required a considerable knowledge of accountancy, it was soon filled by Copts or converted

[1] Bundārī, *Zubda*, pp. 59, 77, 79, 92; Horst, *Die Staatsverwaltung*, pp. 21–2, 51–2, 57, 126–7, 133; Quatremère, op. cit., i. i, pp. 202–5 n. 85; Levy, article 'Mustawfī' in *EI*[1]; Cahen, article 'Bayt al-māl' in *EI*[2]; id., *Pre-Ottoman Turkey*, pp. 41, 225–6;B āshā, *Funūn*, iii, p. 1085.

[2] Ibn al-Furāt, iv, p. 149; Qalqashandī, *Ṣubḥ*, iii, p. 496.

[3] Maqrīzī, *Khiṭaṭ*, i, p. 401.

[4] Ibn Mammātī, ed. Atiya, p. 301, ed. Najjār, pp. 8–9; Rabī', *Nuẓum*, p. 85.

[5] Nābulsī, *Luma'*, pp. 36–7, tr. Cahen, 'Quelques aspects', p. 104; see also Nābulsī's *Tajrīd*, fol. 209v.

[6] Nuwayrī, viii, pp. 301–3; Qalqashandī, *Ṣubḥ*, v, p. 466.

[7] Qalqashandī, *Ṣubḥ*, iv, p. 30, xi, p. 355; Gaudefroy-Demombynes, *La Syrie*, pp. lxviii–lxix.

Muslims of Coptic origin. The *mustawfī al-dawla* of Baybars was Hibat Allāh al-Naṣrānī, known for his skill in such work. After his death in 681/1282–3, Qalāwūn appointed to this office Hibat Allāh's son Jirjis, who soon attained his father's status.[1] Sometimes the office of *istīfā' al-dawla* was filled by two or more *mustawfī*s; this occurred in 711/1312 when both al-Tāj Isḥāq and al-Muwaffaq Hibat Allāh were appointed to this office by al-Nāṣir and in 713/1313, when it was filled by three persons.[2]

There was a special office called *istīfā' al-ṣuḥba*, whose holder, called *mustawfī al-ṣuḥba*, was attached to the person of the sultan, on whose behalf he supervised the work of the *kuttāb* and checked all accounts.[3] It is said that, in 729/1329, al-Nāṣir fined some officials, among them Ibn Qarwīna, the then *mustawfī al-ṣuḥba*, 600,000 *dirham*s for failing to check an increase in the tax arrears of the Jīza province.[4]

As to the office of the *mu'īn* which is found in some, but not all Fāṭimid *dīwān*s, it survived under both the Ayyūbids and the Mamluks.[5] Ibn Mammātī states that the *mu'īn* was a clerk who helped the *mustawfī* in his work.[6] It is implied in *Ṣubḥ* that, under the Mamluks, a *mu'īn* was attached not only to the *mustawfī*, but also to other *dīwānī* officials.[7]

The *nāsikh* was, according to Ibn Mammātī, a lower clerk whose task it was to copy the reports and correspondence of the *dīwān*.[8] The office of *al-mushārafa*, held by the *mushārif*, was Fāṭimid in origin, and is found mentioned in an inscription from the year 532/1138.[9] At the beginning of the Ayyūbid era, the *mushārif*,

[1] Nuwayrī, xxix, fol. 25; Ibn al-Furāt, vii, p. 257.

[2] Maqrīzī, *Sulūk*, ii, pp. 107, 124.

[3] See the advice to *mustawfī al-ṣuḥba* in 'Umarī, *Ta'rīf*, pp. 115–16; see also Qalqashandī, *Ṣubḥ*, iv, p. 29; Gaudefroy-Demombynes, *La Syrie*, lxviii; Quatremère, op. cit., i. ii, p. 140 n. 171; Ibn Wāṣil (*Mufarrij*, MS. 1703, fol. 94r) mentions an office called *naẓar al-dīwān bi al-ṣuḥba*, the holder of which seems to have been a *nāẓir* appointed to accompany the sultan on his campaigns; see also, Ibn Ḥajar, *Durar*, iii, pp. 214–15.

[4] 'Aynī, *Badr*, fol. 24r; Maqrīzī, *Sulūk*, ii, p. 312.

[5] Cf. Ibn al-Furāt, iv, pp. 144, 149; Maqrīzī, *Khiṭaṭ*, i, p. 402; Qalqashandī, *Ṣubḥ*, iii, p. 496.

[6] Ibn Mammātī, ed. Atiya, pp. 301–2, ed. Najjār, p. 9.

[7] Qalqashandī, *Ṣubḥ*, v, p. 466.

[8] Ibn Mammātī, ed. Atiya, p. 302, ed. Najjār, p. 9; Rabī', *Nuẓum*, p. 85. The term *nāsikh* was also used to denote a scribe copying books; cf. Subkī, *Mu'īd*, pp. 186–7; Björkman, article 'Diplomatic' in *EI*²; Bāshā, *Funūn*, iii, p. 1177.

[9] Bāshā, *Funūn*, iii, p. 1092; cf. Ibn al-Ṣayrafī, *Qānūn*, pp. 137, 143.

whom even Ibn S͟hīt͟h rates next to the *nāẓir* in the *bayt al-māl*, was an important figure in the *dīwān*. His signature appears on receipts and accounts. He was entrusted with the revenue of the *dīwān* after it was sealed, a usage which, according to Nuwayrī, survived at least until the end of the period under study. On his appointment, the *mus͟hārif* had the right to ask for the lists of taxes, estimates, revenue, arrears, reserves, etc., to enable him to check the accounts with the *'āmil*.[1]

The *'āmil* was—under both the Ayyūbids and the Mamluks— responsible for keeping the accounts in detail. His signature was necessary for the ratification of each account. Under the Ayyūbids, the work of the *'āmil* remained under the control of both the *nāẓir* and the *mus͟hārif*. In case of dismissal, the *'āmil* was required to investigate the arrears, obtain witnessed statements from the debtors, and deliver them to the *dīwān*.[2] The significance of the function of the *'āmil* is reflected in the *Maḥkama* documents, in some of which a *wāqif* refers to the appointment of a salaried *'āmil* for the purpose of keeping the accounts of the revenue and expenditure of the *waqf*.[3]

As for the *kātib* (scribe), Ibn Mammātī mentions that he performed the duties of the *'āmil* where there was none, and if there was an *'āmil* 'any function that was required of a *kātib*'.[4] Qalqas͟handī states that in his time the term '*kātib*' was used to denote '*kātib al-māl*' (financial scribe). This implies that the function of the *kātib* continued in existence for a very long period.[5]

Ibn Mammātī and Ibn S͟hīt͟h mention a *dīwānī* employee called the *jahbad͟h*, a term of Persian origin, perhaps derived from the *gahbad͟h* of the Sāsānid administration. The *jahbad͟h* was known in Abbasid Iraq as a person of some importance in the fiscal administration, a kind of banker in government service, performing the tasks of cashier or treasurer, money-changer, and accountant.[6] In

---

[1] Ibn S͟hīt͟h, p. 30; Ibn Mammātī, ed. Atiya, pp. 302–3, ed. Najjār, p. 9; Nuwayrī, viii, p. 304; Rabī', *Nuẓum*, p. 85.

[2] Ibn Mammātī, ed. Atiya, p. 303, ed. Najjār, p. 9; Ibn S͟hīt͟h, pp. 30–1; Nuwayrī, viii, pp. 304–5; Qalqas͟handī, *Ṣubḥ*, v, p. 466. The title *'āmil* as used in the inscriptions seems to refer to several offices; for details, cf. Bās͟hā, *Funūn*, ii, pp. 745–69.

[3] Cf. *Ḥujjat waqf* Baybars al-Jās͟hnikīr, *Maḥkama*, Box 4, no. 22.

[4] Ibn Mammātī, ed. Atiya, p. 303, ed. Najjār, p. 9.

[5] Qalqas͟handī, *Ṣubḥ*, v, p. 452.

[6] Fischel, *Jews*, pp. 2–4; id., article 'Djahbad͟h' in *EI²*; Cahen, article 'Bayt al-māl', in *EI²*; Lambton, 'The merchant in medieval Islam', in *A Locust's*

Egypt the *jahbadh* was known before the advent of the Fāṭimids. This is confirmed by the occurrence of the term '*jahbadh*' in a fragment found among the Vienna papers which represents a receipt of 10 *dīnārs* paid by Abū Jamīl Mirqūra ibn Mīnā *al-Jahbadh* as his *kharāj* tax for the year 345/956–7.[1] It is fortunate that the same Abū Jamīl *al-Jahbadh* is also mentioned in a receipt for 23 *dīnārs kharāj* for 346/958, preserved in the papyrus collection of the Egyptian Library.[2] Relying on several fragments from the Geniza, Professor Goitein states that the *jahbadhs* seem to have worked as cashiers in Fāṭimid Egypt. They had to be present whenever payments were made to government offices, and were probably permitted to engage in business on their own account.[3]

In Ayyūbid times, the Egyptian *jahbadh* ceased, according to Ibn Mammātī and Ibn Shīth, to be a high official in the *dīwāns* and was reduced to the position of a subaltern, whose work was merely to receive cash payments and make out receipts.[4] The Mamluk counterpart to the Ayyūbid *jahbadh* was called the *ṣayrafī*.[5]

The *shāhid*, as an employee of the *dīwān*, was known under both the Ayyūbids and the Mamluks.[6] His main function was to keep, correct, and witness the day-book, *taʿlīq al-muyāwama*, otherwise described as the *rūznāmaj*, which was a list of all items of the daily revenue. Besides, he had to sign receipts and accounts, and record all details of revenue and expenditure in the *jarīda* (register).[7]

Ibn Mammātī mentions two subordinate clerks of the *dīwān*, the *nā'ib* and the *amīn*, whose functions somewhat overlapped. The

leg. Studies in honour of S. H. Taqizadeh, pp. 128–30; Imamuddin, 'Bayt al-mal and banks', pp. 18–19; Dūrī, *Studies*, pp. 173–85; id., *Tārīkh al-ʿIrāq*, pp. 159–69; for *dīwān al-jahbadha*, cf. Qudāma, *Kharāj*, fol. 20^{r-v}.

1 A.Ch. 10, fol. 7852.

2 Grohmann, *Arabic papyri*, iii, pp. 183–4 and plate XVII. The *jahbadh* is frequently mentioned in papyri from the pre-Fāṭimid era, cf. ibid., iii, p. 169, v, pp. 15–16.

3 Goitein, *Med. Soc.*, i, pp. 248–50. It seems that, under al-Mustanṣir, the *jahbadh* was quite an important official in the Fāṭimid *dīwāns*; cf. Maqrīzī, *Ighātha*, p. 21.

4 Ibn Mammātī, ed. Atiya, p. 304, ed. Najjār, p. 9; Ibn Shīth, p. 31; Cahen, 'Contribution', p. 250 n. 4, p. 269; Rabīʿ, *Nuẓum*, pp. 85–6.

5 Qalqashandī, *Ṣubḥ*, v, p. 466.

6 *Shuhūd* (pl. of *shāhid*) was a term designating registered witnesses in judicial courts; cf. Bāshā, *Funūn*, ii, pp. 618–22.

7 Ibn Mammātī, ed. Atiya, p. 304, ed. Najjār, p. 9; Nuwayrī, viii, p. 304; Qalqashandī, *Ṣubḥ*, v, p. 466; Rabīʿ, *Nuẓum*, p. 86; for *taʿlīq al-muyāwama* and *rūznāmaj* see above, pp. 135–6 and n. 1, p. 135; for *shāhid bayt al-māl* under the Ayyūbids, cf. Ibn Shīth, pp. 28–30.

nā'ib seems to have been a minor secretary not concerned with accountancy; so was the *amīn* who replaced the *shāhid* in some *dīwāns*. The office of the *amīn* proved capable of development, as the *emīn* of the Ottoman administration was a salaried government intendant or commissioner, appointed by or in the name of the sultan 'to administer, supervise, or control a department, function or source of revenue'.[1]

Four other clerks, the *dalīl*, the *māsiḥ*, the *ḥā'iz*, and the *khāzin*, seem to have dealt chiefly with the estimation and collection of the *kharāj* tax. The *dalīl*, frequently referred to in papyri from the 3rd/9th century, had, apart from his above-mentioned role in the collection of the *jawālī* tax, essential duties in the estimation of the *kharāj* tax.[2] As pointed out already, the *māsiḥ* (surveyor) used to prepare the yearly pre-harvest survey under the supervision of the *'āmil* and the *mushārif*.[3] Ibn Mammātī suggests that it was not the *māsiḥ* who undertook the measurement in person, but the *qaṣṣāb*, who measured the cultivated land by means of the *qaṣaba* (unit of length). Thus the role of the *māsiḥ* who was a *kātib* consisted merely in calculating the surface area from these measurements.[4] In later times, however, it was, according to Qalqashandī, the *māsiḥ* who independently performed the survey of cultivated land.[5]

The *ḥā'iz* was a *kāṭib* in charge of the threshing floor. It was his duty to record the yield of the harvest, even before it was brought in, and keep the threshing floors closed at night to prevent the peasants from getting hold of the crop before the *dīwān* had taken its share. The *khāzin* (storekeeper)—referred to in a very flimsy fragment in the Vienna papers—was the collector of taxes paid in kind to the state granaries and storehouses, and the storekeeper in charge of the *a'māl* (inventories) and the distribution of the grain, responsible for any deficit and, according to Professor Cahen, for the quality of the crops. He was entitled to an additional fixed measure for his own benefit. Professor Cahen also states that the

[1] Ibn Mammātī, ed. Atiya, pp. 304–5, ed. Najjār, p. 9; for the Ottoman *emīn*, cf. Lewis, article 'Emīn' in *EI*²; Heyd, *Ottoman documents*, pp. 20, 59–60, 93, 111, 113, 118, 123, 133, 137, 141, 172; Shaw, *The financial and administrative organization*, pp. 21, 26, 62; id., *Ottoman Egypt*, pp. 45 n. 4, 47 n.

[2] Grohmann, *Arabic papyri*, iii, p. 130, iv, pp. 90, 122, 193; see above, p. 73 and p. 135.

[3] See above, p. 74.

[4] Ibn Mammātī, ed. Atiya, p. 305, ed. Najjār, pp. 9–10; Rabī', *Nuẓum*, p. 86. There is a mention of the *qaṣṣāb* in a papyrus from the 3rd/9th century; cf. Grohmann, *Arabic papyri*, v, pp. 4, 6.

[5] Qalqashandī, *Ṣubḥ*, v, p. 466.

khāzin accepted deliveries in the presence of one or two witnesses, giving *barā'āt*, and received the repayments for the *taqāwī* (seeds) which had been lent to the peasants for sowing.[1]

The functions of the last two employees named in Ibn Mammātī's list, the *ḥāshir* and the *ḍāmin*, have already been discussed in some detail.[2]

[1] A.Ch. 10227; Ibn Mammātī, ed. Atiya, p. 305 and n. 14, p. 306 and n. 3, ed. Najjār, p. 10; Ibn Shīth, pp. 31–2; Cahen, 'Contribution', pp. 269, 270 and n. 1.

[2] See above, pp. 134–7.

V

THE MONETARY SYSTEM

'To pronounce the word "pure gold *dīnār*" was like mentioning the name of a wife to a jealous husband, while to hold such a coin in one's hand was like crossing the doors of paradise.' This quotation, copied by Maqrīzī from al-Qāḍī al-Fāḍil's account of the monetary crisis which occurred immediately after the collapse of the Fāṭimid regime, has been often commented on, but it still needs clarification and interpretation.[1] For this purpose it will be necessary to go back to the pre-Ayyūbid era.

A. *The monetary system of Egypt in the pre-Ayyūbid era*

In the Umayyad and ʿAbbāsid periods, Egypt had no independent coinage. What was in circulation in the country was the official currency of the Caliph who resided in Syria or Iraq. In 170/786–7 gold, and from 181/797–8 silver coins were minted in Egypt, but the legends they bore were exactly the same as those on the coins minted in Baghdad.[2] The first step towards emancipation from central control was taken by Aḥmad ibn Ṭūlūn, who coined the highly valued Aḥmadī *dīnār*. This may be ascribed to Ibn Ṭūlūn's political ambitions or to the undeniable economic prosperity of Egypt under his rule or to both, especially as there was a marked gradual deterioration in the ʿ*iyār* of later Ṭūlūnid *dīnārs*.[3]

[1] Maqrīzī, *Sulūk*, i, p. 46, tr. Blochet, 'B', p. 503; id., *Shudhūr*, p. 59, tr. Silvestre de Sacy, *Traité des monnoies musulmanes*, p. 43; M. de Boüard, 'Sur l'évolution monétaire de l'Égypte médiévale', *EC*, xxx (1939), p. 446; Ehrenkreutz, 'The crisis of *dīnār* in the Egypt of Saladin', *JAOS*, lxxvi (1956), p. 178; id., 'Arabic *dīnārs* struck by the Crusaders', *JESHO*, vii (1964), p. 179; Rabīʿ, *Nuẓum*, pp. 94–6.

[2] Maqrīzī, *Shudhūr*, p. 54, tr. S. de Sacy, p. 37; Balog, 'History of the dirhem in Egypt', *Revue Numismatique*, 6e série, iii (1961), p. 111.

[3] Makhzūmī, fols. 138v–139r; Balawī, *Sīra*, p. 196; Maqrīzī, *Shudhūr*, pp. 54–7, tr. S. de Sacy, pp. 37–40; Qalqashandī, *Ṣubḥ*, iii, pp. 465–6; ʿAlī Mubārak, *Khiṭaṭ*, xx, p. 3; Sauvaire, 'Matériaux pour servir à l'histoire de la numismatique et de la métrologie musulmanes', *JA*, 7e série, xv (1880), pp. 271–2; Zaky M. Hassan (Zakī M. Ḥasan), *Les Tulunides*, pp. 211–12; Grabar, *The coinage of the*

When Muḥammad ibn Ṭughj seized power in Egypt, there was a revival of economic prosperity. Internal peace and security were re-established.[1] Professor Ehrenkreutz believes that it was this prosperity which was reflected in the high standard of fineness of the Ikhshīdid *dīnār*s struck in Egypt.[2] However, it seems that this prosperity did not last until the end of the Ikhshīdid period, as there was a monetary crisis in Egypt on the eve of the Fāṭimid invasion. Evidence of this crisis may be found in the *amān* granted to the people of Egypt in Shaʿbān 358/July 969 by Jawhar al-Ṣiqillī on behalf of the Caliph al-Muʿizz, which contains a promise of a reform of the coinage by adjusting its intrinsic quality to the Fāṭimid standard, and eliminating debased coins from circulation.[3]

Jawhar did indeed take steps to fulfil his promise by striking, in 358/969, the Muʿizzī *dīnār*, which seems to have been of high quality.[4] He introduced, in the years 359/969–70, 361/971–2, and 362/972–3, three consecutive series of administrative measures which aimed at the withdrawal of other types of gold coins from circulation.[5] Consequently, the *Kharāj* tax in Muḥarram 363/October 973 was collected only in Muʿizzī *dīnār*s, equivalent to 15½ *dirham*s

Ṭūlūnids, p. 59 and n. 3; M. de Boüard, 'Évolution monétaire', pp. 436–41; Ehrenkreutz, 'Studies in the monetary history of the Near East in the middle ages', (I), *JESHO*, ii (1959), pp. 131, 149–51; Fahmī, *Nuqūd*, p. 56. The meaning of the Arabic word *ʿiyār* is 'the principle determining the metallic composition of coins' or briefly 'the standard of fineness'. E.g. the fineness of a gold *dīnār* depends on the proportion of gold in it. The metallic composition of coins is interesting to the student of economic history because changes in the purity of the coins were mostly related to and indicative of the economic situation of the time and place; cf. Sauvaire, 'Matériaux', *JA*, xix (1882), pp. 97 ff.; Ehrenkreutz, 'Monetary aspects', pp. 45–6; id., 'Studies' (II), *JESHO*, vi (1963), pp. 244–8; see above, p. 23.

1 Masʿūdī, *Murūj*, i, pp. 287–321; Wiet, *L'Égytpe arabe*, p. 135; Sayyida Kāshif, *Miṣr*, pp. 233 ff.

2 On the basis of an investigation of the standard of fineness of 14 Ikhshīdid *dīnār*s, he found that 5 (or 35·7 per cent) have the standard of 99 per cent, six (or 42·8 per cent) the regular standard of 98 per cent, two of 97 per cent, and one of 96 per cent of fineness. See Ehrenkreutz, 'Studies' (I), pp. 152–3; see also Balog, 'Tables de références des monnaies ikhchidites', *Revue belge de Numismatique*, ciii (1957), pp. 107–34.

3 Maqrīzī, *Ittiʿāẓ*, fol. 16^{r-v}; Ibn Ḥammād, *Akhbār*, p. 42; Ehrenkreutz, 'Studies', ii, p. 258.

4 Maqrīzī, *Shudhūr*, p. 58, tr. S. de Sacy, p. 40; Sauvaire, 'Matériaux', *JA*, 7e série, xix (1882), pp. 48–9; Grohmann, *Einführung*, p. 196; Ashtor, 'La recherche des prix dans l'orient médiéval', *SI*, xxi (1964), p. 110 and n. 10; Cahen, 'Quelques problèmes', pp. 399–400.

5 Maqrīzī, *Ittiʿāẓ*, fols. 19^r–20^v.

each. This action decreased the value of other *dīnār*s, especially the Rāḍī *dīnār*, and resulted in heavy losses to the population.[1] In addition to their own efficient minting organization in North Africa, plentiful gold imports from West African and Nubian auriferous regions facilitated the successes of the Fāṭimids in the sphere of gold coinage, at the very outset of their rule in Egypt.[2] It is also worth noting that the transfer of the Fāṭimid capital from North Africa to Cairo was coupled with the transfer of huge amounts of gold to the new capital. What corroborates it is that, on his arrival in Egypt in 361/972, al-Muʿizz was accompanied by a hundred camels laden with gold ingots shaped like millstones.[3]

The Fāṭimids found additional sources of gold in the mines of al-ʿAllāqī in Southern Egypt, and in the tombs of the Pharaohs.[4] Thus they had no difficulties, especially in the first decades of their rule in Egypt, in maintaining a fixed standard of weight for their gold *dīnār*s which were seemingly handled by tale.[5] Relying on the material provided by numismatic catalogues, Professor Ehrenkreutz has reached the conclusion that the majority of the available Fāṭimid *dīnār*s (311 out of 466 or 69·7 per cent) weighed between 4·06 gm. and 4·0 gm., so that they did not materially differ in weight from the legal *dīnār* with a prescribed weight of 4·233 gm.[6] As to the standard of fineness, 142 Fāṭimid *dīnār*s belonging to the American Numismatic Society in New York, struck in Egypt

[1] Maqrīzī, *Ittiʿāẓ*, fol. 23r; Ibn Muyassar, p. 45; Maqrīzī, *Shudhūr*, p. 58; tr. S. de Sacy, p. 41; Maqrīzī, *Khiṭaṭ*, ii, p. 6; Sauvaire, 'Matériaux', *JA*, xv (1880), p. 449, xix (1882), pp. 49–50; Fahmī, *Nuqūd*, p. 62; Sayyida Kāshif, 'Dirāsāt fī al-nuqūd al-Islāmiyya', *MTM*, xii (1964–5), p. 91; Grohmann (*Einführung*, p. 197) has found in the papyri frequent mention of an exchange rate of 15½ for the Muʿizzī *dīnār*. The Rāḍī *dīnār* is said to have been coined by the ʿAbbāsid Caliph al-Rāḍī (died 329/940) cf. Muqaddasī, *Aḥsan*, p. 204; Sauvaire, 'Matériaux', *JA*, xv (1880), p. 449; S. de Sacy, *Traité*, p. 41 and n. 78.

[2] Ehrenkreutz, 'Studies' (II), pp. 261–2. Having established their dynasty in North Africa in the early years of the 10th century, the Fāṭimids became for a while the masters of the three Sahara gold routes: Sijilmāsa ,Tichit, the Sudan; from Ouargla along the bend of the Niger; Djerada, Tripoli; Ghadamès, Aīr to the Sudan. This enabled the Fāṭimids to collect important reserves of precious metals for the realization of the projected conquest of Egypt, cf. Lombard, 'L'or musulman du VIIe au XIe siècle', *Annales* (*E.S.C.*), ii (1947), pp. 150–1.

[3] Nuwayrī, xxvi, fol. 43; Maqrīzī, *Ittiʿāẓ*, fol. 15v.

[4] See below, pp. 169–70.

[5] Muqaddasī, *Aḥsan*, p. 240; Ehrenkreutz, 'The crisis of *dīnār*', p. 178. There is a mention of 5 *danānīr* Ḥākimiyya in a flimsy fragment from the Vienna papers dated 412/1021–2; cf. A.Ch. 10, fol. 7921.

[6] Ehrenkreutz, 'The crisis of *dīnār*', p. 180 and n. 7. In a similar attempt Prof. Ashtor reaches similar results. Cf. 'La recherche des prix', pp. 112–13.

before the end of the eleventh century A.D., were found to be of excellent intrinsic quality, 121 out of 142 or 85·2 per cent showing a standard of fineness of 98 per cent and above.[1]

The fixed-weight standard and the high degree of fineness of the Fāṭimid *dīnār*s were among the reasons which prompted the Crusaders to strike gold coins in imitation of Fāṭimid *dīnār*s, with al-Mustanṣir's and al-Āmir's *dīnār*s as prototypes.[2] Thus the Fāṭimid endeavour to preserve the quality of Egyptian gold coinage seems to have been a defensive measure. In 514/1120, al-Āmir instituted an inquiry 'to investigate the secrets of gold production in the mint which resulted in establishing the standard of the gold at a level which could not be surpassed'.[3] To test the quality of the Āmirī *dīnār*, Professor Ehrenkreutz investigated 91 Egyptian specimens from al-Āmir's reign and found that 69 specimens fell within the excellent category of 96 per cent and above, and that none were inferior to a standard of fineness of 90 per cent after A.D. 1124.[4]

In its latest period, the Fāṭimid Caliphate became both politically and economically too weak to offer sufficient backing for its *dīnār*, already shaken in its prestige by the circulation of Crusaders' coins. The situation was aggravated by a decrease in the supply of gold. It was on the eve of the advent of the Ayyūbids that this acute scarcity of gold occurred, to which al-Fāḍil refers in the words quoted at the beginning of this chapter. Thus, even before the collapse of the Fāṭimid caliphate, the fate of the Muslim 'dollar of the Middle Ages' had been sealed.[5]

The history of the Fāṭimid silver *dirham*s was quite different.

[1] Ehrenkreutz, 'Arabic *dīnārs*', pp. 173–4. The high standard of fineness of the Fāṭimid *dīnār*s does not seem to have been affected by the terrible economic upheavals of the reign of al-Mustanṣir, cf. ibid., pp. 176–7; id., 'Studies' (II), p. 262.

[2] Ehrenkreutz, 'Arabic *dīnārs*', pp. 175–6.

[3] Ibn Ba'ra, pp. 49–50: 'ووقف (الآمر) من أسرار الذهب على أصل لا يجوز لغيره أن يتعداه، وبالغ فى الاستقصاء عنه الى حد لم يصل اليه سواه، وصار قدوة يقتدى به من بعده، وعيارا قد استوعب الممكنات في التحرير وهو العمدة، ولا الوقوف الا عنده'. Cf. Sauvaire, 'Matériaux', *JA*, xix (1882), p. 102; Ehrenkreutz, 'The standard of fineness of gold coins circulating in Egypt at the time of the Crusades', *JAOS*, lxxiv (1954), p. 164; id., 'Studies' (I), p. 131; id., 'Arabic *dīnārs*', p. 178.

[4] Ehrenkreutz, 'Arabic *dīnārs*', pp. 176–7. According to Dr. G. Miles (article 'Dīnār' in *EI*²), the standard of fineness of the *dīnār* under al-Āmir approximated 100 per cent purity.

[5] Ehrenkreutz, 'Arabic *dīnārs*', p. 179.

Muqaddasī, writing about the second half of the 4th/10th century, states that, for some undetermined time after the Fāṭimid invasion, the value of the Fāṭimid *dirham* was low.[1] This statement is confirmed by a piece of evidence from the Geniza collection. Relying on a fragment from a day-to-day account of the income of a textile merchant in 393/1003 from Fusṭāṭ, Professor Goitein reached the conclusion that the exchange rate of the *dīnār* for that year was 1:37·7.[2] As numismatic evidence points to the high quality of the Fāṭimid *dīnār*, it is the silver *dirham* that must have depreciated until it reached this low value. Moreover, the Geniza evidence proves that the crisis of the silver coinage which is said to have occurred in the year 397/1006, goes back to 393/1003.

On this crisis Maqrīzī quotes a statement by al-Musabbiḥī to the effect that the value of the *dirham* depreciated in Rabīʿ I 397/ December 1006 until its rate of exchange reached 34 *dirhams* to 1 *dīnār*. To remedy this situation, the Caliph al-Ḥākim replaced the substandard *dirhams* by new ones at the rate of four old *dirhams* to one new *dirham* and eighteen new *dirhams* to one *dīnār*. It had been announced that all old *dirhams* should be returned to *dār al ḍarb* (the mint) within three days.[3]

The question arises here what was the cause of the depreciation of silver *dirhams*. There is a statement by al-Hamdānī from the tenth century A.D. to the effect that the silver mines were situated in Najd, the Yemen, Khurāsān, or in unknown parts of Arabia. He makes no mention of silver mines in any part of Egypt, which indicates that Egypt had to import its silver.[4] In about A.D. 975, owing to internal decay and Turkish infiltration, the Samanid

[1] Muqaddasī, *Aḥsan*, p. 240.

[2] T.-S. Arabic Box 30, fol. 284 in Goitein, 'The exchange rate of gold and silver money in Fatimid and Ayyubid times', *JESHO*, viii (1965), pp. 4–5; id., *Med. Soc.*, i, p. 369.

[3] Maqrīzī, *Ittiʿāẓ*, fol. 61^{v}; id., *Ighātha* pp. 64–5, tr. Wiet, 'Le traité des famines', pp. 63–4; M. de Boüard, 'Évolution monétaire', pp. 443–4; Balog, 'History of the dirhem', p. 115; Maqrīzī (*Shudhūr*, p. 59) locates the crisis in Rabīʿ I 399, a date which is accepted by Grohmann, *Einführung*, p. 209.

[4] Hamdānī, *Jawharatayn*, fols. 24^{v}–25^{r}, ed. C. Toll, pp. 143–5; Ḥamad al-Jāsir, 'Kitāb al-Jawharatayn', *MMIA*, xxvi (1951), pp. 533–44; Dunlop, 'Sources of gold and silver in Islam according to al-Hamdānī', *SI*, viii (1957), pp. 40–1; see also Qudāma ibn Jaʿfar, *Kharāj*, fol. 36^{r-v}; Abū Dulaf, *al-Risāla al-thāniya*, p. 2, tr. Minorsky, p. 31; Ibn Ḥawqal, *Ṣifa*, fols. 158, 165, 246, 253–5, 264, 272, 296, 299, 303. Prof. Goitein (*Med. Soc.*, i, p. 233) states that huge quantities of silver coins were imported to Egypt under the Fāṭimids 'from the Muslim West year after year, and some came from Arab Asia too'.

dynasty lost control of the most important silver mines in Zarafshān. Later, after the Punjab had been conquered by the Muslims, the silver was drawn off from Turkestan and exported to India. When the sources of silver in Turkestan had been exhausted, the silver was drained off all the Islamic East.[1] Andrew M. Watson attempts to explain the disappearance of the vast quantities of silver which were in circulation before the onset of the famine. He states that they went, probably, partly to India and China, but most certainly to Europe. Hoards discovered in Russia and Scandinavia permit the mapping out of the direction of one such outflow of silver, when Samanid coins moved across the Caspian Sea and then by caravan into Russia, Poland, Sweden, Finland, and Norway, and thence to Western Europe and even to Iceland. The size of these hoards of silver indicates that the loss of silver in this direction alone was enormous. On the other hand, the low price of gold in the West, which minted virtually no gold until the middle of the thirteenth century, may have attracted silver from regions which valued it less highly, while in the East the high price of gold in terms of silver continued, perhaps owing to the abandonment of silver coinage.[2] Thus Egypt was affected by the general silver famine. The shortage of silver in Egypt led to the disappearance of pure silver *dirhams* which were replaced by debased *dirhams* of lower value.

The silver coinage continued to depreciate until the end of the Fāṭimid era. From a Geniza fragment preserved in the Bodleian, which is a handwritten report sent by Nahray ibn Nissīm in 437–8/1045–6 from Egypt to his partner Barhūn ibn Isaac in Qayrawān, it emerges that the rate of exchange was $33\frac{1}{3}:1$. In another fragment of the same report, in Cambridge University Library, a reference to a business transaction concluded in Būṣīr, Upper Egypt, mentions the rate as 32:1.[3] To judge by some other fragments from the same collection from the reign of al-Mustanṣir, the value of the silver *dirham* seems to have fallen to 40:1 in about 448/1056, and to have persisted at this low level without change for at least four years.[4] By the middle of the twelfth century, the

[1] Blake, 'The circulation of silver in the Moslem East down to the Mongol epoch', *HJAS*, ii (1937), pp. 309–10; Miles, article 'Dirham' in *EI*[2]; for silver mines in Turkestan cf. Barthold, *Turkestan*, pp. 65, 164, 168–9, 171–2.

[2] Watson, 'Back to gold and silver', *EHR*, xx (1967), pp. 4–5.

[3] Bodleian MS. Heb. e. 98, fol. 65[a]; T.-S., Box K15, fol. 53 in Goitein, 'The exchange rate', pp. 9–10; id., *Med. Soc.*, i, p. 372.

[4] T.-S., Box Misc. 8, fol. 65; T.-S., Box J1, fol. 1; T.-S., N.S., J28, J111,

silver rate of exchange of the *dīnār* varied between 34·3, 39·5, 40, 42 *dirhams*.[1] In an unpublished daily account book for the year 554/1159 in the Geniza a retail merchant, dealing in flour, flax, wheat, cotton, clothes, etc., refers, on page 9, to outstanding debts of 16 *dirhams* and 23 *dirhams* respectively which he calculates as one *dīnār* and one *dirham*. This proves conclusively that the exchange of one *dīnār* was 38 *dirhams*.[2]

The data found in the Geniza on the depreciation of the Fāṭimid *dirhams* are supported by numismatic evidence. As to the standard of weight, Professor Balog infers from a test made on silver coins in his possession as well as the description of some coins in numismatic catalogues (164 silver coins in all), that the Fāṭimids reduced the weight of the *dirham* by about ten per cent, so that the Fāṭimid *dirham* weighs approximately 2·60 gm., and the half-*dirham* about 1·38 gm.[3] Concerning the standard of fineness, Professor Balog found, by committing 13 Fāṭimid *dirhams* to the furnace of the assayer, that the standard of fineness of the *dirham*, as compared with 81 to 88 per cent of pure silver under al-ʿAzīz, had dropped

J127, and J198 in Goitein, 'The exchange rate', pp. 13–14; id., *Med. Soc.*, i, pp. 373–4.

[1] T.–S., 8J9, fol. 19; T.–S. Misc., Box 8, fol. 66; T.–S., 8J17, fol. 18; T.–S. Box K6, fol. 149 in Goitein, 'The exchange rate', pp. 26–7; id., *Med. Soc.*, i, p. 381. A fragile unpublished fragment from the Geniza (T.–S. Arabic, B40, fol. 129v) from the same period mentions the rate of exchange of 65 *dirhams* per *dīnār*: 'هذا بخطى أنا أبو العلا . . . لابو الحسن عندى كل له عندى من الدراهم الجدد ماية وتسع واربعين . . . صرف خمسه وستين بدينا . . .' 'This is in my own hand, I Abū al-ʿAlā . . ., I owe Abū al-Ḥasan all that. I owe him 149 new *dirhams* exchangeable at the rate of 65 per *dīnā*(*r*).'

[2] T.–S., Arabic B40, fol. 39; this daily account book consists of 12 pages about 3½ × 7 inches. An entry on page 5 refers to a debt of 16 *dirhams* contracted by Abū Wakīm on 1 Muḥarram 552; on p. 6 the date of Wednesday, the first day of Ramaḍān is mentioned without specifying the year. As the first of Ramaḍān in the year 554 (16 Sept. 1159) fell on Wednesday, the document seems to have been written a few days after that.

[3] Balog, 'History of the dirhem', pp. 117–22; according to Musabbiḥī (*Akhbār*, xl, fols. 255v, 260v–261r) the Fāṭimid *dirhams* were never accepted by tale but by weight, and bakers and other dealers who falsified the glass coin-weights were punished by the *muḥtasib* (inspector of the markets). For the glass coin-weights cf. W. Airy, *On the Arabic glass weights*, pp. 3–6; G. Miles, *Early Arabic glass weights*, pp. 1–12. Prof. Balog ('The Ayyūbid glass jetons and their use', *JESHO*, ix (1966), pp. 242–56) tries to prove that the Fāṭimid and the Ayyūbid glass jetons could not have been coin-weights, in the sense of Umayyad and ʿAbbāsid *sanajāt*, but were intended to circulate as 'fiduciary currency to substitute the copper coinage'. However, the idea is difficult to accept or refute, as there is no reference in textual sources to the use of glass jetons as currency.

gradually to 25 to 30 per cent of pure silver content under al-ʿĀḍid.[1] As the Fāṭimid *dirhams* in circulation on the advent of Saladin not only considerably deviated from the theoretical weight of the *dirham*, but were also of extremely poor metallic quality, Saladin was faced by problems resulting from the lack of both gold and silver.

B. *The effect of the decrease in gold supplies on the standard of weight and purity of Saladin's* dīnār*s*

The cause of the decrease of the supply of Egyptian gold at the beginning of the Ayyūbid era was complex. First, there was the exhaustion of the indigenous sources of gold. According to al-Idrīsī (twelfth century), the productivity of the Egyptian gold mines in al-ʿAllāqī, a valley in lower Nubia between the Nile and the shore of the Red Sea, operated by individual effort with very primitive means, continued to decrease, and the Fāṭimid caliphs found that its exploitation hardly covered the costs of production.[2] Besides al-Idrīsī, there is al-Yaʿqūbī's ninth-century account of the successes of the gold-seekers in al-ʿAllāqī,[3] and al-Hamdānī's tenth-century description of the wealth of the mines in al-ʿAllāqī, Qifṭ, al-Aqṣur (Luxor), Armant, and Aswān.[4] Together, these three accounts led to the conclusion that the yield of the Egyptian mines, so rich in the ninth and tenth centuries. had vastly decreased when Saladin came to power. This is also true of the amount of gold derived from Pharaonic tombs (*al-maṭālib*). Ibn Ṭūlūn made the exploitation of this gold source a state monopoly, and it seems that

[1] Balog, 'History of the dirhem', pp. 122–3. In his *Coinage of the Mamluk sultans*, p. 40 n. 1, Prof. Balog gives a description of his method of analysing coins. A determined amount of silver (0·5 gm.) is cut off the coin, weighed, and melted in the presence of lead in a porous terracotta container. The container absorbs the lead which carries with it the non-precious elements from the molten drop of metal, so that only the pure silver remains. The fineness is calculated from the difference of weight between the original alloy and the remaining pure silver. For other methods, see below, p. 172 n. 3.

[2] Idrīsī, *Nuzha*, pp. 26–7; M. de Boüard, 'Évolution monétaire', p. 447; Rabīʿ, *Nuẓum*, p. 95.

[3] Yaʿqūbī, *Buldān*, pp. 334–5, tr. Wiet, *Le Pays*, pp. 189–91; Lombard, 'L'or musulman', p. 149; it would not be justified to infer from Yaʿqūbī's account that new beds of Nubian gold were discovered, since these had already been known and accessible long before the advent of the Arabs, cf. Cahen, 'Quelques problèmes', p. 404 and n. 35; Lopez, 'The dollar of the middle ages', *JEH*, xi, no. 3 (1951), p. 227.

[4] Hamdānī, *Jawharatayn*, fol. 24^{v}, ed. C. Toll, p. 143; Dunlop, 'Sources of gold and silver', p. 40; see also Ibn Ḥawqal, *Ṣifa*, fols. 41, 76; id., *Ṣūra*, i, p. 162; Ibn Saʿīd, *Basṭ*, p. 50; Wiet, article 'al-ʿAllāḳī' in *EI*^{2}.

by the time the controls were removed, this source was already exhausted.[1] Al-Baghdādī, who visited Egypt in 590/1194, describes in detail how the people searching for gold destroyed monuments but found only mummies, bandages, and remains of animals and birds.[2]

Secondly, there was the decrease in Egyptian exports, especially in textiles, owing to a certain lack of stability and security in the last decades of the Fāṭimid regime, confiscations, high taxation, and the frequent looting of Tinnīs by the Franks. Thus Egypt suffered not only a loss of gold imports through the fall of textile exports, but even had to pay out gold for the import of goods for her own use.[3]

Thirdly, Egypt paid large amounts of gold in ransom and tributes. Every incursion of Amalric, the king of Jerusalem, and of the Zangids was accompanied by a loss of gold. When the Fāṭimid vizier Shāwar asked for Amalric's help in expelling Shīrkūh from Egypt in 559/1164, he paid him 27,000 gold *dīnār*s.[4] It is said that, in 562/1167, Shāwar paid Shīrkūh 50,000 *dīnār*s to induce him to return to Syria, and engaged to pay the Crusaders a yearly tribute of 100,000 *dīnār*s.[5] It is also said that, when Amalric conquered Egypt in 564/1168, Shāwar agreed to pay him a million *dīnār*s, of which he actually paid an advance of 100,000 *dīnār*s.[6] Caution is advisable in dealing with these figures, but they indicate, in one way or another, that much Egyptian gold went to Syria on these occasions. A similar loss occurred under Saladin who, after the

[1] Balawī, *Sīra*, pp. 194–6; Maqrīzī, *Shudhūr*, pp. 55–7, tr. S. de Sacy, pp. 38–40; Zaky Hassan, *Les Tulunides*, pp. 211–12. On the gold in the Pharaonic tombs cf. Mas'ūdī, *Murūj*, i, pp. 211–13; Lombard, 'L'or musulman', pp. 148–9.

[2] Baghdādī, *Ifāda*, pp. 158–74, tr. S. de Sacy, pp. 196–204; M. de Boüard, 'Évolution monétaire', pp. 447–8; Rabī', *Nuẓum*, p. 95.

[3] M. de Boüard, 'Évolution monétaire', p. 448; Rabī', *Nuẓum*, p. 95; Labib, *Handelsgeschichte*, p. 264.

[4] Abū Shāma, *Rawḍatayn*, i. ii, p. 421; Ibn Abī al-Damm (*Tārīkh*, fol. 151^{r}) states that Shāwar decided to pay the Crusaders 400,000 *dīnār*s for their help.

[5] Ibn Wāṣil, *Ṣāliḥī*, fols. 193^{v}–194^{r}; Ibn Abī al-Damm, fol. 152^{r}; Abū Shāma, *Rawḍatayn*, i. ii, p. 366; Ibn al-'Adīm, *Zubda*, ii, p. 324; *Chronique de Michel le Syrien* (French transl.), iii, p. 329.

[6] Iṣfahānī, *Sanā*, fol. 169^{v}; Ibn Abī al-Hayjā', fol. 164^{v}; Ibn Wāṣil, *Ṣāliḥī*, fol. 194^{r}; Ibn Qāḍī Shuhba, *Durr*, fol. 84^{r-v}; Nuwayrī, xxvi, fol. 102; Abū Shāma, *Rawḍatayn*, i. ii, pp. 391–2; *Chronique de Michel le Syrien*, iii, p. 333; Schlumberger, *Compagnes du Roi Amaury Ier de Jérusalem en Égypte*, pp. 205–6. According to William of Tyre (*A History of deeds*, Engl. transl., ii, p. 353) Shāwar promised Amalric two million pieces of gold for the release of his son and nephew and the withdrawal of the troops to their own country.

collapse of the Fāṭimid regime, in 567/1171 sent part of his spoils from Fāṭimid palaces to Nūr al-Dīn, obviously to prove his loyalty.[1] Saladin repeated this gesture in 568/1172–3. Although this second present is said to have contained 60,000 gold *dīnār*s, it failed to satisfy Nūr al-Dīn who sent al-Qaysarānī to Egypt to check the resources and expenses.[2] The latter took back to Nūr al-Dīn in 569/1174 a third present, said to have included ten boxes of Egyptian gold.[3] According to Maqrīzī, the value of this last present was estimated at 225,000 *dīnār*s. However, Nūr al-Dīn died before he received it; part of it was sent back to Saladin.[4]

Finally, after the end of the Fāṭimid era and the advent of the Ayyūbids, wealthy Egyptians, especially merchants, felt anxious as to what was in store for them. It is very probable that they converted their fortunes to jewels hung round the necks of their wives and daughters and into gold bars buried in walls or underground.[5]

The shortage of gold did not prevent Saladin from coining new *dīnār*s. Following the abolition of the Fāṭimid caliphate, he decreed on 7 Rabīʿ II 567/8 December 1171 that the legend on Egyptian coins should bear the names of both the ʿAbbāsid Caliph al-Mustaḍīʾ and Nūr al-Dīn.[6] In 570/1174, to proclaim the establishment of the new dynasty on the death of Nūr al-Dīn, Saladin coined a *dīnār* bearing the name of the ʿAbbāsid Caliph as well as his own. Saladin continued to issue gold *dīnār*s until the end of his reign.[7]

It is a controversial point whether the lack of gold influenced the standard of weight and purity of Saladin's *dīnār*s. Professor Ehrenkreutz states that Saladin abandoned the fixed-weight standard of the Fāṭimid coinage, since when the coins could no longer be taken

[1] Dawādārī, *Durr maṭlūb*, fol. 19ᵛ; Ibn Iyās, *Badāʾiʿ*, i, p. 69.

[2] Iṣfahānī, *Sanā*, fol. 175ʳ⁻ᵛ; Abū Shāma, *Rawḍatayn*, i. ii, pp. 524–5; Ibn Wāṣil, *Mufarrij*, i, pp. 224–5; Maqrīzī, *Sulūk*, i, p. 50, tr. Blochet, 'B', p. 507.

[3] Ibn Qāḍī Shuhba, *Durr*, fols. 113ʳ–114ᵛ; ʿAynī, *ʿIqd*, 'A', xii, fol. 183ᵛ; Ibn Kathīr, xii, p. 274.

[4] Maqrīzī, *Sulūk*, i, pp. 54–5, tr. Blochet, 'B', pp. 512–13.

[5] Rabīʿ, *Nuẓum*, p. 95; see below, pp. 176–7; Prof. Goitein surmises that well-to-do people who were near death hoarded hard cash in quantities representing a very substantial part of their wealth. Besides, in times of insecurity and political unrest even commercial cash receipts were buried in the earth. As, by its very nature, this economic attitude required utmost secrecy, not much can be learned about it from the Geniza, cf. *Med. Soc.*, i, pp. 264–5.

[6] Maqrīzī, *Sulūk*, i, p. 45, tr. Blochet, 'B', p. 501; Rabīʿ, *Nuẓum*, p. 97.

[7] Lane-Poole, *Catalogue of the collection of Arabic coins preserved in the Khedivial Library*, pp. 203–6; id., *Catalogue of oriental coins in the British Museum*, iv, pp. 63–6; Lavoix, *Catalogue*, pp. 173–7.

by tale, but had to be weighed.[1] Relying on information available in some numismatic catalogues and tests on some Ayyūbid *dīnār*s from the collection of the American Numismatic Society, he infers that the *dīnār*s of Saladin and of his successors lacked a fixed standard of weight, and that the Ayyūbids ordered their *dīnār*s to be struck outside the weight limits current under the Fāṭimids.[2] It is, on the whole, possible that Saladin was forced to decrease the weight of the *dīnār* as a result of the prevailing gold shortage.

As regards the purity of Saladin's *dīnār*s, Professor Ehrenkreutz analysed 44 specimens issued by Saladin to judge their standard of fineness by their specific gravities.[3] He found that the largest group of the specimens consisting of 13 *dīnār*s fell below the 90 per cent purity. Simultaneously, however, the Egyptian administration maintained the exchange rate between the Egyptian and foreign coinage at the old Fāṭimid rate. Professor Ehrenkreutz quotes Ibn Jubayr to show that in Alexandria in 578/1183 every leader of *ṣalāt* in the mosques earned five Egyptian *dīnār*s, the equivalent of ten Mu'minī *dīnār*s of the Almohades. As the Mu'minī *dīnār* weighed half as much as the Fāṭimid *dīnār*, Saladin seems to have insisted, despite the debasement of his *dīnār*, on a maintenance of the exchange rate of 2:1.[4]

By the operation of Gresham's law, the Fāṭimid *dīnār* was super-

[1] Ehrenkreutz, 'Contributions to the knowledge of the fiscal administration of Egypt in the middle ages', *BSOAS*, xvi (1954), pp. 502–3; id., 'The standard of fineness', p. 163 n. 6.

[2] Ehrenkreutz, 'The crisis of *dīnār*', p. 180; Prof. Cahen (article 'Ayyūbids' in *EI*²) maintains that Saladin's desire 'to eliminate all traces of the Fāṭimid régime, led him to replace the coinage by a new one, of variable weight'.

[3] The application of specific gravity measurements to the study of the *dīnār*s and *dirhams* is one of the oldest known methods of assay, as Archimedes used it to detect the adulteration of the gold in the crown of Hieron of Syracuse, cf. E. R. Caley, 'Validity of the specific gravity method for the determination of the fineness of gold objects', *Ohio Journal of Science*, xlix (1949), pp. 73–82; id., 'Estimation of composition of ancient metal objects', *Analytical Chemistry*, xxiv, no. 4 (1952), pp. 676–81. There are two other methods of inquiry into the nature of the alloy of numismatic specimens. The use of X-ray spectrographic analysis for the study of *dirhams* and the application of the method of radioactivation which reveals the total composition and percentage of all elements in the alloy structure of examined specimens, cf. Ehrenkreutz, 'Monetary aspects', p. 46; see also Bacharach and Gordus, 'Studies on the fineness of silver coins', *JESHO*, xi (1968), pp. 298–307.

[4] Ehrenkreutz, 'The crisis of *dīnār*', pp. 181–2 and n. 14; Dr. Miles also states (article 'Dīnār' in *EI*²) that the fineness of the *dīnār* under Saladin fell below 90 per cent; for the Mu'minī *dīnār* cf. Ibn Jubayr, p. 43; Sauvaire, 'Matériaux', *JA*, xix (1882), p. 55; Goitein, *Med. Soc.*, i, p. 234.

seded by the debased *dīnār* of Saladin. It may be assumed that hoarding of the Fāṭimid *dīnār*s by the inhabitants was, if not the sole, at least a contributory cause of the disappearance of the Fāṭimid *dīnār*s from circulation.[1] It is also probable that the continuous Syrian campaigns aggravated the drain of Egyptian gold as the majority of the Egyptian army—as has been said in Chapter II—had to be equipped and supplied from Egyptian *iqṭā*ʿs. Obviously, the Egyptian soldiers spent the money in Syrian towns. Moreover, the Egyptian treasury had to supply the necessary currency for the expenses of the army and navy, fortifications, and the purchase of war material from Europe.

c. *Saladin's monetary reform of 583/1187*

However, a serious monetary crisis developed in S͟hawwāl 583/December 1187. It was in this month, if the anti-Saladin historian Ibn al-At͟hīr is to be credited, that Saladin was forced to leave Tyre for Acre and adjourn his campaign, since the rich amirs feared that, his treasuries having been emptied of *dirham*s and *dīnār*s, he would call on them for financial support.[2] Ibn al-At͟hīr's account is supported by a reply from al-Qāḍī al-Fāḍil to a communication from Saladin complaining of financial difficulties. Al-Fāḍil ascribes Saladin's difficulties to an excess of military expenses, gifts, and hospitality.[3]

Saladin seems to have sought a solution in an Egyptian monetary reform in the same month, S͟hawwāl 583. According to Maqrīzī, he abandoned the Egyptian coins in circulation, striking new *dīnār*s from Egyptian gold, and replacing the black *dirham* (*al-dirham al-aswad*) by the Nāṣirī *dirham* made of 50 per cent silver and 50 per cent copper.[4]

[1] See below, pp. 176–7; Prof. Udovitch doubts the applicability of Gresham's law to the medieval Islamic monetary context. In his opinion, there is no observable trend of bad coins driving good ones out of circulation. See his remark concerning the exchange rate in *Settimane di studio del Centro Italiano di studi sull'alto medioevo*, xii (1965), i, pp. 488–9; id., 'England to Egypt', p. 125. In point of fact one can find cases where the law seems to have applied and cases where it does not, see below, pp. 177, 185 n. 4, 186–8, 194–5.

[2] Ibn al-At͟hīr, *Kāmil*, xi, pp. 368–9.

[3] *al-Muk͟htār min kalām al-Fāḍil* (MS. Brit. Mus., Add. 7465 Rich) fols. 10^{v}–11^{r}.

[4] Maqrīzī, *S͟hud͟hūr*, p. 60, tr. S. de Sacy, p. 44; Sauvaire, 'Matériaux', *JA*, xix (1882), pp. 58, 301; Grohmann, *Einführung*, p. 210; Balog, 'Études numismatiques de l'Égypte musulmane' I, *BIE*, xxxiii (1950–1), p. 19. Maqrīzī errs

This monetary reform changed the monetary standard of Egypt. As gold had become too scarce to satisfy the needs of circulation and Saladin's expensive campaigns, silver was chosen as the new standard coinage. It was presumably to emphasize this change that he struck a new type of *dirham*. Gold, considered from then on only as a commodity with a daily fluctuating market price to be calculated in silver *dirhams*, lost its position as the standard of currency.[1] Thus, for example, the salary of the lecturer of Shāfiʿī *fiqh* in the Nāṣirī school, amounting to 40 *dīnār*s monthly, used to be paid not in *dīnār*s but in *dirhams*, each *dīnār* equalling 13½ *dirhams*.[2]

D. *The silver* dirham *under Saladin*

On the eve of the Ayyūbid era there was an acute shortage of silver in Egypt.[3] On 11 Rabīʿ I 567/12 November 1171, Saladin had all silver sashes removed from the prayer-niches of Cairo mosques as well as the mosque of ʿAmr ibn al-ʿĀṣ in Fusṭāṭ. He obviously wanted to kill two birds with one stone, that is, to remove the titles of the Fāṭimid caliphs from the mosques, and to get hold of a huge amount of silver to alleviate the endemic silver famine. It is said that the weight of silver obtained from the Azhar mosque alone amounted to 5,000 *nuqra dirhams*.[4]

when he states in *Kitāb al-sulūk*, i, p. 99, tr. Blochet, 'C', p. 35, that the new *dirhams* of Saladin were struck of pure silver; for the black *dirham* see below, p. 175 n. 1.

[1] Prof. Balog ['History of the dirhem', p. 132; id., 'Observations on the metrology of the Mamlūk fals', *The Numismatic Chronicle*, 7th series, ii (1962), p. 263] takes the view that Saladin decided to change the monetary standard when he took over the administration of Egypt, i.e. A.H. 567. It seems, however, that he did not carry out this decision before 583/1187, i.e. approximately 16 years after the establishment of the Ayyūbid dynasty. This assumption may be confirmed by a letter sent by al-Fāḍil to Saladin during the siege of Acre in A.H. 586, in which the former refers to the success of the introduction of the new silver standard, as follows: 'ولو لم تكن الدراهم سلعة لا تخرج من مصر كما يخرج الدينار لما وجدت كما لا يوجد الدينار . . .' 'If *dirhams* were not a commodity restricted to the country, and if they were just as unrestricted as *dīnārs*, *dirhams* would not have been generally available, just as *dīnār*s are not available . . .'; see Abū Shāma, *Rawḍatayn*, ii, p. 177; Rabīʿ, *Nuẓum*, p. 96.

[2] Ibn al-Furāt, vii, p. 272; Maqrīzī, *Khiṭaṭ*, ii, p. 400; Suyūṭī, *Ḥusn*, ii, p. 157; Rabīʿ, *Nuẓum*, p. 97.

[3] See above, pp. 166–9.

[4] *Khiṭaṭ*, ii, pp. 251, 275. The word *nuqra* designates 'ingot of fine silver or gold'; cf. Ibn Manẓūr, *Lisān*, vii, p. 87; Dozy, *Supp. Dict. Ar.*, ii, p. 710. In medieval Egypt, the term *dirham nuqra* was used to indicate coins struck of pure silver, whose exchange value was 13⅓ *dirhams* per gold *dīnār*, cf. T.–S., B.42, fol. 70; T.–S. N.S., J. 375; Ibn Baʿra, pp. 75–6; Sauvaire, 'Matériaux', *JA*. xix

This seems to have enabled Saladin to continue issuing the black or *waraq dirham* with its low silver content.[1] Professor Balog suggests that this *dirham* only differed from the latest Fāṭimid black *dirham* by the inscriptions it bore, while its quality was essentially the same. He also thinks that black *dirhams* constituted the bulk of the entire silver currency until 622/1225. To prove this assumption he examined for fineness 17 specimens of black *dirhams*, namely 7 issued by Saladin, 4 by al-ʿAzīz ʿUthmān, one by al-Manṣūr Muḥammad, one by al-ʿĀdil I, and 4 by al-Kāmil before 622, and found that each contained 28 per cent of fine silver, that is, about the same percentage as the black *dirham* issued by the Fāṭimid Caliph al-ʿĀḍid.[2] Thus Maqrīzī's statement that the Nāṣirī *dirham* successfully replaced the black *dirham* is to be treated with considerable caution.

As to the rate of exchange of the Nāṣirī *dirham* with 50 per cent silver content, it is assumed to have been $26\frac{2}{3}$ *dirhams* to the *dīnār*.[3]

(1882), pp. 61 ff.; Grohmann, *Einführung*, p. 213; Ehrenkreutz, 'Extracts from the technical manual on the Ayyūbid mint in Cairo', *BSOAS*, xv (1953), pp. 438–40; id., 'Contributions to the knowledge of the fiscal administration', p. 503 and nn. 3–5; Balog, 'History of the dirhem', pp. 123–4. The information given by Qalqashandī (*Ṣubḥ*, iii, pp. 443, 466–7) and tr. by Gaudefroy-Demombynes (*La Syrie*, pp. 137–8) is misleading. Data found in some unpublished fragments from the Vienna papers indicate that this type of *dirham* was known in Egypt as 'the *nuqra*' or *al-darāhim al-nuqra al-jayyida* 'the excellent *nuqra dirhams*' or *al-darāhim al-nuqra al-bayḍā' al-maskūka* 'the white coined *nuqra dirhams*', names which all imply purity; cf. A.Ch. fol. 10214ᵛ, fol. 10216, fol. 10228, fol. 12477 (dated 724/1324); fol. 23050 (dated 674/1276). Moreover, *dirhams* of this type are sometimes described in the Geniza by the term '*fiḍḍat dhahab*' 'golden silver', cf. T.–S. Arabic, Box 30, fol. 215 in Goitein, 'Bankers' accounts', pp. 57, 58 n. 2.

[1] It seems that, from the Umayyad period onwards, the term '*dirham aswad*' (black *dirham*) denoted a *dirham* whose silver content was poor. In Egypt the term was used to identify the *waraq dirham* which is frequently mentioned in the papyri, the Geniza, and the Vienna papers; cf. Grohmann, 'New discoveries', ii, pp. 161, 163, 164; T.–S., B.40, fol. 126; A.Ch. 5, fol. 4133; A.Ch. 8, fol. 7229. Ibn Baʿra (*Kashf*, pp. 83–4) states that its alloy consisted of 30 per cent silver and 70 per cent copper. Prof. Ehrenkreutz ('Extracts', p. 425 n. 1, 'Contributions to the knowledge of the fiscal administration', p. 503) states that these *dirhams* were struck for the use of the internal Egyptian market, to meet the needs of the local retail trade; see also Maqrīzī, *Shudhūr*, p. 33, tr. S. de Sacy, p. 14; id., *Ighātha*, p. 65, tr. Wiet, p. 64; Sauvaire, 'Matériaux', *JA*, xv (1880), pp. 275–6; Ashtor, 'Les prix', p. 112; Qalqashandī (*Ṣubḥ*, iii, p. 443) describes the black *dirham* as a fictitious *dirham*, the same as the *jayshī dīnār*. It is, however, probable that Qalqashandī refers to the contemporary black *dirham*.

[2] Balog, 'History of the dirhem', pp. 123, 128–30.

[3] Prof. Ehrenkreutz ('Contributions to the knowledge of the fiscal administration', p. 504) bases this assessment on the exchange rate of $13\frac{1}{3}$: 1 *dīnār* for the

This conjecture can neither be refuted nor accepted, since the historical sources contain no mention of the rate of exchange of such Nāṣirī *dirhams* as were periodically issued during all the Ayyūbid period. That Nāṣirī *dirhams* continued to be issued is proved by the existence of 7 Nāṣirī *dirhams* coined in Cairo, one issued by Saladin in 586/1190, another by al-ʿĀdil I in 600/1203–4, and five struck by al-Ṣāliḥ Ayyūb around 645 or 646/1247–9.[1] The Nāṣirī *dirhams* remained in circulation in the Baḥrī Mamluk era until 662/1264 or even longer.[2]

E. *The monetary system in post-Saladin times*

It seems that, after Saladin until the reign of al-Kāmil, Egypt remained faithful to the silver standard, gold remaining a commodity. Thus there was no need to debase the gold *dīnār*. The fact that 6 out of 9 *dīnār*s from al-ʿAzīz's reign investigated by Professor Ehrenkreutz were found to fall within the 100 per cent purity limit support this assumption.[3] The high standard of the *dīnār* of al-ʿAzīz by no means reflects an increase in the amount of gold in the country. The shortage of gold was such that even the Ayyūbids tried to confiscate the gold *dīnār*s hoarded by the inhabitants. An unpublished document from the Geniza, dated Tuesday 4 Rabīʿ II 595/3 February 1199, which represents a report sent to the amīr Bahāʾ al-Dīn Qarāqūsh, the then *atābak* of the Sultan Nāṣir al-Dīn Muḥammad ibn al-ʿAzīz ʿUthmān, states that, according to the order of Qarāqūsh to procure the gold preserved in the house of ʿĀbid or ʿĀrim ibn ʿĪsā in Manūf al-ʿUlyā, a representative (*mandūb*) went with witnesses on Sunday 2 Rabīʿ II/1 February. They entered ʿĀbid's house where the latter's wife took from a cache in the wall and handed to them, to be sent to Qarāqūsh in a sealed purse, 170 gold *dīnār*s, which when weighed were found to be worth 161 currency *dīnār*s.[4]

silver *nuqra dirham* with a 100 per cent silver content, and 40:1 *dīnār* for the black *dirham* with a 30 per cent silver content, see below, p. 187 n. 2; cf. Ashtor, 'Quelques indications sur les revenus dans l'orient musulman au haut moyen âge', *JESHO*, ii (1959), p. 265 n. 1.

[1] Balog, 'Études numismatiques' ii, *BIE*, xxxiv (1951–2), pp. 26–8; id., 'History of the dirhem', pp. 129–30.

[2] See below, pp. 187–8.

[3] Ehrenkreutz, 'The crisis of *dīnār*', p. 181.

[4] T.-S. Arabic, B.42, fol. 171; for the *atābak*, cf. Qalqashandī, *Ṣubḥ*, iv, p. 18; Cahen, article 'Atabak' in *EI*[2]; id. *Pre-Ottoman Turkey*, pp. 37, 47, 221–2; for *atābak al-ʿasākir* (commander-in-chief) in the Mamluk army; cf. Ayalon, 'Studies', iii, pp. 58–9; id., article 'Atābak al-ʿAsākir' in *EI*[2]. During the period

This proves one of two possibilities: these *dīnār*s had either been struck by the last Fāṭimid caliphs, which would indicate that gold *dīnār*s were hoarded even after 28 years of the Ayyūbid regime, and explain, indirectly, why they disappeared from circulation on the eve of this regime. Or they were *dīnār*s, struck by Saladin before his reform of 583/1187, which implies that peasants were reluctant to accept the silver standard but believed in the value of gold to which they had been used for centuries.

F. *The monetary reforms of al-Kāmil*

The accession of al-Kāmil to the Ayyūbid sultanate marks the beginning of a new era in the Egyptian monetary system. Ibn Baʿra states that al-Kāmil was interested in the standard of fineness of al-Āmir's *dīnār*s and was eager to surpass it. Consequently, no *dīnār* either in the East or in the West was superior in standard to that of al-Āmirī al-Kāmilī.[1]

This significant statement has been confirmed by two subsequent attempts of Professor Ehrenkreutz to examine the degree of fineness of Egyptian Kāmilī *dīnār*s. In 1954 he found that, of 18 *dīnār*s coined between 1219 and 1237 and preserved in the British Museum and the Ashmolean Museum, four were inferior in purity of alloy to 95 per cent, and the standard of the remaining fourteen fluctuated between 96·29 and 98·83 per cent, that is to say, remained well within the limits of 23 to 24 carats.[2] In 1956, of 27 Kāmilī *dīnār*s, five coins fell within the 100 per cent limit, six showed the high standard of 99 per cent, four were of 98 per cent purity, and none fell under 93 per cent.[3]

under review, money seems to have been largely handled in sealed purses, indicating on their outside the exact number and weight of the coins they contained, a system which also prevailed in contemporary Christian Europe. Two types of purses can be distinguished in the Geniza records; those bearing the seal of a certified money-assayer, of a government office, or of a semi-official exchange, and those referred to by the names of individual merchants; cf. Lopez and Raymond, *Medieval trade*, pp. 15, 148; Goitein, *Med. Soc.* i, pp. 231 ff.

[1] Ibn Baʿra, MS., fol. 2r; ed. Fahmī, p. 50: 'ولما علم مولانا السلطان الملك الكامل علق الدينار عن الآميريه أراد بعلق همته البروز عنها، وحيف عيار الدنانير المختومة باسمه عن الآميريه وهى أعلى منها، ولا فى شرق الأرض ولا مغربها دينارا أعلى من عيار الآميرى الكاملى', see also Ehrenkreutz, 'The standard of fineness', p. 164; Miles, article 'Dīnār' in *EI*².

[2] Ehrenkreutz, 'The standard of fineness', pp. 164–5.

[3] Ehrenkreutz, 'The crisis of *dīnār*', p. 181.

The reasons for the improvement of the *ʿiyār* of these *dīnār*s, which is probably indicative of economic stability under al-Kāmil, are by no means obvious. It is known that, under al-Kāmil, intensified trade relations with Europe led, in one way or another, to an increase in the influx of gold to Egypt. It is also said that frequently European merchants who came to Egypt to trade used to deliver to the mint the gold they brought with them to be coined in the form of official Egyptian currency to pay their custom duties and buy the goods they could not obtain by barter. This practice went back to pre-Saladin times.[1] Moreover, the stern measures of al-Kāmil who personally supervised the monetary administration of Egypt seem to have contributed to the high reputation of his *dīnār* which spread outside Egypt. Ibn al-Mujāwir, who lived in the first quarter of the 7th/13th century, states that the coins struck in Mecca were coined from Egyptian gold and possessed the same standard of fineness as the Egyptian *dīnār*s.[2] It would appear from Ibn al-Mujāwir's statement that a large amount of these high-quality Egyptian *dīnār*s went abroad, and that the standard of silver continued to be the Egyptian monetary standard.

As to the silver *dirham* under al-Kāmil, Maqrīzī mentions a monetary reform in Dhū al-Qaʿda 622/November–December 1225. In that month Sultan al-Kāmil substituted *dirham*s of a new type, called *al-darāhim al-Kāmiliyya* or *al-mustadīra* (Kāmilī or rounded *dirhams*), for the *waraq* and Nāṣirī *dirham*s. The alloy of the new *dirham*s consisted of $\frac{2}{3}$ silver and $\frac{1}{3}$ copper.[3] Both al-Dawādārī and Nuwayrī state that, when al-Kāmil abandoned the pre-reform *dirham*s, he ordered the inhabitants to deliver the silver coins in

[1] Makhzūmī, fols. 139ʳ–140ʳ; Ibn Mammātī, pp. 331–3; Nābulsī, *Lumaʿ*, pp. 52–4, tr. Cahen, 'Quelques aspects', pp. 113–14; T. Iskandar, 'Niẓām al-muqāyaḍa', *MTM*, vi (1957), p. 38; Labib, *Handelsgeschichte*, pp. 273–4; Goitein, *Med. Soc.*, i, p. 267 and p. 466 n. 2.

[2] Ibn al-Mujāwir, i, p. 12.

[3] Maqrīzī, *Shudhūr*, p. 60, tr. S. de Sacy, p. 44; id., *Ighātha*, pp. 65–6, tr. Weit, pp. 64–5; id., *Khiṭaṭ*, i, p. 110. There are some erroneous statements based on Maqrīzī's account of the proportions of the Kāmilī *dirham* alloy, cf. Sauvaire, 'Matériaux', *JA*, xix (1882), pp. 29, 127; M. de Boüard, 'Évolution monétaire', p. 450; Grohmann, *Einführung*, p. 210; Popper, *Systematic notes*, ii, p. 51; Rabīʿ, *Nuẓum*, p. 100 and n. 4; Fahmī, *Nuqūd*, p. 73. Prof. Gottschalk (*al-Malik al-Kāmil von Egypten*, p. 129) rightly states that al-Kāmil's reform of 622/1225 implied a debasement of the existing silver coinage, but seems to be mistaken in assuming that the new *dirham*s which consisted of $\frac{2}{3}$ silver and $\frac{1}{3}$ copper were intended to replace the pure silver *dirhams* which were then in circulation, see below, p. 180; Balog, 'History of the dirhem', pp. 112–13.

their possession at the low exchange rate of 60 *dirhams* per 1 *dīnār*, and sent them to the mint to be struck in the form of new Kāmilī *dirhams*, to the loss of the public and his own substantial gain.[1]

However, it does not seem that gain was al-Kāmil's motive in the introduction of that reform. Professor Balog suggests that, as his black *dirhams* struck before 622/1225 were inferior to those issued by al-ʿĀdil I, Manṣūr Muḥammad, al-ʿAzīz ʿUthmān, and Saladin, it is probable that the reform originated in the wish to put an end to continuous difficulties caused by worthless coinage.[2] That he did not quite succeed in the undertaking is another matter.

Professor Balog's theory seems to be supported by evidence from the Geniza. In his study of the exchange rate of gold and silver money, Professor Goitein describes the contents of three fragments from the Geniza. The first, which is a detailed account of a religious slaughterer from Fusṭāṭ, in or around 1179 or 1183, quotes the exchange rate of 65 *dirhams* for $1\frac{3}{4}$ *dīnārs*, that is, $37\frac{1}{2}:1$. The second fragment, also from Fusṭāṭ, dated October 1194–July 1199,

[1] Dawādārī, *Durr maṭlūb*, fol. 109^{v}; id., *Durar*, fol. 200^{r}; Nuwayrī, xxvii, fol. 27. Regarding the annual output of individual Islamic mints, there is a new method which has been applied by a seminar team at the University of Michigan. Cf. the report on the procedures and results of this experiment entitled 'Early Islamic mint output. A preliminary inquiry into the methodology and application of the "coin-die count" method', in *JESHO*, ix (1966), pp. 212–41. This method involves two phases: the estimation of the number of dies employed in the production of a coinage series, and the estimation of the quantity of coins which the dies were capable of producing, the product of both indicating the quantity of coins manufactured in the series in question. It will not be amiss to refer here to Prof. Balog's statement that the *sikka* (coin-die) was manufactured by casting as it would have been impossible to engrave the inscription on the hard surface of the die. Prof. Ehrenkreutz opposes this view maintaining that the dies were engraved, not cast. Dr. Fahmī, however, relying on a test performed on a group of Ayyūbid *dīnārs* as well as on two engraved lead discs preserved in the Islamic Museum in Cairo, concludes that there were two types of coin-dies in existence: direct engraved dies, made by engraving the inscriptions in reverse, as well as dies made by engraving inscriptions on lead plaques, whose cast, taken in clay, was subsequently baked in the oven and used to produce unlimited numbers of iron and bronze stamp-dies. Since it is impossible, with this second type of die, to assess how many dies were made from clay cast, the quantity of coins produced by the dies might be almost unlimited, and can hardly be estimated. Cf. Balog, 'Aperçus sur la technique de monnayage musulman au moyen âge', *BIE*, xxxi (1948–9), pp. 95–105; id., 'Études numismatiques' I, *BIE*, xxxiii (1950–1), pp. 34 ff.; id., *The coinage of the Mamluk Sultans*, pp. 54–6; Ehrenkreutz, 'Contributions to the history of the Islamic mint in the middle ages' (Ph.D., London, 1952), pp. 106–10; id., 'Extracts', p. 437; Dr. Fahmī's introduction to Ibn Baʿra's *Kashf*, pp. 11–16.

[2] Balog, 'History of the dirhem', p. 130.

concerning the rent of a *qā'a* (ground floor), presupposes an exchange rate of 40:1. The third, dated February–March 1223, concerning the auction of the books of a scholar after his death, qualifies the sums of 4¾ and 3 *dīnār*s respectively by the remark '*ṣarf* 40'.[1] These two rates of exchange, 37½:1 and 40:1 before al-Kāmil's reform, seem to indicate debasement in the silver *dirhams*.[2]

Concerning the rounded *dirhams* of al-Kāmil, Professor Balog analysed a certain number of them in order to ascertain their content of pure silver. He found that the Kāmilī *dirhams*, struck after the reform of 622, contained only between 23 and 30 per cent silver, that is, a little less than the *dirham waraq*. In other words, the content of the rounded *dirham* was ⅓ silver to ⅔ copper, and not, as Maqrīzī says, the reverse. Professor Balog came to the conclusion that al-Kāmil's reform was in reality 'a huge fraud or camouflage'.[3] Professor Ehrenkreutz states that, as the exchange rate of the rounded *dirhams* was fixed by al-Kāmil at 37:1, and later at 35:1, they contained no more than 32·4 and 34·2 per cent silver respectively, a conclusion which is the same as Professor Balog's.[4] However, it would seem that al-Kāmil's reform changed, not the intrinsic value of the coin, but merely its aspect. The old square type of inscription on Egyptian coins was temporarily replaced by a round legend, executed in *naskhī* script instead of the usual *kufic* characters.[5]

[1] T.–S. 16.39; T.–S. 10 J.28, fol. 13, T.–S. 20.44 in Goitein, 'The exchange rate', pp. 27–9; id., *Med. Soc.*, i, pp. 381–2; for T.–S. 20.44 cf. E. J. Worman, 'Two book-lists from the Cambridge Genizah fragments', *JQR*, xx (1907–8), pp. 450–63; Ashtor, 'Le coût de la vie dans l'Égypte médiévale', *JESHO*, iii (1960), pp. 71–2. For the term *ṣarf* 'the rate of exchange or conversion-charge' cf. Grohmann, 'New discoveries', i, pp. 167–9; ibid., ii, pp. 161–4.

[2] In an unpublished document from Ushmūnayn found among the Vienna papers which represents a kind of promissory note dated 2nd Ramaḍān 616/11th November 1219, 'Abd al-Qādir ibn 'Abd al-Ḥakam states that he has contracted the debt of 17 *dirhams* from Ibn Ḥamūd and undertakes to settle it in weekly instalments of 4¼ *dirhams*. Unfortunately, the document does not name the type of the *dirhams* in question which seem to have been *waraq dirhams*; cf. A.Ch. 12441.

[3] Balog, 'History of the dirhem', pp. 112, 130–1; id., *The coinage of the Mamluk Sultans*, p. 40.

[4] Ehrenkreutz, 'Contributions to the knowledge of the fiscal administration', p. 504.

[5] Balog, 'Études numismatiques', i, pp. 28–30 and plate v; id., 'History of the dirhem', p. 130; Ehrenkreutz, 'Contributions to the history of the Islamic mint', pp. 119–20; id., 'Contributions to the knowledge of the fiscal administration', p. 504. Some round-legend *dirhams* are preserved in the collection of the Bibliothèque Nationale, cf. Lavoix, op. cit., pp. 245–7.

Maqrīzī states that the Kāmilī *dirhams* remained in circulation during the rest of the Ayyūbid period and under the Mamluks, until the amir Maḥmūd al-Ustādār replaced silver with copper *fulūs* in 781/1379–80. He added that expensive goods were evaluated in Kāmilī *dirhams*, in which business was generally conducted. Even the *kharāj* tax and the rents of houses were collected in Kāmilī *dirhams*.[1] This does not prove that the Kāmilī *dirhams* were the only remaining currency after al-Kāmil's reform of 622. There is ample evidence that other *dirhams*, especially the *waraq dirhams*, continued to circulate after 622/1225. Nuwayrī states that, in 627/1230, there was a low flood and Sultan al-Kāmil set the price of 20 *dirhams waraq* per *ardabb* of wheat, ordering the clerks of the sultani granaries (*al-ahrā' al-sulṭāniyya*) to sell it as 25 *dirhams waraq* per *ardabb*.[2] In a fragment from the Geniza, written in Minyat Ziftā Jawād in Lower Egypt in March 1232, which represents a claim for 35 *dīnārs* before the rabbinical court, the amount is calculated in *waraq* silver coins as 1,400 *dirhams*.[3] An unpublished fragment from the Geniza dated 25 Rabī' II 630/9 February 1233, is a receipt for 22 *dirhams waraq* given to Faraj Allāh ibn Abū al-Baqā ibn Abū Sa'īd al-Naṣrānī for the purchase price of a Nubian slave girl.[4]

According to Maqrīzī, copper *fulūs* were in circulation in Egypt until 622/1225, as a local currency for the purchase of cheap goods, but were not legal tender in the same sense as *dīnārs* or *dirhams*. It appears that their circulation was limited, as the coining of the *fulūs* was in the hands of the local *wālīs*, without centralized control.[5]

[1] Maqrīzī, *Ighātha*, p. 66; tr. Wiet, p. 65; Maqrīzī, *Khiṭaṭ*, i, p. 110; Sauvaire, 'Matériaux', *JA*, xix (1882), pp. 29–31.

[2] Nuwayrī, xxvii, fol. 35.

[3] T.-S. N.S., J.30 in Goitein, 'The exchange rate', p. 29; id., *Med. Soc.*, i, p. 382.

[4] T.-S. Arabic, B.39, fol. 245; 22 *dirhams waraq* is a very low price to pay for a slave girl, who must have been very old or ill to have fetched so little. For prices of slave girls in other documents from the same collection cf. Goitein, 'Slaves and slave girls in the Cairo Geniza records', *Arabica* ix (1962), pp. 8–11; id., *Med. Soc.*, i, pp. 137–9.

[5] Maqrīzī, *Ighātha*, pp. 66–7, tr. Wiet, pp. 65–6; id., *Shudhūr*, pp. 67–8, tr. S. de Sacy, pp. 53–5; Sauvaire, 'Matériaux', *JA*, xv (1880), pp. 257–8; for the *fals* in early Islamic period cf. Udovitch, article 'Fals' in *EI*². It is worth mentioning that copper *fulūs* are often published by numismatists without recording their weight. Prof. Balog ('A hoard of late Mamlūk copper coins', *The Numismatic Chronicle*, 7th series, ii (1962), p. 243) quotes the opinion of most numismatists that, as the *fulūs* were produced without attention to metrological order,

After 622/1225, copper *fulūs* attained the status of official currency. According to Dawādārī and Nuwayrī, Sultan al-Kāmil ordered copper *fulūs* to be struck in Cairo and Miṣr (Fusṭāṭ), and they became valid currency.[1] Maqrīzī states in *Ighātha* that the main purpose of striking large numbers of copper *fulūs* was to put a coin into circulation which would facilitate daily shopping for household items worth less than one *dirham* or part of it. He tells the story of a woman who asked Abī al-Ṭāhir al-Maḥallī, the *khaṭīb* (preacher) of the mosque of Miṣr, if drinking water was legal. When he asked her in turn what prevented her from drinking it, she said that the sultan had coined *dirhams* (she may have had Kāmilī *dirhams* in mind) and she had bought a waterskin at ½ *dirham*, paid the water-carrier one *dirham*, and received ½ *dirham waraq* change. This obviously means that she had obtained from him water and ½ *dirham waraq* in exchange for one (Kāmilī) *dirham*, and was plagued by remorse that she had underpaid the water-carrier who was, perhaps, unaware of the difference in the value of two coins of the same denomination. It is possible that al-Maḥallī knew nothing of transactions of this kind, either because it was wrong to give the water-carrier a Kāmilī *dirham* with its poor silver content instead of a *dirham waraq*, or because he feared that they might lead to usury. Thus he consulted Sultan al-Kāmil, who ordered *fulūs* to be issued.[2] This story indicates that *fulūs* fulfilled a real need, as there were no half or quarter Kāmilī *dirhams* in existence.

After they had become valid coinage, and could be used for the payment of taxes and in settlement of debts, the number of *fulūs* in circulation increased in quantity. But it seems that, as copper coins were made of cheap metal and were easier to counterfeit than gold or silver coins, they gave forgers an opportunity to profit by the difference between the monetary value of the *fals* and its intrinsic quality. Besides, *fulūs* were debased by the addition of cheaper

their weight was of no importance. Prof. R. N. Frye ('Soviet historiography on the Islamic Orient', in Lewis and Holt, *Historians*, p. 369) points out that, in Western museums, only silver and gold coins have been found artistically worthy of collection. As to the copper coins, Marxist-oriented scholars, interested in such basic source-material for economic history, have studied this 'coinage of the masses', and that is why the Russians were the first to study in detail Islamic copper coinage.

[1] Dawādārī, *Durar*, fol. 200r; Nuwayrī, xxvii, fol. 27.

[2] Maqrīzī, *Ighātha*, p. 67, tr. Wiet, p. 66; Sauvaire, 'Matériaux', *JA*, xv (1880), pp. 258–9; Rabīʿ, *Nuẓum*, p. 101 n. 1.

metals, such as lead, or simply by decreasing their weight. The officials refused to accept copper money for the payment of taxes. The debasement of copper *fulūs* led to a monetary crisis in Egypt in 630/1233, in consequence of which Sultan al-Kāmil withdrew the *fulūs* from circulation in Cairo and Fusṭāṭ, and ordered the inhabitants to deliver those in their possession to the money-changers, who accepted them by weight, estimating a pound at approximately 2¼–2½ Kāmilī *dirhams*. This action injured the people who lost a considerable proportion of their wealth.[1]

According to M. de Boüard, the crisis of 630/1233 marked an important date in the monetary history of Egypt, since it was then that copper money became for the first time an important factor in exchange markets, where it caused confusion by its very abundance.[2] However, al-Kāmil issued in 634/1236–7 another large quantity of *fulūs*. This action was profitable for the sultan who put into circulation, at the usual rate of exchange, copper which he had bought at a very low price four years before.[3] According to Maqrīzī, copper *fulūs* were abandoned in 635/1237–8 by Sultan al-ʿĀdil II, possibly owing to the prevalence of forgeries.[4]

The silver currency seems to have remained in favour until the end of the Ayyūbid period. The Kāmilī *dirhams* continued to be issued after the reign of al-Kāmil. Having committed to assay some rounded *dirhams* (Kāmilī) from the reigns of al-ʿĀdil II and al-Ṣāliḥ Ayyūb, Professor Balog found that this type of *dirham*

[1] Nuwayrī, xxvii, fol. 27; Maqrīzī, *Sulūk*, i, p. 247, tr. Blochet, 'D', p. 269; Rabīʿ, *Nuẓum*, p. 101. Each of the great Egyptian cities such as Cairo, Alexandria, etc., had an exchange market, *sūq al-ṣarf* or *sūq al-ṣarrāfīn*, where the money-changers dealt with the change of currencies in special shops called *ḥawānīt al-ṣarf*, cf. T.–S., B.38, fol. 123; T.–S. B.40, fol. 53; Musabbiḥī, fols. 239^{r-v}, 276^{v}–277^{r}: Nuwayrī, xxviii, fol. 66; Shayzarī, *Nihāya*, pp. 74–5; Maqrīzī, *Khiṭaṭ*, ii, p. 97; Subkī, *Muʿīd*, pp. 198–9; Worman, 'Notes on the Jews in Fustāt', p. 19; Labib, *Handelsgeschichte*, pp. 277, 282; Goitein, *Med. Soc.*, i, p. 238.

[2] M. de Boüard, 'Évolution monétaire', p. 451.

[3] Nuwayrī, xxvii, fol. 27; Maqrīzī, *Sulūk*, i, p. 254, tr. Blochet, 'D', p. 284; M. de Boüard, 'Évolution monétaire', p. 451; Rabīʿ, *Nuẓum*, p. 101. It appears that the monetary crises caused by the circulation of copper *fulūs* affected only the inhabitants of Cairo and Fusṭāṭ, e.g., Maqrīzī states that, up to the year 770/1368–9, the population in Alexandria used bread as legal tender in their daily purchases of vegetables and other goods. Maqrīzī saw Egyptian villagers barter cheap merchandise and food for chickens, bran, and flax. He was told that in Upper Egypt, seashells were used as money for the purchase of cheap goods, cf. *Ighātha*, p. 69, tr. Wiet, p. 68.

[4] Maqrīzī, *Sulūk*, i, p. 274, tr. Blochet, 'D', p. 302.

averaged about 27 per cent pure silver.[1] But Professor Balog's assumption that the Kāmilī *dirham* constituted the only Egyptian silver currency up to the end of the Ayyūbid dynasty is not acceptable.[2] Ibn Saʿīd al-Andalusī, who visited Egypt during the reign of al-Ṣāliḥ Ayyūb, mentions that the common currency in Cairo and Fusṭāṭ consisted of black *dirhams*, each of them equal to $\frac{1}{3}$ of the Nāṣirī *dirham*. This shows that both the black *dirham* and the Nāṣirī *dirham* continued to circulate beside the Kāmilī *dirham*. Al-Andalusī's account implies that the quality of the black or *waraq dirham* under al-Ṣāliḥ Ayyūb was poor. If the previous estimation of the exchange rate of different *dirhams* according to their intrinsic quality is correct, the exchange rate between the Nāṣirī *dirham* and *waraq dirham* which had been 1 : 1½ rose at the end of the Ayyūbid era to 1 : 3, which means that the silver content of the black *dirham* had fallen to 15 per cent silver. Since Ibn Saʿīd states that the black *dirhams* caused trouble, loss, and quarrels in buying and selling, this may be correct. Ibn Saʿīd adds that the *fulūs* were abandoned, though not as he wrongly assumes, under al-Kāmil.[3]

G. *The monetary system of the Mamluks*

1. *From the beginning of the Mamluk period until al-Nāṣir's reign*

Maqrīzī remarks that the Mamluks adopted the currency of the Ayyūbids, as if taking pride in their relationship with this great dynasty.[4] This is significant and has been confirmed by numismatic evidence. Professor Balog states that the coins of the first Mamluk sultans resembled those of the last Ayyūbids, and calls them 'pseudo-Ayyūbid issues'. The legends on the *dīnārs* of Shajar al-Durr, al-Ashraf Mūsā, Aybak, al-Manṣūr ʿAlī, and Quṭuz were still engraved in a manner similar to al-Ṣāliḥ Ayyūb's gold coinage.[5] As to the weight, the gold *dīnārs* of the Baḥrī Mamluks have quite irregular, individual weights, obviously because, as has been already stated, there was an obligatory standard only for silver coinage, while gold was assessed at its market price.[6]

[1] Balog, 'History of the dirhem', p. 128. [2] Ibid., p. 131.

[3] Maqrīzī, *Khiṭaṭ*, i, p. 367; see above, p. 175 n. 3.

[4] Maqrīzī, *Shudhūr*, p. 60, tr. S. de Sacy, pp. 44–5.

[5] Balog, *The coinage of the Mamluk Sultans*, pp. 12, 71, 73–6, 78–9, 82–3.

[6] The weight of 9 *dīnārs* from the reign of ʿAlī ibn Aybak ranges between 5·75 and 7·22 gm., and that of 24 *dīnārs* from the reign of Quṭuz between 4·63 and 9·38 gm.; cf. Balog, 'Quelques dinars du début de l'ère Mamelouke Bahrite', *BIE*, xxxii (1949–50), pp. 234–49; id., 'History of the dirhem', p. 136.

Concerning the silver *dirhams* in which all transactions were carried out, it is worth noting that Shajar al-Durr and al-Ashraf Mūsā issued rounded *dirhams* which differ neither in design nor in general appearance from those struck by al-Ṣāliḥ Ayyūb. Though Aybak, al-Manṣūr 'Alī, and Quṭuz imitated the Ayyūbid *dirhams*, there was an improvement in their standard of fineness.[1]

There is no mention in the textual sources of the copper *fulūs* at the beginning of the Mamluk era.[2] But in view of the existence of two copper coins struck in Cairo in 658/1259–60 under the short rule of Quṭuz—one preserved in American Numismatic Society, New York (weight 3·87 gm.) and the other in the Staatliche Münzsammlung, Munich (weight 3·12 gm.)—one may assume that the Mamluk sultans found it as difficult as Sultan al-Kāmil the Ayyūbid to abandon the copper coinage. These two specimens are heavier than the theoretical weight of the *fals*, which is 2·975 gm.[3] This superior weight may have been the reason why copper money caused no monetary crisis during the first ten years of the Baḥrī Mamluk period.

The reign of Sultan al-Ẓāhir Baybars initiates a new era in the history of the Mamluk coinage. According to Maqrīzī's *Khiṭaṭ*, the exchange rate of the *dīnār* was, at the beginning of his reign, 28½ *dirhams nuqra*, that is, more than double the normal rate, which indicates that, possibly owing to the shortage of gold in Egypt at the beginning of Baybars' reign, the price of gold was very high.[4]

[1] Balog, *The coinage of the Mamluk Sultans*, p. 12; id., 'History of the dirhem', pp. 139–40; see also Grohmann, *Einführung*, p. 210.

[2] Various copies of MSS. of *Ighātha* by Maqrīzī contain the statement that, after A.H. 750, the production of copper *fulūs* used to be assigned as *ḍamān*, while the weight of the *fals* was raised to one *mithqāl*, i.e. *dīnār*, cf. *Ighātha*, p. 70 n. 1 and Sauvaire, 'Matériaux', *JA*, xv, p. 260. The two editors, M. M. Ziada and J. al-Shayyal, p. 70, took the view that this occurred after A.H. 650, but there is no authority for this statement. It is repeated by Prof. Wiet in his translation of the book ('Le traité des famines', p. 68), and recurs in Dr. Fahmī's booklet, *Nuqūd*, p. 105. However, the event must definitely be dated after A.H. 750, more precisely A.H. 759, during the reign of al-Nāṣir Ḥasan; for details cf. Qalqashandī, *Ṣubḥ*, iii, pp. 443–4, 467; Balog, 'Observations', p. 265 and p. 272.

[3] These two specimens are described by Prof. Balog, *The coinage of the Mamluk Sultans*, p. 84 and Plate II, 26; id., 'Observations', p. 266. In theory, the weight of the *fals* remained at 2·975 gm. until about A.H. 759, cf. ibid., pp. 264, 265, 273.

[4] Maqrīzī, *Khiṭaṭ*, i, pp. 345–6; ii, p. 298; see also Qalqashandī, *Ṣubḥ*, iii, p. 442; Sauvaire, 'Matériaux', *JA*, xix (1882), p. 129; for the rate of exchange cf. Lane-Poole, 'The Arabian historians on Mohammadan numismatics', *Numismatic Chronicle*, 3rd series, iv (1884), p. 87. Prof. Ayalon ('The system of

M. de Boüard attributes the gold shortage of that time mainly to the fact that it was then that Europe turned to gold coinage, and it is probable that a good number of Egyptian *dīnār*s went to Europe, especially as Egypt had to pay in gold for the import of many commodities.[1] As to the statement of Abū al-Fidā (672–732/1273–1331) that there was a gold mine in the mountain of al-ʿAllāqī which was still worth exploiting, it may be discounted as it is well known that most medieval Arabic geographers copied from their predecessors without stating their source, and Abū al-Fidā's information may well derive from a reference previous to the exhaustion of Egyptian gold mines.[2] However, it is possible that Egypt lived on its diminishing stocks until the reign of al-Nāṣir Muḥammad, when another source of gold, Bilād al-Takrūr, was discovered.[3]

Be it as it may, Baybars adhered to the silver standard, and even tried to raise the silver content of the *dirham*s by issuing *dirham*s of a new type, called *al-darāhim al-Ẓāhiriyya*, in 658/1260. Maqrīzī states that the alloy of the Ẓāhirī *dirham* consisted of 70 per cent silver and 30 per cent copper, and that these new *dirham*s circulated in Egypt and Syria parallel with the Kāmilī *dirham*s until the reign of Sultan Barqūq.[4]

Numismatic evidence shows that the percentage of purity of the alloy of the Ẓāhirī *dirham* amounted to 67·2 per cent which almost exactly corresponds to that of the Ẓāhirī *dirham* as mentioned in the literary sources.[5] Besides, some Ẓāhirī *dirham*s were shown, on examination, to possess a standard of fineness which varied between 62 and 77 per cent.[6]

payment', p. 47), states that, during the Baḥrī period and the first two or three decades of the Circassian period, there existed a more or less fixed ratio between the *dirham* and the *dīnār*, and that when changes did occur they were usually slight (up to 28 *dirhams* to the *dīnār*). This may need some clarification, as *nuqra*, Nāṣirī, Kāmilī, and Ẓāhirī *dirhams* existed side by side for much of the Baḥrī Mamlūk era. However, they all varied considerably in their rate of exchange, in proportion to their intrinsic quality and in consequence of changing economic conditions in general.

[1] M. de Boüard, 'Evolution monétaire', p. 452.

[2] Abū al-Fidā, *Taqwīm*, pp. 121, 163; see above, p. 169.

[3] See below, pp. 191–2.

[4] Maqrīzī, *Shudhūr*, p. 61, tr. S. de Sacy, p. 45; cf. Qalqashandī, *Ṣubḥ*, iii, p. 467; Sauvaire, 'Matériaux', *JA*, xv (1880), p. 476; xix (1882), pp. 103, 128–9; Grohmann, *Einführung*, p. 210; Popper, *Systematic notes*, ii, p. 51; Balog, 'History of the dirhem', p. 133.

[5] Ehrenkreutz, 'Contributions to the knowledge of the fiscal administration', p. 505; see also Bacharach and Gordus, 'Studies', pp. 309–10.

[6] Balog, 'History of the dirhem', pp. 139, 140; in another place (*The coinage of the Mamluk Sultans*, p. 44) Prof. Balog mentions a silver content of 66–77 per cent.

As to the source from which Baybars obtained sufficient silver to produce these superior Ẓāhirī *dirhams*, it seems that, with the rise of the Mongols in the mid 7th/13th century, silver suddenly reappeared in vast quantities from China and Central Asia. Thanks to its trade relations with countries around the Red Sea, the Indian Ocean, the Black Sea, and the Mediterranean, it was possible for Egypt to obtain considerable amounts of silver, and the quality of the Ẓāhirī *dirhams* improved.[1]

As for the exchange rate of the Ẓāhirī *dirhams*, Professor Ehrenkreutz calculates that, as 100 per cent silver *dirhams* were rated at $13\frac{1}{3}$: 1, 50 per cent silver *dirhams* at about $26\frac{2}{3}$: 1, and 30 per cent silver *dirhams* at 40: 1, the exchange rate of the Ẓāhirī *dirhams* must have been 20: 1, a ratio which appears most frequently in the sources dealing with the exchange rates between the monetary types of the Baḥrī Mamluks.[2]

However, as the Ẓāhirī *dirham* was superior in quality to the Nāṣirī *dirham* and the Kāmilī *dirham*, the value of the latter two rapidly decreased. The *ḍāmins* of the mint even petitioned Sultan Baybars in 662/1264 to abandon the Nāṣirī *dirhams*, but the latter, obviously apprehensive that, if he abandoned the Nāṣirī *dirhams*, their value would fall and the population would be exposed to considerable loss in exchanging their Nāṣirī *dirhams* for the new issue, preferred to reduce their *ḍamān*.[3] It is worth noting that the refusal of Sultan al-Ẓāhir to abandon the Nāṣirī *dirhams* perpetuated a certain confusion in the Egyptian monetary system. In any previous monetary reform such as those of Saladin and al-Kāmil, the old types of coins with higher or lower weight and different alloy were kept in circulation parallel with the new ones. The Nāṣirī

[1] Blake, 'The circulation of silver', p. 291; Miles, article 'Dirham' in *EI*^{2}; Labib, *Handelsgeschichte*, p. 265; Watson, 'Back to gold', p. 6.

[2] The pattern of the rates of exchange of Ayyūbid and Baḥrī Mamluk *dirhams*, with the exclusion of Kāmilī *dirhams* whose alloy is controversial, is illustrated by Prof. Ehrenkreutz ('Contributions to the knowledge of the fiscal administration', p. 505) as follows:

Type of dirhams	*Alloy*	*Exchange rate per 1 gold unit*	
nuqra	100%	$13\frac{1}{3}$	
		correct	*reported*
Ẓāhirī	70%	20	20
Nāṣirī	50%	$26\frac{2}{3}$	25 and $28\frac{1}{2}$
waraq	30%	40	40 and $35\frac{1}{4}$

[3] See above, p. 117.

dirhams continued to be legal coinage as late as eighty years from the date of their issue, and so did the Kāmilī *dirhams*.[1] The simultaneous existence of different types of silver *dirhams* with their different alloys and rates of exchange resulted in frequent monetary crises, which al-Ẓāhir's reform, for very noble motives, failed to terminate.

It would seem that the population preferred the *dirham nuqra*, which was no doubt superior in quality to the others. It figures as money of account, especially in deeds of *waqf*. Thus, for example, in the *ḥujjat waqf* of the amir al-Ḥājj Bahā' al-Dīn Sunbul, dated 17 Rajab 687/17 August 1288, the amir Bahā' al-Dīn postulates that some of the rents of his properties should be paid, after his death, to some *shaykhs* and reciters of the Qur'ān in *nuqra* or equivalent *dirhams*.[2]

Copper *fulūs* struck in Cairo by Sultan Baybars and his successors before Kitbughā's reign are scarce in the known numismatic collections. Only Professor Balog has been able to ascertain the weight of 8 specimens which, though issued during Baybars' reign, are undated and without reference to their *dār al-ḍarb* (mint). They all remain below the theoretical weight of the *fals*. This is also true of two other specimens from Balog's collection, deriving from the reign of Sultan Qalāwūn.[3] A comparison of Professor Balog's data with the weight of the *fulūs* struck by Quṭuz leads to the inference that underweight *fulūs* began to be struck by individuals in enormous quantities as early as the reign of Sultan Baybars, possibly as a result of the confusion caused by the circulation of different types of silver *dirhams*. These underweight *fulūs* increased in numbers until they caused a monetary crisis during the year 695/1296 in the reign of Sultan Kitbughā, when people re-

[1] A fragment from the Geniza, written in Fusṭāṭ in the spring of 1261, refers to a woman who offered for sale a quarter of a house for 300 Kāmilī *dirhams*. In another fragment from the same collection, dated January 1268, a *divorcée* agrees to accept 30 instead of 70 Kāmilī *dirhams* due to her, cf. T.–S. 16.355; Mosseri Collection A18 in Goitein, 'The exchange rate', pp. 35–6; id., *Med. Soc.*, i, p. 386.

[2] *Maḥkama*, Box 3, no. 16. The use of *dirhams nuqra* as money of account is frequently mentioned in documents from the *Maḥkama* collection, cf. *Ḥujjat waqf* Ḥusām al-Dīn Lājīn (21 Rabī' II 397/5 February 1298), Box 3, no. 17; *Ḥujjat waqf* Sayf al-Dīn Baktamur al-Nāṣirī (14 Muḥarram 707/16 July 1307), Box 4, no. 20; *Ḥujjat waqf* Baybars al-Jāshnikīr (26 Shawwāl 707/20 April 1308), Box 4, no. 22.

[3] Balog, 'Observations', p. 266; id. *The coinage of the Mamluk Sultans*, pp. 103–6, 118–19, and Plates IV–V.

fused to accept underweight *fulūs* in their transactions. It was then that it was announced, for the first time in Egypt, that copper *fulūs* would be dealt with by weight and not by tale, each *raṭl* (unit of weight) being equal to 2 *dirhams* and each *ūqiya* ($\frac{1}{12}$ of the *raṭl*) to $\frac{1}{6}$ *dirham*. To secure the success of this action it was decreed that one *fals* should be equal in weight to one silver *dirham*.[1] However, these measures miscarried as the counterfeiters debased the *fulūs* by the use of cheaper metals such as bronze and lead which led to the aggravation of the monetary situation under Sultan al-Nāṣir Muḥammad, despite occasional increase in the number of gold *dīnārs*.

2. *The monetary system in the reign of al-Nāṣir*

Two reasons seem to account for the increase in the circulation of gold *dīnārs* in Egypt under al-Nāṣir. In this relatively long period in the history of the Mamluk sultanate agriculture, inland and foreign trade flourished, and this prosperity was reflected in the increase of the amount of gold *dīnārs* in the country. Secondly, the activities of al-Nāṣir himself contributed to an increase in the circulation of gold coins. According to Nuwayrī and Maqrīzī, large numbers of *dīnārs* came into circulation in the year 699/1299–1300, after al-Nāṣir's defeat by the Mongols at Ḥimṣ. In order to regain military power, al-Nāṣir not only spent large amounts of money from his private purse, but also imposed additional taxes on merchants and wealthy people, which were mainly collected in gold, each individual concerned paying between 10 and 100 *dīnārs*. This levy was distributed to the various ranks of the army in gold, each cavalry-man receiving 40 *dīnārs* *nafaqa*. Obviously, a considerable amount of this gold was spent by the troops in Egypt before the campaign. Consequently, the value of gold fell and its rate of exchange sank to 17 *dirhams* per *dīnār*, instead of the previous rate of $25\frac{1}{2}$ *dirhams*.[2]

According to the contemporary historian al-Dawādārī, the low

[1] Maqrīzī, *Ighātha*, pp. 37, 70, tr. Wiet, pp. 39, 69; id., *Sulūk*, i, p. 810, tr. Quatremère, ii. ii, p. 26; Sauvaire, 'Matériaux', *JA*, xv (1880), pp. 260–1, 267–8; xix (1882), p. 130; Grohmann, *Einführung*, p. 217; Popper, *Systematic notes*, ii, p. 67. This evidence seems to refute Prof. Balog's idea ('Observations', p. 273) as repeated by Prof. Udovitch ('England to Egypt', p. 124) that it was only after 759/1357–8 that copper coins, which had hitherto passed by tale, began to be weighed.

[2] Nuwayrī, xxix, fol. 117; Maqrīzī, *Sulūk*, i, p. 899, tr. Quatremère, ii. ii, pp. 167–8; for the *nafaqa*, see above, pp. 33–4.

price of gold in that year encouraged some soldiers to speculate. For instance, Sunqur Shāh al-Ḥusāmī, the mamluk of the amir Ḥusām al-Dīn Ṭuruntāy, bought 100,000 *dīnār*s at 18 *dirhams* per *dīnār*, and sold them after the campaign at 25 *dirhams* per *dīnār*, thus making a gain of 700,000 *dirhams*.[1] Others must have similarly benefited, as the Mamluk sultanate tried to mitigate the economic consequences of the depreciation of gold by enforcing the existing fixed exchange rate at 20 *dirhams* per *dīnār*.[2]

It is worth noting that, despite or because of the abundance of gold, the gold standard was never re-established. It seems that the people trusted silver more than gold, as silver remained the Egyptian monetary standard. This assumption is supported by the circumstance that, in the title-deed of the amir Shams al-Dīn Sunqur Jāh ibn ʿAbd Allāh al-Manṣūrī, dated 13 Shawwāl 699/3 July 1300 and preserved in the 'Personal status court' in Cairo, the total sum paid to the heirs of the famous amir Badr al-Dīn Baysarā al-Shamsī al-Ṣāliḥī as purchase price of a stable is mentioned as 19,443¾ *dirhams nuqra* and not as the equivalent sum in gold *dīnār*s.[3] However, it seems that the shortage of gold recurred after a mere two years. The crisis was so severe that the authorities did not oppose the invasion of the Venetian ducat in 1302.

The Venetian gold ducat was first issued in 1284, at a time of gold scarcity in Egypt, and just after the withdrawal of the Byzantine *nomisma*, the currency in which all large commercial operations in the Mediterranean had previously been accounted. The success of the ducat was very swift, owing to the strength and expansion of the Venetian economy and to the role of Venice in the system of international transactions and exchanges which supported the intrinsic stability of the ducat.[4] Obviously, the Venetian ducat had great ascendancy over the Egyptian gold *dīnār*, owing to its purity

[1] Dawādārī, *Durr fākhir*, pp. 37–8.

[2] Maqrīzī, *Sulūk*, i, p. 900, tr. Quatremère, ii. ii, p. 168.

[3] *Maḥkama*, Box 4, no. 19. Baysarā, who died on 19 Shawwāl 698/20 July 1299, was one of the important amirs of Sultan al-Ẓāhir Baybars. In 690/1291, Sultan Khalīl ibn Qalāwūn conferred upon him Minyat banī Khaṣīb as a *darbastā iqṭā*ʿ, cf. above, p. 43.

[4] Cipolla, *Money, prices, and civilisation*, pp. 20–1, 24; M. de Boüard, 'Évolution monétaire', pp. 456–7. Though Genoa—interested in North African trade—issued a gold coin of its own in 1252, and Florence the florin about the same time, neither coinage had an impact on the Egyptian *dīnār* at that time; cf. Lopez, 'The dollar of the middle ages', p. 213; Atiya, *Crusade*, p. 188; Labib, *Handelsgeschichte*, p. 271.

as well as to the volume of Egypt's trade with Venice.[1] The ducat achieved importance in the Egyptian internal market because it was struck in pure gold, of stable weight 3·56 gm., and was circulated in large regions south and east of Venice in the eastern Mediterranean and as far as India. It had the advantage over the Mamluk *dīnār* that it had a perfect circular shape of constant dimension, on which the legend could be figured entirely, so that it could be circulated by tale and not by weight as the Mamluk *dīnār*. In 701/1302, eighteen years after the first ducat issue, the Egyptian customs officially accepted ducats in settlement of taxes imposed on imported goods.[2]

The spread of the ducat, with its purity and stable weight, encouraged Egyptian counterfeiters to debase the gold coins in circulation. Forgeries of this kind were so profitable that even high state officials engaged in them. For example, a number of forgers was found at work in the house of the vizier Nāṣir al-Dīn Muḥammad al-Shaykhī, after his dismissal in 704/1305.[3]

An important source of gold, namely Bilād al-Takrūr, was opened to Egypt in the first half of the 14th century, which obviously delayed the success of the ducat for several years.[4] The visits of the kings of Bilād al-Takrūr to Egypt, on the occasion of their pilgrimage to Mecca, and the following trade relations,

[1] Labib, *Handelsgeschichte*, p. 272.

[2] M. de Boüard, 'Évolution monétaire', p. 457; Ives and Grierson, *The Venetian gold ducat*, pp. 1–2, 5; Labib, *Handelsgeschichte*, p. 274; Iskandar, 'Niẓām al-muqāyaḍa', p. 44.

[3] Ibn Abī al-Faḍā'il, p. 614; coins were debased in many ways in the Islamic world. Some counterfeiters used to strike *dīnārs* from silver and coat them with gold, others hollowed them out, replacing the removed gold with cheap metals, cf. Karmalī, *Nuqūd*, p. 17 n. 3; al-Naqshbandī, *al-Dīnār al-Islāmī*, i, p. 14. It was one of the functions of the *muḥtasib* to prevent the circulation of counterfeit coins, cf. Shayzarī, *Nihāya*, pp. 74–6; Ibn al-Ukhuwwa, *Maʿālim*, pp. 143–4.

[4] Some medieval Arabic geographers and writers provide information on the eponymous capital of the state of Takrūr, which flourished for a brief period in the middle ages (*c.* A.D. 1000); cf. Yāqūt, *Muʿjam*, i, p. 861; Ibn Saʿīd, *Basṭ*, pp. 24–6; Qazwīnī, *Āthār*, p. 17; Abū al-Fidā, *Taqwīm*, pp. 2, 153; Qalqashandī, *Ṣubḥ*, v, pp. 286–7; Nagar, 'Takrūr', paper read on 23 February 1966, Institute of Commonwealth Studies and S.O.A.S., London University. Delafosse (article 'Takrūr' in *EI*[1]) locates the town of Takrūr near the arm of the Senegal in the vicinity of the present site of Podor. Qalqashandī (*Ṣubḥ*, v, p. 282) states that Mali was known among the 'common people' as Bilād al-Takrūr, which is an indication that, in his time, the term Bilād al-Takrūr was circulated by popular usage, certainly in Egypt and possibly in other countries of the Middle East. Some Arabic classical texts on Bilād al-Takrūr are found in *Mamlakat Mali ʿind al-jughrāfiyyīn al-Muslimīn* by Ṣ. al-Munajjid, Beirut, 1963.

resulted in a considerable influx of gold. In Rajab 724/July 1324, King Mūsā ibn Abī Bakr al-Takrūrī visited Egypt. According to *Masālik al-abṣār* in *Ṣubḥ*, he presented Sultan al-Nāṣir with a *ḥiml* of ore and distributed gold among all the amirs and sultani officials. All in all, he is said to have spent, on the occasion of his visit, 100 *ḥiml* of gold.[1] All the members of King Mūsā's retinue exchanged their gold for Egyptian goods, so that the volume of gold in the hands of the people increased.[2] The generosity of King Mūsā even caused him financial trouble, so that he had to borrow from the Egyptian merchants. It is by no means strange that Egyptian merchants were often paid in gold for the goods they exported to Bilād al-Takrūr, which became the most important source of gold for Egypt.[3] This obviously reduced the value of the gold *dīnār* by two *dirhams*, and enabled the sultan to issue gold coinage whose weight satisfied the theoretical requirements.[4]

Despite the influx of gold from Bilād al-Takrūr, the Egyptian did not abandon the silver *dirhams* in favour of gold *dīnārs*. This is borne out by information found in two unpublished fragments from the Vienna papers. In the first fragment, dated 733/1333–4, Nāṣir al-Dīn Muḥammad ibn ʿIzz al-Dīn Aybak confirms the receipt of an amount of 8 *nuqra* (*dirhams*) less 14 *fals* from al-Ḥājj Yūsuf as part-payment for ramming the floor of his house. In the second fragment, dated 26 Rabīʿ II 734/4 January 1334, provision is made by one person for another (both names are missing) by undertaking to pay him, at the end of every month, the amount of $4+\frac{1}{2}+\frac{1}{3}=4\frac{5}{6}$ *dirhams nuqra*.[5]

[1] Qalqashandī, *Ṣubḥ*, v, pp. 295–6. The *ḥiml* is the average load. According to Makhzūmī, the *ḥiml* for certain kinds of wood was 600 *raṭls miṣrī*, for pepper 500, and for ginned cotton 553⅓; cf. *Minhāj*, fol. 137ʳ; Cahen, 'Douanes', p. 277; Hinz, pp. 13–14; see also Goitein, *Med. Soc.*, i, p. 220.

[2] Ibn Ḥajar, *Durar*, iv, p. 383.

[3] Dawādārī, *Durr fākhir*, pp. 316–17; Qalqashandī, *Ṣubḥ*, iii, p. 465, v, p. 296; Labib, *Handelsgeschichte*, p. 267. Ibn Baṭṭūṭa (*Tuḥfa*, iv, pp. 431–2) states that Sultan Mūsā and his amirs borrowed money from the Egyptian merchant Sirāj al-Dīn ibn al-Kuwayk. Sirāj al-Dīn went to collect his money which, in fact, was paid to his son, as he himself died before reaching Mali, see also Ṣafadī, *Aʿyān* (MS. A.S. 2966), fol. 147ᵛ. For Banū Kuwayk, cf. Jacqueline Sublet, ' 'Abd al-Laṭīf al-Takrītī', pp. 193–6.

[4] Yāfiʿī, *Mir'āt*, iv, p. 271; Ibn Kathīr, xiv, p. 112; Maqrīzī (*Sulūk*, ii, p. 255 and *Dhahab*, p. 113) states that the value of the *dīnār* decreased by 6 *dirhams*. The weight of an undated quarter *dīnār*, possibly deriving from the year A.H. 724, is 1·18 gm., which corresponds almost exactly to the legal weight of the *dīnār*, cf. Balog, 'Un quart de dinar du Sultan Naser Mohamed Ben Qalaoun', *BIE*, xxxii (1949–50), pp. 255–6.

[5] A.Ch. 10216ʳ; A.Ch. 10228.

In the course of time, the amount of gold in circulation was considerably reduced. Whether he was anxious to preserve the silver standard, or because he realized that the large influx of gold was merely temporary, or because it was in line with his general tendency of confiscating what he could, Sultan al-Nāṣir made the attempt to withdraw the gold in circulation to his treasury. According to ʿUmarī and Maqrīzī, in 736/1336 al-Nashw, *nāẓir al-khāṣṣ*, forced goldsmiths and the officials of the mint to discontinue their purchases of gold. All the gold had to be sent to the mint to be struck in shape of *dīnār*s, which were made of refined gold (*danānīr haraja*) and bore the legend of the sultan. This type of *dīnār* could be exchanged for *dirhams*. Thanks to this stratagem, the *nāẓir al-khāṣṣ* collected a large amount of gold in the treasury. He confiscated the gold of the merchants and the public which was already in the mint, compensating them with goods. Maqrīzī says that all the Egyptian gold found its way to the mint, so that it was not obtainable in the market.[1]

In consequence, the price of gold rose. In 737/1336–7 Sultan al-Nāṣir bought the amir Sayf al-Dīn Ṣarghitmish for 200,000 *dirhams fiḍḍa* (*nuqra*), equal to 4,000 *mithqāl* (= *dīnār*), which means that the exchange rate of the gold *dīnār* had risen to 1:50 *dirhams* in one year.[2] This appears to have led, in turn, to a scarcity of silver, which was still the Egyptian standard money. In search of a solution, al-Nāṣir introduced a bimetallic monetary gold and silver standard which, according to al-ʿAynī, resulted in great losses to the population. Al-ʿAynī relates that the exchange rate of the *dīnār* was fixed at 25 *dirhams* in 739/1338–9, and that the value of goods in all transactions was calculated half in silver and half in gold.[3] The price of gold remained dear, as there was no silver coinage

[1] ʿUmarī, *Masālik* (MS. A.S. 3434), fols. 107ʳ–108ʳ; Maqrīzī, *Sulūk*, ii, p. 393; the term *haraja* denotes refined Islamic gold, cf. Ibn Baʿra, pp. 68–9; Ehrenkreutz, 'Extracts', p. 434 and n. 3.

[2] Maqrīzī, *Khiṭaṭ*, ii, p. 404. The *mithqāl*, by which gold coins were weighed, corresponds to the Roman *solidus*, a unit of the Byzantine system adopted by the Arabs. In practice, the word *mithqāl* was synonymous with the *dīnār* of full weight standard, cf. Ibn Khaldūn, *Muqaddima*, pp. 219–20; Ibn al-Ukhuwwa, *Maʿālim*, pp. 81–2; Maqrīzī, *Awzān*, pp. 19–21; id., *Shudhūr*, pp. 28–30, tr. S. de Sacy, pp. 9–10; Ḥakīm, *Dawḥa*, pp. 47–8; Sauvaire, 'Matériaux', *JA*, xiv (1879), pp. 489 ff.; Allan, article 'Mithḳāl' in *EI*¹; Lane-Poole, 'The Arabian historians', pp. 74–5; Grohmann, 'New discoveries', (I), p. 165, (II), p. 162; Ehrenkreutz, 'The standard of fineness', p. 163 n. 6; Frey, *Dictionary of numismatic names*, p. 151.

[3] ʿAynī, *ʿIqd*, 'C', xxiv. i, fol. 34; id., *Badr*, fol. 37ᵛ.

available to cover half of the markets' needs. At the end of the year (739), al-Nāṣir decreased the value of the *dīnār* to 20 *dirhams*, only to raise it again to 25 *dirhams* in the following year (740/1339). It is said that, as the sultan owed the merchants 1,000,000 *dīnārs*, he hoped to be able to settle the debt faster on the new basis. But the shortage of silver, coupled with the rise in the gold price, resulted in a monetary crisis, which brought all trade to a halt.[1]

All silver having disappeared from the market, Sultan al-Nāṣir was forced to distribute 2,000,000 silver *dirhams* from his treasury among the money-changers, to be exchanged for gold—which revived the economy of the country. But the relief was only temporary.[2] It is probable that these two million silver *dirhams*, put in circulation by Sultan al-Nāṣir in 740/1339, were part of the yearly silver tribute from Armenia.[3] They failed to remedy the situation, presumably because they were rejected by the market owing to their poor silver content. This assumption is supported by numismatic evidence. Professor Balog's examination of the purity of al-Nāṣir's *dirhams* showed that some contained only 46 per cent fine silver.[4]

Both the rise in the price of gold and the shortage of silver after 736/1336 indicate that the heyday of the Egyptian gold *dīnār* was over. The Venetian gold ducat spread in great quantities all over Egypt, and was followed by the Florentine florin, the term '*ifrantī*' denoting both the ducat and the florin. In a repeated attempt to counteract the influence of these European coins, Sultan Faraj ibn Barqūq (801–15/1399–1412) and Sultan Barsbāy (825–41/1422–38) coined new gold *dīnārs* imitating the *ifrantī*, and of approximately

[1] 'Aynī, '*Iqd*, 'A', xvii, fol. 155[v]; Maqrīzī, *Sulūk*, ii, p. 488; one *dīnār* to twenty *dirhams* is frequently quoted by Maqrīzī as the exchange rate in al-Nāṣir's reign, cf. *Khiṭaṭ*, i, p. 226, ii, pp. 33, 64, 209, 306, 422; see also Grierson, *The Venetian gold ducat*, p. 3; Labib, *Handelsgeschichte*, p. 266.

[2] Maqrīzī, *Sulūk*, ii, p. 494.

[3] In 723/1323, King Leo V (1320–42) agreed to pay an annual regular tribute to Sultan al-Nāṣir to the amount of 100,000 silver *dirhams*. Only a part of these Armenian *trams* was put into circulation without alteration; some were melted down to be struck as Mamluk *dirhams*, while the majority were overstruck with an Arabic legend. These three kinds of silver coins have been found together in hoards from this period. Cf. Maqrīzī, *Sulūk*, ii, p. 246; Balog, *The coinage of the Mamluk Sultans*, pp. 41–2, 146–7; id., 'History of the dirhem', p. 141; for the treaty of 1323 cf. Issaverdens, *Armenia and the Armenians*, i, p. 347; id., *Histoire de l'Arménie*, p. 233; the *tram*, a silver coin of Armenia representing half the value of the silver *tahégan*, corresponded to the *dirham*, cf. Langlois, *Numismatique de l'Arménie*, pp. 12–13; Frey, *Dictionary*, pp. 234, 246.

[4] Balog, 'History of the dirhem', pp. 139, 141; id., *The coinage of the Mamluk Sultans*, p. 44.

the same weight. However, these failed to displace the Italian coins, which continued to circulate parallel with the Egyptian *dīnār*s until the end of the Mamluk era.[1]

The edict of Sultan Kitbughā, decreeing that the *fulūs* should be circulated by weight not by tale, had grievous consequences during the long reign of al-Nāṣir Muḥammad, when there were many monetary crises owing to the vicissitudes of the copper *fulūs*.[2] These crises recurred, with certain variations, over and over again. There is a distinctly discernible vicious circle. The *fulūs* of fixed weight, that is, weight of a *dirham*, to be handled by tale, were debased by counterfeiters, and ensuing orders to sell them by weight resulted in heavy losses to the public, especially the dealers who in certain cases, had to go out of business. Then new full-weight *fulūs* used to be issued only to be debased and counterfeited in their turn, whereupon the vicious circle continued. In 705/1305 there were great numbers of underweight and debased *fulūs* in circulation. *Fulūs* of normal weight seemed to have disappeared from the markets. When al-Nāṣir issued new *fulūs*, he fixed the value of the underweight ones at 2½ *dirhams* per *raṭl*.[3] It seems that the inhabitants dealt with the new normal-weight *fulūs* by tale, 48 *fals* equalling 1 *dirham*, a rate of exchange which probably continued until 720/1320, when activities of counterfeiters, reducing the *fals* to ⅙ of the weight of the *dirham*, caused a new monetary crisis. What added to the confusion was that al-Nāṣir abandoned in Syria the underweight *fulūs*, which were subsequently brought to Egypt by merchants and bankers. When it was decreed that the *fulūs* must be circulated by weight, a *raṭl* equalling 3 *dirhams*, some retailers, who had to sell the *fulūs* they obtained by tale in exchange for their goods so cheaply by weight, had to close their shops. Though it was proclaimed that only *fulūs* minted under the supervision of the sultan and bearing the sultani legend were acceptable,

[1] Qalqashandī, *Ṣubḥ*, iii, pp. 441–2; Gennep, 'Le ducat vénitien en Égypte, son influence sur le monnayage de l'or dans ce pays au commencement du XVe siècle', *Revue Numismatique*, 4e série, i (1897), pp. 373–81, 494–508; Ives and Grierson, *The Venetian ducat*, p. 3; M. de Boüard, 'Évolution monétaire', pp. 457–8; Popper, *Systematic notes*, ii, pp. 45–50; Labib, *Handelsgeschichte*, p. 274; Udovitch, 'England to Egypt', pp. 124–5.

[2] See above, pp. 188–9.

[3] Baybars al-Manṣūrī, *Zubda*, fol. 246^v; 'Aynī, *'Iqd*, 'C', xxi. ii, fol. 365; Zetterstéen, p. 132. Maqrīzī, *Sulūk*, ii, p. 17; Sauvaire, 'Matériaux', *JA*, xv (1880), p. 268; Grohmann, *Einführung*, p. 217; Popper, *Systematic notes*, ii, p. 67; Balog. 'Observations', p. 264; Labib, *Handelsgeschichte*, p. 268.

the counterfeiters (*al-zughaliyya*) forged the sultani legend on their underweight *fulūs*, so that the value of the *raṭl* of *fulūs* had to be reduced to 2½ *dirhams*. The success of the new measure lasted a mere few days, after which the shops were closed again. The sultan had new *fulūs* of *dirham* weight to be circulated by tale. Meanwhile the underweight *fulūs* continued to circulate by weight, the *raṭl* at 3 *dirhams*. This caused renewed hardship as these *fulūs*, which were worth 7 *dirhams* by tale, were worth only 3 *dirhams* when sold by weight.[1]

The effect of the sultan's reform in Dhū al-Ḥijja 720/January 1321 lasted only one month. In Muḥarram 721/February 1321, according to al-'Aynī, Cairo stopped dealing in copper *fulūs*, probably because the counterfeiters had succeeded in debasing all the *fulūs* in circulation.[2] The lack of copper money caused obvious difficulties in daily shopping, so that al-Nāṣir was forced to permit the circulation of the *fulūs*, but by weight not by tale,[3] and the circulation of debased *fulūs* increased to the extent that the merchants, for fear of exchanging their goods for coins of lesser value, closed their shops again, and the *ardabb* of wheat rose from 10 to 17 *dirhams*. In Muḥarram 724/January 1324, the inhabitants were called upon to exchange their copper coins at the mint into silver *dirhams*. Such action, harmful to the population, benefited the sultan, who had reduced the price of the *raṭl* of copper from 3 and 2½ to 2 *dirhams*. About 200,000 new copper *fulūs*, each weighing 1⅛ *dirhams* instead of the normal weight of 1 *dirham*, were distributed among the money-changers of Cairo and Fusṭāṭ, and soon disappeared from the market, causing another monetary crisis.[4]

Twelve years later, business in Cairo came to a halt on 13 Rajab 736/26 February 1336, possibly owing to lack of full-weight copper coins. Wheat prices increased once more, and the average consumer had difficulty in buying bread.[5] Finally, in 738/1337–8, al-Nashw,

[1] Nuwayrī, xxx, fol. 141; 'Aynī, *'Iqd*, 'C', xxiii. ii, fols. 227–9, 259–60; id., *Badr*, fol. 12^{r}; Maqrīzī, *Sulūk*, ii, pp. 205–6.

[2] 'Aynī, *'Iqd*, 'C', xxiii. ii, fols. 259–60; id., *Badr*, fol. 12^{r}.

[3] Maqrīzī, *Sulūk*, ii, p. 233.

[4] 'Aynī, *'Iqd*, 'C', xxiii. iii, fol. 439; id., *Badr*, fol. 15^{r}; Maqrīzī, *Sulūk*, ii, p. 253; Ibn Taghrī Birdī, *Nujūm*, ix, p. 77; Maqrīzī (*Khiṭaṭ*, ii, pp. 148–9) states that on the 1st of Ramaḍān 724/23 August 1324 the amir Sayf al-Dīn Qadādār, appointed by Sultan al-Nāṣir as *wālī* of Cairo, tried to settle the trouble by flogging the bakers and sellers to punish them for refusing to accept debased *fulūs*. He went so far as to threaten to crucify them.

[5] Maqrīzī, *Sulūk*, ii, pp. 391–2.

nāẓir al-khāṣṣ, forced the merchants and dealers to buy 200,000 *dirhams* of copper *fulūs* struck in Alexandria, Tarūja, Fuwwa, and other cities in Upper Egypt. The *fulūs* of the cities concerned were debased by lead and other cheap metals. The expedient of cutting the big *fals* into three parts proved useless, the *fulūs* were refused again, and the price of wheat increased by another 3 *dirhams* per *ardabb*.[1] Both the cut *fals* and the lead *fals* were abolished, but the problem remained.[2]

It may be worth noting that the frequent copper monetary crises led to a gradual increase of the total amount of copper in circulation. As a result—towards the end of the Baḥrī Mamluk era—the *fals* remained the only currency available in sufficient quantities for commercial transactions, and became the sole currency. In the words of Maqrīzī: 'the *fulūs* increased in excessive numbers in the hands of the population and were favoured to such an extent that they became the dominant currency in the country'. Gold continued to be a mere commodity, and silver became extremely scarce, because the European merchants exported it to their countries in exchange for the copper which they brought to Egypt. The Mamluks used silver mostly for jewellery and ornaments.[3]

[1] This appears to contradict Prof. Ashtor's statement that there were no changes in wheat prices under al-Nāṣir ibn Qalāwūn, cf. 'Prix et salaires à l'époque mamlouke', *REI* (1949), p. 61.

[2] Maqrīzī, *Sulūk*, ii, p. 444. According to Mayer's 'Some problems of Mamlūk coinage', in *Transactions of the International Numismatic Congress*, held in London, 1936, p. 441, lead Mamluk coins are exceedingly rare. However, it seems that both the Mamluk sultanate and the public tried to prevent the debasement of the quality of the copper *fulūs*. The results of chemical (nitric acid) tests made on a large number of different Baḥrī and Circassian *fulūs* leave no doubt that most of them were made of pure copper, and only a few of Qānṣūh al-Ghawrī's *fulūs* were made of bronze, cf. Balog, *The coinage of the Mamluk Sultans*, p. 55.

[3] Maqrīzī, *Ighātha*, p. 71, tr. Wiet, p. 70; see also Maqrīzī, *Shudhūr*, p. 69, tr. S. de Sacy, p. 56; Balog, 'Observations', p. 264; id., *The coinage of the Mamluk Sultans*, p. 42; Labib, *Handelsgeschichte*, pp. 270–1; the term *fulūs* (plural of *fals*) is still in use in colloquial speech in Egpyt to denote money in general.

BIBLIOGRAPHY

1. *Cairo Geniza documents*

BM: British Museum

BM. Or. 5535 II (Shaked, *A tentative bibliography of Geniza documents*, p. 173).

BM. Or. 5549 III, fol. 5 (Shaked, p. 176)

BM. Or. 5566D, fol. 6 (Shaked, p. 179)

T.–S.: Taylor–Schechter Collection, University Library, Cambridge

T.–S. [Glasses] 16.215 (Shaked, p. 69)

T.–S. [Bound volumes] 10 J5, fol. 2 (Shaked, p. 98)

T.–S. [Bound volumes] 10 J28, fol. 13 (Goitein, *Med. Soc.*, i, p. 382, sec. 59)

T.–S. [Bound volumes] 10 J29, fol. 14 (Shaked, p. 110)

T.–S. [Arabic boxes]:

B.38, fol. 14
B.38, fol. 95
B.38, fol. 123
B.38, fol. 137
B.39, fol. 25
B.39, fol. 57
B.39, fol. 118
B.39, fol. 133
B.39, fol. 189
B.39, fol. 219
B.39, fol. 245
B.39, fol. 280
B.39, fol. 342
B.39, fol. 372
B.39, fol. 386
B.39, fol. 444
B.39, fol. 480
B.39, fol. 492
B.40, fol. 37
B.40, fol. 39
B.40, fol. 53
B.40, fol. 56
B.40, fol. 126
B.40, fol. 129
B.40, fol. 184
B.41, fol. 49
B.41, fol. 107
B.41, fol. 109r–v
B.41, fol. 111
B.42, fol. 24
B.42, fol. 51
B.42, fol. 70
B.42, fol. 94
B.42, fol. 129
B.42, fol. 130
B.42, fol. 171
B.42, fol. 209
B.42, fol. 210
B.42, fol. 214

T.–S. Boxes [miscellaneous]:

Box 28, fol. 33 (Shaked, p. 147)

T.–S. New Series:

Box 297, fol. 1
Box 306, fol. 1^{r-v}
Box 321, fol. 23^{r-v}
J30 (Goitein, *Med. Soc.*, i, p. 366, sec. 24, p. 382, sec. 61)
J117 (Shaked, p. 161)
J136 (Shaked, p. 162)
J297 (Goitein, *Med. Soc.*, i, p. 386, sec. 79)
J375, fol. 1^{r}–2^{r}
$J383^{r}$
J412 (Goitein, *Med. Soc.*, i, p. 383, sec. 64)

2. *Vienna papers*

A.Ch. 1, fol. 627
fol. 667
fols. 906–921
A.Ch. 3, fol. 2002
fol. 2007
fol. 2032
fol. 2038
fol. 2039
fol. 2050
A.Ch. 4, fol. 3049
fol. 3111
fol. 3306
fol. 3439
A.Ch. 5, fol. 4074
fol. 4122
fol. 4133
A.Ch. 8, fol. 7113
fol. 7133
fol. 7140
fol. 7229
fol. 7277
A.Ch., fol. 7379
A.Ch. 8, fol. 7425
fol. 7476
fol. 7487
A.Ch. 10, fol. 7816
fol. 7852
fol. 7921
A.Ch., fol. 8052
A.Ch., fol. 8137
A.Ch., fol. 9277
A.Ch., fol. 9284
A.Ch., fol. 9531
A.Ch., fol. 9533
A.Ch., fol. 10216^{r-v}
A.Ch., fol. 10217^{r-v}
A.Ch., fol. 10218
A.Ch., fol. 10219
A.Ch., fol. 10220
A.Ch., fol. 10227
A.Ch., fol. 10228
A.Ch., fol. 12185
A.Ch., fol. 12340^{r-v}
A.Ch., fol. 12436
A.Ch., fol. 12437
A.Ch., fol. 12439
A.Ch., fol. 12441
A.Ch., fol. 12446
A.Ch., fol. 12477
A.Ch., fol. 12479
A.Ch., fol. 12483
A.Ch., fol. 12484^{r-v}
A.Ch., fol. 12485
A.Ch., fol. 12487
A.Ch., fol. 12506^{r-v}
A.Ch., fol. 12507

A.Ch., fol. 12508
A.Ch., fol. 12509^{r-v}
A.Ch., fol. 15311^{r-v}
A.Ch., fol. 17785
A.Ch., fol. 23050
A.Ch., fol. 28750^{r}

3. Maḥkama *collection*

(i) *Ḥujjat waqf* of al-Ṣāliḥ Ṭalā'i' ibn Ruzzīk (20 Rabī' II 554/11 May 1159), Box 1, no. 1.
(ii) *Ḥujjat waqf* of Jamāl al-Dīn Muḥammad's daughter (1 Dhū al-Qa'da 637/25 May 1240), Box 1, no. 4.
(iii) *Ḥujjat tamlīk* and *waqf* of Sadīd al-Dīn Abī Muḥammad 'Abd Allāh (19 Sha'bān 649/7 November 1251), Box 1, no. 5; see H. Rabie, 'Ḥujjat tamlīk wa waqf'.
(iv) *Ḥujjat waqf* of Fakhr al-Dīn Ya'qūb ibn Abī Bakr ibn Ayyūb (12 Shawwāl 651/5 December 1253), Box 1, no. 6.
(v) *Ḥujjat waqf* of Majd al-Dīn 'Alī ibn Bahā' al-Dīn (12 Rajab 659/11 June 1261), Box 1, no. 7.
(vi) *Ḥujjat waqf* of Abī al-Ma'ālī Yāqūt ibn al-qadi Sa'd, known as Ibn al-Būrī (15 Jumādā II 661/26 April 1263), Box 2, no. 8.
(vii) *Ḥujjat bay'* al-Sayfī Barqūq ibn 'Abd Allāh (6 Ṣafar 667/15 October 1268), Box 2, no. 10.
(viii) *Ḥujjat tamlīk* and *waqf* of the qadi Ḥamza ibn Abī Bakr (27 Ramaḍān 671/16 April 1273), Box 2, no. 13.
(ix) *Ḥujjat waqf* of the amir al-Ḥājj Bahā' al-Dīn Sunbul (17 Rajab 687/17 August 1288), Box 3, no. 16.
(x) *Ḥujjat waqf* of Sultan Ḥusām al-Dīn Lājīn (21 Rabī' II 697/5 February 1298), Box 3, no. 17.
(xi) Title-deed of the amir Shams al-Dīn Sunqur Jāh ibn 'Abd Allāh al-Manṣūrī (13 Shawwāl 699/3 July 1300), Box 4, no. 19.
(xii) *Ḥujjat waqf* of Sayf al-Dīn Baktamur al-Nāṣirī (14 Muḥarram 707/16 July 1307), Box 4, no. 20.
(xiii) *Ḥujjat waqf* of Badr ibn 'Abd Allāh al-Ḥusaynī (14 Rajab 707/9 January 1308), Box 4, no. 21.
(xiv) *Ḥujjat waqf* of Sultan Baybars al-Jāshnikīr (26 Shawwāl 707/20 April 1308), Box 4, no. 22.

4. *Literary sources*

al-'Abdarī, Muḥammad b. Muḥammad (inception of journey 688/1289), *al-Riḥla al-Maghribiyya*, MS. B.N. (Paris), no. 2283 Arabe, edited by M. al-Fāsī, Rabat, 1968.

Abū Dulaf, Mis'ar b. Muhalhil (4th/10th c.), *al-Risāla al-thāniya*, edited and translated into English by V. Minorsky, Cairo, 1955.

Abū al-Fidā, Ismā'īl b. 'Alī (d. 732/1331),
(i) *al-Mukhtaṣar fī akhbār al-bashar*, 4 vols., Istanbul, 1286/1870.
(ii) *Taqwīm al-buldān*, ed. M. Reinaud and M. de Slane, Paris, 1840.

Abū Makhrama, 'Abd Allāh al-Ṭayyib b. 'Abd Allāh (947/1540–1), *Tārīkh thaghr 'Adan*, ed. O. Löfgren, 2 vols., Leiden, 1936.

Abū Ṣāliḥ al-Armanī (still alive at the outset of the 13th c. A.D.), *Akhbār min nawāḥī Miṣr wa iqṭā'ihā*, attributed to Abū Ṣāliḥ, edited and translated by B. T. A. Evetts, *The churches and monasteries of Egypt and some neighbouring countries*, Oxford, 1895.

Abū Shāma, 'Abd al-Raḥmān b. Ismā'īl (d. 665/1268),
(i) *Kitāb al-rawḍatayn fī akhbār al-dawlatayn*, 2 vols., Cairo, 1287/1870; ed. M. H. M. Aḥmad, vol. i. i–ii, Cairo, 1956, 1962.
(ii) *Mukhtaṣar al-rawḍatayn*, MS. Köprülü (Istanbul), no. 1153.
(iii) *'Uyūn al-rawḍatayn*, MS. B.M., no. Or. 1537.
(iv) *al-Dhayl 'alā al-rawḍatayn*, ed. I. al-'Aṭṭār, Cairo, 1947.

Abū 'Ubayd, Qāsim b. Sallām (d. 224/838), *Kitāb al-amwāl*, Cairo, 1353/1935.

Abū Yūsuf, Ya'qūb b. Ibrāhīm (d. 182/798), *Kitāb al-kharāj*, Cairo, 1352/1933–4.

al-Andalusī, Muḥammad b. Abī al-'Āṣ, *Risāla fī taḥqīq al-wabā'*, MS. B.N. (Paris), no. 3027 Arabe.

Anonymous, *Awrāq jumi'at fīhā faḍā'il Miṣr*, MS. Cambridge U.L., no. Qq. 91.

Anonymous (Moroccan writer, 6th/12th c.), *Kitāb al-istibṣār fī 'ajā'ib al-amṣār*, ed. S. Zaghlūl 'Abd al-Ḥamīd, Alexandria, 1958.

Anonymous, *Tārīkh al-dawla al-Turkiyya* (A.H. 650–805), MS. Cambridge U.L., Qq. 147.

Arnold of Lübeck, Abbot of the Monastery of St. John, Lübeck (d. 1211–14), *Arnoldi Chronica Slavorum*, ed. G. H. Pertz, Hanover, 1868, Lib. VII, 8, pp. 264–77.

al-'Askarī, Abū Hilāl al-Ḥasan b. 'Abd Allāh (latest known biographical date 395/1005), *Kitāb al-awā'il*, MS. B.N. (Paris), no. 5986 Arabe.

al-Asnawī, 'Abd al-Raḥīm b. al-Ḥasan (d. 772/1370), *al-Kalimāt al-muhimma fī mubāsharāt ahl al-dhimma*, MS. B.M., no. Or. 11581, fols. 6–14; cf. Perlmann, 'Asnawī's tract'.

al-'Aynī, Maḥmūd b. Aḥmad (d. 855/1451),
(i) *'Iqd al-jumān fī tārīkh ahl al-zamān*, (A) vols. xii, xvii, MSS. Ahmed III (Istanbul), no. 2911, (B) vols. xiii, xv, MSS. Veliyuddin (Istanbul), nos. 2390, 2392, (C) vols. xviii–xxii, MSS. Dār al-Kutub (Cairo), no. 1584 *tārīkh*.
(ii) *Tārīkh al-Badr fī awṣāf ahl al-'aṣr*, MS. B.M., no. Add. 22360.

al-Baghdādī, ʿAbd al-Laṭīf b. Yūsuf (d. 629/1231–2), *Kitāb al-ifāda wa al-iʿtibār*, reproduced in the form of a photographic facsimile by K. H. Zand and others as '*The Eastern key, Kitāb al-ifādah wa'l-iʿtibār*', Cairo, London, 1964, see above, p. 22 n. 3; French translation by Silvestre de Sacy, *Relation de l'Égypte, par Abd-Allatif, médecin arabe de Bagdad*, Paris, 1810.

al-Balawī, ʿAbd Allāh b. Muḥammad (4th/10th c.), *Sīrat Aḥmad ibn Ṭūlūn*, Damascus, 1939.

al-Balawī, Khalīl b. ʿĪsā (inception of journey 737/1336, completion of journey 741/1340), *Tāj al-mafriq fī taḥliyat ʿulamā' al-mashriq*, MS. B.N. (Paris), no. 2286 Arabe.

Baybars al-Manṣūrī, the amir Rukn al-Dīn (d. 725/1325),
(i) *al-Tuḥfa al-mulūkiyya fī al-dawla al-Turkiyya*, MS. Österreichische Nationalbibliothek (Vienna), no. Mixt 665.
(ii) *Zubdat al-fikra fī tārīkh al-hijra*, MS. B.M., no. Add. 23325, II.

Benjamin of Tudela (completion of journey A.D. 1173), *The itinerary of Benjamin of Tudela*, translated into English by M. N. Adler, London, 1907, translated into Arabic by E. H. Haddad, Baghdad, 1945.

al-Bundārī, Fatḥ b. ʿAlī, *Zubdat al-nuṣra* and *Sanā al-barq* see Iṣfahānī.

al-Dawādārī, Abū Bakr b. ʿAbd Allāh b. Aybak (contemporary of Sultan al-Nāṣir b. Qalāwūn; last known biographical date: 736/1335–6),
(i) *Durar al-tījān wa ghurar tawārīkh al-zamān*, MS. Damad Ibrahim Paşa (Istanbul), no. 913.
(ii) *Kanz al-durar wa jāmiʿ al-ghurar*,
vol. vi, *al-Durra al-muḍiyya fī akhbār al-dawla al-Fāṭimiyya*, ed. Ṣ. al-Munajjid, Cairo, 1961,
vol. vii, *al-Durr al-maṭlūb fī akhbār banī Ayyūb*, MS. Sarayı (Istanbul), no. 2932 VII,
vol. viii, *al-Durra al-zakiyya fī akhbār dawlat al-mulūk al-Turkiyya*, MS. Sarayı, no. 2932 VIII,
vol. ix, *al-Durr al-fākhir fī sīrat al-Malik al-Nāṣir*, ed. H. R. Roemer, Cairo, 1960.

al-Dhahabī, Muḥammad b. Aḥmad (d. 748/1348),
(i) *al-ʿIbar fī khabar man ghabar*, ed. Ṣ. al-Munajjid and F. al-Sayyid, 5 vols., Kuwait, 1960–6.
(ii) *Tārīkh al-Islām wa ṭabaqāt al-mashāhīr wa al-aʿlām*, MSS. B.M., nos. Or. 49–52, 1540, 5578, MSS. B.N. (Paris), nos. 1581–2 Arabe, MSS. Bodleian (Oxford), nos. Laud Or. 279, 305.

al-Dimashqī, Jaʿfar b. ʿAlī (11th or 12th c. A.D.), *Kitāb al-ishāra ilā maḥāsin al-tijāra*, Cairo, 1318/1900–1.

al-Fāsī, Muḥammad b. Aḥmad (d. 832/1429), *Shifā' al-gharām bi-akhbār al-balad al-ḥarām*, ed. F. Wüstenfeld, Leipzig, 1859.

al-Ḥakīm, 'Alī b. Yūsuf (8th/14th c.), *al-Dawḥa al-mushtabika fī ḍawābiṭ al-sikka*, ed. Ḥ. Mu'nis, Madrid, 1960.

al-Ḥamawī, Muḥammad b. 'Alī (d. after 631/1234), *al-Tārīkh al-Manṣūrī*; edited and annotated by P. A. Gryaznevich; photographic facsimile, Moscow, 1960.

al-Hamdānī, al-Ḥasan b. Aḥmad (d. 334/945), *Kitāb al-jawharatayn al-'atīqatayn al-mā'i'atayn min al-ṣafrā' wa al-bayḍā'*, photocopy of the Upsala MS., Dār al-Kutub (Cairo), no. 907 *ṭabī'a*, edited by C. Toll, Upsala, 1968; cf. Dunlop and Ḥamad al-Jāsir.

al-Ḥanbalī, Aḥmad b. Ibrāhīm, *Shifā' al-qulūb fī manāqib banī Ayyūb*, MS., B.M., no. Add. 7311 (attributed to al-Ḥanbalī by M. Kurd 'Alī, 'al-Shāmiyyūn wa al-tārīkh', *MMIA*, xvii (1942), p. 101).

al-Harawī, 'Alī b. Abī Bakr (d. 611/1215), *Kitāb al-ishārāt ilā ma'rifat al-ziyārāt*, ed. J. Sourdel-Thomine, Damascus, 1953.

al-Ḥijāzī, Aḥmad b. Muḥammad (9th/15th c.), *Kitāb al-nayl al-rā'id fī al-Nīl al-zā'id*, MS. B.M., no. Add. 23333.

al-Ḥijāzī, Shams al-Dīn, *Juz' fī al-ṭā'ūn*, MS. Dār al-Kutub (Cairo), no. 102 *majāmī'*, fols. 147–55.

Hilāl al-Ra'y, Hilāl b. Yaḥyā (d. 245/859), *Aḥkām al-waqf*, Hyderabad, 1936.

Ibn 'Abd al-Ḥakam, 'Abd al-Raḥmān b. 'Abd Allāh (d. 257/871), *Kitāb futūḥ Miṣr*, ed. C. C. Torrey, Leiden, 1920.

Ibn 'Abd al-Ẓāhir, Muḥyī al-Dīn Abū al-Faḍl 'Abd Allāh (d. 692/1292),
(i) *al-Alṭāf al-khafiyya min al-sīra al-sharīfa al-Sulṭāniyya al-Malakiyya al-Ashrafiyya*, ed. A. Moberg, Leipzig, 1902.
(ii) *al-Rawḍ al-zāhir fī sīrat al-Malik al-Ẓāhir* (complete text, ed. by Abdul Azīz al-Khowayter, 'A critical edition of an unknown source for the life of al-Malik al-Ẓāhir Baibars', London, Ph.D. thesis, 1960).
(iii) *Tashrīf al-ayyām wa al-'uṣūr fī sīrat al-Malik al-Manṣūr*, ed. M. Kāmil, Cairo, 1961.

Ibn Abī al-Damm al-Ḥamawī, Ibrāhīm b. 'Abd Allāh (d. 642/1244), *al-Tārīkh al-Muẓaffarī*, MS. Bodleian (Oxford), no. Marsh 60.

Ibn Abī al-Faḍā'il, al-Mufaḍḍal (wrote about 759/1358), *Kitāb al-nahj al-sadīd wa al-durr al-farīd fīmā ba'd tārīkh ibn al-'Amīd*, ed. E. Blochet, *PO* xii, xiv, xx (1919–28).

Ibn Abī Ḥajala, Aḥmad b. Yaḥyā (d. 776/1375), *al-Ṭib al-masnūn fī daf' al-ṭā'ūn*, MS. Dār al-Kutub (Cairo), no. 102 *majāmī'*, fols. 141–6.

Ibn Abī al-Hayjā' (contemporary of Saladin), *Tārīkh ibn Abī al-Hayjā'*, MS. al-Aḥmadiyya (Tunis), no. 4915, available as Microfilm no. 16, Ma'had al-Makhṭūṭāt al-'Arabiyya (Cairo).

Ibn Abī Sharīf al-Kāmilī, Muḥammad b. Muḥammad (d. 906/1500),
 (i) *Kitāb fī aḥkām al-ṭā'ūn*, MS. Dār al-Kutub (Cairo), no. 102 *majāmī'*, fols. 156–63.
 (ii) *Fatāwā fī al-ṭā'ūn*, MS. Cambridge U.L., no. Add. 3257, fols. 173v–185r.

Ibn al-'Adīm, 'Umar b. Aḥmad (d. 660/1262),
 (i) *Bughyat al-ṭalab fī tārīkh Ḥalab*, MS. B.N. (Paris), no. 2138 Arabe.
 (ii) *Zubdat al-ḥalab min tārīkh Ḥalab*, ed. S. al-Dahhān, 2 vols., Damascus, 1951, 1954; and MS. B.N. (Paris), no. 1666 Arabe.

Ibn al-Akfānī, Muḥammad b. Ibrāhīm (d. 749/1348), *Nukhab al-dhakhā'ir fī aḥwāl al-jawāhir*, ed. A. M. al-Karmalī, Cairo, 1939.

Ibn al-'Amīd, al-Makīn Jirjis (d. about 672/1274), *Akhbār al-Ayyūbiyyīn*, ed. C. Cahen, 'La chronique des Ayyoubides', *BEO*, xv (1955–7), pp. 109–84.

Ibn al-Athīr, 'Alī b. Muḥammad (d. 630/1233),
 (i) *al-Kāmil fī al-tārīkh*, ed. C. J. Tornberg, 14 vols. Leiden, 1851–76.
 (ii) *Tārīkh al-dawla al-Atābakiyya*, ed. M. de Slane and B. de Meynard, *RHC* (*Hist. Or.*), ii. ii, Paris, 1876; newly edited by A. A. Tolaymat, *al-Tārīkh al-bāhir fī al-dawla al-Atābakiyya*, Cairo, n.d. (preface dated 1963).

Ibn Bahādir, Muḥammad b. Muḥammad (d. 877/1472), *Kitāb futūḥ al-naṣr fī tārīkh mulūk Miṣr*, MS. Ayasofya (Istanbul), no. 3344.

Ibn Ba'ra, Manṣūr al-Dhahabī al-Kāmilī (contemporary to Sultan al-Kāmil), *Kitāb Kashf al-asrār al-'ilmiyya bi-dār al-ḍarb al-Miṣriyya*, MS. Dār al-Kutub, no. 21 *ṭabī'a*, ed. A. Fahmī, Cairo, 1966.

Ibn Bassām, Muḥammad b. Aḥmad (late 6th and early 7th c. A.H.), *Kitāb anīs al-jalīs fī akhbār Tinnīs*, ed. by J. al-Shayyāl in *MMII*, xiv (1967), pp. 151–89.

Ibn Baṭṭūṭa, Muḥammad b. 'Abd Allāh (d. 779/1377), *Tuḥfat al-nuẓẓār fī gharā'ib al-amṣār wa'ajā'ib al-asfār*, 4 vols., Paris, 1853–8.

Ibn Dāwūd, Nūr al-Dīn al-Miṣrī, *Kitāb al-lu'lu' al-manḍūd fīmā bi-Miṣr min ma'dūm wa mawjūd*, MS. Süleymaniye (Istanbul), no. 838.

Ibn Duqmāq, Ibrāhīm b. Muḥammad (d. 809/1406),
 (i) *al-Intiṣār li-wāsiṭat 'iqd al-amṣār*, ed. Vollers, vols. iv. v, Cairo, 1893.

(ii) *al-Jawhar al-thamīn fī sīrat al-mulūk wa al-salāṭīn*, MS. Bodleian (Oxford), no. Digby Or. 28.

Ibn al-Furāt, Muḥammad b. ʻAbd al-Raḥīm (d. 807/1405), *Tārīkh al-duwal wa al-mulūk*, vols. i–iii, MSS. Österreichische Nationalbibliothek (Vienna), nos. AF 117–19; vol. iv. i, ed. H. M. al-Shammāʻ, Basra, 1967; vols. v–vi, MSS. AF. 121–2; vol. vii, ed. Q. Zurayq, Beirut, 1942; vol. viii, ed. Q. Zurayq and N. ʻIzz al-Dīn, Beirut, 1939; vols. ix. i, ed. Q. Zurayq, Beirut, 1936; ii, ed. Q. Zurayq and N. ʻIzz al-Dīn, Beirut, 1938.

Ibn al-Fuwaṭī, ʻAbd al-Razzāq b. Aḥmad (d. 723/1323), *al-Ḥawādith al-jāmiʻa*, ed. M. Jawād, Baghdad, 1932.

Ibn Ḥabīb, al-Ḥasan b. ʻUmar (d. 779/1377),
(i) *Durrat al-aslāk fī dawlat al-Atrāk*, MS. Bodleian (Oxford), nos. Marsh 223, 319, 591.
(ii) *Tadhkirat al-nabīh fī ayyām al-Manṣūr wa banīh*, MS. B.M., no. Add. Rich. 7335.

Ibn Ḥajar al-ʻAsqalānī, Aḥmad b. ʻAlī (d. 852/1448),
(i) *Badhl al-māʻūn fī fawā'id al-ṭāʻūn*, MS. S.O.A.S., no. 13998.
(ii) *al-Durar al-kāmina*, 4 vols., Hyderabad, 1929–32.
(iii) *Rafʻ al-iṣr ʻan quḍāt Miṣr*, 2 parts, Cairo, 1957, 1961.

Ibn al-Ḥājj, Muḥammad b. Muḥammad (d. 737/1336), *al-Madkhal*, 4 vols., Cairo, 1929.

Ibn Ḥammād, Muḥammad b. ʻAlī (d. 628/1230), *Akhbār mulūk banī ʻUbayd*, ed. M. Vonderheyden, Alger–Paris, 1927.

Ibn Ḥawqal, Abū al-Qāsim al-Naṣībī (d. after 367/977),
(i) *Kitāb ṣūrat al-arḍ*, 2nd ed., Part I, ed. J. H. Kramers, Leiden, 1938–9.
(ii) *Ṣifat al-aqālīm al-Islāmiyya*, MS. Ahmed III (Istanbul), no. 3012.

Ibn al-ʻIbrī (Bar-Hebraeus), Gregory Abū al-Faraj (d. 685/1286), *Tārīkh mukhtaṣar al-duwal*, Beirut, 1890.

Ibn al-ʻImād, ʻAbd al-Ḥayy b. Aḥmad (d. 1089/1679), *Shadharāt al-dhahab fī akhbār man dhahab*, 8 vols., Cairo, 1350–1/1931–3.

Ibn Iyās, Muḥammad b. Aḥmad (d. 930/1524),
(i) *Badā'iʻ al-zuhūr*, 3 vols., Cairo 1893–6.
(ii) *Jawāhir al-sulūk fī akhbār al-khulafā' wa al-mulūk*, MS. Cambridge U.L., no. Qq. 74.
(iii) *Nashq al-azhār fī ʻajā'ib al-aqṭār*, MS. B.M., no. Add. 7503.

Ibn al-Jīʻān, Yaḥyā ibn Shākir (d. 885/1480), *al-Tuḥfa al-saniyya bi-asmā' al-bilād al-Miṣriyya*, ed. B. Moritz, Cairo, 1898.

Ibn Jubayr, Muḥammad b. Aḥmad (d. 614/1217), *Tadhkira bi al-akhbār ʿan ittifāqāt al-asfār*, ed. W. Wright, E. J. W. Gibb Memorial Series, vol. v, Leiden, 1907.

Ibn Kathīr, Ismāʿīl b. ʿUmar (d. 774/1373), *al-Bidāya wa al-nihāya*, 14 vols., Cairo, 1932–9.

Ibn Khaldūn, ʿAbd al-Raḥmān b. Muḥammad (d. 808/1406), *Kitāb al-ʿibar*, 7 vols., vol. i, *al-Muqaddima*, Cairo, 1284/1867.

Ibn Khallikān, Aḥmad b. Muḥammad (d. 681/1282), *Kitāb wafayāt al-aʿyān*, 2 vols, Cairo, 1299/1882.

Ibn Khurradādhbih, ʿUbayd Allāh b. ʿAbd Allāh (d. about 300/912), *Kitāb al-masālik wa al-mamālik*, ed. M. G. De Goeje, Leiden, 1889.

Ibn Mammātī, al-Asʿad b. al-Khaṭīr (d. 606/1209), *Kitāb qawānīn al-dawāwīn*, ed. M. A. al-Najjār, Cairo, 1299/1882, ed. A. S. Atiya, Cairo, 1943.

Ibn Manẓūr, Muḥammad b. Mukarram (d. 711/1311), *Lisān al-ʿArab*, 20 vols., Cairo, 1300–8/1882–91.

Ibn al-Mujāwir, Yūsuf b. Yaʿqūb (d. 690/1291), *Ṣifat bilād al-Yaman wa Mecca wa baʿḍ al-Ḥijāz* (*Tārīkh al-mustabṣir*), ed. O. Löfgren, 2 parts, Leiden, 1951, 1954.

Ibn Muyassar, Muḥammad b. ʿAlī (d. 677/1278), *Akhbār Miṣr*, vol. 2, ed. M. H. Massé, Cairo, 1919.

Ibn Nujaym, Zayn al-ʿĀbidīn b. Ibrāhīm (d. 970/1562), *Rasāʾil fiqhiyya Ḥanafiyya*, MS. Cambridge U.L., no. Add. 3690(6), including *Risālat al-tuḥfa al-marḍiyya fī al-arāḍī al-Miṣriyya*, fols. 48–61, *Risāla fī al-iqṭāʿāt*, fols. 131–5.

Ibn Qāḍī Shuhba, Abū Bakr Aḥmad b. Muḥammad (d. 851/1448), *Ṭabaqāt al-Shāfiʿiyya*, MS. B.M., no. Or. 3039.

Ibn Qāḍī Shuhba, Muḥammad b. Abī Bakr Aḥmad (d. 874/1469), *al-Durr al-thamīn fī sīrat Nūr al-Dīn*, MS. Ayasofya (Istanbul), no. 3194.

Ibn al-Rāhib, Buṭrus b. Abī al-Karam (7th/13th c.), *Tārīkh ibn al-Rāhib*, ed. L. Cheikho, Beirut, 1903.

Ibn al-Sāʿī, ʿAlī b. Anjab (d. 674/1275), *al-Jāmiʿ al-mukhtaṣar*, Baghdad, 1934.

Ibn Saʿīd, ʿAlī b. Mūsā (d. 673/1274 or 685/1286),
(i) *Kitāb basṭ al-arḍ fī al-ṭūl wa al-ʿarḍ*, ed. J. V. Gines, Tetuan, 1958.
(ii) *Kitāb al-mughrib fī ḥulā al-Maghrib*, vol. i, ed. Z. M. Ḥasan and others, Cairo, 1953, vols. ii, iii, MS. Dār al-Kutub (Cairo), no. 2712 *tārīkh*, vol. iv, ed. Knut L. Tallqvist, Leiden, 1898–9.

Ibn al-Ṣayrafī, ʿAlī b. Munjib (d. 542/1147 or after 550/1155),
(i) *al-Ishāra ilā man nāl al-wizāra*, ed. ʿAbd Allāh Mukhliṣ, Cairo, 1924.
(ii) *Qānūn dīwān al-rasāʾil*, ed. A. Bahjat, Cairo, 1905.

Ibn Shaddād, Bahāʾ al-Dīn Yūsuf b. Rāfiʿ (d. 632/1234), *al-Nawādir al-sulṭāniyya, Sīrat Ṣalāḥ al-Dīn*, ed. J. al-Shayyāl, Cairo, 1962.

Ibn Shaddād, Muḥammad b. Ibrāhīm (d. 684/1285), *al-Rawḍa al-zāhira fī al-sīra al-Ẓāhira*, MS. Selimiye (Edirne), no. 2306; there is a Turkish translation in existence by M. Şerefüddin Yaltkaya, entitled *Baypars tarihi*, Istanbul, 1941.

Ibn Shīth al-Qurashī, ʿAbd al-Raḥīm b. ʿAlī (d. 625/1228), *Maʿālim al-kitāba*, ed. Q. al-Bāshā, Beirut, 1913.

Ibn Taghrī Birdī, Abū al-Maḥāsin Yūsuf (d. 874/1470),
(i) *al-Manhal al-ṣāfī*, vol. i, ed. A. Y. Najātī, Cairo 1956; MS. B.N. (Paris), 2068–72 Arabe; cf. G. Wiet, *Les biographies du Manhal safi*, *MIE*, xix, Cairo, 1932.
(ii) *Mawrid al-laṭāfa*, ed. J. D. Carlyle, Cantabrigiae, 1792.
(iii) *al-Nujūm al-zāhira fī mulūk Miṣr wa al-Qāhira*, 12 vols., Cairo, 1929–56.

Ibn Taymiya, Aḥmad b. ʿAbd al-Ḥalīm (d. 728/1328),
(i) *al-Ḥisba fī al-Islām*, Cairo 1318/1900–01.
(ii) *al-Siyāsa al-sharʿiyya*, Cairo, 1951; cf. H. Laoust, *Le traité de droit public d'Ibn Taimīya*, Beirut, 1948.

Ibn al-Ukhuwwa, Muḥammad b. Muḥammad (d. 729/1329), *Maʿālim al-qurba fī aḥkām al-ḥisba*, ed. R. Levy (E. J. W. Gibb Memorial Series, New Series, xii), London, 1938.

Ibn ʿUnayn, Muḥammad b. Naṣr Allāh (d. 630/1233), *Dīwān*, ed. Khalīl Mardam, Damascus, 1946.

Ibn al-Wardī, ʿUmar b. al-Muẓaffar (d. 749/1348),
(i) *Kharīdat al-ʿajāʾib wa farīdat al-gharāʾib*, Cairo, 1939.
(ii) *Tatimat al-mukhtaṣar fī akhbār al-bashar* (*Tārīkh ibn al-Wardī*), 2 vols., Cairo, 1285/1868.

Ibn Waṣīf Shāh, al-Masʿūdī Ibrāhīm (7th/13th c.), *Kitāb jawāhir al-buḥūr wa waqāʾiʿ al-ʾumūr wa ʿajāʾib al-duhūr wa akhbār al-diyār al-Miṣriyya*, MS. B.M., no. 25731.

Ibn Wāṣil, Muḥammad b. Sālim (d. 697/1298),
(i) *Mufarrij al-kurūb fī akhbār banī Ayyūb*, vols. i–iii, ed. J. al-Shayyāl, Cairo, 1953–60, MS. B.N. (Paris), nos. 1702, 1703 Arabe; the *dhayl* under al-Muẓaffarī.
(ii) *al-Tārīkh al-Ṣāliḥī*, MS. Fatih (Istanbul), no. 4224.

Ibn Ẓāfir al-Azdī, Abū al-Ḥasan ʿAlī (d. 613/1216), *Akhbār al-duwal al-munqaṭiʿa*, MS. B.M., no. Or. 3685.

Ibn Ẓuhayra, Muḥammad b. Muḥammad (d. 888/1483), *al-Faḍāʾil al-bāhira bi-maḥāsin Miṣr wa al-Qāhira*, MS. B.M., no. Or. 1285.

al-Idfuwī, Jaʿfar b. Thaʿlab (d. 748/1347), *al-Ṭāliʿ al-saʿīd bi-asmāʾ al-fuḍalāʾ wa al-ruwāh bi-aʿlā al-Ṣaʿīd*, Cairo, 1914.

al-Idrīsī, Muḥammad b. Muḥammad (d. 560/1165), *Ṣifat al-Maghrib wa arḍ al-Sūdān wa Miṣr wa al-Andalus*, derived from the *Kitāb nuzhat al-mushtāq*, Leiden, 1864–6.

al-ʿIṣāmī, ʿAbd al-Malik b. Ḥusayn (d. 1111/1699), *Simṭ al-nujūm al-ʿawālī*, 4 vols., Cairo 1380/1960–1.

al-Iṣfahānī, ʿImād al-Dīn Muḥammad b. Muḥammad (d. 597/1201),
(i) *al-Barq al-Shāmī*, MS. Bodleian (Oxford), vol. iii, no. Bruce II and vol. v, no. Marsh 425.
(ii) *Sanā al-barq al-Shāmī* (*al-Barq* as abridged by Fatḥ b. ʿAlī al-Bundārī), MS. Esʿad Efendi (Istanbul), no. 2249/2 fols. 163^{v}–242^{r}.
(iii) *Dīwān rasāʾil al-Kātib al-Iṣfahānī*, MS. Nuruosmaniye (Istanbul), no. 3745.
(iv) *Nuṣrat al-fatra*, as abridged by al-Bundārī, *Zubdat al-nuṣra* (*Tārīkh dawlat āl Saljūq*), Cairo, 1900.
(v) *Kitāb al-fatḥ al-qussī fī al-fatḥ al-qudsī*, Leiden, 1888.

al-Jawālīqī, Mawhūb b. Aḥmad (d. 539/1144), *al-Muʿarrab min al-kalām al-aʿjamī*, Leipzig, 1867.

al-Jawharī, ʿAlī b. Dāwūd (d. 887/1482), *Kitāb al-durr al-thamīn al-manẓūm fīmā warada fī Miṣr wa aʿmālihā bi al-khuṣūṣ wa al-ʿumūm*, MS. B.N. (Paris), no. 1813 Arabe.

al-Jazarī, Muḥammad b. Ibrāhīm (d. 739/1339), *Tārīkh al-Jazarī*, MS. Köprülü (Istanbul), no. 1147.

al-Khafājī, Aḥmad b. Muḥammad (d. 1069/1659), *Shifāʾ al-ghalīl fīmā fī kalām al-ʿArab min al-dakhīl*, Cairo 1282/1865.

al-Khālidī, Muḥammad b. Luṭf Allāh (9th/15th c.), *Kitāb al-maqṣid al-rafīʿ al-manshā al-hādī ilā ṣināʿat al-inshā*, MS. B.N. (Paris), no. 4439 Arabe.

al-Khaṣṣāf, Aḥmad b. ʿAmr al-Shaybānī (d. 261/874–5),
(i) *Kitāb aḥkām al-waqf*, Cairo, 1904.
(ii) *Kitāb al-ḥiyal wa al-makhārij*, ed. J. Schacht, Hanover, 1923.

al-Khazrajī, Muḥammad b. Ibrāhīm (7th/13th c.), *Tārīkh dawlat al-Akrād wa al-Atrāk*, MS. Hekimoglu Ali Paşa (Istanbul), no. 695.

al-Khwārizmī, Muḥammad b. Aḥmad (second half of the 4th c. A.H.), *Mafātīḥ al-ʿulūm*, ed. von Vloten, Leiden, 1895.

al-Kindī, Muḥammad b. Yūsuf (d. 350/961), *Kitāb al-wulā wa kitāb al-quḍā*, ed. R. Guest (E. J. W. Gibb Memorial Series, vol. xix), Beirut–London, 1908–1912.

al-Kindī, ʿUmar b. Muḥammad b. Yūsuf, *Faḍāʾil Miṣr*, MS. Kiliç Ali Paşa (Istanbul), no. 756.

al-Kutubī, Muḥammad b. Shākir (d. 764/1363),
(i) *Fawāt al-wafayāt*, Cairo, 1283/1866.
(ii) *ʿUyūn al-tawārīkh*, MS. Fatih (Istanbul), no. 4439, MS. Köprülü (Istanbul), no. 1121, MS. Cambridge U.L., no. Add. 2923.

al-Maḥallī, Muḥammad b. Aḥmad (d. 864/1459),
(i) *Mabdaʾ al-Nīl wa muntahā*, MS. B.M., no. Or. 1535.
(ii) *al-Qawl al-mufīd fī al-Nīl al-saʿīd*, MS. B.N. (Paris), no. 2259 Arabe.
(iii) *Muqaddima fī Nīl Miṣr al-mubārak*, MS. Ayasofya (Istanbul), no. 3446.

al-Makhzūmī, ʿAlī b. ʿUthmān (6th/12th c.), *Kitāb al-minhāj fī ʿilm kharāj Miṣr*, MS. B.M., no. Add. 23483.

al-Manṣūrī, see Baybars al-Manṣūrī.

al-Maqrīzī, Aḥmad b. ʿAlī (d. 845/1442),
(i) *al-Bayān wa al-iʿrāb ʿammā bi arḍ Miṣr min al-aʿrāb*, ed. A. ʿĀbidīn, Cairo, 1961.
(ii) *al-Dhahab al-masbūk*, ed. J. al-Shayyāl, Cairo, 1955.
(iii) *Ittiʿāẓ al-ḥunafā*, MS. Ahmed III (Istanbul), no. 3013, incomplete edition by J. al-Shayyāl, Cairo, 1940.
(iv) *Kitāb al-awzān wa al-akyāl al-sharʿiyya*, ed. O. G. Tychsen, Rostock, 1800.
(v) *Kitāb ighāthat al-umma bi-kashf al-ghumma*, ed. M. M. Ziada and J. al-Shayyāl, Cairo, 1940; French translation by G. Wiet, 'Le traité des famines de Maqrīzī', *JESHO*, v (1962), pp. 1–90.
(vi) *Kitāb al-mawāʿiẓ wa al-iʿtibār* (*Khiṭaṭ*), 2 vols., Cairo, 1270/1853–4.
(vii) *Kitāb al-sulūk*, ed. M. M. Ziada, 2 vols., in 6 parts, Cairo, 1934–58; French translation E. Blochet, 'Histoire d'Égypte de Makrizi', in *ROL*, 'A', vol. vi (1898), pp. 435–89, 'B', vol. viii (1900–1), pp. 165–212, 501–53, 'C', vol. ix (1902), pp. 6–163, 466–530, 'D', vol. x (1903–4), pp. 248–371, 'E', vol. xi (1905–8), pp. 192–239; and Quatremère, *Histoire des Sultans Mamlouks, de l'Égypte*, 2 vols., Paris, 1837–45.
(viii) *Kitāb thaghr Dimyāṭ*, MS. Bodleian (Oxford), no. Pocock 361, fols. 20–61.

(ix) *Shudhūr al-ʿuqūd fī dhikr al-nuqūd*, ed. by A. M. al-Karmalī in *al-Nuqūd al-ʿArabiyya*, pp. 21–73, Cairo, 1939, French translation by S. de Sacy, *Traité des monnoies musulmanes, Traduit de l'Arabe de Makrizi*, Paris, 1797.

al-Masʿūdī, ʿAlī b. al-Ḥusayn (d. 345 or 346/956–7), *Murūj al-dhahab*, 4 vols., Cairo, 1938.

al-Māwardī, ʿAlī b. Muḥammad (d. 450/1058) *al-Aḥkām al-sulṭāniyya*, Cairo, 1298/1881.

Michael the Syrian (d. 1199), *Chronique de Michel le Syrien patriarche jacobite d'Antioche*, ed. and trans. by J.-B. Chabot, 4 vols., first published 1899–1910, Paris; reprinted, Bruxelles, 1963.

Miskawayh, Aḥmad b. Muḥammad (d. 421/1030), *Tajārib al-'umam*, ed. H. F. Amedroz, 7 vols., Cairo–Oxford, 1920–1.

al-Mundhirī, ʿAbd al-ʿAẓīm b. ʿAbd al-Qawī (d. 656/1258), *Kitāb al-takmila li-wafayāt al-naqla* (582–642 A.H.), MS. Ayasofya (Istanbul), no. 3163.

al-Muqaddasī, Muḥammad b. Aḥmad (4th/10th c.), *Kitāb aḥsan al-taqāsīm*, ed. M. J. de Goeje, Leiden, 1906.

al-Musabbiḥī, al-Amīr al-Mukhtār ʿIzz al-Mulk Muḥammad b. ʿUbayd Allāh (d. 420/1029), *Akhbār Miṣr*, vol. xl, MS. Escorial Library (Spain), Cod. 534, part 2.

al-Muẓaffarī, ʿAlī b. ʿAbd al-Raḥīm (7th/13th c.), *Dhayl mufarrij al-kurūb* (A.H. 660–95), MS. B.N. (Paris), no. 1703 Arabe, fols. 172r–216r.

al-Nābulsī, ʿUthmān b. Ibrāhīm (d. 660/1261),

(i) *Kitāb lumaʿ al-qawānīn al-muḍiyya*, ed. by C. Becker and C. Cahen in *BEO*, xvi (1958–60); cf. C. Cahen, 'Quelques aspects de l'administration égyptienne médiévale vus par un de ses fonctionnaires', *BFLS*, 26e année (1948), pp. 97–118.

(ii) *Tajrīd sayf al-himma*, MS. B.M., no. Add. 23293; cf. C. Cahen, 'Histoires coptes d'un cadi médiéval, Extraits du *Kitāb tadjrīd saïf al-himma li'stikhrādj mā fī dhimmat al-Dhimma*', BIFAO, lix (1960), pp. 133–50.

(iii) *Tārīkh al-Fayyūm*, ed. B. Moritz, Cairo, 1899.

Nāṣir-i Khusraw, Abū Muʿīn Nāṣir b. Khusraw (d. after A.D. 1087), *Safar nāma*, Arabic translation by Y. al-Khashshāb, Cairo, 1945.

Niẓām al-Mulk, al-Ḥasan b. ʿAlī (d. 485/1092), *The Siyāsat-nāma* or *Siyar al-mulūk*, English translation by H. Darke, London, 1960.

al-Nuʿmān ibn Ḥayyūn, al-Qāḍī al-Nuʿmān b. Muḥammad (d. 363/974), *Daʿā'im al-Islām*, ed. by A. A. A. Fyzee, 2 vols., Cairo, 1951–60.

al-Nuwayrī, Aḥmad b. ʿAbd al-Wahhāb (d. 732/1332), *Nihāyat al-arab fī funūn al-adab*, vols. i, viii, Cairo, 1923, 1931; vols. xxvi–xxx, MS. Dār al-Kutub (Cairo), no. 549 *maʿārif ʿāmma*.

al-Qāḍī al-Fāḍil, ʿAbd al-Raḥīm b. ʿAlī al-Baysānī (d. 596/1200),
(i) *al-Fāṣil min kalām al-Qāḍī al-Fāḍil*, MS. B.M., no. Add. 7307 Rich.
(ii) *Inshaʾāt al-Qāḍī al-Fāḍil*, MS. Cambridge U.L., no. Qq. 232.
(iii) *ʿUyūn al-rasāʾil al-Fāḍiliyya*, MS. B.M., no. Add. 25756.
(iv) *Collection of al-Fāḍil's correspondence*, MS. B.M., no. Add. 7465 Rich.
(v) *Collection of al-Fāḍil's correspondence*, MS. B.M., no. Add. 25757.
(vi) *Fāḍiliyyāt al-Fāḍil*, MS. Leiden, Cod. Or. 994, fols. 135–79.

al-Qalqashandī, Aḥmad b. ʿAlī (d. 821/1418),
(i) *Maʾāthir al-ināfa fī maʿālim al-khilāfa*, ed. A. A. Farrāj, 3 vols., Kuwait, 1964.
(ii) *Ṣubḥ al-aʿshā*, 14 vols., Cairo, 1919–22.
(iii) *Ḍawʾal-ṣubḥ*, Cairo, 1906.

al-Qazwīnī, Zakariyyā b. Muḥammad (d. 682/1283), *Āthār al-bilād wa akhbār al-ʿibād*, ed. F. Wüstenfeld, Göttingen, 1848.

Qudāma b. Jaʿfar, al-Kātib (d. 337/948), *Kitāb al-kharāj*, MS. Köprülü (Istanbul), no. 1076; A. Ben Shemesh, *Taxation in Islām, volume II, Qudāma b. Jaʿfar's Kitāb al-kharāj*, part seven, Leiden–London, 1965.

al-Qurashī, Yaḥyā b. Ādam (d. 203/818), *Kitāb al-kharāj*, ed. A. M. Shākir, Cairo, 1929; A. Ben Shemesh, *Taxation in Islam, volume I, Yaḥyā ben Ādam's Kitāb al-kharāj*, Leiden, 1958.

Rashīd al-Dīn, Faḍl Allāh Rashīd al-Dīn b. ʿImād al-Dawla (d. 718/1318), *Taʾrīḫ-i-Mubārak-i-Ġāzānī* (1265–1295), ed. K. Jahn, 's-Gravenhage, 1957.

al-Ṣafadī, al-Ḥasan b. ʿAbd Allāh (8th/14th c.),
(i) *Kitāb fī dhikr Miṣr*, MS. B.N. (Paris), no. 1931 Arabe, fols. 211–52.
(ii) *Nuzhat al-mālik wa al-mamlūk*, MS. B.M., no. Or. 6267.

al-Ṣafadī, Khalīl b. Aybak (d. 764/1363),
(i) *Aʿyān al-ʿaṣr wa aʿwān al-naṣr*, MS. Ayasofya (Istanbul), nos. 2962 to 2970.
(ii) *Kitāb al-wāfī bi-al-wafayāt*, 4 vols., Istanbul–Damascus, 1931–59.

al-Sakhāwī, Muḥammad b. ʿAbd al-Raḥmān (d. 902/1497), *al-Ḍawʾ al-lāmiʿ*, 12 vols., Cairo 1353–5/1934–6.

Ṣāliḥ b. Yaḥyā (the Buḥturid Druze prince, d. about 840/1436), *Tārīkh Bayrūt*, Beirut, 1902.

al-Shābushtī, ʿAlī b. Muḥammad (d. 390/1000), *Kitāb al-diyārāt*, ed. by G. ʿAwād, Baghdad, 1951.

Shāfiʿ ibn ʿAlī, Naṣīr al-Dīn al-ʿAsqalānī (d. 730/1330),
(i) *al-Faḍl al-maʾthūr min sīrat al-Sultan al-Malik al-Manṣūr*, MS. Bodleian (Oxford), no. Marsh 424.
(ii) *Ḥusn al-manāqib al-sariyya al-muntazaʿa min al-sīra al-Ẓāhiriyya*, MS. B.N. (Paris), no. 1707 Arabe.

al-Shāfiʿī, Aḥmad b. ʿImād, *Risāla fī bayān faḍl Nīl Miṣr*, MS. Cambridge U.L., no. Qq. 85.

al-Shayzarī, ʿAbd al-Raḥmān b. Naṣr (d. about 589/1193),
(i) *Kitāb al-manhaj al-maslūk fī siyāsat al-mulūk*, Cairo, 1326/1908.
(ii) *Kitāb nihāyat al-rutba fī ṭalab al-ḥisba*, ed. E. E. al-ʿArīnī, Cairo, 1946.

al-Shirbīnī, Yūsuf b. Muḥammad (still alive in 1098/1687), *Hazz al-quḥūf fī sharḥ qaṣīd abī shādūf*, ed. M. al-Baqlī, Cairo, 1963.

Sibṭ b. al-Jawzī, Yūsuf b. Qizughlū (d. 654/1257), *Mirʾāt al-zamān*, ed. J. R. Jewett, Chicago, 1907.

al-Subkī, ʿAbd al-Wahhāb b. ʿAlī (d. 771/1370),
(i) *Muʿīd al-niʿam wa mubīd al-niqam*, Leiden, 1908.
(ii) *Ṭabaqāt al-Shāfiʿiyya al-kubrā*, 6 vols., Cairo 1324/1906–7.

al-Suyūṭī, ʿAbd al-Raḥmān b. Abī Bakr (d. 911/1505),
(i) *al-Ḥāwī li al-fatāwī*, 2 vols., Cairo, 1352/1933–4.
(ii) *Ḥusn al-muḥāḍara fī akhbār Miṣr wa al-Qāhira*, 2 vols., Cairo, 1321/1903.
(iii) *Kitāb mā rawāhu al-wāʿūn fī aḥkām al-ṭāʿūn*, MS. Dār al-Kutub (Cairo), no. 102 *majāmīʿ*, fols. 172–95.
(iv) *Risāla fī dhamm al-maks*, MS. Dār al-Kutub (Cairo), no. 1416 *ḥadīth*.
(v) *Risālat al-inṣāf fī tamyīz al-awqāf*, MS. B.N. (Paris), no. 4588 Arabe, fols. 88ʳ–89ᵛ.

al-ʿUmarī, Aḥmad b. Yaḥyā b. Faḍl Allāh (d. 749/1349),
(i) *Masālik al-abṣār fī mamālik al-amṣār*, MS. Ayasofya (Istanbul), nos. 3415–39; MS. B.N. (Paris), nos. 2325, 2328 Arabe.
(ii) *al-Taʿrīf bi-al-muṣṭalaḥ al-sharīf*, Cairo, 1312/1894.

William, Archbishop of Tyre (d. A.D. 1185 or 1186), *A history of deeds done beyond the sea*, English translation by E. A. Babcock and A. C. Krey, 2 vols., New York, 1943.

al-Yāfiʿī, ʿAbd Allāh b. Asʿad (d. 768/1367), *Mirʾāt al-janān wa ʿibrat al-yaqẓān*, 4 vols., Hyderabad, 1919–21.

al-Yāfi'ī, Ḥasan b. Ibrāhīm (contemporary of Sultan Qalāwūn), *Kitāb jāmi' al-tawārīkh* (A.H. 621–79), MS. B.N. (Paris), no. 1543 Arabe.

Ya'qūbī, Aḥmad b. Abī Ya'qūb (d. 284/897), *Kitāb al-buldān*, ed. M. J. de Goeje, Leiden, 1891–2, French translation by G. Wiet, *Les pays*, Cairo, 1937.

Yāqūt al-Rūmī, b. 'Abd Allāh al-Ḥamawī (d. 626/1229),
(i) *Irshād al-arīb ilā ma'rifat al-adīb*, ed. D. S. Margoliouth (E. J. W. Gibb Memorial Series, vi), 7 vols., Leiden–London, 1907–31.
(ii) *Mu'jam al-buldān*, 6 vols., Leipzig, 1866–70.

al-Yūnīnī, Mūsā b. Muḥammad (d. 726/1326), *Dhayl mir'āt al-zamān*, 2 vols., Hyderabad, 1954–5; MS. Sarayı (Istanbul), no. 2907E, vols. iii, iv.

al-Ẓāhirī, Ghars al-dīn Khalīl b. Shāhīn (d. 872/1468), *Zubdat kashf al-mamālik*, Paris, 1894.

Zetterstéen, Karl v., *Beiträge zur Geschichte der Mamlūkensultane in den Jahren 690–741 der Hiǵra nach arabischen Handschriften*, Leiden, 1919.

5. *Modern books and articles in periodicals*

Abbott, Nabia, 'A new papyrus and a review of the administration of 'Ubaid Allāh B. al-Ḥabḥāb', in Makdisi, *Arabic and Islamic studies*, pp. 21–35.

Adler, E. N., *Jewish travellers*, London, 1930.

Ahmad, M. H. M.,
(i) 'Studies on the works of Abū Shāma', Ph.D. thesis, London, 1951.
(ii) 'Some notes on Arabic historiography during the Zengid and Ayyubid periods', in Lewis and Holt, *Historians*, pp. 79–97.

Airy, W., *On the Arabic glass weights*, London, 1920.

Alarcón y Santón, M. A., and García de Linares, R., *Los documentos árabes diplomáticos del Archivo de la Corona de Aragón*, Madrid and Granada, 1940.

Amari, M.,
(i) *I diplomi arabi del R. Archivio Fiorentino*, Florence, 1863.
(ii) *Nuovi ricordi arabici su la storia di Genova*, in *Atti della Società Ligure di Storia Patria*, vol. v, 1873.

al-'Arīnī, E. E., *Miṣr fī 'aṣr al-Ayyūbiyyīn*, Cairo, 1960.

Ashtor (Strauss), E.,
(i) 'Prix et salaires à l'époque mamlouke', *REI* (1949), pp. 49–94.
(ii) 'The social isolation of Ahl adh-dhimma', *Études orientales à la mémoire de Paul P. Hirschler*, Budapest, 1950, pp. 73–94.
(iii) 'The Kārimī merchants', *JRAS*, 1956, pp. 45–56.

(iv) 'Quelques indications sur les revenus dans l'orient musulman au haut moyen âge', *JESHO*, ii (1959), pp. 262–80.
(v) 'Le coût de la vie dans l'Égypte médiévale', *JESHO*, iii (1960), pp. 56–77.
(vi) 'Some unpublished sources for the Baḥrī period', *Studies in Islamic history and civilization* (*Scripta Hierosolymitana*, ix), Jerusalem, 1961, pp. 11–30.
(vii) 'L'évolution des prix dans le Proche-Orient à la basse-époque', *JESHO*, iv (1961), pp. 15–46.
(viii) 'Matériaux pour l'histoire des prix dans l'Égypte médiévale', *JESHO*, vi (1963), pp. 158–89.
(ix) 'La recherche des prix dans l'orient médiéval', *SI*, xxi (1964), pp. 101–44.

'Āshūr, S., *al-Mujtama'al-Miṣrī fī 'aṣr Salāṭīn al-Mamālīk*, Cairo, 1962.

Atiya, A. S.,
(i) *Egypt and Aragon*, Leipzig, 1938.
(ii) *The Arabic manuscripts of Mount Sinai*, Baltimore, 1955.
(iii) *Crusade, commerce and culture*, Bloomington–London, 1962.

Ayalon, D.,
(i) 'The plague and its effects upon the Mamlûk army', *JRAS*, 1946, pp. 67–73.
(ii) 'The Wafidiya in the Mamluk kingdom', *IC*, xxv (1951), pp. 89–104.
(iii) 'Studies on the structure of the Mamluk army,' *BSOAS*, xv (1953), pp. 203–28, 448–76, xvi (1954), pp. 57–90.
(iv) 'The system of payment in Mamluk military society', *JESHO*, i (1958), pp. 37–65, 257–96.

Bacharach, J. L., and Gordus, A. A., 'Studies on the fineness of silver coins', *JESHO*, xi (1968), pp. 298–317.

Bahgat, A.
(i) 'Les forêts en Égypte et leur administration au moyen âge', *BIE*, 4e série, no. 1 (1900), pp. 141–58.
(ii) 'Les manufactures d'étoffe en Égypte au moyen âge', *BIE*, 4e série, no. 4 (1903), pp. 351–61.

Bailey, H. W.,
(i) 'Turks in Khotanese texts', *JRAS* (1939), pp. 85–91.
(ii) 'Indo-Turcica', *BSOAS*, ix (1937–9), pp. 289–302.

Bakhīt, M. A., 'Mamlakat al-Karak fī al-'ahd al-Mamlūkī', M.A. thesis, The American University of Beirut, 1965.

Balog, P.,
(i) 'Aperçus sur la technique de monnayage musulman au moyen âge', *BIE*, xxxi (1948–9), pp. 95–105.

(ii) 'Deux dinars inédits du dernier roi Ayoubite d'Égypte Al-Malek Al-Achraf Abou'l Fath Moussa', *BIE*, xxxi (1948–9), pp. 187–90.
(iii) 'Quelques dinars du début de l'ère Mamelouke Bahrite', *BIE*, xxxii (1949–50), pp. 229–52.
(iv) 'Un quart de dinar du Sultan Naser Mohamed Ben Qalaoun', *BIE*, xxxii (1949–50), pp. 255–6.
(v) 'Études numismatiques de l'Égypte musulmane', *BIE*, xxxiii (1950–1), pp. 1–42; xxxiv (1951–2), pp. 17–55; xxxv (1952–3), pp. 401–29.
(vi) 'Monnaies islamiques rares Fatimites et Ayoubites', *BIE*, xxxvi (1953–4), pp. 327–46.
(vii) 'Dirhems Ayoubites inédits du Yemen', *BIE*, xxxvi (1953–4), pp. 347–55.
(viii) 'Tables de références des monnaies ikhchidites', *Revue belge de Numismatique*, ciii (1957), pp. 107–34.
(ix) 'History of the dirhem in Egypt from the Fāṭimid conquest until the collapse of the Mamlūk empire', *Revue Numismatique*, 6e série, iii (1961), pp. 109–46.
(x) 'A hoard of late Mamlūk copper coins and observations on the metrology of the Mamlūk fals', *The Numismatic Chronicle*, 7th series, ii (1962), pp. 243–73.
(xi) *The coinage of the Mamlūk Sultans of Egypt and Syria*, New York, 1964.

Barrāwī, R., *Ḥālat Miṣr al-iqtiṣādiyya fī 'ahd al-Fāṭimiyyīn*, Cairo, 1948.

Barthold, W., *Turkestan down to the Mongol invasion* (E. J. W. Gibb Memorial Series, N.S., v), 3rd ed., London, 1968.

al-Bās͟hā, Ḥ.,
(i) *al-Alqāb al-Islāmiyya*, Cairo, 1957.
(ii) *al-Funūn al-Islāmiyya wa al-waẓā'if 'alā al-āt͟hār al-'Arabiyya*, 3 vols., Cairo, 1965–6.

Becker, C. H., *Islamstudien*, 2 vols., Leipzig, 1924, 1932.

Bekhit, M., 'De l'institution du wakf', *EC*, xviii (1927), pp. 403–21.

Ben Shemesh, A., see Qudāma b. Ja'far and al-Quras͟hī.

Berchem, Max van, and others, *Matériaux pour un Corpus Inscriptionum Arabicarum* (*CIA*), Part one, *Egypt*, 2 vols.: vol. i, M. van Berchem, *Le Caire*, Mémoires de la Mission Archéologique Française au Caire, xix (1894–1903); vol. ii, G. Wiet, *Le Caire* (*suite*), *Mémoires de l'Institut Français d'Archéologie Orientale*, lii (1930).

Bishai, W. B., 'Coptic lexical influence on Egyptian Arabic', *JNES*, xxiii (1964), pp. 39–47.

Blake, R. P., 'The circulation of silver in the Moslem East down to the Mongol epoch', *HJAS*, ii (1937), pp. 291–328.

Bloch, Marc, *Feudal society*, translated from the French by L. A. Manyon, London, 1961.

Bosworth, C. E., 'Military organisation under the Būyids of Persia and Iraq', *Oriens*, 18–19 (1967), pp. 143–67.

Boüard, M. de, 'Sur l'évolution monétaire de l'Égypte médiévale', *EC*, xxx (1939), pp. 427–59.

Cahen, C.,

(i) 'Quelques aspects de l'administration égyptienne médiévale', see al-Nābulsī, *Kitāb luma' al-qawānīn.*

(ii) 'L'évolution de l'iqta' du IXe au XIIIe siècle', *Annales* (*E.S.C.*), viii (1953), pp. 25–52.

(iii) 'Review of Løkkegaard's *Islamic taxation*', *Arabica*, i (1954), pp. 346–53.

(iv) 'L'histoire économique et sociale de l'Orient musulman médiéval', *SI*, iii (1955), pp. 93–115.

(v) 'Le régime des impôts dans le Fayyūm Ayyūbide', *Arabica*, iii (1956), pp. 8–30.

(vi) 'Notes pour l'histoire de la ḥimāya', *Mél. L. Massignon*, i, Damascus, 1956, pp. 287–303.

(vii) 'Réflexions sur l'usage du mot de "Féodalité" ', *JESHO*, iii (1960), pp. 2–20.

(viii) 'Histoires coptes d'un cadi médiéval', see al-Nābulsī, *Tajrīd sayf al-himma.*

(ix) 'Réflexions sur le waqf ancien', *SI*, xiv (1961), pp. 37–56.

(x) 'Un traité financier inédit d'époque Fatimide–Ayyubide', *JESHO*, v (1962), pp. 139–59.

(xi) 'Contribution à l'étude des impôts dans l'Égypte médiévale', *JESHO*, v (1962), pp. 244–78.

(xii) 'L'alun avant Phocée, un chapitre d'histoire économique islamo-chrétienne au temps des Croisades', *RHES*, xli (1963), pp. 433–47.

(xiii) 'Douanes et commerce dans les ports méditerranéens de l'Égypte médiévale d'après le *Minhādj* d'al-Makhzūmī', *JESHO*, vii (1964), pp. 217–314.

(xiv) 'Quelques problèmes concernant l'expansion économique musulmane au haut moyen âge, *Settimane di studio del Centro Italiano di studi sull'alto medioevo*, xii (1965), i, pp. 391–432.

(xv) *Pre-Ottoman Turkey*, translated from the French by J. Jones-Williams, London, 1968.

Caley, E. R.,
(i) 'Validity of the specific gravity method for the determination of the fineness of gold objects', *Ohio Journal of Science*, xlix (1949), pp. 73–82.
(ii) 'Estimation of composition of ancient metal objects. Utility of specific gravity measurements', *Analytical Chemistry*, vol. xxiv, no. 4 (1952), pp. 676–81.

Cipolla, C. M., *Money, prices and civilization in the Mediterranean world*, Princeton, 1956.

Combe, E., Sauvaget, J., and Wiet, G., *Répertoire chronologique d'épigraphie arabe* (*RCEA*), 15 vols., Le Caire, 1931–56.

Cook, M. A., ed., *Studies in the economic history of the Middle East from the rise of Islam to the present day*, London, 1970.

Coulson, N. J., *A history of Islamic law*, Edinburgh, 1964.

Darrāg, A., *L'Égypte sous le règne de Barsbay*, Damascus, 1961.

Dennett, D. C., *Conversion and the poll tax in early Islam*, Cambridge, Mass., 1950.

Dietrich, A., *Arabische Papyri aus der Hamburger Staats- und Universitäts-Bibliothek*, Leipzig, 1937.

Dozy, R., *Supplément aux dictionnaires arabes*, 2 vols., Leiden, 1881.

Dunlop, D. M., 'Sources of gold and silver in Islam according to al-Hamdānī (10th century A.D.)', *SI*, viii (1957), pp. 29–49.

Duplessy, J., 'La circulation des monnaies arabes en Europe occidentale du VIIIe au XIIIe siècle', *Revue Numismatique*, Ve série, xviii (1956), pp. 101–63.

Dūrī, A.,
(i) 'Studies on the economic life of Mesopotamia in the 10th century', Ph.D. thesis, London, 1942.
(ii) *Tārīkh al-ʿIrāq al-iqtiṣādī fī al-qarn al-rābiʿ al-hijrī*, Baghdad, 1948.
(iii) *Muqaddima fī al-tārīkh al-iqtiṣādī al-ʿArabī*, Beirut, 1969.

Ehrenkreutz, A. S.,
(i) 'Contributions to the history of the Islamic mint in the middle ages', Ph.D. thesis, London, 1952.
(ii) 'Extracts from the technical manual on the Ayyūbid mint in Cairo', *BSOAS*, xv (1953), pp. 423–47.
(iii) 'Contributions to the knowledge of the fiscal administration of Egypt in the middle ages', *BSOAS*, xvi (1954), pp. 502–14.
(iv) 'The standard of fineness of gold coins circulating in Egypt at the time of the Crusades', *JAOS*, lxxiv (1954), pp. 162–6.

(v) 'The place of Saladin in the naval history of the Mediterranean Sea in the middle ages', *JAOS*, lxxv (1955), pp. 100–16.

(vi) 'The crisis of *dīnār* in the Egypt of Saladin', *JAOS*, lxxvi (1956), pp. 178–84.

(vii) 'Studies in the monetary history of the Near East in the middle ages. The standard of fineness of some types of *dinars*', *JESHO*, ii (1959), pp. 128–61; 'The standard of fineness of Western and Eastern *dīnārs* before the Crusades', *JESHO*, vi (1963), pp. 243–77.

(viii) 'Arabic *dīnārs* struck by the Crusaders', *JESHO*, vii (1964), pp. 167–82.

(ix) 'Monetary aspects of medieval Near Eastern economic history', in Cook (ed.), *Studies*, pp. 37–50.

Elisséeff, N., *Nūr Ad-Dīn un grand prince musulman de Syrie au temps des croisades (511–569 H./1118–1174)*, 3 vols., Damascus, 1967.

Ernst, H., *Die Mamlukischen Sultansurkunden des Sinai–Klosters*, Wiesbaden, 1960.

Fahmī, A., *al-Nuqūd al-ʿArabiyya*, Cairo, 1964.

Fattal, A., *Le statut légal des non-Musulmans en pays d'Islam*, Beirut, 1958.

Fischel, W.,

(i) *Jews in the economic and political life of mediaeval Islam*, London, 1937.

(ii) 'The Bait Māl al-Khāṣṣa' in *Atti del XIX Congresso Internazionale degli Orientalisti*, Rome, 1938, pp. 538–41.

(iii) 'The spice trade in Mamluk Egypt. A contribution to the economic history of medieval Islam', *JESHO*, i (1958), pp. 157–74.

Forand, P. G., 'Notes on ʿušr and maks', *Arabica*, xiii (1966), pp. 137–41.

Frey, A. R., *Dictionary of numismatic names*, New York, 1947.

Frye, R. N.,

(i) 'Ṭarxūn∼Türxün and Central Asian history', *HJAS*, xiv (1951), pp. 105–29.

(ii) 'Soviet historiography on the Islamic Orient', in Lewis and Holt, *Historians*, pp. 367–74.

Gabrieli, G., *Manuale di bibliografia Musulmana*, Rome, 1916.

Gardiner, A., *Theban ostraca*, Oxford, 1913.

Gaudefroy-Demombynes, M.,

(i) *La Syrie à l'époque des Mamelouks d'après les auteurs arabes*, Paris, 1923.

(ii) *Les institutions musulmanes*, 3rd ed., Paris, 1946, English translation by J. P. MacGregor, *Muslim institutions*, 2nd ed., London, 1954.

Ghaleb, K. O., 'Le miḳyâs ou Nilomètre de l'Île de Rodah', *MIE*, liv (1951), pp. 1–175.

Gennep, A. Rangé van, 'Le ducat venitien en Égypte, son influence sur le monnayage de l'or dans ce pays au commencement du XVe siècle', *Revue Numismatique*, 4e série, i (1897), pp. 373–81, 494–508.

Gibb, H. A. R.,
(i) *Studies on the civilization of Islam*, London, 1962.
(ii) *Arabic and Islamic studies in honor of Hamilton A. R. Gibb*, see Makdisi.

Goitein, S. D.,
(i) 'The Cairo Geniza as a source for the history of Muslim civilisation', *SI*, iii (1955), pp. 75–91.
(ii) 'L'état actuel de la recherche sur les documents de la Geniza du Caire', *REJ*, Troisième série, i (cxviii) (1959–60), pp. 9–27.
(iii) 'The documents of the Cairo Geniza as a source for Mediterranean social history', *JAOS*, lxxx (1960), pp. 91–100.
(iv) 'The main industries of the Mediterranean area as reflected in the records of the Cairo Geniza', *JESHO*, iv (1961), 168–97.
(v) 'Slaves and slave girls in the Cairo Geniza records', *Arabica*, ix (1962), pp. 1–20.
(vi) 'Evidence on the Muslim poll tax from non-Muslim sources. A Geniza study', *JESHO*, vi (1963), pp. 278–95.
(vii) 'Letters and documents on the India trade in medieval times', *IC*, xxxvii (1963), pp. 188–205.
(viii) 'The exchange rate of gold and silver money in Fatimid and Ayyubid times', *JESHO*, viii (1965), pp. 1–46.
(ix) 'Bankers' accounts from the eleventh century A.D.', *JESHO*, ix (1966), pp. 28–66.
(x) *Studies in Islamic history and institutions*, Leiden, 1966.
(xi) *A Mediterranean society*, vol. i, *Economic foundations*, Berkeley and Los Angeles, 1967.

Gottschalk, H. L., *al-Malik al-Kāmil von Egypten und seine zeit*, Wiesbaden, 1958.

Grabar, O., *The coinage of the Ṭūlūnids*, New York, 1957.

Grierson, P., *Numismatics and history*, The Historical Association, General series, G.19, London, 1951.

Grohmann, A.,
(i) *Arabic papyri in the Egyptian Library*, 6 vols., Cairo, 1934–62.

(ii) 'New discoveries in Arabic papyri. An Arabic tax-account book', *BIE*, xxxii (1949–50), pp. 159–70; *BIE*, xxxv (1952–3), pp. 159–69.

(iii) *From the world of Arabic papyri*, Cairo, 1952.

(iv) *Einführung und Chrestomathie zur arabischen Papyruskunde*, Prague, 1955.

Guest, A. R., 'A list of writers, books, and other authorities mentioned by El Maqrīzi in his K̲h̲iṭaṭ', *JRAS* (1902), pp. 103–25.

Ḥamad al-Jāsir, 'Kitāb al-jawharatayn al-'atīqatayn', *MMIA*, xxvi (1951), pp. 533–44.

Haq, M., 'al Qaḍi-ul-Fadil and his diary', *Proceedings and Transactions of the tenth All-India Oriental Conference*, March 1940, pp. 724–5.

Ḥasan, Y. F., *The Arabs and the Sudan*, Edinburgh, 1967.

Ḥasan (Hassan), Z. M.,
  (i) *Les Tulunides*, Paris, 1933.
  (ii) *al-Raḥḥāla al-Muslimūn fī al-'uṣūr al-wusṭā*, Cairo, 1945.

Heers, Marie-Louise, 'Les Génois et le commerce de l'alun à la fin du moyen âge', *RHES*, xxxii (1954), pp. 31–53.

Helbig, A. H., *Al-Qāḍī al-Fāḍil, der Wezīr Saladin's*, Berlin, 1909.

Heyd, U., *Ottoman documents on Palestine*, Oxford, 1960.

Heyd, W., *Histoire du commerce du Levant au moyen âge*, 2 vols., Leipzig, 1923.

Hinz, W., *Islamische Masse und Gewichte*, Leiden, 1955.

Horst, H., *Die Staatsverwaltung der Grosselǧūqen und H̲ōrazmšāhs (1038–1231)*, Wiesbaden, 1964.

Ḥusayn, M. A., *al-Wat̲h̲ā'iq al-tārīk̲h̲iyya*, Cairo, 1954.

Hussey, Joan M., *The Byzantine world*, 3rd ed., London, 1967.

Imamuddin, S. M., 'Bayt al-mal and banks in the medieval Muslim world', *IC*, xxxv (1961), pp. 12–20.

'Īsā, A., *Mu'jam asmā' al-nabāt (Dictionnaire des noms des plantes)*, Cairo, 1930.

Iskandar, T., 'Niẓām al-muqāyaḍa fī tijārat Miṣr al-k̲h̲ārijiyya fī al-'aṣr al-wasīṭ', *MTM*, vi (1957), pp. 37–46.

Issaverdens, J.,
  (i) *Armenia and the Armenians*, 2 vols., Venice, 1875, 1878.
  (ii) *Histoire de l'Arménie*, Venice, 1888.

Ives, H. E., *The Venetian gold ducat and its imitations*, edited and annotated by Philip Grierson, New York, 1954.

Kabir, M., *The Buwayhid dynasty of Baghdad (334/946–447/1055)*, Calcutta, 1964.

Karabacek, J., and others, *Papyrus Erzherzog Rainer, Führer durch die Ausstellung*, Vienna, 1894.

al-Karmalī, Anastase-Marie, *al-Nuqūd al-ʿArabiyya*, Cairo, 1939.

Kāshif, Sayyida Ismāʿīl,
(i) *Miṣr fī ʿaṣr al-Ikhshīdiyyīn*, Cairo, 1950.
(ii) 'Dirāsāt fī al-nuqūd al-Islāmiyya', *MTM*, xii (1964–5), pp. 59–110.

Khaṣbāk, J. H.,
(i) 'Aḥwāl al-ʿIrāq al-iqtiṣādiyya fī ʿahd al-Īlkhāniyyīn', *Majallat Kulliyat al-Ādāb*, University of Baghdad, iv (1961), pp. 117–72.
(ii) *al-ʿIrāq fī ʿahd al-Mughūl al-Īlkhāniyyīn*, Baghdad, 1968.

Labib, S.,
(i) 'al-Tujjār al-kārimiyya wa tijārat Miṣr fī al-ʿuṣūr al-wusṭā', *MTM*, iv (1952), pp. 5–63.
(ii) *Handelsgeschichte Ägyptens im Spätmittelalter (1171–1517)*, Wiesbaden, 1965.
(iii) 'Egyptian commercial policy in the middle ages', in Cook (ed.), *Studies*, pp. 63–77.

Lambton, Ann K. S.,
(i) 'Contributions to the study of Seljūq institutions', Ph.D. thesis, London, 1939.
(ii) *Landlord and peasant in Persia*, London, 1953.
(iii) 'The merchant in medieval Islam', in *A locust's leg. Studies in honour of S. H. Taqizadeh*, London, 1962, pp. 121–30.
(iv) 'Reflections on the *iqṭāʿ*', in Makdisi, *Arabic and Islamic studies*, pp. 358–76.

Lane-Poole, S.,
(i) *Catalogue of oriental coins in the British Museum*, vols. iv, ix, London, 1879, 1889.
(ii) 'The Arabian historians on Mohammadan numismatics', *Numismatic Chronicle*, 3rd series, iv (1884), pp. 66–96.
(iii) *Catalogue of the collection of Arabic coins preserved in the Khedivial Library at Cairo*, London, 1897.

Langlois, V., *Numismatique de l'Arménie au moyen âge*, Paris, 1855.

Lapidus, I. M.,
(i) *Muslim cities in the later middle ages*, Cambridge, Mass., 1967.
(ii) 'The grain economy of Mamluk Egypt', *JESHO*, xii (1969), pp. 1–15.

Lavoix, H., *Catalogue des monnaies musulmanes de la Bibliothèque Nationale*, vol. iii, Paris, 1896.

Levy, R., *The social structure of Islam*, Cambridge, 1965.

Lewis, B.,
(i) 'The Fatimids and the route to India', *RFSE* Univ. Istanbul, xi (1949–50), pp. 50–4.
(ii) 'The Ottoman Archives as a source for the history of the Arab lands', *JRAS* (1951), pp. 139–55.
(iii) 'The sources for the history of the Syrian Assassins', *Speculum*, xxvii (1952), pp. 475–89.
(iv) *Notes and documents from the Turkish Archives*, Jerusalem, 1952.
(v) 'Studies in the Ottoman Archives—I', *BSOAS*, xvi (1954), pp. 469–501.
(vi) 'The use by Muslim historians of non-Muslim sources', in Lewis and Holt, *Historians*, pp. 180–91.
(vii) 'Government, society and economic life under the Abbasids and Fatimids', in *The Cambridge Medieval History*, second edition, 1966, vol. iv, part I, pp. 638–61.
(viii) 'Sources for the economic history of the Middle East', in Cook (ed.), *Studies*, pp. 78–92.
(ix) 'Jaffa in the 16th century, according to the Ottoman tahrir registers', in *Necati Lugal Armağani*, Ankara, 1969, pp. 435–46.

Lewis, B., and Holt, P. M., eds., *Historians of the Middle East*, London, 1962.

Liagre, L., 'Le commerce de l'alun en Flandre au moyen-âge', *Le Moyen Âge*, lxi (1955), pp. 177–266.

Lichtheim, M., *Demotic ostraca from Medinet Habu*, The University of Chicago, Oriental Institute Publications, lxxx (1957).

Løkkegaard, F., *Islamic taxation in the classic period*, Copenhagen, 1950.

Lombard, M., 'L'or musulman du VIIe au XIe siècle', *Annales (E.S.C.)*, ii (1947), pp. 143–60.

Lopez, R. S.,
(i) 'The dollar of the middle ages', *JEH*, xi, no. 3 (1951), pp. 209–34.
(ii) 'Back to gold 1252', *EHR*, 2nd series, ix, no. 2 (1956), pp. 219–40.

Lopez, R. S., and Raymond, I. W., *Medieval trade in the Mediterranean world*, New York and London, 1961.

Lucas, A., *Ancient Egyptian materials and industries*, 4th edition, revised and enlarged by J. R. Harris, London, 1962.

Mājid (Magued), A. M.,
(i) *Nuẓum al-Fāṭimiyyīn wa rusūmuhum*, vol. i, Cairo, 1953.

(ii) 'L'organisation financière en Égypte sous les Fatimides', *EC*, liii (1962), pp. 47–57.

Majid, S. A., 'Wakf as family settlement among the Mohammedans', *JSCL*, N.S., ix (1908), pp. 122–41.

Makdisi, G., ed., *Arabic and Islamic studies in honor of Hamilton A. R. Gibb*, Leiden, 1965.

Mann, J., *The Jews in Egypt and in Palestine under the Fāṭimid Caliphs*, 2 vols., Oxford, 1920–2.

Mas-Latrie, L. de, *Traités de paix et de commerce et documents divers concernant les relations des Chrétiens avec les Arabes d'Afrique septentrionale au moyen âge*, Paris, 1866; *Supplément*, 1872.

Mattha, G., *Demotic ostraka*, Publications de la Société Fouad I de Papyrologie Textes et Documents, vi (1945).

Mayer, L. A.,
(i) 'Some problems of Mamlūk coinage', in *Transactions of the International Numismatic Congress*, London, 1938, pp. 439–41.
(ii) *Mamluk costume*, Geneva, 1952.
(iii) *Bibliography of Moslem numismatics*, 2nd ed., London, 1954.

Mazuel, J., *Le sucre en Égypte. Étude de géographie historique et économique*, Cairo, 1937.

Meyerhof, M., and Schacht, J., *The Theologus autodidactus of Ibn al-Nafīs*, Oxford, 1968.

Michel, B., 'L'organisation financière de l'Égypte sous les sultans mamelouks d'après Qalqachandi', *BIE*, vii (1924–5), pp. 127–47.

Miles, G. C.,
(i) *Early Arabic glass weights and stamps*, New York, 1948; *A supplement*, New York, 1951.
(ii) *Fāṭimid coins in the collections of the University Museum, Philadelphia, and the American Numismatic Society*, New York, 1951.
(iii) 'Islamic numismatics: a progress report', in *Congresso Internazionale di Numismatica*, Rome, 1961, vol. i, pp. 181–92.

Minovi, M., and Minorsky, V., 'Naṣīr al-Dīn Ṭūsī on finance', *BSOAS*, x (1940–2), pp. 755–89.

Mubārak, ʿAlī, *al-Khiṭaṭ al-Tawfīqiyya*, 20 vols., Cairo 1306/1888–9.

al-Munajjid, Ṣ., *Mamlakat Mali ʿind al-jughrāfiyyīn al-Muslimīn*, Beirut, 1963.

Musharrafa, A. M., *Nuẓum al-ḥukm bi-Miṣr fī ʿaṣr al-Fāṭimiyyīn*, Cairo, *c.* 1949.

Nagar, O., 'Takrūr', paper read on 23 February 1966, Institute of Commonwealth Studies and S.O.A.S., London University.

al-Naqshbandī, N. M., *al-Dīnār al-Islāmī fī al-Mathaf al-'Irāqī*, vol. i, Baghdad, 1953.

Ostrogorsky, G.,
(i) *Pour l'histoire de la féodalité byzantine*, Bruxelles, 1954.
(ii) *Quelques problèmes d'histoire de la paysannerie byzantine*, Bruxelles, 1956.
(iii) *History of the Byzantine state*, translated by Joan Hussey, 2nd ed., Oxford, 1968.

Perlmann, M.,
(i) 'Notes on anti-Christian propaganda in the Mamlūk Empire', *BSOAS*, x (1940–2), pp. 843–61.
(ii) 'Asnawī's tract against Christian officials', *Goldziher memorial vol.*, ii, Jerusalem, 1958, pp. 172–208.

Pétis de la Croix, F., *The history of Genghizcan the Great*, London, 1722.

Poliak, A. N.,
(i) 'Les révoltes populaires en Égypte à l'époque des Mamelouks et leurs causes économiques', *REI*, viii (1934), pp. 251–73.
(ii) 'Le caractère colonial de l'état mamelouk dans ses rapports avec la Horde d'Or', *REI*, ix (1935), pp. 231–48.
(iii) 'La féodalité islamique', *REI*, x (1936), pp. 247–65.
(iv) 'Some notes on the feudal system of the Mamlūks', *JRAS* (1937), pp. 97–107.
(v) *Feudalism in Egypt, Syria, Palestine and the Lebanon*, London, 1939.
(vi) 'The Ayyūbid feudalism', *JRAS* (1939), pp. 428–32.
(vii) 'The influence of Chingiz-Khān's Yāsa upon the general organization of the Mamlūk state', *BSOAS*, x (1940–2), pp. 862–76.

Popper, W.,
(i) *The Cairo nilometer* (*Studies in Ibn Taghrî Birdî's chronicles of Egypt*): I, Berkeley and Los Angeles, 1951.
(ii) *Egypt and Syria under the Circassian Sultans 1382–1468* A.D. *Systematic notes to Ibn Taghrî Birdî's chronicles of Egypt*, 2 vols., Berkeley and Los Angeles, 1955, 1957.

Quatremère, M., *Histoire des sultans mamlouks*, see Maqrīzī, *Kitāb al-sulūk*.

Rabī' (Rabie), H. M.,
(i) *al-Nuẓum al-māliyya fī Miṣr zaman al-Ayyūbiyyīn*, Cairo, 1964.
(ii) 'Ḥujjat tamlīk wa waqf', *MTM*, xii (1964–5), pp. 191–202.
(iii) 'The size and value of the *iqṭā'* in Egypt 564–741 A.H./1169–1341 A.D.', in Cook (ed.), *Studies in the economic history of the Middle East*, pp. 129–38.

Ramzī, M., *al-Qāmūs al-jughrāfī*, 2 parts in 5 vols., Cairo, 1953–63.

al-Rayyis, M. Ḍ., *al-Kharāj wa al-nuẓum al-māliyya li-al-dawla al-Islāmiyya*, Cairo, 1961.

Riasanovsky, V. A., *Fundamental principles of Mongol law*, Tientsin, 1937.

Rodinson, M., 'Histoire économique et histoire des classes sociales dans le monde musulman' in Cook (ed.), *Studies*, pp. 139–55.

Roemer, H. R., 'Documents et archives de l'Égypte islamique', *MIDEO*, v (1958), pp. 237–52.

Saʿdāwī, N. Ḥ., *al-Tārīkh al-ḥarbī al-Miṣrī fī ʿahd Ṣalāḥ al-Dīn*, Cairo, 1957.

Sahillioğlu, H., '*Sıvış* year crises in the Ottoman Empire', in Cook, *Studies*, pp. 230–52.

Sauvaget, J.,
- (i) 'Décrets mamelouks de Syrie', *BEO*, ii (1932), pp. 1–52; iii (1933), pp. 1–29; xii (1947–8), pp. 5–60.
- (ii) 'Noms et surnoms de Mamelouks', *JA*, ccxxxviii (1950), pp. 31–58.
- (iii) *Jean Sauvaget's introduction to the history of the Muslim East: a bibliographical guide, based on the second edition as recast by Claude Cahen*, Berkeley and Los Angeles, 1965.

Sauvaire, H., 'Matériaux pour servir à l'histoire de la numismatique et de la métrologie musulmanes', *JA*, 7e série, xiv (1879), pp. 455–533, xv (1880), pp. 228–77, 421–78, xviii (1881), pp. 499–516, xix (1882), pp. 23–77, 97–163, 281–327; 8e série, iv (1884), pp. 207–321, vii (1886), pp. 124–77, 394–468.

Schacht, J., 'Early doctrines on waqf', *Mélanges Fuad Köprülü*, Istanbul, 1953, pp. 443–52.

Schlumberger, G., *Compagnes du Roi Amaury Ier de Jérusalem en Égypte, au XIIe siècle*, Paris, 1906.

Serjeant, R. B., 'Material for a history of Islamic textiles up to the Mongol conquest', *AI*, xiii–xiv (1948), pp. 75–117.

Shafei, Ali, 'Fayoum irrigation as described by Nabulsi in 1245 A.D.', *BSRGE*, xx (1940), pp. 283–327.

Shaked, S., *A tentative bibliography of Geniza documents*, Paris–The Hague, 1964.

Shaltūt, M., *al-Fatāwā*, Cairo, 1964.

Shaw, S. J.,
- (i) *The financial and administrative organization and development of Ottoman Egypt 1517–1798*, Princeton, 1962.
- (ii) *Ottoman Egypt in the eighteenth century*, Cambridge, Mass., 1962.

al-Shayyāl, J.,
(i) *Dirāsāt fī al-tārīkh al-Islāmī*, Beirut, 1964.
(ii) *Tārīkh Miṣr al-Islāmiyya*, 2 vols., Alexandria, 1967.

Silvestre de Sacy, Baron,
(i) Pièces diplomatiques tirées des Archives de la République de Gênes', in *Notices et extraits des manuscrits de la Bibliothèque du Roi et autres bibliothèques*, xi (1827), pp. 1–96.
(ii) *Traité des monnoies musulmanes*, see al-Maqrīzī, *Shudhūr*.
(iii) *Relation de l'Égypte, par Abd-Allatif*, see al-Baghdādī, *Kitāb al-ifāda*.

Singer, C., *The earliest chemical industry. An essay in the historical relations of economics and technology illustrated from the alum trade*, London, 1948.

Stephenson, C., *Mediaeval feudalism*, Ithaca, New York, 1963.

Stern, S. M.,
(i) 'An original document from the Fāṭimid chancery concerning Italian merchants', *Studi . . . Levi Della Vida*, ii (1956), pp. 529–38.
(ii) 'A Fāṭimid decree of the year 524/1130', *BSOAS*, xxiii (1960), pp. 439–55.
(iii) 'Three petitions of the Fāṭimid period', *Oriens*, xv (1962), pp. 172–209.
(iv) 'Petitions from the Ayyūbid period', *BSOAS*, xxvii (1964), pp. 1–32.
(v) *Fāṭimid decrees*, London, 1964.
(vi) *Documents from Islamic chanceries*, Oxford, 1965.
(vii) 'Petitions from the Mamlūk period', *BSOAS*, xxix (1966), pp. 233–76.

Sublet, Jacqueline, ' 'Abd al-Laṭīf al-Takrītī et la famille des Banū Kuwayk, marchands kārimī', *Arabica*, ix (1962), pp. 193–6.

Tafel, G. L. and Thomas, G. M., *Urkunden zur älteren Handels- und Staatsgeschichte der Republik Venedig mit besonderer Beziehung auf Byzanz und die Levante*, 3 vols. (*Fontes Rerum Austriacarum*, vols. xii–xiv), Vienna, 1856–7.

Thiriet, F.,
(i) *Régestes des délibérations du Sénat de Venise concernant la Romanie, I (1329–1399)*, Paris–The Hague, 1958.
(ii) *Délibérations des assemblées vénitiennes concernant la Romanie, I (1160–1363)*, Paris, 1966.

Tritton, A. S.,
(i) *The Caliphs and their non-Muslim subjects*, Oxford, 1930; Arabic translation by Ḥ.Ḥabashī, *Ahl al-dhimma fī al-Islām*, Cairo, n.d.

(ii) 'Notes on the Muslim system of pensions', *BSOAS*, xvi (1954), pp. 170–2.

Ṭūssūn, U.,
(i) *Māliyyat Miṣr min ʿahd al-farāʿina ilā al-ān*, Alexandria, 1931.
(ii) *Tārīkh khalīj al-Iskandariyya*, Alexandria, 1942.

Udovitch, A. L.,
(i) 'Credit as a means of investment in medieval Islamic trade', *JAOS*, lxxxvii (1967), pp. 260–4.
(ii) 'England to Egypt, 1350–1500: long-term trends and long-distance trade, part IV, Egypt', in Cook (ed.), *Studies*, pp. 115–28.

Vernadsky, G.,
(i) 'The scope and contents of Chingis Khan's Yasa', *HJAS*, iii (1938), pp. 337–60.
(ii) *O sostave velikoi Yasui Chingis Khana*, Bruxelles, 1939.

Watson, A. M., 'Back to gold—and silver', *EHR*, xx (1967), pp. 1–34.

Wiet, G.,
(i) 'Les inscriptions arabes d'Égypte', *Comptes rendus de l'Académie des Inscriptions et Belles-lettres*, 1913, pp. 500–5.
(ii) *L'Égypte arabe*, in *Histoire de la nation égyptienne*, edited by G. Hanotaux, iv, Paris, 1937.
(iii) 'Les marchands d'épices sous les sultans mamlouks', *CHE*, vii (1955), pp. 81–147.
(iv) 'Un décret du sultan mamlouk Malik Ashraf Shaʿban à la Mecque', *Mélanges Louis Massignon*, iii (1957), pp. 383–410.
(v) *Les Biographies du Manhal Safi*, see Ibn Taghrī Birdī, *al-Manhal*.
(vi) 'Le traité des famines de Maqrīzī', see al-Maqrīzī, *Kitāb ighāthat al-umma*.
(vii) *Matériaux pour un Corpus Inscriptionum Arabicarum*, part one, vol. ii, see Berchem, Max van.

Worman, E. J.,
(i) 'Notes on the Jews in Fusṭāt from Cambridge Genizah documents', *JQR*, xviii (1905–6), pp. 1–39.
(ii) 'Two book-lists from the Cambridge Genizah fragments', *JQR*, xx (1907–8), pp. 450–63.

Yūsuf, J. N., 'Dirāsa fī wathā'iq al-ʿaṣrayn al-Fāṭimī wa al-Ayyūbī', *BFA*, xviii (1964), pp. 179–208.

Zaghlūl, S. A., 'Mulāḥaẓāt ʿan Miṣr', *BFA*, viii (1954), pp. 91–118.

al-Zayyāt, Ḥ., 'al-Jawālī', *al-Mashriq*, xli. ii (1947), pp. 1–12.

Ziada, M. M.,
(i) 'Dīwān al-zakāt', *al-Thaqāfa*, no. 211 (1943).
(ii) 'al-Sujūn fī Miṣr fī al-ʿuṣūr al-wusṭā', *al-Thaqāfa*, nos. 260, 262, 279 (1943–4).

INDEX